Richard Wagner

Derek Watson

RICHARD WAGNER

A Biography

J. M. Dent & Sons Ltd

London   Melbourne   Toronto

Phototypeset in V.I.P. Palatino by
Western Printing Services Ltd, Bristol.

Printed in Great Britain by
Billing & Sons Ltd
London, Guildford and Worcester
for J. M. Dent & Sons Ltd
Aldine House, Welbeck Street, London

British Library Cataloguing in Publication Data

Watson, Derek
  Richard Wagner.
  1. Wagner, Richard
  2. Composers – Germany – Biography
  3. Opera – Germany – Biography
  782.1'092'4   ML410.W1
  ISBN 0-460-03166-X

Contents

We recently had a very serious conversation on the subject of Richard Wagner. I merely stated that Wagner was the greatest man who had ever existed, and I went no further. I didn't say that he was God himself, though indeed I may have thought something of the sort.

Debussy to Pierre Louÿs

There has probably never been a more complex artist, and certainly never anything like so complex a musician. A soul and a character so multiform are an unending joy to the student of human nature.

Ernest Newman, *Wagner as Man and Artist*

In memory of my father

Acknowledgments

The author and publishers would like to thank the following for permission to reproduce photographs: Radio Times Hulton Picture Library (Plates 1, 2, 5, 6, 9, 11–15, 18, 19, 22–6, 29–35, 37, 43–6, 52–61); Wilhelm Altmann (*Letters of Richard Wagner*) and J. M. Dent & Sons Ltd (Plates 3, 8, 10, 16, 17, 27, 28, 36); Richard Wagner Gedenkstätte, Bayreuth (Plates 4, 20); William Heinemann Ltd for the drawing of Alberich and the Rhinemaidens from *The Ring of the Nibelungs*, illustrated by Arthur Rackham (Plate 21); Robert L. Jacobs (*Wagner* – Master Musicians series) and Breitkopf and Härtel (Plate 42); Archive of the Royal Opera House, Covent Garden (Plates 47–9); Theatermuseum, Munich (Plate 50); Foundation Swiss Theatre Collection, Berne (Estate of Adolphe Appia) (Plate 51).

List of Illustrations

Preface

IT HAS BECOME customary to apologize to readers for foisting more words upon them concerning the subject of this biography. Some tales twice told can be tedious: not so that of the life of Richard Wagner, nor, I hope immodestly, my re-telling of it. My aim has been to write an approachable chronological account of the man, of the circumstances from which his art arose, and of his friends and enemies who shaped the course of his career – in a manageable span. To turn from the music of Wagner to Wagner the man is not easy for many people. It is hard to reconcile the greatness of his art with the unworthiness of some of his deeds and writings. His music is banned in at least one country today. There is an understandable tendency, even among the admirers of his stage works, to shrink away from the baseness of much of what the biographer must dutifully reveal. Yet the biographer must believe that a study of the muddy soil from which the riches sprang can lead to greater awareness and understanding, not only of the history of the times, but of the mysteries of the creative process itself.

I have assumed the reader knows, or will be able to find in one of many reference books, the plots of the Wagner operas from *Rienzi* onwards. For anyone new to the Wagner story, the number of *dramatis personae* involved can seem bewildering. With this in view, I have appended a glossary containing short biographies of 140 of the characters who take the stage from time to time through the length of the history that follows.

To my friends and colleagues, perfect and imperfect Wagnerites among them, who inspired, encouraged, criticized, typed, read and guided my thoughts, to those who lent me material and those who kindly gave permission to reproduce photographs, my grateful thanks. I wish to acknowledge especially, Michael Anderson of the Reid Music Library, University of Edinburgh; the staff of the British Library, London, and the National Library of Scotland; John and Jane Blackie; Nic Carter; the late Deryck Cooke; Manfred Eger of the Richard Wagner Gedenkstätte, Bayreuth; Joan James; Neil Mackay; Avril Mathison; Kay Nichols; Sue Powell; Will Scott; B. J. Skidelsky, Archivist of the Royal Opera House, Covent Garden; Eileen Skinner; Ronald Stevenson; Winifred Wagner; and my mother.

DW *Edinburgh 1979*

Sources

A LIST OF ALL the sources I have consulted will be found at the end of this book. But the pattern in which the most important material on Wagner has unfolded since the composer's death is a fascinating one. It is part of the Wagner story and is best related here. More has been written concerning Richard Wagner than about any other composer or artist in history. Over ten thousand Wagnerian books and articles existed even before his death. Of these, the official biography was that of Karl Friedrich Glasenapp which was prepared from material at Wahnfried, Wagner's Bayreuth home. Glasenapp's *Das Leben Richard Wagners* was ultimately expanded into a six-volume edition appearing between 1894 and 1911, written under the watchful eye of Cosima, the composer's widow. Glasenapp and his English translator William Ashton Ellis were pious partisans of the Wagner cause and, although their patience, energy and tireless pursuit of the subject must be admired, their writings present a false picture – the portrait of Richard Wagner as he himself wanted it to be seen. Distortion of truth, glossing-over of evidence and suppression of facts were the hallmark of subsequent 'official' writing about Wagner, notably so in the work of Wagner's son-in-law Houston Stewart Chamberlain.

Wagner himself was naturally careful to provide posterity with his own self-portrait. From 1835 onwards he kept a diary in a large red pocket book, known as the 'Red Book'. With the aid of this he provided the two autobiographical resumés that appeared in his lifetime, the *Autobiographical Sketch* (1843) and *A Communication to my Friends* (1851). The Red Book was also the main source for his full-length autobiography *Mein Leben* (My Life) which takes his story to the year 1864. *Mein Leben* was written at the request of Ludwig II of Bavaria and was taken down by Cosima from Wagner's dictation. By April 1867 the book had progressed to the year 1846. Wagner realized that many of his subsequent activities in Dresden, his debts, his revolutionary activities, and the affairs of the Zurich years with Jessie Laussot and Mathilde Wesendonck would be a startling revelation to Ludwig. So, early in 1868, he decided to extract the notes he needed from the Red Book and transfer these 'Annals' into his new diary, known as the 'Brown Book'. Thereupon the Red Book was destroyed, all except the first four pages which reveal how remarkably concise the entries were, and contain his diary from August 1835 to September 1839. Thus in *Mein Leben* Wagner himself set the precedent for falsified biography. Many of his darker doings, activities he understandably wanted to conceal from both Ludwig and Cosima, are glossed over or the facts concerning them artfully manipulated. Between 1870 and 1875 the first three parts of *Mein Leben* were privately printed in Basel – an undertaking which was surrounded with the deepest secrecy. Wagner chose an Italian printer, Bonfantini, for the principal reason that he understood no German, and took great care that the eighteen copies of this strictly limited edition reached only his most trusted friends. The fourth part of the autobiography was dictated between 1876 and 1880 and published privately at Bayreuth in 1881. After Wagner's death in 1883 Cosima recalled all the copies of *Mein Leben* and apparently destroyed most of them. In 1911 she gave permission for a public edition to appear. Considerable speculation surrounded this book before and after the 1911 publication, and it was even suggested that Cosima had falsified much of it. But the appearance in 1963 of a critical edition based on Cosima's manuscript of *Mein Leben* as dictated by Wagner, showed that the 1911 edition was in all essentials faithful to the original, the main differences being a few attempts by Cosima to soften Wagner's less kind opinions of certain contemporaries.

Until 1911, then, all the biographical writing on Wagner available to the public, that of Glasenapp, Ellis, Chamberlain and other acolytes of Wahnfried, was of a somewhat spurious nature, and even the long-awaited *Mein Leben* only served to thicken the mysterious mists that surrounded the Master of Bayreuth. The Honourable Mrs Mary Burrell had tried to remedy this situation in the years immediately following Wagner's death. An English admirer of Wagner's music, and a lady of means, she set out on a mission of travel and research during which she was to reap an undreamt of harvest of Wagner material. She explored every back alley of Wagner's career that she could uncover, followed one clue to the next, awakened memories in men and women who had known him from his earliest Dresden days onwards, corresponded, cajoled, bribed, made friends with and pursued every ghost of Wagner's past which could be traced. One of her richest finds was the widow of the printer of *Mein Leben*. The artful Bonfantini had sensed amid the mystery and secrecy of his dealings with Wagner that it might be worth his while to have an extra copy of the first three parts of *Mein Leben* struck off. This he did, and Mrs Burrell bought the uncut and unbound sheets from his widow in 1892. This provided her with an insight into a host of episodes of Wagner's career that lay unknown except to the widow of Bayreuth and to friends such as Glasenapp and Chamberlain, who drew a veil over them. Two years before, Mrs Burrell had contacted Natalie Bilz-Planer, the illegitimate daughter of Wagner's first wife, Minna. After persuading her that she was not an agent of Cosima, whom Natalie loathed, Mrs Burrell won the confidence of this old lady and, item by item, extracted from her a large collection of letters principally from Wagner to Minna, which shed the greatest light on his earlier career. Mrs Burrell's intention was to write a complete Life of Wagner based on the documents she had amassed. But when she died in June 1898 her biography had only taken Wagner to the age of twenty. Her husband and daughter immediately published one hundred private copies of the fragment, including a reproduction of the title page and preface to *Mein Leben*, which presumably gave Cosima Wagner an unpleasant surprise. But 'fragment' is not a suitable word to describe Mrs Burrell's book which is a profusely illustrated, lavish work of art, with hand-engraved script printed on hand-made paper, each page watermarked with a facsimile of Wagner's signature, and bound in white vellum embossed with gold-leaf lettering. Vast in size, it is indeed, as her family desired 'a worthy Foundation for the Monument she had hoped to erect to the Genius of Richard Wagner'. Unfortunately the rest of Mrs Burrell's material, known as the Burrell Collection and consisting of 840 valuable items (mostly letters), was not released to the world for another fifty-three years. In 1951 the contents of the collection, which is housed at the Curtis Institute of Music in Philadelphia, were published in English.

King Ludwig had been anxious for Wagner to continue his autobiography beyond 1864. For a number of reasons, not least his vacillatory behaviour towards Ludwig himself and his adultery with Cosima von Bülow, Wagner refused. But he intended that Cosima should write an account of his life from 1864 onwards. To this end she kept a detailed diary from 1 January 1869 until 12 February 1883, that is, from her earliest days with him at Tribschen until the night before his death. In October 1869 Wagner wrote to Ludwig, 'For our son's benefit she keeps an exceptionally precise diary in which she records each day my health, my work, my conversation and so forth.' Thus we have in twenty-one quarto notebooks, a scrupulous, minutely faithful account of Wagner's doings from the loftiest to the most trivial, seen through the eyes of the woman who adored every facet of his being. Wagner's own later diary, the Brown Book, was rarely used as such. It contains entries from 10 August 1865, in the nature of stray thoughts, as well as sketches for poems and articles. There are few entries for 1866–7. As mentioned above the 'Annals' (the uncontroversial material of the years 1846–67) from the old Red Book were transcribed to the Brown Book. At the end of 1868 Wagner entered the 'Annals' of that year. There are no entries for the years 1874–80, but subsequently a series of notes on art, religion and man; mainly sketches for essays, including his last and incomplete tract *Über das Weibliche im Menschlichen*. Both Cosima's diaries and the Brown Book cast valuable light on Wagner's later years, and only recently have scholars had access to them, with the exception of those favoured by Cosima such as Glasenapp and her own biographer Count Richard du Moulin-Eckart.

Both documents passed to Wagner's daughter Eva who, at her death in 1942, willed that they should remain in the vaults of a Munich bank for thirty years. An example of the old Wahnfried spirit is seen in Eva's treatment of the Brown Book. Five pages were pasted over by her in an attempt to conceal Wagner's outbursts of ill-temper, and another seven pages were cut out of the book and are lost. The Brown Book was published in 1975 and Cosima's Diaries in 1976–7.

Faced with the abundance of inaccurate literature about Wagner, decades before the nature of material such as the Burrell Collection and Cosima's Diaries was known, it was the task of another English admirer, Ernest Newman, to reveal the truth about the composer's life. Newman's first study of Wagner appeared in 1899 and over the next half century or so he devoted his energies to establishing what was fact and what was fiction about Wagner. His four-volume *Life of Richard Wagner* (1933–46) is a monument to scholarship, detective-work and fine English prose, laced with wit and humour. Except on a very few counts, it is a frank and remarkably level-headed survey to which every subsequent writer on Wagner is deeply indebted. Newman's sustained sense of balance is all the more commendable as the picture of Wagner that he slowly uncovered was at times a horrifying image. Largely thanks to Newman, together with the Burrell Collection and recent meticulous German scholarship, we have today a fairly complete picture of the real Richard Wagner.

This real Wagner can also be found in his letters, speaking with a freshness and honesty that is lacking in *Mein Leben* or in the cumbersome prose of his twelve mighty volumes of collected writings. Unfortunately the history of Wagner's letters, their appearance in abridged and censored form, the fact that they are widely scattered in dozens of volumes according to the different recipients, or isolated in private collections, is the most jumbled maze of all. However, a critical edition, in fifteen projected volumes, of Wagner's complete letters (numbering about 5000) is now under way, and three volumes have appeared to date, covering the years 1830–51.

Finally the Wagner scholar can look forward to the completion of another current project – the edition of Wagner's complete musical works, with volumes devoted to his sketches and drafts. Recent musicology has shown how much the biographer can learn from a systematic study of the evolution of a score from its earliest stages to its finished state. The complete publication of this huge musical legacy is a task that defeated previous generations and is but the latest stage in the unfolding of Wagner source material – a process that is unabated almost a century after the composer's death. An absorbing interest in his own self-history is seen in Wagner's *Autobiographical Sketch* of the early 1840s. An absorbing fascination with the spectacle of Wagner's life inspired the quests of Mrs Burrell and Ernest Newman, and a similar fascination with that unfolding story has inspired this present volume.

One

The Cossack

In the lexicon of youth, which fate reserves
For a bright manhood, there is no such word
As – *fail*.

Edward Bulwer-Lytton, Richelieu

AT BAYREUTH IN 1813 the writer and poet Jean Paul mused on his idea of the artist of the future. Until then, he reflected, the Creator had on the one hand provided poets and on the other composers, yet the two stood apart from one another. So, he confided to his diary, the man who was both versifier and composer – the creator of the complete art-work of opera – was still awaited. Unknown to this Romantic visionary, Richard Wagner, born that very year, was to fulfil the requirement, half a century later, bringing his life-work to fruition in the same quiet, provincial Bavarian backwater of Bayreuth that he, Jean Paul, had made his home.

Two years before, two other wise men were unconsciously seeking the same star. In 1811 E. T. A. Hoffmann and Weber had a conversation on the future of art. Hoffmann's view, as he expressed it in an essay, was that 'all the arts must act together in a Romantic opera, to produce the highest illusion, to bring the moment of action to the spectator'. E. T. A. Hoffmann* and Jean Paul* are remembered today as literary men, and Carl Maria von Weber* as a composer; yet both Hoffmann and Jean Paul composed, and Weber wrote a novel. All three were pioneers of an age that had ceased to look upon the artist as a mere artisan, that had freed composers from allegiance to the narrowness of court and church, and had loosed them on a society that allowed them to be respected, revered and even worshipped in a manner that had hitherto been the privilege of deities and princes.

Not only was the cultural ethos of Europe changing, but also its political map, on account of the Napoleonic Wars. Our musical hero was to dream of a conquest of the world through the theatre. At the time of Wagner's birth Napoleon's more radical attempt at a similar conquest was devastat-

---

* A biographical note will be found in the Glossary for all names marked with an asterisk.

ing Europe. In later years Wagner saw a profound significance in the fact that Napoleon was defeated at Leipzig five months after his birth. The 'Battle of Nations' at Leipzig from 16–19 October 1813 was the decisive event of a bloody year. In February, in the wake of the failure of Napoleon's Russian Campaign, Prussia had agreed to conduct a joint campaign with the Russians against Napoleon and the Confederation of the Rhine. Saxony had been a member of the French Confederation of the Rhine since the Peace of Posen of 1806. King Friedrich of Saxony still refused to fight against Napoleon, and when on 27 March the combined Russo-Prussian force occupied the Saxon capital, Dresden, to meet the advancing French, he was forced to flee to Prague. Prussian militarism, which was to fascinate Wagner in the days of the Reich, was in its heady youth. The Berlin statesmen Stein and Hardenburg had in a handful of years transformed Prussia from a near-feudal state to an aware, patriotic, self-determinate people, with an army well trained in tactics and sufficiently armed. This nation now felt confident to lead the War of Liberation in central Europe. Despite his recent chain of disasters Napoleon rallied sufficiently to defeat the Allies in three battles. He routed the Prussians and Russians at Lützen (Gross-Gorschen) on 2 May. Another French victory occurred later that month at Bautzen, after which Napoleon fortified Dresden. In August the big French victory of the Battle of Dresden forced the Allies to flee. Failing to take advantage of this by following the retreat was a tactical error by Napoleon, and as a result the Allies gathered their strength, and the Prussians, Austrians, Russians and Swedes overwhelmed the French at Leipzig in October. Saxon troops deserted their King (who was made prisoner) and refused to fight for Napoleon. The French forces fled across Germany with the Allies pursuing, and shortly Napoleon faced the inevitable invasion of France from the Allies in the east and the English, approaching from Spain, in the south.

During these dark and decisive days, on 22 May, Wilhelm Richard Wagner was born in a house in the Brühl, Leipzig, called the 'Red and White Lion'. He was the ninth child of a police official, Carl Friedrich Wilhelm Wagner, whose knowledge of French had made him a useful ally of the occupying Napoleonic troops. Carl Friedrich was born on 17 June 1770 and descended from a line of village schoolmasters (see Genealogical Table). In December 1780 he enrolled at St Thomas's School, Leipzig, in 1789 entered University as a student of jurisprudence, becoming a notary in 1793, and was employed thereafter as a vice-actuary (assistant registrar) with the Leipzig town court. One of the many mysteries of Richard Wagner's family background is that no marriage certificate has been traced to establish when and whether Carl Friedrich was wedded to Johanna Rosine Pätz (1774–1848). Stranger still is the mystery surrounding the birth and early life of this lady, the composer's mother. Officially she was the fourth child of Johann Gottlieb Pätz, a Weissenfels baker, and

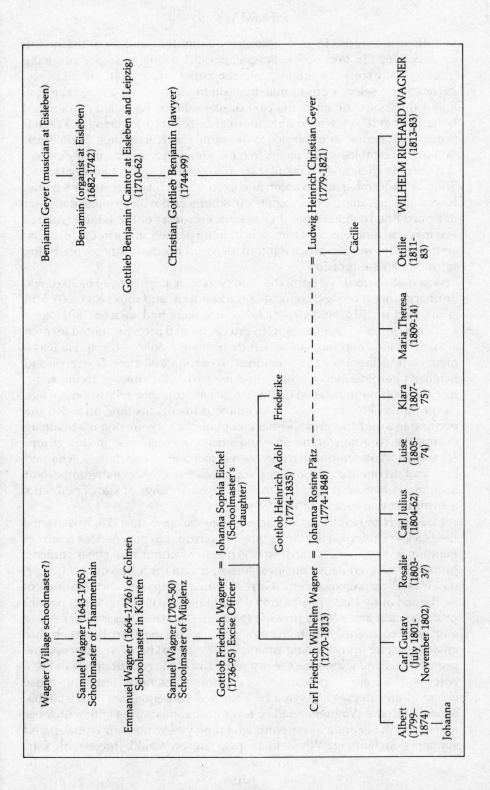

Dorothea Erdmuthe Iglisch, a tanner's daughter, who were married in January 1763. In *Mein Leben* Wagner speaks of her reticence in giving information about her origins, and the curious fact 'that she had been placed in a select educational institution in Leipzig where she had enjoyed the advantage of the care of one whom she called "an exalted fatherly friend" to whom she afterwards referred as being a Weimar prince who had been of service to her family in Weissenfels. Her education in this establishment seems to have been interrupted by the death of this fatherly friend.' As a result it seems, 'her education was very faulty'. She was also embarrassed about and even uncertain of her maiden name. It seems likely, then, that Wagner's mother was the illegitimate daughter of Prince Friedrich Ferdinand Constantin (brother of the Grand Duke of Weimar), an amateur musician, who having perpetrated a youthful indiscretion with Frau Dorothea Pätz, made good his paternity by providing for the child's education.

When Richard was born the family was a large one. He had two brothers, Albert being the eldest of the children, and four sisters. (A fifth sister died in 1814, and one of Johanna's sons had died in 1802, aged sixteen months.) Their father, Carl Friedrich, had been promoted to town actuary in 1805 and had subsequently become a police official. He was a man of fine literary taste, naming his daughters after Goethe's and Schiller's heroines and taking a close interest in the theatre. In his diary, E. T. A. Hoffmann recalled Carl Friedrich as 'an exotic fellow' who was a clever mimic. He was involved in amateur theatricals, and attended the performances of the professional company that was resident in Leipzig during the summer, Franz Seconda's troupe. An actress in this group, Friederike Wilhelmine Hartwig seems to have particularly enchanted him, and on her account Johanna was often led to believe that important documents had kept him late at the office! Another of Carl Friedrich's theatrical friends was Ludwig Geyer.

Ludwig Heinrich Christian Geyer, who was born in 1779, had started life as a law student at the University of Leipzig, but pursued his hobby of painting with greater enthusiasm. While he was still a first year student, his father suffered heavy business losses, and in the following year, 1799, had a fatal carriage accident. Geyer's family were left with his load of debts, so young Ludwig was forced to use his talents as a portrait painter professionally in order to provide for them. He based himself in Leipzig and became friendly with the Wagners, following Carl Friedrich into amateur acting and showing such talent for it that he eventually became professional and joined the theatre company in Magdeburg early in 1805. After maintaining a precarious actor's life in various towns in those economically depressed years he returned to Leipzig in August 1809, stayed with the Wagners, made a few guest appearances and in October joined Franz Seconda's company which played winters in Dresden and summers in Leipzig. When in Leipzig Geyer would lodge with Carl

Friedrich and Johanna. In 1813 Seconda decided to avoid Leipzig for the summer season owing to the proximity of the war and moved instead to the Bohemian spa of Teplitz.

Meanwhile in Leipzig Richard's father found himself fully occupied with extra duties which the French occupation and the threatened Allied attack entailed. In July, when her baby Richard was only two months old, Johanna made an extraordinary journey of 150 miles from Leipzig to Teplitz, possibly with her child, in order to see Geyer. This journey by a lone woman across dangerous country occupied by foreign troops must have been an urgently necessary one.[1] Why else should she face such hazards just after her confinement to visit a friend of the family? Or was her relation with Geyer of an especially intimate kind? In fact, could he perhaps have been the father of her latest child? Why was the baby Richard's baptism mysteriously delayed for three months, until 16 August, when he was christened Wilhelm Richard Wagner at the Thomaskirche, Leipzig?

In *Mein Leben* Wagner acknowledges Friedrich Wagner as his father. Yet it is certain that to several intimate friends he expressed the possibility that Geyer might have been his real father. Richard had no memory of Carl Friedrich who, strained and weakened by overwork, fell victim to an epidemic of typhus that resulted from the insanitary conditions and the carnage left by the Battle of Leipzig and died on 23 November. We possess no portrait of him, although Mrs Burrell obtained a description of him as small and crooked but with a fine head. Geyer had returned from Teplitz to Dresden with the theatre troupe on 15 August. After Carl Friedrich's death he appears to have hastened to Leipzig to comfort the widow Johanna, who was left very badly off. A number of letters from Geyer in Dresden to Johanna were copied by Mrs Burrell. One of these, of 22 December, breaks off in the middle of a verb. Was there some reference to his intimacy with her? Earlier, this letter of Christmas greetings asked Johanna to 'light a beautiful tree for the Cossack – I should like to rough it up with that lad on the sofa'. Another letter of 14 January 1814 ends, 'The Cossack's wildness can be nothing else than divine; for the first window he smashes he shall have a silver medal. God protect you! Greetings and kisses to all the friends and to my Albert from your ever faithful friend – Geyer.' The 'Cossack' refers to the baby boy Richard, and with the wild Czarist troops at that time terrorizing the German countryside, it is likely, as Mrs Burrell surmised, that every *enfant terrible* in Saxony earned the nickname 'Cossack'. The references to Richard in these letters certainly show a father-like affection, but the mystery of Richard Wagner's paternity remains unsolved, one of the secrets his mother took to her grave.[2]

---

[1] Her son Richard never knew of this strange journey. It was discovered in 1933 during a perusal of the Teplitz Strangers' list for 21 July 1813.

[2] The possibility of Geyer's paternity is fully discussed in Newman's *Life*: vol. I, pp. 3–21; vol. II, pp. 608–13; vol. III, pp. 558–62.

Two points must be stressed, however. Firstly, Ludwig Geyer was not Jewish. In view of the composer's later virulent anti-Semitism and the persistent rumours that were spread about his supposed Jewish origin (by Nietzsche and others) this is an important fact to establish. There is documentary evidence that Geyer's family had been Protestants for generations and had married into Protestant families. His grandfather (who may well have studied music with J. S. Bach at Leipzig in the 1730s) married the daughter of the Cantor of Eisleben. Secondly, both candidates for Richard's paternity, Carl Friedrich and Ludwig Geyer, were men of the theatre: one a dedicated amateur, the other a professional by compulsion. It is certain, then, that the young Cossack had the theatre in his blood.

Johanna married Ludwig Geyer on 28 August 1814 at the parish church of Pödewitz bei Zeitz, near Weissenfels, and six months later, on 26 February 1815, bore him a daughter, Cäcilie. A month after their marriage they set up house in Dresden where Geyer became a member of the Hoftheater, supplementing his income by portrait painting. Geyer was a competent actor of intelligence and some versatility, suited more to character parts than heroic ones, and utilizing his artistic talents in the designing of his own costumes. He was a good father to Johanna's children and worked hard to keep them in a comfortable manner. Albert, the eldest son, was already away from home, studying in Leipzig. Luise also remained in Leipzig in the care of the actress Friederike Hartwig, and made her debut as a child actress in 1814. Never close to his brother Julius, the young Richard was to grow up with his sisters Rosalie, Klara and Ottilie as playmates, and had a special fondness for the youngest of the family, Geyer's daughter Cäcilie. Richard had no memories of his mother being young and pretty as an early portrait records her; he knew her as the woman who had borne ten children and struggled to maintain them as a conscientious housewife during lean financial years. Like him she was diminutive in size, quick-tempered and somewhat eccentric: she apparently suffered from what is described as 'head-gout' and wore nine caps one over the other to keep her head warm. Richard too had a lifelong hatred of the cold.

The political state of Europe changed significantly during 1814 and 1815, years which saw the births of two very different men who were to shape its later course and involve Wagner in their actions, Mikhail Bakunin* and Otto von Bismarck. Napoleon was banished to Elba in April 1814. One of the problems for the Allies following the defeat of France was the fate of Saxony. In November 1814 Russia handed Saxony over to Prussia, the Czar wishing to obtain Poland in exchange. This action was opposed by Austria and the other German states. In January of the new year a secret treaty was concluded between Austria, Britain and France to form a defensive alliance against Prussian and Russian plans to solve the Saxon and Polish problems. In May 1815, during Napoleon's 'Hundred

Days', a peace treaty was concluded by Prussia, Russia and Austria with the King of Saxony who returned to his Dresden capital early in June, although forced by the Congress of Vienna to forfeit the northern region of his country to Prussia. An innocent participant in the celebrations for the return of Friedrich August the Just was the baby Richard Wagner, dressed as an angel as part of a festive play with music by Weber. For this début he was rewarded with an iced cake.

The versatile Geyer was not only an actor and painter, but a modestly talented playwright too. His *oeuvre* included a number of small domestic dramas written to celebrate anniversaries in the household (anticipating Wagner's predilection for similar pantomimes at Tribschen and Wahnfried in later years) and a few large-scale works for the theatre including *Der bethlehemitische Kindermord* (The Massacre of the Innocents), produced at Dresden in 1821 and over the next few years at Berlin, Breslau, Hamburg, Leipzig and elsewhere, earning praise from no less a critic than Goethe. The plot of this tragi-comedy concerns the life of a struggling painter who is torn between his visions and a nagging wife. One wonders if Wagner recalled it during his days with Minna. At the end of 1816 Weber was called to form a new German opera company in Dresden, and occasionally he asked Geyer, who had a pleasant tenor voice, to take a minor singing part, usually in a light Singspiel. Geyer also took part in Méhul's *Joseph*, Weber's first production in Dresden. But from this time his health began to fail, several of his letters speak of the hypochondria to which he had fallen victim, and he tried a cure at Carlsbad in 1817.

At the age of four Richard made his one and only appearance as an actor. This was in Schiller's *Wilhelm Tell* in which he deputized for a girl in the part of Tell's youngest son Wilhelm. In the first scene of Act Three, Tell takes leave of his wife and departs with Walther. Little Wilhelm clings to his mother and has one line to say: 'Mother, I stay with you!' But when young Richard saw his sister Klara as Walther leaving the stage with Tell, he ran after her crying 'Klara, if you're going, I'll go too!', and the curtain fell to thunderous applause. Geyer made the somewhat sardonic remark that the boy had at least a gift for improvisation, and no plans were made to prepare him for a stage-career. Rosalie, however, made her debut in March 1818 in Geyer's tragedy *Das Erntefest* at the Dresden Theatre, and joined the Hoftheater in May 1820.

Recalling that his own studies had been prematurely cut short, Geyer determined that Richard should have the benefit of a sound education. Already the boy showed a tendency to talk fluently and at great length, to grasp new ideas quickly and take an eager interest in the cultural life around him. Perhaps one of the learned professions might be suitable. The idea of Richard following Geyer's path as a painter was quickly ruled out. Characteristically the boy wanted to start painting on the scale of Geyer's canvasses and showed no interest in and no talent for learning the elementary techniques of drawing. As Newman has pointed out, this attitude is typical of the budding genius who was to plan dramas on a Shakespearean scale before he had scarcely learned to read, and to emulate Beethoven before grasping more than the simple rudiments of music. In 1820 the boy was sent to the village school in Possendorf, where he was in the care of Pastor Christian Ephraim Wetzel.

By the end of the year Geyer's health had weakened, and tuberculosis was now well advanced. As his general condition deteriorated he became overwrought and morbidly depressed. He spent part of the winter with Carl Friedrich Wagner's brother Adolf. Uncle Adolf, as he was known to Richard, was the intellectual of the family. E. T. A. Hoffmann sketched him in his diary as 'a learned man – speaks 1700 languages – but it doesn't work out right'. As Mrs Burrell said, 'The description of Adolf's varied gifts looks as if the family had already tried to produce a Richard and failed.' Richard's uncle, who had known Fichte, Goethe, Schiller and Tieck, led an ascetic, strictly moral life, and frowned upon the theatrical profession. It was all very well for him to read plays in the seclusion of his large library, or to translate great works of drama in and out of various languages, but he disliked the vulgar, tawdry world of the stage itself. During this winter he found Geyer very moody, and the two men probably discussed the precarious nature of the theatrical careers that most of Johanna's children seemed destined for. On 20 February 1821 Geyer was back in Dresden to take part in his play *Der bethlehemitische Kindermord* but was too ill to appear again for several weeks. The performances of this work in Breslau saw the last happy interlude of his life. On his return to Dresden he attempted to continue work despite his broken health. A report of a performance on 5 September noted that 'Herr Geyer was visibly fighting against physical disabilities'. He took a short holiday with Rosalie at Pillnitz, returning home on 21 September. Although suffering acutely from asthmatic attacks he attempted to work at new ideas for dramas and paintings. As his condition grew daily weaker, Richard was brought back from school to be at home. Johanna asked him to play the piano in the room next to her husband's bedroom. The eight-year-old boy strummed a folk-tune and an air from *Der Freischütz*, and Geyer turned to Johanna and asked, 'Is it possible that he has a talent for music?' The next morning, 30 September, Johanna, for the second time a widow, told her children of Geyer's death and gave each of them his blessing. To Richard she said, 'Of you he hoped to make something.'

After Geyer's death, Rosalie and the other older children became the family breadwinners, and Johanna secured a little income by taking in lodgers, including the composer Spohr for a while. Soon Luise became an actress with the Breslau theatre, where Albert, who had taken to a stage career on Weber's advice, was also engaged. Julius was apprenticed to Geyer's younger brother Karl Friedrich Wilhelm, a goldsmith of Eisleben. Rosalie still lived at home with the youngest children, Klara (who had a child's part in Geyer's play and was training to be a singer), Ottilie,

Richard and Cäcilie. To ease Johanna's load, Richard was shortly sent for a year to Eisleben to join Karl Geyer, a bachelor who lived with his mother and who promised to look after the boy's education. After some tuition from Karl, Richard attended the school of Pastor Alt where he studied with the headmaster Weiss. He liked provincial Eisleben and was especially thrilled at the presence in the town of a famous tight-rope walker, Kolter. In a small way, Richard tried to emulate the great man's acrobatic feats. For most of the time, the 'Cossack' seems to have been a bundle of energy and to have exhibited typical boyish traits, including a passion for sweets and cream puffs, but there were signs that marked him out as different. He was abnormally sensitive and imaginative, and a prey to nightmares. Each night he would startle the household by wakening out of ghostly dreams and screaming, so that none of his brothers or sisters would sleep near him. All through his life Wagner loathed being on his own, except when composing, and as a child, loneliness held special terrors. As he recalled in his autobiography, 'If left alone in a room for long, my attention would become fixed on inanimate objects, such as items of furniture, which would suddenly seem to be alive, and I would shriek out with fright.' In the Dresden house, stone beer bottles seemed to grin at him and change their shape every moment. He fell victim to a number of childhood illnesses, one of which seems to have left him so weak that his mother often wished him dead, so unlikely was it that his strength would ever return. But Ludwig Geyer patiently and courageously helped him grow fit and his later energy astonished everyone.

The interlude at Eisleben came to an end with Karl Geyer's decision to marry. Uncle Adolf was unwilling to take on Richard because of his confirmed bachelor ways and the pressures of his literary work. But the boy did stay for a few days with Adolf, his sister Friederike and their mother in their strange old house in Leipzig, where the vastness of his bedroom and the gloomy ancestral pictures thoroughly frightened him. On returning to Dresden he entered the second division of the fifth (and lowest) class of the Kreuzschule on 2 December 1822 as a day-scholar, living at home. For conduct Wilhelm Richard Geyer was given good marks throughout his career here, but with academic matters he proved less consistent. He was unwilling to apply himself to subjects he disliked, and with subjects he enjoyed he employed an odd approach. Rudimentary introductions bored him: he would plunge into the centre of a subject, only to find himself lost and irritated, so he would be forced back to the elementary stages. But in this strange way he acquired an impetus that gave him an insight into things that were to affect him deeply – Greek mythology, for example. The grammar of Latin and Greek was 'a bothersome obstacle' and his ability to understand the original classics probably did not proceed very far. But Greek mythology did excite him, and the translations of Uncle Adolf and the pseudo-classical tragedies of the latter's friend August Apel contributed to his enthusiasm.

Richard Wagner

Weber's opera *Der Freischütz*, first performed in Berlin, in June 1821, reached Dresden in the following January, and was setting young Germany alight with enthusiasm. Much of this filtered through to Richard who would watch Weber passing along the street on his way to the theatre. Occasionally, the composer stopped to chat with the widow of his old friend Geyer, but Johanna assured him she had noticed no real signs of musical talent in her youngest son. Certainly the boy was no infant prodigy. Nothing in those years hinted that he would be specially gifted in any particular direction, but rich and varied forces were working upon him, particularly that of the theatre. Everything about the theatre bewitched him: he was transported far from the dull reality and routine of everyday life to a realm of illusion, of mystery and of intoxicating fantasy. To this imaginative child there seemed something magical about the very dressing rooms and stores of props. This world of make-believe had an intense attraction for him, and it was here that the strongly erotic side of his nature first awakened. The contents of his actress-sisters' wardrobe, for example, 'exercised a subtle charm over my imagination; nay, my heart would beat madly at the very touch of one of their dresses'. In May 1824 his sister Klara made her debut in Rossini's *La Cenerentola* at the Italian opera in Dresden, but her career lasted only a short number of years owing to the fact that she over-used her voice before it was fully developed. Richard's chief companion was Cäcilie, his younger sister, and a deep affection drew them together with a common love for animals and for childish pranks.

At Easter 1825 Richard moved up to the Fourth Class at the Kreuzschule and from this date seems to have made fairly steady progress. About that time too he had his first regular piano lessons from a tutor named Humann. Johanna had until then avoided music lessons as she wanted to prevent artistic traits in the boy leading him, like most of her other children, into the theatre world. Again impatience seized him and his distracted teacher, on hearing Richard plunge into attempts to play the *Freischütz* overture by ear before he had mastered even rudimentary technical exercises, declared that nothing would ever come of him. Apart from Weber the household received visits from the castrato singer Sassaroli. Wagner recalls him in *Mein Leben*:

> The Italian male-soprano, a huge pot-bellied giant, horrified me with his high effeminate voice, his astonishing volubility, and his incessant screeching laughter. In spite of his boundless good nature and amiability . . . I took an uncanny dislike to him. On account of this dreadful person, the sound of Italian either spoken or sung, seemed to my ears almost diabolical; and when . . . I heard them talking about Italian intrigues and cabals, I conceived so strong a dislike for everything connected with this nation that even in much later years I used to feel myself carried away by an impulse of utter detestation and abhorrence.

1826 brought the death of Richard's idol Carl Maria von Weber, and a disruption in the Dresden household. Rosalie was given a more profitable engagement at Prague and Johanna, with Ottilie and Cäcilie, followed her there. In Prague Rosalie showed her talents in such roles as Gretchen, Ophelia and Portia. Richard moved into lodgings in Dresden with a noisy, rather poor family named Böhme, whose sons were his school-mates and somewhat overfond of horseplay. 'I lost the quiet necessary for work and the gentle imaginative influence of my sisters' companionship,' recalls the autobiography. Soon, however, he began to find pleasure with other girls. One such, Amalie Hoffmann, made him speechless with her beauty; and often he would pretend to fall asleep in the evening so that the girls in the house would carry him up to bed, and thus he was brought 'into closer and more gratifying proximity with them'.

At the end of the year his mother returned to Dresden and took him with her to Prague for a holiday. His first glimpse of the world beyond Saxony fascinated him. An aristocratic family, that of Count Pachta, had befriended Ottilie, and Richard soon found himself at home in this circle, listening to conversations about the tales of Hoffmann, to whose fantastic world he became an immediate convert, and admiring the Count's pretty daughters Jenny and Auguste.

In the spring of 1827 Richard rose to the Second Class at the Kreuz-schule, and was confirmed in the Kreuzkirche (this occasion being the last recorded use of the surname Geyer). In high spirits that Easter, he set out on an adventurous walking holiday with Rudolph Böhme to Prague, remembering the new and dazzling society he had seen there on his last visit. Finding himself without money *en route*, Richard showed no hesitation in stopping the first elegant carriage that came along and begging from its occupants. Unknown to these good people they were the first of an untold, incalculable number of gullible victims who were to provide Richard Wagner with cash on demand. Once more Jenny and Auguste entranced him in Prague, and his grief at leaving them was such that on the return journey he threw himself to the ground and wept until his companion despaired of ever reaching home.

During the summer, his mother and the two youngest girls moved to Leipzig, where Luise now worked at the theatre. Richard took another holiday on foot with schoolfellows as far as Grimma, and from there proceeded to Leipzig in the restful comfort of a carriage. This return visit to his birthplace brought him into closer contact with Uncle Adolf and his world of books. He was thrilled to find that Geyer's library had been preserved for him and sent several of these volumes of literature to Dresden. His own return to Dresden was very unwilling. He missed his family, he had been excited by the sight of the colourful students of Leipzig, and felt stirring within him vague notions of creative plans. To assert his independence he left the Böhmes' house, took a room in a garret and settled down to write a colossal tragedy in verse, while sustained by supplies of thin Saxon coffee from his landlady, 'a Court dishwasher's widow'. Determined to return to Leipzig, because of the aristocratic-looking students there, join his Uncle Adolf's literary circle, and devote himself to reading Hoffmann and writing tragic dramas, he feigned to the school authorities in Dresden that he had been called back urgently to his family. The ruse worked: he was discharged from school and rejoined his family in Leipzig at Christmas 1827.

Although literature dominated his thoughts, the principal advantage of returning to Leipzig was that more music was available to his young ears. Until that time Weber was his main musical interest. He was prejudiced against Mozart because of the Italian texts. He had already heard the overture to *Fidelio*, but a true appreciation of the recently deceased Beethoven grew during these Leipzig years. At the famous Gewandhaus concerts he was introduced to Beethoven's Seventh Symphony which had an 'indescribable' effect on him. He soon equated Beethoven with Shakespeare in his sleeping and waking thoughts: 'I used to meet them both in ecstatic dreams, saw them and spoke to them; on awakening I was bathed in tears.' A performance of Mozart's *Requiem* converted him to a worship of that master too. Marschner's operas were another discovery. *Der Vampyr* appeared in Leipzig in March 1828 and *Der Templer und die Jüdin* the following year. Goethe was at that time largely a closed world to Wagner. In Cosima's Diary for 1873 she records that he knew very little about the great German master at the time of his death in 1832, and thought of him as 'one of those people who are always pouring out books. Such is youth!' He seems to have thought more of Schiller. *Mein Leben* records that he wished to read Goethe's *Faust* but his uncle considered him too young to understand it.

Richard was wounded to find that he had been relegated to the Third Class at his new school, St Nicholas in Leipzig, having come from the Second Class at Dresden. (The famous St Thomas School was being rebuilt at that time.) It marked the beginning of a resentment against his Leipzig tutors, whom he blamed all his life for spoiling his study of Greek. This may indeed have been the case, but it is well to remember that Wagner never displayed much aptitude for languages, and during the Leipzig years he largely abandoned his studies and turned to the theatre, his own creative plans and various youthful dissipations. Yet all his days he bore a grudge against his Nicholai teachers, who clearly struck a blow at the already sensitive Wagnerian self-esteem. Uncle Adolf's library was the principal source for Richard's first monumental romantic drama, *Leubald und Adelaide*. This bloodthirsty epic drew upon elements from *Hamlet*, *King Lear*, *Macbeth*, *Romeo and Juliet*, Goethe's *Götz von Berlichingen* and other sources. Almost all the characters are murdered in the course of the action, so the youthful playwright is compelled to bring them back as ghosts for the final act. The word 'Schurke' (knave) occurs 104 times! Curiously though, Leubald and Adelaide anticipate Tristan and Isolde in a number of ways: a Brangäne-like character, Gundchen, sinks down weeping, and Astolf, in the manner of King Mark, plays the role of the disappointed lover who stands watching the climax of the tragedy, deeply moved. Richard worked in secret on his masterpiece, intending it as a surprise for Uncle Adolf and the family. None of them was impressed, unfortunately, and the only message they read from the drama was the clear sign that Richard had been neglecting his school studies.

One more influence on *Leubald* was the world of E. T. A. Hoffmann. Through his reading of Hoffmann's tales, hearing them discussed at Uncle Adolf's and the Pachta's, and visiting the popular stage adaptations of them in which his sisters appeared, the boy Wagner absorbed an enduring influence. Furthermore he read Hoffmann's musical criticisms and gained an insight into the Romantic view of the art. Music for Hoffmann was the language of the soul, 'the art that teaches us to feel feeling'. Music was the most Romantic of all the arts in Hoffmann's view 'because its theme is but the infinite, the mysterious language of Nature. . .' And Richard found in Hoffmann's musical writings an enthusiastic admiration for Beethoven that paralleled his own. He had discovered a score of *Egmont* belonging to his sister Luise, and this stirred him to plan a musical setting for his own tragedy *Leubald*. First he had to unravel the secrets of musical theory. To this end he borrowed Johann Bernhard Logier's *Method of General-Bass* from the lending library of Friedrich Wieck, father of Clara and future father-in-law of Schumann.* Wieck became the first recorded creditor of Richard Wagner as the loan of the harmony book extended into weeks and months. Ultimately, after sending many reminders, Wieck received his dues – from Richard's mother. Young Wagner began to take some lessons in harmony with Christian Gottlieb Müller,* a theatre violinist and director of the Euterpe Society concerts.

Luise married Friedrich Brockhaus,* a wealthy Leipzig publisher, in June 1828. Brockhaus proved kind to his poorer relatives, but his new wife seems to have been something of a snob, and relations cooled between her and her young scapegrace brother. Klara married a singer, Heinrich Wolfram, in the following year; he later became a businessman. Rosalie returned to Leipzig in 1829 to take part in *Julius Caesar* at the newly formed Royal Court Theatre, and also appeared as Gretchen in Goethe's *Faust* as part of the eightieth birthday celebrations in honour of the poet.

Gradually music replaced drama as Richard's dominant interest. In April 1829 he heard the great dramatic soprano Wilhelmine Schröder-Devrient* in *Fidelio*, performing the role in which she had been admired by Beethoven himself. Wagner was later to call this first experience of her art the most powerful impression of his whole life. She was 'an artist whose like I have never seen on the stage since'. He sent her an ebullient letter, declaring that from that day his life had assumed a new significance and that should the world ever hear anything of him, it would be thanks to her, as she had made him what, he now swore, it was his destiny to become. In this enthusiastic state of mind he found himself alone in the house during part of the summer and able to devote himself unhindered to music. He wrote an aria for soprano, two piano sonatas (in D minor and F minor), studied Haydn quartets and obtained, during a visit to Klara in Magdeburg, a score of Beethoven's Quartet in E flat, opus 127. Soon a quartet of his own, in D major, was on paper. He planned a pastoral play and wrote incidental music for it before he had even considered the text. This music he orchestrated after studying a full score of *Don Giovanni*. Not one of these fruits of youthful industry survives. In order to complete this work-load, and to his family's horror, Richard avoided school for half the year. Clearly there was no alternative but to recognize his enthusiasm and allow him to study music – on condition he returned to his classes. Friedrich Brockhaus offered to send him to Weimar to study piano with Hummel. This did not appeal to the boy but he did agree to take violin lessons from the Gewandhaus player Robert Sipp (born 1806). Sipp was to attend the first Bayreuth festival as a guest of honour, and he survived Wagner by sixteen years. He told Mrs Burrell with amusement that Richard was his very worst pupil: he 'understood quickly, but was lazy and would not practise'. Pedantic harmony lessons with Müller also continued, and although Wagner later remembered this teacher with respect, he felt nothing but boredom and contempt for the rules and regulations of strict harmony. He returned to school but learned little more: 'My continued attendance was a pure sacrifice on my part out of consideration for my family: I took no notice of what was taught in the lessons, instead using the time for secret reading, which had a special attraction for me.' And his thoughts would stray towards the evening's pleasures at the theatre, whether a play of Shakespeare or Schiller, or an opera of Marschner* or Auber.*

He longed to become a university student. There was no hope of an academic recommendation from the St Nicholas school, so in June 1830 he embarked on six months of private study at St Thomas's school, where he made little more progress, but was able to browse through the Greek classics, including Sophocles. Political fervour seized him in the wake of the July Revolution in Paris, which was followed by revolts in Brussels, Warsaw and certain German and Italian states. There was an uprising in Leipzig in September, and recalling the destruction and riots in *Mein Leben*, Wagner admits that 'the historical world began for me from this day; and naturally I was wholeheartedly for the revolution'. During the disturbances the Leipzig students proved useful and popular by doing a form of police work and, though not yet one of them, Richard willingly joined in this task. At school he helped to organize a club modelled on the patriotic university ones. At its initial meeting Wagner presided, dressed in white leather breeches and jackboots. He would roam the town for nights without returning home, frequently drank too much, joined packs of similar hooligans and on one occasion assisted a mob that attacked various town brothels. The following morning he awoke as if from a nightmare to find he possessed a tattered red curtain as a token of his exploit. In more sober hours he earned useful pocket money, and learned probably more than he did at school, by proof-reading history books for Friedrich Brockhaus, mainly volumes on the Middle Ages and the French Revolution.

With an energy characteristic of his whole career he continued to find time for composition. At a period when most musicians made little of Beethoven's later music, Wagner made a study of the scores. The Ninth Symphony received an inadequate and largely uncomprehended performance in Leipzig on 14 April. Before the advent of the photo-copying machine, the transcription of a full score by hand was less of a chore than an educational experience. It was probably the finest way to learn, and by this method Wagner steeped himself in 'Beethoven's last glorious Symphony'. When his task was complete he set about arranging a pianoforte version, as he was dissatisfied with the existing four-hand transcription by Czerny. Wagner sent his manuscript to the publisher Schott at Easter 1831, but they refused it on the grounds that it would have no market. A year later he approached them again and they retained, but did not publish, his work. As payment they sent him a score of Beethoven's Mass in D.

Two overtures (in C major and B flat major) were also products of 1830. The overture in B flat survives, and it was performed at the Leipzig theatre on Christmas Day under Heinrich Dorn.* Dorn seems to have thought the boy's work worthy of attention, although it was obviously derivative of Beethoven, and somewhat peculiarly notated in black, red and green ink. Odder still, every four-bar phrase was followed by an extra fifth bar, announced each time by a loud bang on the kettle drum. In his *Autobiographical Sketch* Wagner remarked that 'Beethoven's Ninth was to be but a Pleyel sonata compared to this wonderfully complex overture'. The young genius grew very apprehensive at the rehearsal, on account of the strange effect of the isolated drum beat inexorably repeated every fifth bar, and decided to keep his identity as the composer a secret from the audience. Dorn recalled in his memoirs that he had great difficulty with the orchestra, who pleaded with him not to foist this insane multi-coloured composition on them and the public. On the fateful evening of the premiere Wagner found himself at the theatre door without the money for a ticket. In a panic he persuaded the doorman that he must be allowed inside as he was the composer of the 'New Overture', and forced his anxious way to a seat in the pit. In torment he heard his black brass music, red strings and green woodwind float before him, and noticed the merriment with which the audience began to anticipate each regular return of the ludicrous drum beat from the black world. Without warning the music stopped abruptly – Wagner having contrived to give his piece 'a trite ending'. This produced the most extraordinary effect on his listeners, as *Mein Leben* reports:

> I heard no exclamations of disapproval, no hissing, no remarks, not even laughter; all I saw was intense astonishment at such a strange occurrence, which impressed them, as it did me, like a horrible nightmare. The worst moment, however, came when I had to leave the pit and take my sister home. To get up and pass through the people in the pit was horrible indeed. Nothing, however, equalled the pain of coming face to face with the man at the door; the strange look he gave me haunted me ever afterwards and for a considerable time I avoided the pit of the Leipzig theatre.

Wagner enrolled at the University of Leipzig as a music student in February 1831. Without any school examination passes he was not eligible for any kind of degree, but he had achieved his chief aim – to join the ranks of the privileged student community. Not that academic life attracted him in the least; it was the exciting social activities of the student class that appealed to him. He joined the popular Saxonia Club and enjoyed dressing up in their colours and wearing a fantastic cap emblazoned with silver. In his behaviour at that period we see the perennial revolt of a middle class youth against his bourgeois background, and a desire to be unconventional at all costs. Drinking and gambling were his principal relaxations. His adventures at the gaming tables were symptomatic of his perpetual need for money. He was already heavily in debt and spending beyond his means. The cure for his gambling mania came after several months of nocturnal addiction. Hoping to win enough to wipe out his debts, he staked his mother's entire pension and lost all but one thaler. His fate depended on hazarding this last coin, and before he played it he vowed that, should he win, he would turn his back on the world of cards and dice forever. He played and won sufficient to present his mother's pension to her (at the same time confessing his guilt) and to pay off his current debts. Wagner felt that God and His angels took a hand that night and that the heavenly powers were also busy protecting him from certain death in pre-arranged duels with other wild bloods, which miraculously never transpired. However much his family was alarmed by his wildness, it was no more than a symptom of his boisterous adolescence and the charged political atmosphere. Revolution was no vague prospect but a daily reality. Polish troops and citizens fleeing to Leipzig from the Warsaw uprising and the Battle of Ostrolenka (May 1831), in which Czarist forces crushed Polish liberal hopes, brought political awareness to young Wagner. He was excited by seeing the expatriate revolutionary leader Count Vincenz Tyszkiewicz one day in the foyer of the Gewandhaus, dressed in tight-fitting coat and red velvet cap. Such refugees of actual human struggle soon showed Wagner how petty and insignificant the much admired student gang-leaders really were.

Occasionally he felt obliged to attend lectures. One such on philosophy was the sum of progress in that direction. He heard several talks on aesthetics by Christian Hermann Weisse, a friend of Uncle Adolf, and renowned for the deliberate impenetrability of his style. Adolf too wrote what Wagner himself called ridiculously pompous and involved prose. The dictum of Adolf Wagner and Weisse, that weighty matters should only be dealt with in a complex and obscure style, may be the root of Wagner's later tortuous prose writing.

Music triumphed over aesthetics and debauchery. The revolutionary repercussions in Saxony inspired a 'Political Overture', which, like an Overture to Schiller's *Braut von Messina* and a piano-duet sonata, is lost. In August 1831 he applied to Breitkopf und Härtel and the Leipzig Bureau of Music (later Peters) for proof-reading or arranger's work, at less than the current rates of pay. To Breitkopf he submitted a piano transcription of a Haydn symphony, but nothing came of any of these approaches. It was Richard's good fortune to find a wise and experienced teacher, Christian Theodor Weinlig,* with whom he studied willingly and happily from October. A mutual respect grew between master and pupil and Wagner began to see the benefit of a sound training in the fundamentals of harmony, counterpoint, fugal writing and the principles of sonata form. Weinlig seems to have been regarded, at any rate locally, as the supreme contrapuntist of his time. He must surely then have known something of the music of his great predecessor as Cantor of the St Thomas Church, Johann Sebastian Bach, and presumably imparted some of this knowledge to his pupil. This limited professional knowledge of Bach (Mozart and Beethoven knew his work) was not shared by the public at large. As recently as March 1829 Mendelssohn* had revived the *St Matthew Passion* in Berlin, for the first time since Bach's death. How much of Bach the future composer of the overture and chorale scene of *Die Meistersinger* learned at this period is not certain. A contemporary Fantasia in F sharp minor for piano certainly shows a firm grasp of the Bach style. Decades later the Master of Bayreuth entertained his family with 'Bach evenings', and exhibited an enthusiasm for *Das Wohltemperiertes Clavier* that may well have been instilled by Weinlig. Wagner's first published compositions were a Pleyel-like Piano Sonata in B flat major and a Polonaise and Trio in D major for four hands (Breitkopf 1832; a contemporary two-handed Polonaise with the same Trio was published by Novello, 1973). A Concert Overture in D minor influenced by Beethoven's *Coriolan*, and written during the autumn of 1831, met with a good reception at an Euterpe Society Concert on Christmas Day. Twelve months had shown a great advance on the 'Colour Overture'. The same society gave another Concert Overture in C (with concluding fugato) early next spring, and this was repeated at a Gewandhaus concert. In March 1832 the first Wagner premiere in a theatrical context occurred with performances of an Overture to Raupach's play *König Enzio*, and the industrious boy, not yet nineteen, produced a more ambitious 'Grosse Sonata' for piano in A major during the same spring, and a 'Scene and Aria' for the soprano Henriette Wüst who performed it in the Hoftheater on 22 April.

After six months of intensive work Weinlig dismissed his pupil with the comment that although Wagner would probably never have to write canons or fugues again, he had mastered independence. A sign of his pleasure with the boy was his refusal to accept any fee for their period together. Wagner was by now ashamed of his association with the Philistine student hordes, and disgusted by their failure to share in his sympathy with the Polish refugees. He had formed a friendship with the exiled Count Tyszkiewicz and joined him on a journey to Brünn in the summer, taking with him the scores of his overtures and a recently completed Symphony in C major, but Brünn was in the grip of a cholera epidemic, and therefore no place to linger. During his night there Wagner experienced a characteristic Hoffmann-esque nightmare: the cholera disease seemed to take visible shape as if he could grasp it in his hands. At midsummer he arrived in Vienna for an enjoyable month's stay during which he made several influential contacts. A new musical world opened before him in the shape of the wildly popular opera *Zampa* by Hérold and the fashionable waltzes of Johann Strauss the Elder. He was bored by a performance of Gluck's *Iphigenia in Tauris* and enchanted with a fairy play at the Theater an der Wien. Some students at the Conservatoire rehearsed his D minor Overture, but soon gave up the attempt. Inevitably he ran out of funds and contracted debts in the Austrian capital that were not settled until he became Kapellmeister at Dresden – over eleven years later!

Bohemia was his next destination, and a visit to the Pachtas at their Pravonin estate, some miles from Prague. Gone was the innocent 'calf-love' for Jenny and Auguste that had reduced him to tears five years before. He now saw them as ostentatious social superiors, wasting their time reading cheap novels, dreaming of advantageous marriages and – most heinous crime of all – singing bad Italian arias! In reality he was head-over-heels in love with Jenny and only too painfully aware of the social gulf between her and himself. The lifelong Wagner method for dealing with this kind of situation was to put the other party in the wrong. He began to tell the sisters how to improve themselves, became 'harsh and offensive' towards them, and later told a friend that Jenny 'was not worthy of my love'. In Prague itself he met the composers Tomašék* and Dionýs Weber.* The latter conducted a private performance of Wagner's Symphony with the conservatoire orchestra in November, having been assured that it was influenced by Mozart and not by the mistrusted modernist Beethoven. But Wagner left Prague with chip on his shoulder: resentment for the Pachtas and a growing hatred for aristrocratic society.

Rich friends were very useful though. Theodor Apel* was his closest friend of the early 1830s and from the correspondence with him we learn much about Wagner's inner feelings. These letters reveal him as hopelessly impractical, constantly in debt, incurably extravagant and yet possessing an extraordinary energy to overcome all the difficulties that such an attitude to life threw across his path. His description to Apel of the end of his love for Jenny is a vivid one, written on 16 December 1832:

> When I sought to warm myself with the last embers of my passion and felt them flicker and pale under the cold breath of death, how hopelessly I gazed into the fiery river of the past, into the glacier of the future!

Apel had ambitions to be a poet and dramatist. A lost work belonging to this year was a setting of one of his poems, *Glockentöne*, modelled on Beethoven's *Liederkreis*, and prompted by the bitter-sweet love for Jenny. Seven songs from Goethe's *Faust* survive and, perhaps due to the inspiring quality of the poetry, show less debt to classical models.

The most significant product of his Prague visit was the sketch for his first projected opera, *Die Hochzeit* (The Wedding). Wagner had been familiar with the source of this tragedy, J. G. Büsching's book on chivalry, *Ritterzeit und Ritterwesen* (Leipzig, 1823) for a year or two, and at first intended to use it as the basis for a novel. This story, medieval in origin, also has links with the mysterious occult world of Hoffmann, with which Wagner was much preoccupied.

Preparations are being made for the marriage of Arindal and Ada, daughter of Hadmar. In an attempt to end a long standing inter-family feud, Cadolt, son of Morar, is invited to the wedding, and received with a chorus of welcome. As Ada's procession approaches Cadolt's glance falls on her, like that of the Flying Dutchman with Senta. During a septet the various characters express their emotions: Cadolt and his companion Admund express distrust as Hadmar extends his friendship; Arindal and a lady of the court sing of love, while Ada and Hadmar's servant reveal that they too are apprehensive. Weinlig praised this Septet, but Rosalie Wagner disliked the entire plot and, accepting her opinion, Wagner destroyed the libretto, leaving only the music for the opening scene and the synopsis of the plot extant. This summary shows that one of Wagner's perpetual dramatic situations was inherent in this early text. Love in *Die Feen*, *Lohengrin*, *Tristan* and the *Ring* is thwarted by the circumstances in which it arises. In *Die Hochzeit* Cadolt fixes his eyes on Ada and on the wedding night forces his way into her chamber where she awaits Arindal. With superhuman strength she struggles with him and flings him out of the tower window through which he has entered and he falls to his death. Admund and his followers demand revenge, but Hadmar averts this by foretelling that God's judgment will fall on the murderer at the time of Cadolt's burial. For this ceremony Ada leaves her seclusion in the tower, and at the sight of Cadolt's corpse sinks lifeless, Isolde-like, upon the body.

Wagner had returned to Leipzig from Prague for an Euterpe Society performance of his Symphony, before Christmas. The work was repeated at the Gewandhaus on 10 January 1833 under Christian August Pohlenz, and was well received by both public and critics. The thirteen-year-old Clara Wieck, who played a concerto during the programme, wrote to her future husband Robert Schumann urging him to hurry on with a symphony himself as 'Herr Wagner has outstripped you'. But young Herr Wagner already knew that his path lay in the direction of opera, not the symphony. At the same Gewandhaus concert he made the acquaintance of Heinrich Laube,* a critic and friendly admirer of Rosalie, who shortly offered Wagner an opera text that he had written with Meyerbeer in mind. But Wagner also realized intuitively that he was to be his own librettist. Only one further step towards his goal had to be taken – a practical initiation in the theatre itself. In search of such experience Wagner left Leipzig after the concert in January and began the career that Johanna and Ludwig Geyer had hoped to prevent.

Two

Years of Apprenticeship

Ich träumt und liebte sonnenklar;
Dass ich lebte, ward ich gewahr.

Goethe, *Der Pantheist*

WÜRTZBURG WAS REPRESENTATIVE of most provincial German opera houses in that it contrived to present an ambitious repertoire each season, despite having only the humblest resources at its disposal. Good singers were thin on the ground, there were the usual cabals and intrigues, the orchestra was of dubious quality, overworked and underpaid, and conductors were, as Beethoven once observed, often no more capable of conducting a score than of conducting their own lives. Yet in this tiny Bavarian town there was an audience that demanded to see and hear the same works that were all the rage in Paris or Vienna. The season which ended late in April 1833 included *Fra Diavolo* and *Masaniello* by Auber, Beethoven's *Fidelio*, Cherubini's *The Water Carrier*, Hérold's *Zampa*, Marschner's *Der Vampyr*, Meyerbeer's *Robert le diable*, Paer's *Camilla*, Rossini's *Tancredi*, and Weber's *Freischütz* and *Oberon*.

Wagner, as an eager new recruit to this world, arrived in Würtzburg for his first taste of practical theatre life late in January. He came partly for the salary of ten gulden per month as chorus master, partly because his brother Albert was a tenor with the Würtzburg company, and partly in order to avoid military conscription in Saxony. Albert arranged for Wagner to conduct one of his overtures with the local music society, on 22 April, and for the first few weeks the new chorus master stayed with his brother. Albert's wife, the soprano Elisa Gollmann, was apparently a formidable creature and largely owing to an intense dislike of her, Wagner soon found modest lodgings for himself. In all probability he lived beyond his paltry means during the three months of his engagement, and no doubt attempted to exercise his young will on improving the state of musical affairs at the theatre.

He had brought to Würtzburg his recently completed libretto of *Die Feen* (The Fairies). This very title evokes Hoffmann and indeed it was he who brought the dramatic tale *La donna serpente* by Carlo Gozzi to public attention in his essay 'The Poet and the Composer'. Adolf Wagner had translated Gozzi into German. That Wagner had considered this subject for some time is clear from his 'Scene and Aria' for Henriette Wüst of early 1832, which is a setting of a dramatic moment for Ada in *Die Feen*, but with different music. In the text of this first opera, Wagner attempted to follow Hoffmann's advice about blending two incompatible worlds: the real, human world and the fantastic spirit world. The aim was not to use fairies and spirits as a device merely to entertain an easily dazzled audience, but to depict the interaction of the two worlds, the cause and effect of their intermingling. Wagner retained the character names from his discarded *Die Hochzeit*.

While hunting, Prince Arindal of Tramond accidentally tumbles into a river, loses consciousness and then awakens in the castle of the beautiful lady Ada, with whom he falls in love. For eight years he stays with her, the stipulation being that he should not enquire about her origins. After this lapse of time he does inquire and immediately Ada and her castle vanish in a thunderbolt. Arindal is found by courtiers from Tramond who urge him to return home, where all is in disorder since the King died with grief at losing him. But Ada, half-fairy, half-mortal, longs to unite with Arindal as his earthly wife. Before she can become mortal, he must endure harsh trials; and if he fails she will turn to stone for a full century. Arindal, who does not understand the reason for all the misfortune that comes his way, curses her. She then reveals her purpose, but he sinks into madness. With the help of a magician, however, he succeeds in penetrating the underworld where he overcomes the guardian spirits, and awakens Ada from her stony condition with a love song accompanied on a magic lyre. He then becomes immortal and together they are enthroned in Fairyland.

Apart from a backward glance to Gluck's *Orfeo*, several significant pointers to later Wagner can be discovered in this drama. Lohengrin, whose identity no one must discover; Parsifal, who undergoes a trial he does not understand before he breaks the spell of evil; and Brünnhilde who is imprisoned in sleep and surrounded by fire until a hero awakens and releases her. Wagner began the music of *Die Feen* on 20 February 1833, inspired by the works of Weber, Marschner and Beethoven he had recently heard. When the theatre season ended in May he remained in Würtzburg for the summer to work on his score. He turned down the offer of a conductorship at Zurich, probably because he could not obtain a passport on account of his liability for military service in Saxony. By 6 August Act One was complete, and at the end of that month his Symphony was performed in Würtzburg.

During that summer, Albert and his wife were in Strassburg, so Wagner occupied their house and kept an eye on the three children. He enjoyed exploring the Bavarian countryside, sampling the local taverns and chasing after the chorus girls. The family of one of these, Therese Riegelmann, a grave-digger's daughter, tried to arrange an engagement, but Wagner took care to avoid that step. With Friederike Galvani, a mechanic's daughter, things became a little more serious. By that time Wagner was realizing just how much women were attracted to him, and *Mein Leben* tells with an air of smug triumph how he snatched Friederike away from her fiancé, a theatre oboist. With pocket money supplied by Rosalie and the pleasures of Friederike, life at Würtzburg rolled by rather pleasantly, despite the fact that he was not re-engaged for the theatre's winter season. An allegro finale of 142 bars for an aria in Marschner's *Der Vampyr* (sung by Albert as Aubry), with text and music by Wagner, was well received at the theatre in September.

On 12 December the Würtzburg music society performed selections from *Die Feen* and on the first day of the new year Wagner completed the full score. The overture was finished on 6 January 1834. The music is predictably derivative but there are several significant turns of phrase, occasional harmonic constructions and a tentative use of 'leitmotif' technique that anticipate the Wagner of the next decade. His task ended, Wagner returned to Leipzig on 15 January to find his family more anxious than ever about his lack of employment. He had high hopes that the Leipzig theatre would take up *Die Feen* and Rosalie interceded with the management on his behalf. But Marschner's *Hans Heiling* (with libretto by Eduard Devrient*) was providing good box office in Leipzig, and the management had no interest in another 'fairy opera', the clumsy first effort of a local boy.[1] Significantly, Wagner now began to criticize Marschner, and his envy at the latter's success contributed to his growing admiration for Italian, as opposed to pedantic German, opera.

In March, Schröder-Devrient, whom Wagner longed to hear as his Ada, brought even greater success to the Leipzig theatre when she sang Romeo in Bellini's *I Montecchi ed i Capuletti*. Bellini became Wagner's new operatic God, and his enthusiasm is evident in his first published literary effort, an article on 'The German Opera', which appeared anonymously in Laube's *Zeitung für die elegante Welt* in June. Another article 'Pasticcio' (signed 'Canto Spianto') appeared in the Leipzig *Neue Zeitschrift für Musik* in November. Wagner's point of view (reiterated in an article 'Bellini', 1837) is that although the melody of Italian opera is flimsy and flippant, it is at least tuneful, well suited to the voice and enjoyable to hear. In comparison, the arias of German operas are laborious, dull and completely lacking in warmth and passion. German singing too lacks quality. As Newman points out, Wagner's apparent *volte-face* concerning the art of his native land is only an echo of the prevailing sentiments expressed in much contemporary writing on German culture. As German national consciousness grew, an inferiority complex became manifest. French and Italian opera were seen to be superior to the home-grown variety; to fulfil its potentially great destiny, German opera must utilize the best elements

---

[1] *Die Feen* received its first performance after Wagner's death, at Munich, 29 June 1888.

of the French and Italian art. Wagner's friend Laube was a leading voice in expressing the political, cultural and musical ideals of 'Young Germany'. The central creed of the 'Young Germany' movement was emancipation from the past, and a disdain for the old-fashioned values of Goethe, Weber and Mozart.

Brimming over with capricious wild spirits, Wagner set off for a holiday in Bohemia with his rich friend Theodor Apel. Both young men had defied their families and forsaken the prospect of a secure career for art – in Apel's case, poetry and drama. Happy in such congenial company Wagner abandoned himself to an indulgent spree of eating, drinking and mad-cap exploits. He seems to have known that this was to be the last carefree episode of his young life, for he wrote to Rosalie: 'Are the happy days I'm now enjoying about to venge themselves on me? For with this coming winter the chill of life will seize me too.' Early one morning at Teplitz Wagner left Apel to breakfast alone, and stole away to sketch a plan for a new opera, *Das Liebesverbot* (The Ban on Love), into which he poured the ideals of 'Young Germany'. In Prague he astonished the Pachtas with his tomfoolery, and one evening climbed out of the window on the second floor of his hotel in a state of undress, balanced on the ledge and bawled the forbidden *Marseillaise* into the night air. Next morning the police had to be gravely assured that this was not an incitement to revolution but merely a wild prank.

Back in Leipzig Wagner was offered the post of conductor at the Magdeburg theatre. His family urged him to go to Lauchstädt for an interview with the director of the company, which was on tour there. Solely to please them, he complied on 1 August. Heinrich Bethmann was a curious individual whose company forever sailed close to financial disaster. He survived comfortably himself on a pension that had been granted to the first Frau Bethmann, an actress who had obliged the King of Prussia in a rather special way. On meeting Herr Bethmann, who was wandering in the village dressed amiably in his dressing-gown and cap, Wagner sized up the situation rapidly – but before he could make a retreat he was presented to the second Frau Bethmann. Wagner recalled in *Mein Leben* that this lady, 'crippled in one foot, lay on an extraordinary couch while an elderly bass, concerning whose excessive devotion Bethmann had already complained to me quite openly, smoked his pipe beside her'. During a conversation with the stage manager Wagner was informed that his first duty would be to conduct *Don Giovanni* on the next Sunday, though there was little chance of a rehearsal. Throughout this bizarre interview the stage manager persistently leaned out of the window to pick cherries from a nearby tree, chew them and spit out the stones with a disagreeable noise. Wagner, who had a lifelong aversion to fruit, found this even more repellent than the prospect of joining such a slap-dash enterprise. Determined to leave for Leipzig as fast as he could, he was first persuaded by an acquaintance to look at a possible lodging in the town. The visit to this house was a fateful turning-point in his life.

In the doorway stood Minna Planer, the celebrated beauty of the Magdeburg company. She took care to see that the landlady would attend to Wagner's every need and then walked off gracefully to her rehearsal. Wagner booked a room immediately and agreed to conduct *Don Giovanni*. He returned to Leipzig to collect his belongings and delighted his family with the news of his appointment, but while there he learned that his friend Laube's political activities had placed him in danger of arrest. Wagner tried to arrange shelter for him on the estate of his friend Apel, but Apel had to refuse this and shortly Laube fled Saxony, was arrested and imprisoned in Berlin.

In the slovenly circumstances of the Lauchstädt *Don Giovanni*, the father of modern conducting made his historic debut as an operatic conductor. Historic in a different sense was Wagner's commencement and abandonment of another symphony. A first movement and twenty-eight bars of an Adagio of this Symphony in E major were sketched during August. The abrupt halt to this project indicates Wagner's greater interest in his new opera, and the poem of *Das Liebesverbot* was written between August and October.

Winton Dean remarked when reviewing this opera's first British performance that 'Wagner turned *Measure for Measure* into an undergraduate frolic in praise of free love'. He converted Shakespeare's play into a surprisingly successful opera buffa, and provided himself with the only comic opera text he ever set, apart from *Die Meistersinger*. Perhaps he needed to work from the model of a great dramatist in order to improve on the hasty and clumsy construction of *Die Feen*. Of note in this poem is the concept of 'redemption', the embryo of a dramatic idea that is inherent in many of Wagner's future works.

From Lauchstädt the company moved to Rudolstadt in September, Wagner travelling via Leipzig to raid the family coffers once more. To Apel he complained of utter boredom and distaste for the tawdry musical fare he was now faced with. The gambling tables and tavern of Rudolstadt were an expensive antidote to this depression. Minna was also a consolation, and as the standards of performance fell and his disillusionment grew, the fascination with this actress sustained him. She was, however, a young woman well experienced in the ways of the world, and the circumstances of her early life had combined to mould a personality that was both sober and practical.

Christine Wilhelmina Planer was born at Oederan on 5 September 1809, the daughter of a poor mechanic. By all accounts she was an exceptional beauty. The harsh realities of the world were forced upon her as a girl of fifteen when she was seduced by Ernst Rudolph von Einsiedel, a captain of the Royal Saxon Guards, and in February 1826 she gave birth to a daughter, christened Ernestine Natalie. Throughout her life Minna pretended that this illegitimate daughter was her younger sister, a secret that Wagner learned early in his acquaintance with her, and which he kept from Natalie all his life. At Lauchstädt, Rudolstadt and their next stopping place, Bernburg, the attentions of the flirtatious young conductor merely amused Minna, accustomed as she was to the advances of eager young men. To support Natalie and her impoverished family she pursued her career as leading actress of the company with a philosophic sense of duty, nurtured by necessity. It appears that she may have considered an engagement with a certain Herr von O. whilst at Rudolstadt, and this resulted in an exhibition of impassioned jealousy by the hot-headed young Wagner. His unconcealed and uncontrolled intoxication with Minna prompted the exhibitionist in him. She naturally had no wish to forsake her commonsense career and obligations to set sail for better or, far more likely worse, on the uncharted voyage of life with an untried, penniless bandmaster. Mistaking her cool and distant complacency for hardness of heart, Wagner therefore abandoned himself to a 'bad life' with undesirable company in the hope of at least attracting her pity. In his autobiography Wagner painted a portrait of Minna coloured by thirty years of the squabbles and schisms of a turbulent married life. His poor opinion of her level of culture and education, and even of her talents as an actress, is distorted. There is no doubt that her bourgeois temperament and homely personality made her a most unsuitable partner for the extravagant, restless genius that was Richard Wagner, but she was no fool, and her documented popularity and reputation as an actress give the lie to Wagner's retrospective sentiments. An examination of his letters of the Magdeburg period indicates the extent of his infatuation with her, and the lengths to which he went to capture her affection.

Once in Magdeburg itself Wagner enjoyed his duties at the conductor's desk together with the sense of his responsibility in rehearsing the operatic repertory. It was not long before he won the respect of the public and the performers (including an intelligent tenor, Friedrich Schmitt*). Throughout the remainder of the decade Wagner was tied to a ceaseless round of Italian and other foreign operas. The advantage of this was the soundest possible training as a conductor of a varied range of music, and a gradual reappraisal of operatic values that turned him into a thinking artist once more. On the debit side, this was a period of uncertain and insufficient earnings; and thrift was never one of Wagner's characteristics. An insatiable need for the comforts and luxuries of life soon brought him into debt, and before long creditors were knocking on Minna Planer's door with a view to repayment. Apparently in order to be certain of any pay at the Magdeburg theatre, Wagner was obliged to be as pleasant as possible to Frau Bethmann. The more he became aware of the sordid conditions of German provincial opera, the more he dreamed of making his fortune elsewhere, and Paris became the clear goal of these dreams. He wrote to Apel in October, 'I shall compose a French opera in Paris –

and God knows where I shall be then! I know *who* I shall be, certainly no longer a German Philistine!'

He observed Minna receiving the flattering attentions of several local noblemen and despaired of mending his apparent estrangement from her. A reconciliation occurred on the last day of 1834, when Wagner threw a lavish New Year's Eve party with champagne, punch and oysters in the hope of impressing her. While the rest of the company relaxed and indulged themselves without restraint, Wagner was impressed by the 'queenly dignity' which Minna retained. She was not in love with him but from this night regarded him with more kindness and affection, and probably pity for his thoughtless, extravagant ways. One evening early in February 1835, he arrived at her house drunk as a wheel-barrow, and several hours late for a pre-arranged tea. Realizing that in this condition he would never reach home, Minna gave up her own bed to the groggy lad. The following morning they partook of a quiet, seemly breakfast, took a long walk together and from that day became openly acknowledged lovers.

The year had commenced with the performance of a cantata by Wagner, *Beim Antritt des neuen Jahres*, consisting of an overture, two interludes and two choruses, which was repeated on 3 January. A performance of his *Die Feen* overture took place a week later. Wagner composed another overture, *Columbus*, as a curtain-raiser for a play by Theodor Apel, and this was heard at a Leipzig Gewandhaus concert, conducted by Pohlenz, on 2 April. In Magdeburg, Bethmann performed Apel's play for the simple reason that its author was willing to buy the scenery and costumes, which the crafty impresario could then utilize in other productions. From Apel's purse Wagner benefited too, with a loan of two hundred thalers.

The principal creative task of this year was the music of *Das Liebesverbot* which Wagner commenced on 23 January. This echoed the styles of the opera composers whose work he was conducting daily: Auber, Bellini, Cherubini, Paisiello and Rossini.

In April Schröder-Devrient made some guest appearances at the theatre in *Fidelio*, *Freischütz*, *I Montecchi ed i Capuletti* and Rossini's *Otello*. Wagner was flattered that she apparently recalled his youthful letter to her, and once more fell under the spell of her powers as an actress. She seems to have returned the compliment by admiring his interpretative skill, for she agreed to return to Magdeburg on 2 May, to take part in the customary end-of-season concert for the conductor's benefit. In recognition of this honour, Wagner planned an ambitious and expensive programme. Unfortunately no one in Magdeburg believed that the great prima donna would appear merely for his sake, and the audience was a tiny one. The only people who seemed to take an interest in the possible results of a benefit concert for Richard Wagner were his creditors. Schröder-Devrient did fulfil her promise and delighted the few who had troubled to attend. The programme had begun with Wagner's *Columbus* overture for which he had proudly arranged an array of six trumpets. In the resounding acoustic of the hotel saloon hired for the concert, the volume was almost unbearable. But the climax of the evening, Beethoven's *Battle of Vittoria*, complete with bugles, cannon and artillery, literally caused a stampede. In Wagner's words (*Mein Leben*):

> Mme Schröder-Devrient had kindly taken a front seat in order to hear the concert to its end. . . . When the English made a fresh desperate assault upon the French position, she took to flight, almost wringing her hands. Her action became the signal for a panic-stricken stampede. Everyone rushed out; and Wellington's victory was finally celebrated in a confidential outburst between myself and the orchestra alone.

The end of the Magdeburg season found Bethmann in his customary state of bankruptcy. Wagner, poorer than ever, went home to Leipzig to try to raise some money in order to appease the more impatient of his creditors. He was accompanied by an intelligent brown poodle, Rüpel ('Bounder'), and Minna joined him later in May for a few days, on her way to visit her parents in Dresden. Wagner told Apel, 'Minna was here, and for my sake stayed three days in the vilest weather, without knowing another soul in the place, merely to give me pleasure. That is touching – it is remarkable what an influence I have acquired over the girl.' While in Leipzig he conducted his *Columbus* overture. Pohlenz had been dismissed as conductor of the Gewandhaus concerts, and his successor Felix Mendelssohn had his own popular following who felt little sympathy towards Wagner's efforts.

Leipzig had nothing to offer Wagner at that or any subsequent time. He visited a music festival at Dessau, and from there proceeded to Magdeburg, Naumburg and Kösen, where he met up with Laube, recently released from prison. Back in Leipzig he found himself quite miserable without Minna, and resolved to call on her in Dresden. On the way there he met a carriage taking Minna and one of her sisters to Magdeburg. He persuaded them on the spur of the moment to join him and, proceeding to Dresden, where he borrowed money from a friend, the three young people then set off for the Saxon Alps, to enjoy what, in retrospect, Wagner called the happiest holiday of his young life. Minna and her sister then resumed their interrupted progress to Magdeburg, and Wagner faced his family in Leipzig once more, without revealing where he had just been. A visit to Magdeburg found that the future of the theatre had taken a turn for the better. The King of Saxony had guaranteed support for Bethmann providing that the management of the company was put in trustworthy hands. Wagner's contract was renewed, with the promise of a higher salary, and in a mood of self-confidence Wagner volunteered to undertake a tour of Germany in search of singers – unwisely at his own expense.

Optimistically, he expected his brother-in-law Friedrich Brockhaus to finance this all-important tour without demur. 'Fritz' did help but not before he had given Wagner a stern lecture on the facts of business life. Wagner wrote to his mother on 25 July:

> Oh, this humiliation before Fritz has bitten deep into my heart and I am tortured by the bitterest self-reproaches that I ever gave him the right to humiliate me. I will make a complete settlement with him, but I will not be reconciled to him now or ever, and if I am wrong in this matter I prefer to die wrong. I will shun them all utterly. Everybody cannot be right and I was wrong, but I will never admit it to *them* and shall adopt the attitude that I have nothing to admit. My worst sin was to have played into their hands and to have got myself into a position where they had the least right over me.

In the course of his hunt for singers, Wagner not only exhausted the Brockhaus loan but incurred new debts and pawned or sold several personal valuables. His incapacity in money matters cannot be over-estimated. A revealing anguished confession to Apel of 21 August illustrates this:

> No one, not even the rich, throw money away as I did. The result has been a regular maelstrom of perplexity and misery, the complexities of which I can only view with dismay. I simply cannot reckon up the details clearly, it is unheard of and inexplicable into what an abyss I have fallen.

And in what Newman calls 'the customary professional borrower's style' he goes on to beg 400 thalers from his friend.

The last week or two of July found him in Teplitz, Prague and Carlsbad. Travelling from Eger to Nuremberg he was impressed by the sight of the little town of Bayreuth, aglow with the light of the setting summer sun. At Nuremberg he met Schröder-Devrient once more, and persuaded his sister Klara and her husband Heinrich Wolfram to come and sing at Magdeburg. But the lasting impression of Nuremberg was an incident that took place one evening at an inn. Wagner and a crowd of tipsy revellers had been cruelly taunting a local master carpenter who imagined himself to be an excellent singer. After making a dupe of this old fellow the excited crowd soon swelled to a clamorous riot, in the midst of which someone was knocked senseless to the ground. Then, as Wagner recalled in *Mein Leben*, the throng broke up with incredible speed. 'Within little more than a minute of the most violent uproar of hundreds of human voices, my brother-in-law and I were able to stroll arm-in-arm through quiet moonlit streets. . . .' The vivid memory of this scene years afterwards prompted the similar events at the close of Act Two in *Die Meistersinger von Nürnberg*.

Wagner called next at Würtzburg where he found his former sweetheart, the unmarried Friederike Galvani, in unfortunate circumstances. 'My girl now has a child – a country bumpkin had been my fortunate rival', he told Apel. After visiting Wiesbaden he arrived at

Frankfort, where he wrote his desperate appeal for funds to Apel and had to surrender his luggage in payment for a hotel bill.

It was in Frankfort that he began to keep his diary – in a large red pocket book. Returning to Leipzig to collect his dog, he learned with regret of Uncle Adolf's death. Apart from his understanding mother, Wagner felt nothing but contempt for the wealthier members of his family at that time.

On 1 September he was back for duties in Magdeburg, and the winter season began on a better footing owing to the arrival of the hand-picked singers from his tour. Wagner attempted to improve the standards of repertory generally and, despite Bethmann's objections, he succeeded in enlarging the small, inadequate orchestra. Before long he was immersed in 'a terrible whirlpool of work and drudgery', as he described it to Apel, with a repertory that included *Norma* and *I Montecchi e Capuletti* by his idol Bellini, Auber's *Lestocq* and Spohr's *Jessonda*. This last he found lengthy, pedantic and sentimental compared with Bellini. He also pressed ahead with the music of his own *Liebesverbot*.

Problems with Minna were his main concern that autumn, however. Her mother had come to stay in Magdeburg and this lady made it abundantly clear to Wagner that she considered her daughter's secure career would only be jeopardized by a liaison with a theatrical novice like himself. Matters were complicated by the appearance of a rival to Minna as actress, Madame Grabowsky, the stage-manager's wife. On the question of marrying Minna, Wagner too was racked with doubts on account of his age and financial circumstances. Refusing to tolerate the presence of Madame Grabowsky Minna unwittingly brought the crisis of her relationship with Wagner to a head, by accepting an engagement at the Berlin Königstadt Theatre. The director there, Karl Friedrich Cerf, had made her a lucrative offer and, lover or no lover, she left Magdeburg at dawn on the morning of 4 November. Wagner had already confessed to Apel on 27 October, 'She loves me and her love is worth a great deal to me now. She is the pivot of my life and gives it consistency and warmth. I cannot relinquish her.'

When he saw Minna's carriage disappearing into the early morning mist, his torment knew no bounds. His innermost feelings were poured out into nine lengthy love letters, the first written at 8.30 on the morning of her departure. His heart is broken, he sobs and cries like a child; he begs her to marry him, and implores her to realize that he has sacrificed his career as an opera composer merely to be with her in Magdeburg. Each day Minna was bombarded with a frank confession of his desires and hopes, addressed to his 'sweet betrothed'. He will devote his life to her if only she will restore his happiness; he has an unshakable faith that, united in marriage, their future together will be secure. He swears he will never chastise her or chide her in any way. Only she can cure his sorrow, only she can fill his emptiness. He tells her that he has completely won over her mother, and has also persuaded the theatre committee to receive her back, unconditionally. Accustomed as she was to receiving love letters, it can safely be hazarded that Minna had read none like these before. The appeals and entreaties worked. Although she had made a good impression in Berlin and had been offered more parts there, she returned to the embraces of her ardent correspondent in Magdeburg. According to Wagner's autobiography they became closer and closer to one another during that winter.

In January 1836 the music of *Das Liebesverbot* was finished, and the completion of the full score occupied him over the next two months. In later years Wagner looked upon his second opera as a nauseating effort. He was repelled by this youthful tribute to everything that was un-German. Yet the score demonstrates a clearer use of the concept of thematic reminiscence, the beginnings of his mastery of 'leitmotif' technique; and another significant hallmark is the appearance of the 'Dresden Amen', later a feature of *Lohengrin* and *Parsifal*.

On 29 March occurred the only performance of *Das Liebesverbot* in Wagner's lifetime, if indeed the word 'performance' can be used to describe the fiasco that ensued. As usual at the end of the season, the Bethmann enterprise was on the verge of financial collapse; many of the singers had given up hope of receiving their salaries and were looking for engagements elsewhere. Wagner did his best to persuade a requisite number to remain behind for the performance of his opera. Bethmann was, like Wagner, heavily in debt and craftily arranged that the profits from the first performance be used to cover the expenses of the production. The second performance would then be a benefit one for Wagner, a privilege to which he was entitled for his work in finding and training singers. Bethmann conveniently forgot to have the libretto printed in time for the first night, and so saved himself further expense. That the first night transpired at all was thanks to Minna, who sold a bracelet in order to redeem the parts from the copyist, who had not been paid. The audience, who knew nothing of the story, must have been sorely perplexed by the first Wagner opera to reach the stage. Not one of the singers had troubled to memorize the music properly and the leading tenor contrived to hide behind his enormous plume of coloured feathers, as he improvised suitable snatches of Auber and Hérold. News of the disaster soon spread through parochial Magdeburg and on the second night, 11 April, there was virtually no audience at all. In fact a total of three Jews occupied the stalls, fifteen minutes before the scheduled starting time. One of these, a Madame Gottschalk, was Wagner's principal creditor, who had therefore a vested interest in that benefit performance for the conductor. Suddenly a fight broke out backstage. A punch-up between the lover of the leading lady, Karoline Pollert, and her husband ended up as a general brawl in which the company members released their pent-up aggression and bitterness after a wearing season. The evening's performance was cancelled, Bethmann's company declared bankrupt and the theatre closed down.

The loss of his benefit put Wagner in danger of imprisonment for debt. He tried to escape to Apel's estate at Ermlitz, but his friend informed him that owing to building operations there he could not entertain him. An appeal to his brother-in-law Heinrich Wolfram was ignored. A visit to Leipzig to negotiate a loan also failed. So Wagner lived in seclusion in Magdeburg, and in constant fear of his creditors. He was not idle though, and sought to improve his fortunes elsewhere. Although he regarded the successful career of Mendelssohn in Leipzig with jealousy, there was surely nothing to prevent the Jewish composer being useful to him. On the day of the abandoned *Liebesverbot* performance, he sent the score of his C major Symphony to Mendelssohn as a gift, but Mendelssohn never performed it and the score is lost. Wagner subsequently believed that Mendelssohn destroyed the score because he was envious of Wagner's symphonic talents. This is inconceivable. Mendelssohn would have found nothing to startle him into jealousy in this unpolished student effort of Wagner's.

Schumann published a lively account of musical life at Magdeburg in his *Neue Zeitschrift für Musik* (3 May). Writing anonymously Wagner provides an amusing description of the poor conditions, but has praise for the capabilities of the orchestra and the good qualities of the soprano Karoline Pollert. Naturally the 'young and gifted artist' Richard Wagner is praised for his skill and imagination as conductor, 'full of fire and nuptial passion'. A few weeks later Wagner sent Schumann an article on the Berlin critic Rellstab,* couched in such libellous language that Schumann was compelled to reject it.

Minna was due to leave Magdeburg for an engagement at Königsberg in East Prussia.[1] She had accepted this offer as there was some hope of arranging a post for Wagner at Königsberg. The days leading up to their separation were full of gloom. They saw a poor wretch drown himself in the River Elbe, and on the very morning of her departure the town was all agog to watch the execution of a criminal, who was to be broken on the wheel. In May, Theodor Apel had a riding accident and suffered appallingly for two years, eventually becoming totally blind.

Thoroughly depressed, Wagner left Magdeburg without regrets, and arrived in Berlin on 18 May where he found his friend Laube and several Magdeburg colleagues. His activities in Berlin are documented in a series of love letters to Minna in Königsberg, which outdo those of the previous November in the intensity of their ardour. He had come to Berlin in the hope of a performance of *Das Liebesverbot* at Cerf's Königstadt Theatre. For a few weeks Wagner believed that Cerf intended to help him: the Berlin director was full of empty promises, which the desperate Wagner was

---

[1] Now Kaliningrad, USSR.

only too ready to regard as genuine. While he lingered in the Prussian capital, bad news filtered through from Königsberg. Minna had been led to believe that Wagner would soon be appointed as conductor, but Louis Schuberth, the present incumbent, showed no desire to leave. Schuberth, whom Wagner had known as first cellist in Magdeburg, was also conductor at Riga, but as the theatre there was being reconstructed he preferred to remain in Königsberg where he had formed a satisfactory liaison with the prima donna, Henriette Grosser.

For the moment Wagner was convinced that Cerf really meant to instal him as conductor at the Berlin Königstadt Theatre and perform his opera, so he lingered in Berlin, spending most of his time writing hysterical, anguished letters to Minna. He met a Jewish tradesman from Magdeburg, one Schwabe, who had previously been in love with Minna. Jealousy, suspicion, frustration and self-pity were fanned as the days passed without a letter from her. When he did hear from her, he was reassured that she was still devoted to him. At the same time he realized that Cerf's smooth-faced assurances were utterly hollow. Berlin had no use for him, and so he resolved to leave for Königsberg without further humiliation. Borrowing money from Laube, he did so on 7 July.

His plan was to persuade Schuberth to return to Riga. On arriving in 'Prussian Siberia', as he described isolated Königsberg, he soon realized that Schuberth would not be a party to this confident scheme. Wagner regarded his former first cellist with intense hatred. He knew that he found himself in this desperate, insignificant outpost of Prussia solely on account of his infatuation with a provincial actress. Instead of storming the opera houses of Paris or Vienna with his works, he was forced to linger in the chilly gloom of Königsberg, and even there an enemy stood in the way of his conductorship. A bleak and miserable winter lay ahead.

Anton Hübsch, the director of the Königsberg theatre, valued Minna as his leading actress. When he learned that she and her lover were about to accept employment in Danzig, he took measures to retain her. Therefore, entirely on account of Minna, the date for Schuberth's departure was arranged for April 1837, when Wagner would fill his post. Meanwhile Wagner was made assistant conductor for a small retaining fee, and had to endure the intrigues of Schuberth, who deliberately set the orchestra against him.

Between Wagner and Minna there was a strong physical attraction. Having abandoned his family, and with recent bitter experiences of the precarious nature of theatrical life, he longed for the security and comfort of a homely marriage. The idea that his restless creative spirit was unsuited to such a future of quiet domestic bliss probably had not occurred to him. He already exhibited the worst characteristics of frustrated young manhood – loss of self-control and a quick and violent temper – but Minna's passion for Wagner was such that she overlooked this. They had frequent violent quarrels throughout the weeks before their marriage and, like many other women throughout his life, she learned to cope with his ill-temper, along with his restless energy and careless spending. They survived the many squabbles of that autumn of 1836, including a heated argument on the very day that they visited the pastor to arrange their wedding. The reverend gentleman was astonished to find the young couple in his hallway engaged in a vicious altercation. Embarrassed, Richard and Minna quickly saw the irony of the situation, and became reconciled once more.

Hübsch had promised Wagner a benefit performance on the eve of his wedding. Wagner chose *Masaniello*, which brought in a large sum. Most of this had to pay off debts, however, as he had already purchased a variety of domestic luxuries in an attempt to make life rosy for Minna. The sun shone brilliantly on the morning of 24 November as Wagner, smartly dressed in a new, dark blue frock-coat with gold buttons, made his way to the little church of Tragheim. The large congregation was composed of frivolous theatrical acquaintances; not one real friend of the couple was present. Throughout the ceremony Wagner felt as if he were in a trance, experiencing a sense of dislocation from reality, in which he seemed to be torn by two opposing forces. One carried his dreaming nature upward, while the other dragged him downwards into a state of unknown fear. Suddenly, the voice of the parson caught his attention. They were to look for an unknown friend during the dark days ahead. Glancing up to hear more about this mysterious patron Wagner was disappointed to hear the pastor sternly pronounce his name: Jesus. A rich and merry banquet followed the ceremony, and Wagner's spirits rose as he viewed the busy, thoughtful hostess who was now his wife.

He had just committed the most imprudent folly of his life. As if to emphasize the pattern for the remainder of his married life, he found himself in the magistrates' court on the following morning, answering a charge brought by the myriad creditors of Magdeburg. Abraham Möller, a local devotee of the theatre who had helped Wagner to secure his appointment in Königsberg, succeeded in staving off these demands temporarily, thanks to a legal technicality.

The years 1836 and 1837 were comparatively barren for creative work, no doubt due to personal problems and uncertainties. During the anxious weeks in Berlin Wagner heard Spontini* conduct an impressive perform-ance of his opera *Ferdinand Cortez*. Spontini's grand heroic style strongly influenced Wagner for a time, and two bombastic overtures attest this: *Polonia* was a belated tribute to the heroic Polish exiles of the Warsaw uprising who had stirred him in his student days; and the grandiloquent *Rule Britannia* overture was completed on 15 March 1837, and dispatched, appropriately, to Sir George Smart of the Philharmonic Society in Lon-don. Sketches for a third overture about Napoleon came to nothing. While he waited for Schuberth to depart he turned his attention to operatic texts. *Die hohe Braut* was a sketch for a libretto, based on a novel of that name by Heinrich König which Wagner had read in Magdeburg. In the autumn of 1836 he had the sketch translated into French, and sent it to Eugène Scribe* in Paris. The dramatist Scribe was the doyen of Grand Opera librettists, and made his fortune in collaboration with Auber and Meyerbeer.* He ventured no reply to Wagner's bold suggestion that he should write a French poem based on the *Hohe Braut* sketch. Wagner tried again in the spring of the following year, enclosing the score of *Das Liebesverbot* in the hope that Scribe would obtain an opinion of it from Meyerbeer and Auber; if *Die hohe Braut* was not to be commissioned for the Paris Opéra, then perhaps Scribe would adapt *Das Liebesverbot* for performance at the Opéra-Comique? To Meyerbeer Wagner wrote a letter of praise, hailing him as a genius who had fulfilled the mission of the Germans by creating works of universal greatness, modelled on the best features of the French and Italian styles. At the same time the editor of the Stuttgart magazine *Europa*, August Lewald, published the *Chant de Carneval* from *Das Liebesverbot* with the impressive information that it was from an opera that had been sent to the renowned Scribe, and was being considered for production in Paris. This Carnival Song achieved quite a vogue in Wagner's day, although he received no royalties for it.

Another sketched libretto, this time for a two-act comic opera with modest Königsberg in mind, *Männerlist grösser als Frauenlist, oder Die glückliche Bärenfamilie* (Man outwits Woman, or the Happy Bear Family), was based on a tale from the Arabian Nights. Only a few sketches for the music were made. The many abandoned fragments of this period show that Wagner was at least full of ideas. Sketches exist of a March and Chorus of Priests that seem to be part of incidental music he supplied to a play about the conflict of paganism and Christianity. He wrote incidental music for another play performed in February by J. Springer. One sketch was to bear significant fruit, however. During the summer of 1837 Wagner read Bärmann's translation of a new novel by Edward Bulwer-Lytton, *Rienzi, the last of the Tribunes*. Impressed with the heroic scale and grandeur of this book, he at once drafted a prose scenario.

Meanwhile the outward circumstances of his life had changed. Schuberth left Königsberg in April, but the theatre was on the verge of bankruptcy. Wagner bravely offered to revive the tottering enterprise, but the orchestra, compelled to accept cuts in salary, thought little of his efforts to restore hard work and discipline. The financial situation was a disaster for the Wagners who were in debt on all fronts. Natalie, Minna's supposed sister, was an additional burden. She stayed with the newly married couple at that time, but her subsequent whereabouts are not known, until she joined them again in Paris in November 1840. Over half a century later Natalie gave Mrs Burrell a vivid account of the grim months of unpleasant bickering and jealous tantrums that followed the wedding. The sickening burden of care, aggravated by Wagner's suspicions concerning Minna's fidelity, led to a succession of tormented disputes. Writing nothing of value and faced with the thankless task of saving Hübsch's company Wagner was irritable and frustrated. Subjected to Minna's criticism of his former lavish ways and the debts he had thereby incurred, he frequently let fly at her in a rough and brutal way.

On 31 May, after six months of married life, she could tolerate no more, and while Wagner was at a theatre rehearsal, she gathered her belongings and left Königsberg with Natalie. Returning home, he learned that she had departed in the company of a local merchant and theatre patron, Dietrich, on the road to Berlin. Wagner had suspected Dietrich of intentions towards Minna for some time, and therefore drew the worst conclusions. With his friend Abraham Möller he embarked on an all-night pursuit of her in an express coach but, on reaching Elbing at break of day, their funds were exhausted and it became clear that Minna's carriage could not be overtaken. Returning to Königsberg, Wagner had plenty of time to brood on the causes of her flight. He soon learned that she had gone to her parents in Dresden, and that Dietrich had only accompanied her on part of the journey. Selling or pawning whatever still belonged to him, Wagner left Königsberg by stealth on 3 June, and four days later wrote to Louis Schindelmeisser* from Leipzig. Schindelmeisser, a friend from Wagner's student days, was conductor at the Königstadt Theatre, Berlin. In his letter, Wagner asked him to do everything he could to arrange an appointment at Riga. He staked everything on Schindelmeisser's influence with the Riga director, Karl von Holtei.* From Dresden on 12 June, Wagner wrote to him again, stressing the importance to him of the Riga engagement, and mentioning the possibility of a divorce from Minna. To the world he was playing the part of the aggrieved and wounded husband. In Dresden he stayed with his sister Ottilie, who was now married to the scholar Hermann Brockhaus.* This couple were always to remain kind and friendly to Wagner. He visited Minna and was received coldly by her parents who thought very little of the behaviour of their new son-in-law but, at the sight of his wife, he broke down and begged forgiveness for his past actions. After spending what he described as an 'anxious and painful week' with her, he travelled to Berlin to sign the contract for Riga with Holtei, at a salary of 800 roubles. From Berlin he wrote to Minna a letter of repentance, assured her that life in Riga would be 'pleasant and carefree', and begged her to forgive him and forget the past.

On his return to Dresden he found her willing to listen to his plans, though she was still reserved and uneasy. Determined to play the part of the kind husband, he persuaded her to leave her parents and live with him at Blasewitz on the banks of the Elbe, a few miles from Dresden. Some weeks passed by, and then the situation grew worse again. Minna left him, apparently to take a 'pleasure trip' with a friend of her family, but did not return.

Some days later, Minna's eldest sister called at Blasewitz to ask Wagner to provide written permission for a passport for his wife. Apprehensively he called on her parents, who refused to give him any information about her plans or her whereabouts. He learned, by letter from Möller, that Dietrich had left Königsberg for Dresden. Calling at his hotel he found that both Dietrich and Minna had disappeared. He now realized that she had forsaken him, and probably faced the fact that there was no purpose in pursuing her further.

Late in August he set out on the long journey to Riga. He travelled first to Berlin, where he met Minna's sister Amalie, and found in her a sympathetic friend. Reaching Lübeck, he waited for a merchant ship to take him to Riga. The voyage was interrupted for a week at Travemünde, because of an unfavourable wind, and Wagner had to stay in a miserable ship's tavern. After four days at sea he landed in Russia at Bolderaa, and made his way to Riga. At this Baltic port, the capital of medieval Livonia, there was a large German community, and a theatre that had sizeable funds at its disposal. Holtei's policy was to present the lightest possible musical fare, and knowing of Wagner's declared preference for French and Italian music, regarded him as the ideal interpreter of the frivolities of the repertory. The theatre, which was well supported, was tiny in size, but three things impressed Wagner in this unpretentious auditorium: the steeply-rising stalls, not unlike the rows of an amphitheatre; the darkness of the auditorium; and the unusually deep orchestra pit. Adapted and refined, these three features were one day to characterize Wagner's theatre on the hill above Bayreuth.

For the want of a leading soprano the first offering of the season, *Norma*, had to be replaced on 16 September by Boieldieu's *La Dame blanche* – a work Wagner admired all his life. The prima donna still failed to appear, so Wagner suggested to Holtei that Minna's sister Amalie be engaged. In reply to this offer Amalie sent news that Minna was now with her parents, seriously ill. In *Mein Leben* Wagner claims that he received this news without emotion, and on account of Minna's infidelity with Dietrich, he intended to divorce her:

> Hereupon Minna herself appealed to me, and wrote me a positively heartrending letter, in which she openly confessed her infidelity. She declared that she had been driven to it by despair, but that the great trouble she had thus brought upon herself having taught her a lesson, all she now wished was to return to the right path.

Overcome with joy, he welcomed her to Riga with the wildest enthusiasm, and she arrived with Amalie on 19 October.

At first Holtei was delighted with Wagner's energetic approach to his duties. The new conductor supplied an aria to words by Holtei, which was inserted into a Singspiel by Carl Blum. Holtei enthused over Wagner's light-hearted libretto *Die glückliche Bärenfamilie*, and expressed a hope that he would complete the music for it. But with the plan for *Rienzi* absorbing him more and more, Wagner made a present of his comic opera text to his worthy assistant conductor, the untalented composer Franz Löbmann. A National Hymn for soloist, chorus and orchestra, with words by Harald von Brackel, achieved popularity in the town, and for several years was performed on the Czar's birthday. An aria Wagner composed for insertion in Weigl's opera *Die Schweizerfamilie* is lost. In his autobiography Wagner remembered that 'it showed signs of the upheaval which was gradually taking place in my musical development'.

This upheaval was a steady inner movement towards musical maturity. Outwardly it was manifest in his growing dislike for the flummery and flimsy of the musical diet at Riga. With the exception of Löbmann, he avoided the company of his theatrical colleagues, and preferred to remain at home working at *Rienzi*. The epic proportion and serious nature of this work reflected his new mood. The poem, cast in five acts, was completed by 6 August 1838; the gigantic task of composition began at once. Wagner's models were *Robert le Diable* and *Les Huguenots* of Meyerbeer, together with two works he had heard at Dresden the previous summer, *La Juive* by Halévy* and Spohr's *Jessonda*. The latter work had now risen in Wagner's estimation. One opera in the Riga repertory also stimulated him: Méhul's *Joseph*. Act One of *Rienzi* was sketched by 6 December and fully scored by 2 February 1839. Act Two was sketched by 9 April 1839 and fully scored by the following month. With his thoughts turning to Paris again, Wagner wrote to the *Europa* editor Lewald in November 1838, asking him to use whatever influence he had to persuade Scribe to come to a decision about *Die hohe Braut*. Lewald published a song by Wagner in the following year, *Der Tannenbaum* (words by Georg Scheuerlin). Another trifle of the Riga period was an orchestral arrangement of *Les Mariniers* from Rossini's *Soirées Musicales*.

Domestic relations with Minna were good in the weeks that followed her arrival, with both of them making a conscious effort to avoid a repetition of past disputes. To compensate for their childless state they acquired a pet in the shape of a Newfoundland dog, Robber. For some weeks they even experimented with a wolf cub, but this pet proved a little difficult to cope with. Amalie also caused problems. At first the sisters seemed almost to revert to the playfulness of childhood, and the *ménage à trois* was happy and cheerful. When Karoline Pollert arrived in Riga, she soon replaced Amalie as the star of the company. Amalie, however, found compensation in the attentions of a young officer in the Russian army, Captain Carl von Meck, to whom she became engaged. For some reason this led to bitter quarrels between the two sisters and Wagner tells us that he 'had the very unpleasant experience of living for a whole year in the same house with two relatives who neither saw nor spoke to each other'.

A move to a more commodious and cheerful lodging in the spring of 1838 provided the comfort necessary for work on *Rienzi*, but inevitably added to the growing pile of debts. Two former sources of financial help were no more: Apel, who had withdrawn from the world after his accident; and Rosalie, Wagner's beloved and generous sister, who died in childbirth in October 1837.

As Wagner ceased to conceal his distaste for the operatic fare at the theatre, Holtei's dissatisfaction with him increased. Wagner's diligent perfectionism in rehearsal was foreign to Holtei. He could hardly complain of Wagner's zeal in the preparing of a considerable number of operas, yet he resented Wagner's ambitious attempts to reform the sleepy old routine. The orchestra became infected by the enthusiasm of their young conductor, however, and each one of the twenty-four players signed a petition, drafted by Wagner, calling for the establishment of a series of winter concerts in the town. This document does credit to Wagner, the practical musician. Recalling the educated audience that had been created by the Leipzig Gewandhaus concerts, and the subsequent benefit to the musician community of such an aware body of connoisseurs, he argued reasonably on behalf of a similar advantageous venture in Riga. Due to the complacent Holtei, nothing was done about the idea.

Holtei apparently had a growing reputation in the town because of homosexual activities. To quieten scandalous rumours he affected to pursue various ladies of the company. Wagner had persuaded Minna to retire from the stage, and he became irritated by Holtei's persistent attempts to wean her back to the theatre. When he learned that Holtei had been calling on Minna in his absence, and that he had actually introduced her to a handsome, rich local merchant, relations between manager and conductor became openly hostile. Late in 1838 the company were due to appear in Mitau. Wagner had a severe cold, but Holtei nonetheless insisted he travel with the others. Working in a freezing theatre at Mitau, Wagner developed typhoid fever which threatened to be fatal. Holtei acknowledged that Wagner was 'on his last legs' and it took all the skill and patience of a homeopathic doctor, Prutzer, to restore him to life and health.

Shortly after the return to Riga, Holtei was forced to leave the town on account of his unsavoury reputation. What appeared to be good news for Wagner soon altered its complexion. For Holtei's successor, Joseph Hoffmann, was appointed by the theatre committee on condition that Wagner be replaced as conductor by Heinrich Dorn, the municipal director of music, and former champion of Wagner's ill-fated colour overture in Leipzig. *Mein Leben* paints Holtei and Dorn in the blackest colours for what Wagner regarded as a conspiracy against him. In reality, the theatre committee, although partly influenced by Holtei's antipathy towards the conductor, regarded Wagner as an unsafe risk. There was every possibility that he would either be imprisoned for old and recently accrued debts, or on account of these make a sudden escape from his creditors to Paris, of which he continually spoke so warmly.

Wagner's situation was now utterly desperate, without any prospect of income, and creditors hemming in on all sides. He wrote a begging letter to Hoffmann:

> I will cheerfully work day and night for the theatre, I will undertake every duty I can possibly cope with, I will orchestrate whole scores and anything else that may be asked of me, but I want to be assured that I am to be remunerated for it . . . I herewith request from you a total remittance of my advance (of course with the exception of the thirty roubles which I recently borrowed from you and which I am to pay off by five roubles each pay-day) and in return I offer to undertake anything you like to heap upon my shoulders, with the sole exception of boot-cleaning and water carrying, which last my heart is not equal to at the moment. I would even copy scores, were it not for the fear that this melancholy occupation would deepen the gloom of my temperament.

Minna was forced to abandon her duties as housekeeper and return to the stage for four guest appearances, which included the fated Mary Queen of Scots in Schiller's tragedy.

The curtain thus fell on another act in Wagner's dramatic life, with stage directions that were to be familiar throughout his career. On this occasion his escape was from one tight corner into a new situation, fraught with more misery, danger and excitement than he had yet dreamed of.

Three

The Lowest Depths

Misswende folgt mir,
wohin ich fliehe.

Siegmund, *Die Walküre*

PARIS HAD FOR LONG been the goal of Wagner's dreams. Now necessity
drove him there. The French capital had brought fame to several foreign
opera composers – the Germans Gluck and Meyerbeer, the Italians
Cherubini, Spontini and Rossini – and it possessed the finest opera house
in Europe, which paid excellent royalties. A successful premiere there
attracted the attention of the operatic world. In Paris Wagner would be
beyond the reach of his creditors, who lay in wait for him in towns all over
Germany.

To escape from Riga posed considerable problems. Wagner gathered
what funds he could, and Minna's guest appearances and the sale of their
furniture provided a few hundred roubles. A flight across the Russian
border was as hazardous then as a similar attempt to cross illegally
from Eastern Europe would be today. Wagner's passport had been
impounded, and to obtain another he would legally be obliged to adver-
tise his intentions publicly – an official ruling designed to forewarn and
protect creditors. Wagner's Königsberg friend, Abraham Möller, aided
the plotting couple. Wagner took Hoffmann into his confidence, and the
new director clearly shared the opinion that Wagner's only way out of his
problems was to flee the country. In June the theatre company appeared
in Mitau where Wagner conducted *Joseph*, *Fidelio* and *Oberon*. From
Mitau, Möller escorted the conductor, his wife, their huge dog, Robber,
together with their few remaining possessions, to a rendezvous with a
friend of his from the Prussian side of the frontier. This friend drove them
through various quiet country roads in the stifling summer heat, while
Möller crossed the border officially, and waited anxiously for his friends.

The Wagners reached a certain point where Möller's friend abandoned
the carriage and conducted them to a smugglers' drinking den, where
they met their guide for the next lap of the dangerous journey. They spent
the evening at this house which, Wagner recalled, 'gradually became
filled to suffocation with Polish Jews of most forbidding aspect'. When

57

darkness had fallen, their guide took them to the border, a ditch which ran the entire length of the Russian frontier, with sentry posts every hundred yards. The Cossack guards had orders to shoot fugitives on sight. The Wagners had to wait anxiously until the sentry left his hut to make a periodic inspection of the border, and then run as fast as they could to the ditch, scramble through it, and continue to run until they were out of firing range. Only when the ordeal was over did Wagner realize the extent of the risks to which they had just been exposed. Neither he nor the anguished, exhausted Minna had realized what hazardous folly their border crossing would be, and Wagner found himself at a loss to convey his regrets to his wife. And worse danger was to come.

Möller's friend awaited them with a carriage on the Prussian side, and they drove to the nearby village of Arnau, a few miles from Königsberg. At an inn there, where they remained a few days, they were joyfully reunited with their saviour Möller. The next stage was to reach the seaport of Pillau and the route they followed was a devious one, by-passing Königsberg, where Wagner was a wanted man. On the way the carriage toppled over in a narrow farmyard. Möller was hurt, Wagner fell onto a manure heap and Minna, caught beneath the vehicle, was severely injured. Mrs Burrell learned from Natalie (who must have heard the story from her mother) that the internal injuries she received made motherhood impossible for Minna. She was dragged to the nearest house, and stayed there overnight in the most squalid conditions. The next day they were compelled to hasten toward Pillau, where Minna had a few days to recover, before the ship was due to sail.

For two reasons, Wagner decided to take advantage of a merchant ship that was sailing to London. The first was a financial one, as the long over-land journey to Paris was beyond their resources. Secondly, their Newfoundland dog, Robber, who had behaved in an exemplary fashion during the frontier crossing, not uttering one bark, would be more easily conveyed by sea. The good beast was so large that he had to be hoisted up the side of the boat. The captain of the small vessel had been persuaded, no doubt by Möller's purse, to accept the Wagners as passengers without passports. His cargo was still to be surveyed by customs officials, however, so the couple had to hide below deck like stowaways until the *Thetis* set sail. The Wagners were relieved as they watched the coast disappear slowly from view, and they relaxed at the prospect of a pleasant voyage to London, which was expected to take eight days, with the prevailing good summer weather.

There followed a nightmare of three-and-a-half weeks at sea. A prolonged calm at first hindered their progress, and after seven days they had only reached Copenhagen. Still in good spirits, Wagner enjoyed the sight of Hamlet's castle of Elsinore as they sailed past, but gradually an unfavourable west wind increased until it became a violent storm. The wooden figure-head of the vessel was torn away, and Minna's trunk, containing some silver and clothing, swept into the sea. For forty-eight hours the ship struggled in the Skagerrak until the captain was forced to seek refuge somewhere on the Norwegian coast. A pilot boat guided them into a fjord, and Wagner forgot his sea-sickness and alarm as the *Thetis* progressed smoothly and quietly between enormous, awe-inspiring walls of rock. The echoes of the sailors' cries that rang through the giant ravine were to be recalled in the rhythmic shape of the seamen's chorus in *The Flying Dutchman*. This legend was vividly brought to Wagner's mind during the voyage to London. On 27 July they landed at a small fishing village, Sandvika, which was later used for the first scene in the opera.

Four days later the captain insisted on leaving this harbour, although the storm had not yet abated. They were driven against a reef, and once more returned to land to examine the damage. This being slight, the *Thetis* set sail once more on 1 August. All was calm for four days and then a good north wind arose which, Wagner thought, would speed them on to the end of their journey, but on 6 August another storm struck them with terrible violence. It reached its peak the following afternoon and a dramatic thunderstorm burst over the vessel as it was hurled up and down by mountainous waves. Minna prayed that they would be killed by the lightning rather than drowned, and begged Wagner to bind her to him, that they might die together. Their terrors lasted for another whole night and, to make matters worse, the crew of the *Thetis* began to look upon the two mysterious passengers as the cause of their ill fate. Even the captain cursed himself for having taken on board the sick and weary pair. On 8 August, the storm gave way to a merely unfavourable wind: apart from the danger of sand-banks, which had to be carefully negotiated, the worst was over. Next day, the English coast was sighted, and on 12 August they entered the Thames. Wagner had a long refreshing sleep, but Minna remained observing the alarming lights and bells which warned of fog, and nervously pointed them out to the sailors. When he awoke he found her and the entire crew slumbering deeply, and alone he watched with growing fascination the approaching landmarks of the famous estuary.

Wagner, Minna and Robber disembarked at Gravesend with what little of their luggage was left – mostly bedding and linen – and took a river steamer to London Bridge. They were fascinated by the strange bustle and excitement of the city. Lodgings were found at the King's Arms in Old Compton Street, for one week, and much of this time was spent sightseeing, during which they exhausted both themselves and most of their money. Wagner travelled by railway train for the first time, on a pleasure trip to Gravesend Park. In London he had hoped to meet Sir George Smart, to whom the score of the *Rule Britannia* overture had been sent, but this gentleman was out of town, as was Edward Bulwer-Lytton.

Wagner had visited the Houses of Parliament to seek Bulwer-Lytton, and experienced an interesting day there during which he heard a debate in the House of Lords on the suppression of the slave trade. He was a little disappointed by the conversational tone of the great Duke of Wellington, dressed in a grey beaver hat, and with his hands stuck deep into his trouser pockets. Although he had not understood a word of the proceedings, Wagner was proud to have glimpsed a little of the famous men of England, including the Prime Minister, Lord Melbourne. After 'experiencing the horrors of a ghastly London Sunday' Wagner and Minna crossed to Boulogne on 20 August, and fervently hoped they would never go to sea again.

On the ferry to Boulogne Wagner had the good fortune to meet two Jewish ladies, friends of the composer Meyerbeer. Wagner had pinned his hopes on the protection of this fellow countryman and was astonished to learn that the great man was in Boulogne at that very time. An introduction was arranged and Meyerbeer received Wagner with kindness and courtesy. He listened patiently as Wagner read him the first three acts of his *Rienzi* poem, and expressed genuine admiration for its dramatic qualities. Wagner left the completed first two acts with him for perusal. Meyerbeer introduced him to various friends in Boulogne, including the virtuoso pianist-composer Ignaz Moscheles, who had known Beethoven and taught Mendelssohn. Wagner remained in Boulogne for almost a month and, inspired by Meyerbeer's praise, pressed on with *Rienzi*. Before he left for Paris he secured from Meyerbeer letters of introduction to the director of the Opéra, Charles-Edmond Duponchel, and its conductor François Habeneck.* Wagner also wrote to Eduard Avenarius, his sister Cäcilie's fiancée, asking him to arrange accommodation in Paris, where Avenarius worked as an agent of the Brockhaus publishing firm.

Forsaking Boulogne for Paris on 16 September, Wagner's first impression of the French capital was unfavourable. The wide streets of Regency London had so recently aroused his admiration that it came as something of a shock to see and smell the dim, dirty, narrow habitations of Paris. Avenarius had found them rooms in a hotel in the Halles quarter. Neither Wagner nor Minna had more than a phrase or two of French between them. In the last month at Riga Wagner had taken lessons in the language, but realizing that he would absorb very little in the time, cleverly managed to use them to provide a French translation of *Rienzi*. This he had inserted into the first two acts, in red ink. Throughout his Paris stay Wagner's acquaintances were limited to the German community there. He had insufficient money, no clothes and a certain roughness of manner which barred him from the circles of the social elite. The close friends he made in Paris were men in much the same position as himself: artists and scholars struggling in a hostile, foreign environment, drawn together by the mutual bonds of poverty.

In the late autumn of 1839 Wagner's high hopes slowly began to wither. The Paris of his youthful, optimistic dreams soon became a waking nightmare. The first rebuff came from Duponchel, the Opéra director. Fixing a monocle to his right eye, he read through the letter from the composer of *Les Huguenots* without displaying the slightest emotion. Wagner left his office and never heard another word from him. Many other contacts proved equally hopeless: some at least feigned interest in his work, which only made the eventual disillusionment all the more bitter. As will be shown, Meyerbeer did a great deal to steer Wagner in the right direction, but during the thirty months Wagner stayed in France Meyerbeer was mostly on tour elsewhere in Europe.

Gottfried Anders* was the first new acquaintance Wagner made in Paris, through an introduction from Avenarius. He was an impoverished, somewhat effeminate bachelor in his fifties, working as a librarian and living under an assumed name (Anders means 'otherwise'). He never revealed his original name but claimed to be a ruined aristocrat. He shared his house with his friend Samuel Lehrs,* a German-Jewish scholar who was equally poor. Lehrs was the first of several Jews with whom Wagner had a deep friendship; indeed, *Mein Leben* speaks of this association as one of the most beautiful of his entire life. He responded particularly to the patient and cultured interest Lehrs took in subjects like philology and medieval poetry. The library of Anders and the researches of Lehrs helped to enrich Wagner's own thinking now that the careless, frivolous attitudes of pre-Riga days receded further and further. Luise and Friedrich Brockhaus were in Paris late in 1839, and through his sister Wagner met Ernst Benedikt Kietz* who soon became a very close friend. Kietz's pursuits were painting and pederasty. He was studying with Delaroche at that time, but when it came to earning a living by his art he proved himself as hopeless as the other members of Wagner's circle; his talents brought him several commissions for portraits but he was temperamentally incapable of ever completing any of them. His unworldly, impecunious and immoral mode of life was a constant source of concern to Wagner. Kietz succeeded in completing a sketch of Wagner and a drawing of Minna, in addition to a number of caricatures. Another painter, Friedrich Pecht,* joined the group of friends at a later date.

Heinrich Laube lived in Paris at that time and proved another stimulating companion. He had married a wealthy widow in Berlin and this lady became friendly with Minna. Laube was to help the Wagners financially by appealing on their behalf to Friedrich Brockhaus and an affluent Jewish merchant, Axenfeld, in Leipzig. Through Laube Wagner met the celebrated and brilliant poet Heinrich Heine.* Wagner admired Heine, but never became close to him personally. In later years Wagner attributed the poet's cynicism to his Jewish origins.

Wagner's friends advised him to compose some songs which might become fashionable as salon pieces. In 1840 the Paris firm of Flaxland published *Trois Mélodies* by R. Wagner: *Dors, mon enfant* (words by a friend of Anders), *Mignonne* (Ronsard) and *L'Attente* (Hugo). At his own expense Wagner published his setting of *Les Deux Grenadiers*, a French translation of the Heine poem which Schumann set as *Die beiden Grenadiere*. Both Wagner and Schumann incorporate *La Marseillaise* in their songs. Two other songs, *Les Adieux de Marie Stuart* and *Tout n'est qu'images fugitives*, like those above, found no one who was interested in performing them, although several singers (including Pauline Garcia, later Viardot*) deigned to glance at them, murmured a few amiable words of praise and then forgot all about them. A grand aria with chorus in the style of Bellini was an attempt to infiltrate the opera world. Wagner hoped that the bass Lablache would include it in performances of *Norma*, but the singer pointed out, in as kindly a fashion as possible, that Bellini's work was too well known to permit this. A vaudeville chorus, *La Descente de la Courtille*, did receive a performance at the Variétés Theatre.

By January 1840 Wagner owed Avenarius 400 francs and when the young man returned to Paris with his bride, Cäcilie (whom he married in Leipzig on 5 March), Wagner turned to him again and again for funds. This led to a temporary coolness between Wagner and his favourite sister. Apart from sums from Axenfeld in Leipzig, Wagner was also dependent upon Kietz, the painter's uncle Eduard Fechner, and Pecht for the occasional loan. In addition, he incurred a debt with another rich Leipzig merchant, Heinrich Schletter. The remnants of Minna's theatrical wardrobe and even their wedding rings were pawned, and the pawn tickets sold. To Wagner's great dismay, poor Robber, the much-loved Newfoundland dog, disappeared, either through hunger or the intuition that he was an extra burden on meagre resources.

It was painful for Wagner to emerge from the utter drudgery of his existence and view the glittering society life of the Paris of Louis Philippe. In April 1840 he had a brief meeting with Franz Liszt,* which came to nothing. Laube mentioned Wagner to Liszt, and had urged his friend to call again on the great virtuoso when he was next in Paris; Liszt had a reputation for generosity to his fellow artists and Laube was convinced that he would find a means of helping Wagner. On arriving at Liszt's hotel one April morning in 1841, Wagner found himself in the company of several other admirers. The conversation that ensued, in fluent French, meant little to him and Liszt was clearly too preoccupied with his own affairs to take more than a polite notice of Wagner. Some days later Liszt's secretary sent Wagner a ticket for one of Liszt's recitals. Everything about this event jarred on the young German. Although he was dazzled by Liszt's virtuosity, the sight of an artist basking in opulence and surrounded by female admirers irritated him. In a letter to his mother he referred contemptuously to the salon talents of Paris: 'I feel bound to despise whomever I have seen succeed in this way.' And in reviewing Liszt's recital for the Dresden *Abendzeitung* he confessed, 'I got such a frightful headache, such painful twitchings of the nerves, that I had to go home early and put myself to bed.'

It is easy to deride Wagner on account of his continual debts, and his enemies have lost no opportunity in doing so, but during the Paris period there can be nothing but admiration for the way in which he struggled, with all the odds against him, to adapt himself to a foreign musical world and yet remain true to his artistic conscience. His industry in the face of poverty and adversity is remarkable. Work on the monumental *Rienzi* advanced steadily throughout 1840: Act Three was sketched between 15 February and 7 July, Act Four between 10 July and 29 August, and Act Five from 5–19 September. The overture was complete by 23 October and the entire work fully scored by 19 November. In addition *A Faust Overture* was finished in February 1840. This work was intended to be the first movement of a Faust Symphony, and Wagner sketched a slow movement theme depicting Gretchen. In the spring, Habeneck rehearsed it with the Conservatoire orchestra, but it was not considered suitable for public performance in Paris on account of its quiet ending.

In addition to his musical creativity, Wagner became busy as a journalist too. Meyerbeer had recommended him to the music publisher Moritz Schlesinger.* Schlesinger, like Meyerbeer a German Jew, published Wagner's song *Les Deux Grenadiers*, for which kindness he charged the composer fifty francs. Unable to pay this sum, Wagner instead wrote an article for Schlesinger's *Gazette Musicale*. So began a long series of essays from Wagner's pen that brought him in an extremely small income – for half the fee for each article went to a translator. His first article for the *Gazette Musicale* was *German Music* (12, 26 July), a clear and comprehensive account of the various forms of music-making in Germany, the greatness of German masters in the direction of instrumental, rather than vocal music and a survey of the historical importance of Bach, Mozart and Weber. Wagner concludes with the hope that a German composer, learning from French models, might create an opera which combines all that is best of both nations. For 'the German more than any other possesses the power to go to another country, develop its art to its highest peak and raise it to the plane of universal validity. Handel and Gluck abundantly proved this and . . . Meyerbeer has provided a fresh example.' Without actually saying so, Wagner optimistically saw himself as the next in this line of succession.

Pergolesi's Stabat Mater (11 October) was a review of a newly published arrangement of that work; and *The Virtuoso and the Artist* (18 October) a light-hearted consideration of musical idols in which Wagner aims a dart or two at popular Italian tenors. In 1841 Wagner contributed articles on *The Overture* (10, 14, 17 January), *The Artist and Publicity* (1 April), *'Der Freischütz' in Paris* (23, 30 May) and, in 1842, *Halévy's 'Reine de Chypre'* (27 February, 18 March, 24 April, 1 May).

In addition Wagner wrote three short stories, *A Pilgrimage to Beethoven*

(19, 22, 29 November, 3 December 1840), *An End in Paris* (31 January, 7, 11 February 1841) and *A Happy Evening* (24 October, 27 November 1841). The first of these is an imaginary account of a visit to the great master in Vienna by a young composer, R . . ., which is almost frustrated by a meddlesome Englishman. It contains the first important reference to the future theory of music drama. The most effective of these stories is the moving, semi-autobiographical *An End in Paris*. The enthusiastic young German composer R . . . is convinced that he will find fame as an opera composer in Paris, but gradually falls victim to disillusionment, poverty and consumption. His beautiful Newfoundland dog deserts him for a new master, the horn-playing Englishman. As in *The Artist and Publicity* Wagner sketches the pain and anguish of an artist struggling for recognition in an alien, Philistine society, and through his struggles discovering his true artistic conscience. The hero of the short story dies affirming his artistic credo, and is buried by three faithful friends: the narrator, a philologist and a painter. He leaves only his debts, and a beautiful dog which returns to mourn beside his grave. *A Happy Evening* is the kernel of the young Wagner's philosophy of music, the reasons for its greatness and unique place among all the arts. All three tales show Wagner attempting to imitate the imagery and prose style of E. T. A. Hoffmann. Although his attempts fall far short of the quality of Hoffmann's work, Wagner achieves a freshness and immediacy in his Paris writings that he never recaptured in his later prose works.

Many of these articles and stories were reprinted in the *Dresdener Abendzeitung* in 1841–2, together with nine *Reports from Paris*. These reports, and a caustic review of the Parisian mistreatment of Weber, *Le Freischütz* (16, 21 July 1841), reflect on the various anomalies and curiosities of Parisian music, the corruption at the Opéra and the activities of Berlioz* and Liszt, with vigour and wit. With the eye of a young idealist, he reveals the pitfalls and prejudices of the French capital and makes his points without the references to politics, anti-Semitism or racial chauvinism that cloud the rhetoric of most of his later essays. Freshness and vitality, and proof that Wagner had attained considerable skill as a natural journalist, if not a born writer, are seen also in two articles submitted to the *Europa* magazine, *Parisian Traps for Germans* (Summer 1841) and *Parisian Amusements* (Autumn 1841); also in an essay reviewing Rossini's *Stabat Mater* and a tenth *Report from Paris*, which appeared in the *Neue Zeitschrift für Musik* (28 December 1841 and 22 February 1842, respectively). The only unpleasant discord is Wagner's adoption of a pseudonym, 'W. Freudenfeuer', for his *Europa* articles. To avoid repercussions Wagner resorted to this sort of anonymity when pursuing a more vitriolic line of attack, in this case of Auber, Dumas, Scribe and various celebrated singers including Giovanni Rubini and Gilbert Duprez. Downright malicious was the use of the name 'H. Valentino' for the article abusing Rossini's *Stabat Mater*, as Henri Valentino was a well-known Paris conductor. Nastier still were the initials 'H.V.' at the end of his Report for the Leipzig *Neue Zeitschrift*, which calls Liszt a buffoon and 'M.' (Meyerbeer) a 'sly, deliberate pickpocket'. This technique of anonymity was later adopted by Wagner whenever he chose a stab-in-the-back attack, for example in the notorious *Judaism in Music* (1850), the shabby invective against his former friend Eduard Devrient (1869) and the base-minded anti-French play *A Capitulation* (1870).

In the spring of 1840 Wagner sketched the scenario of *Der Fliegende Holländer* (The Flying Dutchman), intending it to be a one-act curtain-raiser for an evening of ballet. In this sketch the heroine is named Minna, later changed to Senta. About that time the Wagners moved into more expensive unfurnished accommodation in the Rue de Helder; the rent was 1200 francs per year and furniture had to be obtained on credit. Wagner was pinning all his hopes on a production of *Das Liebesverbot* at the Théâtre de la Renaissance, and Meyerbeer arranged for three singers from the Opéra to learn some extracts from it in French translation. No sooner was Wagner installed in his new surroundings when news came that the Renaissance Theatre was bankrupt. Afterwards Wagner suspected that Meyerbeer had known of this impending bankruptcy and had therefore duped him all along. As Meyerbeer was to be instrumental in helping Wagner make a success in Germany a few years later, it does not seem feasible that he would purposely delude his young fellow country-man in this way. Wagner's retrospective opinion of Meyerbeer's help is grossly unfair, and the treatment of Meyerbeer in *Mein Leben* simply does not square with the facts. Not even Meyerbeer's influence could open every door in Paris for Wagner. This failure, the bitter memory of months of hardship, jealousy of the popular success of works like *Les Huguenots* and an irrational anti-Semitism distort Wagner's later view of his benefac-tor. The above-mentioned reference to Meyerbeer as a 'pickpocket' shows that Wagner's private feelings about him as a successful composer were already antagonistic, but a letter to Schumann of 29 December 1840 tells a different story: 'Don't pitch into Meyerbeer so vigorously. I have that man to thank for everything, and more especially for the fame so shortly to be mine.'

In a last-ditch attempt to have *Das Liebesverbot* mounted, an audition was arranged before Eduard Monnais (temporary director of the Opéra since Duponchel's retirement) and the illustrious Scribe. As Wagner accompanied the singers at the piano a sense of shame at this early superficial work crept over him. Monnais and Scribe were charming and polite about it, and although he appreciated their kindness, Wagner knew that Scribe's offer to arrange the libretto for him as soon as the Opéra decided to accept the work was empty flattery.

As the summer of 1840 approached life at the Rue de Helder became grim. A season of hard work in Paris had brought Wagner little or no return. Now at every door he was greeted with the same monotonous phrase, 'Monsieur est à la campagne', and, not for the last time in his life, Wagner's thoughts turned towards America and the idea of starting a new career there. The larger part of their new apartment had to be let, first to a miserly spinster, Fräulein Leplay, and afterwards to an amiable commercial traveller, Herr Brix, whose only fault was a tendency to practise the flute during all his leisure hours. Minna had to serve the lodgers, and even blacked their boots. One day a mysterious parcel arrived with a London postmark. Wagner's hopes instantly rose – Providence had remembered him. But it contained only the score of his overture *Rule Britannia* – rejected by the Philharmonic Society. Furthermore, Wagner was expected to pay seven francs for the carriage. Angrily, he told the courier to take it to a music publisher: they could do what they liked with it.

On another occasion Wagner was wandering the streets of the city in search of funds to appease the occasional merchant whose bill had fallen due. It was a densely foggy day, but through the gloom Wagner discerned Robber, his lost dog. He ran towards him with outstretched arms, whereupon the animal drew timidly away. As Wagner pursued him, Robber ran faster until man and dog raced through a labyrinth of streets. Eventually, hot and breathless, Wagner abandoned the chase and returned home sad and shaken at the sight of this canine ghost from the past.

On 20 September 1840 Wagner wrote to Theodor Apel from the lowest depths of poverty. He recounted his utter misery and destitution, the failure of all the hopes that had brought him to Paris:

> But I wish now that I could buy medicine for my poor wife! Will she survive this misery and shall I be able to bear hers? Lord God, help me! I no longer know how to help myself! I have exhausted everything, everything, every last resource of the starving. I, unfortunate, never knew mankind until now. Money – it is the curse that annihilates everything noble.

He beseeched Apel to send him 300 thalers. No money and no reply came. In October Wagner was imprisoned for debt for several weeks and, in the ignoble surroundings of a debtors' jail, the scoring of the heroic *Rienzi* was completed. On 28 October Minna wrote a letter to Apel that was drafted by Wagner. It too dwells on the frustration of every goal they had striven towards in Paris, and cries in despair:

> To my horror I learned some time ago how much Richard already owes you. You used to get money for him by your credit; but what was his situation then compared to ours now? Wouldn't this sacrifice be much more apposite now, since there is a sure prospect of paying off such a debt within one or two years at most? Believe me I usually fail to share Richard's exalted hopes, but I know now . . . that he is within one step of reaching his goal. My God, what more can I say? I am not composed enough to explain clearly all that I want to, but I will make up for that later – all I can say is: Help! Help!

On 17 November Minna wrote to Apel again, this time in her own words. Apparently Apel then sent enough money to secure Wagner's release. Natalie appears to have joined the household when they were at this lowest ebb.

Wagner's first task on leaving prison was to send his completed score of *Rienzi* to Baron von Lüttichau,* director of the Dresden Court Theatre, together with a recommendation from Meyerbeer. On 1 December he petitioned King Friedrich August of Saxony with the request that he order a production of the opera. In a letter to Laube two days later Wagner mentions the possibility of further imprisonment and the seizure of his property unless he is provided with funds. He had by now accepted various forms of hack work from Schlesinger in addition to journalism. First Schlesinger asked him to concoct a 'method' for the cornet à pistons. Wagner admitted that he simply knew nothing about this instrument, which was then fashionable among amateur musicians in Paris. Schlesinger's reply was to send him five different published 'Methods' with the request that he devise a new sixth one. Fortunately for Wagner's sanity Schlesinger shortly relieved him of this task and also from another project of arranging fourteen suites for the cornet à pistons.

The publisher's next suggestion was that Wagner should make various arrangements of Donizetti's deathless inspiration *La Favorita*. The task was to make a complete vocal score; a complete piano arrangement without vocal parts; and complete arrangements for piano duet, string quartet, two violins and finally cornet à pistons. For this enormous and humiliating chore he received 500 francs in advance and 600 francs on completion. In addition he received 300 francs for correcting the proofs of the full score of Donizetti's opera. To save money and fuel, Wagner, Minna and Natalie all huddled together in the bedroom during the day so, in addition to eating and sleeping in that room, Wagner applied himself to his hack work in cramped and miserable conditions. At night Natalie slept on the sofa in the cold salon.

New Year's Eve at the end of the eventful year 1840 evokes images of Puccini's *La Bohème*. The consumptive Lehrs arrived at the Rue de Helder with a leg of veal, Kietz with rum, sugar and a lemon, Pecht with a goose and Anders with two bottles of champagne that had been gifted to him. For once a fire was lit in the salon and a merry evening ensued. Wagner freely indulged in champagne and punch, mounted a chair, then a table and preached a sermon in praise of the American Free States. The following morning he faced *La Favorita* again. On 14 January 1841 he told Schlesinger in a letter that he was so busy he had no time even to leave the house, but thanked the publisher for effectively saving his life and raising him a little out of his misery. Perhaps Schlesinger would now further the process of redemption by lending him 1000 francs? – 'If it is difficult for you to do this for me, look upon it as a great sacrifice that you are making for me.'

On 4 February occurred the only public presentation of a work by Wagner during this Paris period. Henri Valentino conducted a poor performance of the feeble *Columbus* overture before a bored, unsympathetic audience.

In the spring of 1841 Wagner moved from his expensive quarters to Meudon, a village not far from Paris. Unfortunately he was one week too late in giving notice to his landlord of his intentions, and was therefore liable for another term of rent. A family was found to occupy the furnished rooms for some months but when they left, the landlord again demanded payment from Wagner. Not gaining satisfaction, he seized the composer's furniture and sold it.

At Meudon life was cheaper and quieter than in the city and Wagner was a safe distance from his creditors. Here he wrote the poem of *The Flying Dutchman* (18–28 May) and sketched the entire score in a mere seven weeks, completing it on 22 August. In July, the new director of the Opéra, Leon Pillet, expressed an interest in the draft of *The Flying Dutchman*. He was not concerned with the idea of Wagner composing the music, but thought of it in terms of one of the composers who already had a contract with the Opéra. Wagner was at first taken aback by this blunt suggestion but, realizing that this was all he could reasonably expect from such an august institution, he sold his plot to Pillet for 500 francs. Ironically this money provided the means for Wagner to work at the music for *The Flying Dutchman*, while his plot was transformed into *Le Vaisseau Fantôme* with music by Pierre Louis Philippe Dietsch,* which met with complete failure at the Opéra in 1842. This same Dietsch was to enter Wagner's life at a crucial moment almost twenty years later.

During 1841 various seeds were sown to cultivate interest in Wagner's works in Germany. In March Meyerbeer wrote to the Dresden director Lüttichau:

> Herr Richard Wagner from Leipzig is a young composer with not only a sound musical education but also much imagination; he has in addition a broad literary culture and his situation deserves the sympathy of his native country in all these respects. His greatest desire is to have the opera *Rienzi* . . . performed in Dresden. I found some sections which he played to me from this work full of imagination and considerable dramatic effect.

Laube helped to interest Schröder-Devrient in a Dresden performance, while Wagner wrote to Lüttichau, and to two old friends of Ludwig Geyer: Hofrath Winkler,* the theatre secretary, and Ferdinand Heine,* the costume designer. Not only was the presence of Schröder-Devrient in Dresden's favour, but also that of Joseph Tichatschek,* who was probably the finest heroic tenor in Germany. In June the Dresden theatre committee agreed to adopt *Rienzi* and to perform it early in 1842. Negotiations dragged on for months, however, and the impatient composer wrote a shoal of letters during the remainder of the year to everyone connected with the Dresden theatre, offering advice on endless trivial details concerning the production. As the months passed by Wagner's excitement increased and Paris seemed more hostile than ever.

The Flying Dutchman marks an important stage in Wagner's musical development. *Rienzi* displayed Wagner's talents in the realm of Grand Opera à la Spontini and Meyerbeer. Its libretto was so wholly idiomatic of that world that Scribe himself was influenced by it in his own libretto *Le Prophète*, written for Meyerbeer. Despite much fine music (notably in the chorus and ensemble numbers) *Rienzi* is overlong, somewhat roughly orchestrated and lacking in thematic variety. *The Flying Dutchman* signified Wagner's spiritual return to Germany. It is the fruit of the period of 'yearning for the German homeland', as he described it in *A Communication to my Friends* of 1851, and Wagner assessed his development succinctly when he wrote that 'so far as my knowledge goes I can find in the life of no artist so striking a transformation, in so short a time, as is evident between *Rienzi* and *The Flying Dutchman*, the former of which was hardly finished when the latter was begun'. *The Flying Dutchman* is not without its flaws but in many respects it marks the beginning of his musical and dramatic maturity, notably in the attempts at a continuous flow of music, telling use of simple, 'elemental' leitmotifs and the dramatic theme of redemption by a woman. Also, like every other opera he wrote afterwards, excepting *Die Meistersinger*, its subject matter is mythological.

On 30 October 1841 Wagner returned from Meudon to Paris, and settled in a wretched little apartment in the Rue Jacob. Kietz lived next door and the two friends could greet each other from their respective windows. Here Wagner completed the scoring of *The Flying Dutchman* on 19 November. At the end of the overture he wrote, 'Paris, 5 November 1841. Per aspera ad astra. God grant it!' With Meyerbeer's help he at once began negotiations with German opera houses for its performance.

Christmas found him destitute once more, and longing to return to Germany. His reading turned to Teutonic literature. After studying Raumer's 'History of the Hohenstaufen' he sketched a five-act opera on the subject of Manfred, *Die Sarazenin* (The Saracen Woman). He became interested in the legends of Tannhäuser and Lohengrin. The festive season was brightened by the gift of a goose from Avenarius, which had in its beak a 500 franc note sent by Schletter of Leipzig. Early in the new year Joseph Dessauer, a Jewish composer and pupil of Dionýs Weber, commissioned a libretto from Wagner. The result was a sketch, *Die Bergwerke zu Falun*, based on a story of that name by E. T. A. Hoffmann. As in *The Flying Dutchman*, Hoffmann's black world of visions and phantoms permeates this sketch, for which Wagner received 200 francs.

Although Dresden seemed to be perpetually postponing the *Rienzi* premiere, Wagner was determined to go there immediately after Easter. Now that he had definite prospects, his relatives were only too pleased to help him with funds for the return to Germany.

Richard Wagner

The thirty months in Paris had been bitter and bleak. Yet despite all the privations and frustrations Wagner gained much during that period. Although he had avoided the Opéra performances, partly from poverty and partly from a distaste for the Italian and French musical fashions, he had experienced a little of truly professional music-making for the first time in his life. Also for the first time he had come into close contact with men of genius. Not least of these was Berlioz, whose *Symphonie fantastique*, *Harold in Italy*, *Romeo and Juliet* and *Symphonie funèbre et triomphale* had greatly impressed him. For the first time too, he had heard Beethoven performed with excellence under Habeneck, whose rehearsals of the Ninth Symphony were a revelation to Wagner. In truth Wagner could write to Ludwig of Bavaria in 1867: '[Paris] occupied so important a place in the development of my relations with the outside world that, whenever I think of such things, I invariably find myself remembering my experiences there . . . and there I was able to grasp at once things which at the wayside stations I would perhaps have taken a lifetime to learn . . .'

On the bright spring morning of 7 April the Wagners took a sad farewell of Anders, the dying Lehrs and the good-hearted Kietz. Before the carriage left, Kietz gave Wagner his last five-franc piece and a packet of good French snuff for the journey. They did not notice the barriers of the city as they drove past, for their eyes were blinded with tears.

Four

Royal Kapellmeister

It is an interesting and noteworthy phenomenon that the cool and unexcitable Dresden theatre public has been transformed by Wagner's operas into a fiery and enthusiastic body, such as may be seen nowhere else in Germany.

Signale für die musikalische Welt, Leipzig, February 1847

AFTER A JOURNEY of five days and nights through snow and rain, with only a vivid glimpse of the Wartburg to lighten his heart, Wagner arrived in Dresden on 12 April 1842. His first task was to find rooms for himself and Minna; Natalie had been left behind in Paris in the care of Cäcilie and Eduard Avenarius. No date had yet been arranged for the *Rienzi* performance so Wagner left Minna in Dresden and set out first for Leipzig to see his family and reassure them that he was now more worthy of a loan, and then, after three days with his mother, on to Berlin to seek after the fortunes of *The Flying Dutchman*.

This opera had been rejected by the directors Ringelhardt*of Leipzig and Küstner* of Munich to whom Wagner had sent the libretto. The Berlin director, Count von Redern* did not even trouble to reply when Wagner sent him a letter about his new work on 27 June 1841, but late in November the score of *The Flying Dutchman* was sent from Paris to Berlin and Wagner begged Meyerbeer to use his influence with Redern. He expressed hearty thanks to Meyerbeer for his successful intervention with Dresden over *Rienzi* and hoped Meyerbeer's kindness would work another miracle with the Berlin management. Meyerbeer did exactly what Wagner requested and personally urged Redern to mount the work of a young composer he considered to be interesting and worthy. Learning that Meyerbeer was willing to help him in this way, Wagner wrote to him, 'That God may give joy to each day of your beautiful life and preserve your eyes for ever from grief is the sincere prayer of your most devoted pupil and servant, Richard Wagner'. On 14 December Berlin acknowledged receipt of *The Flying Dutchman* score and referred to Meyerbeer's particularly warm recommendation. Again Wagner wrote an effusive letter of thanks to Meyerbeer, wishing him all success and happiness, yet within two months Wagner was describing his benefactor as a 'pickpocket' in the columns of the *Neue Zeitschrift für Musik*, and before the end of the decade Wagner was to attack Meyerbeer in less uncertain language. But for the moment duplicity was essential. He could ridicule him in the press under the careful cover of a pseudonym, but to his face he continued to grovel and flatter for as long as Meyerbeer might be of use to him.

On arriving in Berlin on 19 April 1842, Wagner discovered that Redern was on the point of retiring from the directorship, and that his successor was to be Küstner – who had already rejected *The Flying Dutchman* as not suited to the German taste. Wagner saw this state of affairs in a grievous light. He desperately needed a Berlin success. A performance at the Dresden opera, even in the fine new theatre built by Gottfried Semper,* was good so far as it went but without a hearing of his work in Berlin he might almost as well have remained in Paris. In *Mein Leben* Wagner suggests that Meyerbeer was responsible for misleading him into believing that he had hope for a performance in Berlin. Once again, Wagner's autobiography cannot be trusted. Meyerbeer, who became a musical director to the King of Prussia in 1842, genuinely did his best to further Wagner's interests in Berlin as he had done in Paris, as is attested by his letter of 5 December 1843 to Küstner, reminding him of the obligation to perform *The Flying Dutchman*. Wagner records that in April 1842 Meyerbeer regretted 'that he was just on the point of "going away", a state in which I always found him whenever I visited him again in Berlin'.

Further negotiations with Redern were clearly pointless and Wagner resolved to return to Berlin when Küstner was established there. Before leaving the Prussian capital he consulted Mendelssohn (with whom he told Avenarius he was 'on very friendly terms') about the fate of *The Flying Dutchman*. Mendelssohn was polite to Wagner, if not exactly enthusiastic about his aspirations. He assured Wagner that Redern would probably be able to persuade Küstner to agree to the performance of the opera. In *Mein Leben* Wagner states that he found Mendelssohn somewhat cold, 'yet it was not so much that he repelled me as that I recoiled from him'. No reference was made to the score of Wagner's Symphony, sent to Mendelssohn in 1836. Wagner also felt repulsed by the critic Rellstab who showed no interest in his affairs when the composer called on him. Altogether this visit to Berlin was a poor beginning to Wagner's new ventures in Germany.

Nothing in the wake of his Paris experiences was going to daunt him, however. France may have denied him her laurels but he returned to Dresden with a grim determination that his homeland would have no opportunity to do the same. On the way back from Berlin he stopped again at Leipzig and secured a loan from Hermann Brockhaus, his understanding brother-in-law who was now Professor of Oriental languages at the university and who, together with Ottilie and Luise, pledged to give him a monthly sum until *Rienzi* was mounted.

The Dresden manager Lüttichau and the conductor Gottlieb Reissiger* were both taken aback by Wagner's arrival in the town. They considered his presence somewhat premature and unnecessary. Even the worthy Hofrath Winkler thought he would have been better to remain in Paris. Winkler, who wrote under the name Theodor Hell, had published many of Wagner's Paris articles in his capacity as editor of the Dresden *Abend-zeitung*. Through these articles he and another old friend of Ludwig Geyer's, Ferdinand Heine, knew a little about the composer of *Rienzi*, but not much. Knowledge of him in Dresden was slight – he was known to be young and reputedly talented, and to have experienced wild adventures and near-starvation in Paris. He was otherwise an unknown quantity, untried and, until his opera was performed, somewhat unwelcome. The very fact that the Dresden management were willing to mount *Rienzi*, with all its problems of scale and interpretation, was a tribute to their spirit of initiative and enterprise. Wagner knew this and was careful to remain helpful and diplomatic. If *Rienzi* succeeded in the Saxon capital then there was every chance that Berlin would take it up, and then the arena of Europe would be open to him. Reissiger, the Dresden conductor, was also a composer of the old school. He found little to interest him in the work of the newly arrived composer. Wagner wrote to Avenarius on 3 May: 'Reissiger is perpetually hanging on my neck and devours me with kisses when he can get hold of me. Everyone assures me, too, that he really means fair by me and is full of good-will. Unfortunately the fellow has become such a rank Philistine that I should be in a terrible way if I had to leave the artistic production of my opera in his hands alone.' *Rienzi* was at that time scheduled for production in August, then postponed until September, and finally delayed until October.

On 5 May Wagner returned to Leipzig to meet the new Berlin director Küstner, and discuss *The Flying Dutchman*. Küstner refused to promise anything definite, so Wagner wrote to him in Berlin early in June, threatening to go there and intervene personally. Küstner again appealed for a little more time before he made a decision. Wagner was insistent that his opera would present no problems in rehearsal – it was short, posses-sed few ensemble numbers and its vocal demands were well within the means of the Berlin singers.

As there was nothing more he could do to hasten the productions of either *Rienzi* or *The Flying Dutchman*, Wagner decided to take a holiday in June. He made a short visit to his brother Albert who was struggling to make a living in Halle, and was impressed by the singing of Albert's fifteen-year-old daughter Johanna.[1] On 9 June Minna and her sister Jette joined Wagner on a visit to Teplitz. Wagner's mother was also on holiday at her favourite spa, so Wagner left the three women together and departed alone for a few days walking in the Erzgebirge mountains. The product of this solitary excursion was a detailed sketch for a three-act

---

[1] Later the famous singer Johanna Jachmann-Wagner.*

libretto *Der Venusberg*, later called *Tannhäuser*: a result of his readings during the last weeks in Paris. Lehrs had provided the impulse for Wagner to turn to old German legend. Another source for *Tannhäuser* was E. T. A. Hoffmann; specifically the tale in *Die Serapionsbrüder* entitled *Der Kampf der Sänger*. Like all his later opera texts, Wagner's *Tannhäuser* poem is the result of his wide reading – a distillation of many elements consciously and unconsciously remembered. The text of the *Ring* cycle is the most complex example of a poem forged from many different historical sources. The evolution of *Tannhäuser* is strikingly similar, however, in its blend of legendary and pseudo-historical elements which originally were unconnected, but in Wagner's poem coalesce as meaningful components of the drama. The principal two independent themes woven together here are the tale of Tannhäuser and Venus and that of the Contest of Song on the Wartburg. The poem of *Tannhäuser* occupied Wagner until April 1843.

Leaving Minna at Teplitz he returned to Dresden on 18 July in the hope that something might be done to arrange rehearsals for *Rienzi* now that Tichatschek and Schröder-Devrient were returning to the town from their tours elsewhere. Reissiger and the management still seemed to be in no hurry, however. A consolation was the return of Schröder-Devrient to the Dresden stage. Wagner's old enthusiasm for her art increased as he had the opportunity of hearing her frequently. Her first role that summer was in Grétry's *Bluebeard* and Wagner recalled nostalgically that this was the first opera he had ever seen, as a child of five in Dresden. Schröder-Devrient was past her best vocally, guilty of several unfortunate mannerisms and attaining a maternal stoutness which made her unsuitable for youthful parts, but Wagner still found her performances incomparably great and was impressed at her ability to sustain her noble qualities as an actress long after her vocal prime. Furthermore she was well disposed towards his *Rienzi* as was the ever-willing, good-natured Tichatschek. The tenor complemented the soprano in several respects: his intelligence as an actor left much to be desired but his musicianship was natural and brilliant. He displayed a childlike excitement at the magnificent costumes in which he was to be arrayed as Rienzi. These costumes were designed by Ferdinand Heine at whose house Wagner spent most of his evenings and where they were joined by the chorus master Wilhelm Fischer* in convivial intellectual debates over a meal of potatoes and herrings.

On 27 July Wagner moved into a furnished apartment at a rent of twelve thalers per month. This sum came from the family loan and Wagner earned a little more pocket money by arranging Halévy's *Reine de Chypre* for Schlesinger in Paris, and by making other arrangements for the French publisher Troupenas. The day after he occupied his new rooms he wrote to Minna in Teplitz begging her to join him again. It appears that she was somewhat reluctant to do this, but she returned to Dresden with Wagner's mother on 1 August.

At last rehearsals of *Rienzi* began. Wagner was lucky in his two principal singers, but the conductor Reissiger had to be handled with more tact and caution. Reissiger confided to Wagner that his own foremost problem as an opera composer was a perpetual difficulty in obtaining a well-devised libretto. Wagner recalled his *Hohe Braut* sketch that had been intended for Scribe. He read it to Reissiger, who seemed delighted with it, and they came to an agreement that Wagner would complete his libretto and in return Reissiger would hold frequent piano rehearsals of *Rienzi*. This arrangement worked admirably but in the end Reissiger did not compose music for *Die hohe Braut*. Apparently Frau Reissiger persuaded her husband that Wagner's offer of this libretto was part of a cunning plot and, suspecting some trap, Reissiger returned the book to Wagner.

The Dresden company expressed immense enthusiasm for *Rienzi*. Tichatschek was convinced that it was the greatest heroic role of his career. Schröder-Devrient created a few difficulties by her slow learning of new music, but responded well to Wagner's patient and tactful coaching. Certain numbers became regular favourites with the singers. Tichatschek declared that a moment of the Act Three finale was so lovely that something ought to be paid for it each time it was sung, and he set the precedent by putting down a silver penny. Thus on each day of rehearsals the cry would be raised, 'Here comes the silver penny part!' and purses were opened. Schröder-Devrient declared that the rehearsals would ruin her. They all looked upon this ritual as a joke and little realized that each silver penny was more than welcome to the young composer: he could pay the hire on his recently acquired grand piano more easily, and Minna could buy more food.

After many delays *Rienzi* opened on 20 October. It commenced at 6 p.m. and the audience did not leave the theatre until about 11.30. Despite this inordinate length there were enthusiastic ovations at the end of each act, and Heine had to push the stunned composer onto the stage to acknowledge them. Heine sent an account to Kietz, stressing that his views were not those of a partisan but mirrored the general ecstatic reaction:

> Our magnificent theatre was full to bursting, despite the increased prices. From the very first note of the overture there was a hushed silence, which was followed by thunderous applause that became more and more intense until the simply soul-stirring end of the fourth act, which was followed by a deep silence, turning into all the more deafening applause after the fifth act. . . . In the intervals I wandered through the foyer, the boxes, the buffet and the stalls to hear what people were saying, and often I did not know whether to believe my ears. There they were, the old minim-mongers and counterpoint codgers, putting their heads together and declaring roundly that with this opera Wagner had earned his place amongst the most worthy classics. . .

Although no one had left before the end, Wagner was compelled to make cuts in the score before the second performance. This reduced Tichatschek to tears and he declared that he would not allow a single note to be removed from his part.

The King attended the second performance six days later. As people crowded into Dresden from as far afield as Leipzig to hear his opera, Wagner became the toast of the town. *Rienzi* had completely eclipsed *Les Huguenots*. Heine was probably not alone in expressing a fear that Meyerbeer might now view the young Wagner as an undesirable enemy and withdraw his support in Berlin, but the Dresden authorities were anxious to follow up this unprecedented success with another. Negotiations with Küstner resulted in the return of *The Flying Dutchman* score from Berlin, and that opera was immediately put into rehearsal at Dresden. Never before had the work of an unknown young composer created such a stir. Lüttichau attempted to solve the problem of *Rienzi's* great length by presenting it in two parts on consecutive evenings. This proved unsuccessful as the public felt it was being cheated into paying twice for one opera, and after a time *Rienzi* reverted to performances on one evening. It retained an undiminished popularity in Dresden until its composer fled the town seven years later.

Critical attention focused on Wagner for the first time. In *Mein Leben* he comments on the breach between himself and the critics, which became wider as the years progressed:

> Though I was always anxious to be gracious to everybody, I felt just then an invincible repugnance for showing special deference to any man because he was a critic. As time went on, I carried this rule to the point of almost systematic rudeness, and was consequently the victim of unprecedented persecution from the press.

On 26 November Wagner accompanied Tichatschek and Schröder-Devrient on a three-day visit to Leipzig, for a benefit concert for the soprano's mother, the actress Sophie Schröder. This concert included extracts from *Rienzi*, conducted by the composer. Wagner again met Mendelssohn, whose *Ruy Blas* overture was included in the programme, but sensed that Mendelssohn was jealous at the success of *Rienzi* and bitterly resentful that Wagner had won instant acclaim in the operatic realm – a world in which he longed to find fame himself. In Leipzig Laube was once more editing the *Zeitung für die elegante Welt*. He commissioned a literary self-portrait from the newsworthy Wagner and in the following February the *Autobiographical Sketch* appeared in his paper.

Another excursion with Schröder-Devrient, this time to Berlin in December, brought Wagner into closer contact with Liszt. The impulsive soprano embarrassed both men by pointedly referring to their previous meeting in Paris when Liszt had virtually ignored the now famous composer of *Rienzi*. Thanks to Wagner's protestations and Liszt's good nature her scornful innuendoes did no damage. Wagner for the first time became aware of Liszt's noble and sincere personality. He had formerly dismissed his popularity as the empty hero-worship of idle flatterers;

only now did he realize the depth of Liszt's artistic nature and the frank and genuine mind that lay behind the façade of the virtuoso. Some years were to pass before they became real friends, but Liszt promised to attend a *Rienzi* performance at the earliest opportunity.

In Dresden the comforts of Wagner's home were enhanced by the acquisition of a spaniel puppy named Peps. Pets of one sort or another were to be a kind of link between Richard and Minna, helping to unite a bond that was all too easily divided. Debts were a major cause of these divisions, and even when the sun shone on a brighter future, such as during these early Dresden months, the spectre of financial ruin hovered around, for news of Wagner's new-found fame quickly reached the ears of old and almost forgotten creditors in Leipzig, Magdeburg, Königsberg, Riga, Paris and elsewhere. Assuming that success had brought him wealth aplenty, demands rolled in for repayment of debts incurred as long ago as his schooldays. Some of these he regarded as debts of honour, such as those to Kietz, Avenarius and Hermann Brockhaus, and endeavoured to alleviate them as quickly as possible.

His material position would be greatly enhanced if he could be assured of a permanent position in Dresden – and circumstances combined by chance to make this possible. Shortly after the premiere of *Rienzi*, Francesco Morlacchi, conductor of the Italian *ensemble* at Dresden, died (on 28 October) and a week or two later the theatre lost its assistant conductor Joseph Rastrelli (he died on 15 November). These posts were much sought after but the obvious candidate was the talented young conductor whose opera *Rienzi* had attracted so much attention to the town. Despite the lure of financial security and the urgings of his wife, family and friends, Wagner was very wary of taking this step. He had had sufficient experience of German theatres to know intuitively that he had outgrown them in his inner artistic nature. He realized that as a conductor he would be tied once more to the exhausting repertoire of uncongenial operas which would leave him little time for the unfolding of the new creative projects hatching in his mind. He told Lüttichau that his artistic freedom mattered more to him than the attainment of a subordinate post such as Rastrelli had occupied. The Intendant then proposed that Wagner would occupy a newly created post, a second Kapellmeister on equal official standing with Reissiger. On 12 December 1842, Reissiger, who was tired and overworked by extra duties following the deaths of his colleagues, handed over his baton to Wagner for the sixth performance of *Rienzi*. Wagner also conducted a performance of Weber's *Euryanthe* and his interpretation met with enthusiastic acclaim. Weber's widow, Caroline, joined the number of friends who persuaded him to accept the proffered appointment. She told him that only he could worthily continue the work her husband had begun at Dresden a quarter of a century before.

On 2 January 1843 Wagner conducted the first performance of *The Flying Dutchman* at the Royal Court Theatre, Dresden. With the exception of

Schröder-Devrient as Senta, he was disappointed with the standard of performance, and particularly by the poor acting of Michael Wächter in the title part. The audience was repelled by the gloomy subject matter of this romantic saga, and regarded it as a poor sequel to the colourful historical drama of *Rienzi*. This attitude hurt Wagner deeply. He knew that *The Flying Dutchman* was in every respect the better opera and a significant step towards the works he now envisaged, but his reputation with the public rested on an immature grand opera, conceived in a style he had long since abandoned. *The Flying Dutchman* survived another three performances. It was then dropped from the repertoire, partly because Schröder-Devrient left the company for a year early in April, and it was not heard again in Dresden for twenty-five years. To the public's joy and Wagner's resigned despair *Rienzi* returned once more and the tale of the accursed mariner was soon forgotten. Shortly after its first Dresden performance Wagner went to Berlin to ascertain what hopes existed for the *Flying Dutchman* production there. He found affairs in Berlin at a low ebb and became convinced that nothing of true artistic worth would flourish in such a demoralized atmosphere.

On 2 February Wagner was appointed Kapellmeister to the Royal Court of Saxony at a salary of 1500 thalers. He was promised an allowance of time to enable him to compose and convinced himself that the task of taking up Weber's work after seventeen years of falling standards was a worthwhile challenge. Minna was overjoyed at the prospect of being the wife of a Royal Kapellmeister, a position that granted instant respectability. As Wagner's appointment was for life she had every cause to look forward to a future of enviable happiness and security. The Court Theatre was a handsome new building with excellent acoustics.[1] The orchestra was comparatively good by contemporary standards. It contained a number of excellent players but also many who were long past their best. The string section of only twenty-nine players was hardly adequate for Wagner's operas, and the quality and size of the rest of the orchestra also left much to be desired.

When Wagner commenced his duties he intended to raise the standards of performance generally, and fully expected that all his suggestions would be unconditionally accepted. He was to be bitterly disappointed. Although his superiors held him in considerable esteem and although his intelligence and zeal won him many admirers in the ranks of the orchestra, his headstrong enthusiasm and his ignorance of human nature soon alienated many of his colleagues. He appeared to want to change too much too quickly. His personal view of the theatre as a kind of temple for the expression of all that was most noble and good in humanity was incomprehensible to those around him, who regarded it simply as a place of entertainment. His exacting demands and insistence upon the

---

[1] Opened in April, 1841; destroyed by fire in 1869.

highest standards of excellence were not welcomed by everyone. The older players and the conservative critics disapproved of his style of conducting, which relied much upon *rubato* and a romantic flexibility of tempo that seemed to them quite inappropriate to the classical repertoire. When it came to replacing members of the orchestra Wagner chose a player solely on his musical merit and not on the grounds of his seniority – and at this the whole orchestra rose against him. In all these respects Wagner was in the right and his opponents displayed mere ignorance and conventional bigotry, but he forced the pace, lacked the important quality of tact and pursued a private life of varied and persistent folly, all of which resulted in continual quarrels and misunderstandings.

The story of Wagner's association with his colleagues in Dresden is by and large a tale of worsening relations, growing mistrust and a steady descent from the high hopes of 1843 to the revolutionary disaster of 1849. In six short years poor Minna's longed-for security and happiness were shattered, and Wagner led her to the edge of a precipice beyond which the horrors they had known in Paris seemed to await them once again.

King Friedrich August II was a cultured monarch, much respected by the people of Saxony. Although his tastes in music lay more in the direction of older masters such as Gluck, he showed a genuine interest in Wagner's work and the composer in turn thought highly of his royal master's qualities. The two men met very rarely during Wagner's Dresden years, although at an audition shortly after Wagner's appointment the King expressed an intelligent and sympathetic opinion of the two operas he had recently heard.

On account of a close relationship formed in the service of King Friedrich, Baron von Lüttichau found himself installed as Intendant of the Court Theatre. He had previously been Saxon Master of Forests but on his health breaking down was given charge of the theatre in order to remain near the Court. His background and early life had provided little experience of the artistic world but had instilled in him the qualities of tact, diplomacy and efficiency which together with a polished manner and refined courtesy enabled him to rule authoritatively over the upredictable theatre personnel. His lack of culture at any rate kept him aloof from the petty jealousies, schemes and rivalries of those in his charge. Wagner frequently crossed swords with Lüttichau but always maintained a regard for his capabilities. On his part the Intendant must have found many of Wagner's activities and ideas sorely trying, but he performed many acts of kindness on his behalf and realized that in his wayward Kapellmeister he possessed a composer and conductor of no ordinary talent. His wife, Ida von Lüttichau, compensated for her husband's lack of musical knowledge and made a point of encouraging Wagner.

Reissiger had succeeded Marschner as musical director at Dresden in 1828 and had since risen to the rank of Kapellmeister. Wagner depicts him in *Mein Leben* as complacent and lazy, and hints that Reissiger became jealous of him and allied himself with Wagner's press enemies. In reality, Reissiger probably was irritated by Wagner's sudden success and totally alien concept of conducting, but it is doubtful whether he saw the young man as a serious threat to his secure relations with the management. Their rivalry was of the rather petty kind that might be expected when two men of different age and outlook are placed on an equal footing in a theatre hierarchy.

The leader of the orchestra, Karl Lipinski,* was one of the most celebrated violinists of his day, and had been compared to Paganini. He was a friend and admirer of Berlioz, and the dedicatee of Schumann's *Carnaval*. At face value a player of this quality would seem an asset to any theatre orchestra, but Wagner found much to irritate him in Lipinski's mannerisms. He was a natural virtuoso but not a natural leader. Indeed Wagner described him as a leader in a dual sense as he persistently entered a moment in advance of the other violins and allowed his penetrating tone to sing out above theirs. While Lipinski admired Wagner as the composer of *Rienzi* he was indignant at any criticism of his own bad habits. After an initial quarrel concerning the proposed import of a bass player from Darmstadt, relations between conductor and leader were restored on a cool and conventional basis.

Of the rest of the orchestra, the leading 'cellist Dotzauer was a noteworthy player, and the first oboist Hiebendahl should be mentioned as a long-term creditor of Wagner's. Berlioz complained that Hiebendahl was incapable of playing a passage as it was written, but invariably ornamented it with trills and grace-notes. Among the violins was Theodor Uhlig* who appears to have disliked Wagner at first but later became his closest friend. An excellent musician and a discriminating and intelligent artist, Uhlig was converted to Wagner by *Tannhäuser* and Wagner's ideas on Beethoven's Ninth. It was rumoured that he may have been an illegitimate son of King Friedrich August II.

Of Wagner's former friends Kietz alone features prominently during and after the Dresden period, but only through correspondence. Kietz remained in Paris until 1870 and up to that time a great number of letters passed between the two friends. Wagner had hoped that Kietz would follow him to Germany but the impractical painter remained tied to his futile portraiture. His younger brother, the sculptor Gustav Adolf Kietz* was in Dresden at the time of Wagner's arrival. His regular visits to the composer are recalled in a volume of reminiscences. Anders seems to have passed out of Wagner's life and Lehrs, Wagner's most significant Paris friend, died of consumption in 1843. Wagner's closest friends of earlier years were now estranged from him. There is no record of any communication with Apel between 1840 and 1853, when Wagner replied to a letter. Laube championed Wagner in a friendly way at the time of the *Rienzi* premiere but as the years passed the two men drifted apart. Later Laube became one of Wagner's most bitter foes.

Berlioz visited Dresden in February 1843, just after Wagner's appointment. By an unlucky coincidence Wagner's *Autobiographical Sketch* also appeared that month in which Berlioz's nature was described as 'repugnant', and his music as a 'grimace' lacking any sense of beauty. It is no surprise that relations were somewhat strained between these two fundamentally different geniuses. Apart from giving several concerts of his own music at the theatre Berlioz was able to hear *The Flying Dutchman* and the last three acts of *Rienzi*. In his *Memoirs* Berlioz praised the enlightened King of Saxony for having rescued an artist of Wagner's rare ability, but he also criticized an over-use of the tremolo in both the operas he heard. Of the production, costumes and scenery, Berlioz considered that they approached the best standards of Paris. His views on the singers are instructive. Schröder-Devrient he considered too full of figure for the part of Adriano in *Rienzi* and preferred her as Senta, despite the occasional affected pose and the spoken phrases she insisted on interjecting. His finest impression was that of the baritone Wächter, and Tichatschek also earned high praise. Of Henriette Wüst as Irene, Rienzi's sister, Berlioz noted that Wagner had gauged her powers to perfection in allotting her a role with almost nothing to sing. In the orchestra Berlioz commended the leader Lipinski, the first 'cellist, the cor anglais player and a fine horn virtuoso Levy, but he noted that 'the ancient bass player . . . can no longer play some of the notes and indeed can barely support the weight of his instrument'. In a letter to Lehrs of 7 April Wagner implied that Berlioz was jealous at the success of his opera. In fact the jealousy was almost certainly on Wagner's side. There is no hint of envy in Berlioz's account of his Dresden visit. Wagner, envious of the Frenchman's orchestral mastery, merely employed the device already used with Mendelssohn and Meyerbeer and threw the accusation of jealousy at the other party. Lehrs had criticized Wagner for his published remarks on Berlioz, to which Wagner somewhat lamely replied that he had not really intended to print them. 'He is an unhappy fellow, and I certainly would not have written anything against him had I first been present at the concerts he gave here! I felt sorry for him.'

Throughout the Dresden years there is plenty of evidence in Wagner's correspondence that he was ever-hopeful of further favours from Meyerbeer. At the same time he was careful to make it plain that he was completely alienated from Meyerbeer as an artist. Schumann had found the influence of Meyerbeer pervading *Rienzi* and *The Flying Dutchman*. Wagner wrote to him on 25 February 1843:

Only one thing startles me and – I admit it – incenses me, and that is that you calmly tell me that I often have a flavour of *Meyerbeer*! Really I simply cannot conceive what in this wide world *could* be called 'Meyerbeerish' except perhaps the artful attempt to win shallow popularity. . . . I submit that it could only be by some amazing freak of nature that I could draw upon a source of which the least whiff wafted from afar nauseates me. It is no more nor less than a death sentence upon my creative power and the fact that you can pronounce it shows me clearly that you still have no really impartial opinion of me but only one deduced from the knowledge of the outer circumstances of my life, for these have brought me into certain relations with Meyerbeer the *man*, for which I owe him a debt of gratitude.

Four years later he wrote in similar tones to Hanslick:

What separates us by a whole world is your high estimate of Meyerbeer. I can say this with the fullest impartiality, for I am personally friendly with him and have every reason to value him as a sympathetic and amiable man.

Wagner at that time admired much of the music of both Schumann and Mendelssohn, but neither of these composers was able to come to terms with Wagner in a critical sense. Wagner blamed Mendelssohn for the fact that he never received favourable notices in the Leipzig *Allgemeine Musikzeitung*; and until 1844 Schumann edited the other Leipzig music journal, the *Neue Zeitschrift für Musik*, and again Wagner felt that his treatment was less than adequate. When Schumann settled in Dresden in 1844 the two men saw a good deal of each other, but they never became in any way close. Schumann claimed he could make little of Wagner's vocal scores but admitted to being greatly moved by seeing his operas in performance. It must be remembered that both Schumann and Mendelssohn desired to become opera composers and failed. Schumann considered a large number of possible subjects for an opera including the *Nibelungenlied* and the Wartburg Song Contest. Finally he settled for *Genoveva* (Dresden, 1847–8) which contained some inspired music but failed on account of the weak libretto. Wagner offered advice about opera texts, as he was later to do with Berlioz, but met with a rebuff from the wounded Schumann.

Another composer, Ferdinand Hiller,* a friend of Berlioz and the dedicatee of Schumann's Piano Concerto, was resident in Dresden for three years from 1844. His house soon became a centre for Dresden artists and intellectuals and Wagner met the young violin virtuoso Joseph Joachim* there. From January 1843 Wagner was conductor of the local Choral Society (*Liedertafel*), and Hiller succeeded him in this post in 1845, but before long Wagner and Hiller parted company. They each had totally different conceptions of the art of conducting and had a low opinion of each other's talents as composers.

Also hostile to Wagner were the local critics Carl Banck and Julius Schladebach. They had no sympathy for his musical idiom, no understanding of his ideas on theatrical reform; they disliked his interpretation of the classics and found Wagner the man antipathetic. Not all press commentary was unfavourable, however. An intelligent admirer, Dr Hermann Franck, wrote a fine article on *Tannhäuser* in the Augsburg *Allgemeine Zeitung*, November 1845. One sympathetic voice was raised in Berlin, too. Carl Gaillard wrote to Wagner in January 1844 with the declared intention of promoting his cause in his new journal the *Berliner*

Musikalische Zeitung. The two men met in September 1844 and became warm friends. Another Berlin champion was Alwine Frommann,* one of Wagner's few female admirers who was able to confine her enthusiasm to the intellectual plane. Through her association with the Prussian Court she advanced Wagner's ideas in Berlin for over thirty years.

Eduard Devrient was dramatic director of the Dresden theatre from August 1844 until February 1846, replacing the poet Tieck who had left for Berlin in the autumn of 1842. Devrient had begun his career as an actor and singer, and his brother Emil was a popular actor in Dresden. His responsibility as director was for both the acting and operatic sides of the company, and in the latter capacity he seems to have co-operated with Wagner in a friendly professional way. It was to Devrient that Wagner turned for help in 1848–9 when he was jeopardizing his career by meddling in revolutionary affairs, but it will be related in subsequent chapters how Wagner gradually turned against this friend and finally had recourse to libelling him in one of his 'anonymous' articles.

On the occasion of Wagner's thirtieth birthday, 22 May 1843, he was serenaded by sixty members of the Dresden Choral Society, who assembled outside his house with coloured lanterns and sang a poem in his honour, to a melody by Weber. One of the participants was Anton Pusinelli,* a young doctor and enthusiastic convert to Wagner's *Rienzi*; he shortly became Minna's physician, Wagner's creditor and a lifelong trusty adherent in whom the composer could confide. Among other friends Wagner acquired in Dresden, who frequently met together at Engel's restaurant in the Postplatz, were the Jewish poet and novelist Berthold Auerbach (1812–82), known especially for his 'Folk Tales of the Black Forest'; the painters Eduard Bendemann, Julius Hübner and Friedrich Pecht (Wagner's friend and financial benefactor of Paris days, who recalled their friendship in two volumes of memoirs); the sculptors Ernst Hähnel and Ernst Rietschel; the painter and poet Robert Reinick; another more famous painter, Julius Schnorr von Carolsfeld, who became director of the Dresden Art Academy in 1846; and Gottfried Semper, the talented architect.

Wagner soured relations with his two principal sopranos because of his borrowings. Henriette Wüst was married to the actor Hans Kriete who was to supply Wagner with funds for the publishing of his scores. During the long delay in the settlement of this debt the second soprano became very antagonistic towards her conductor. Schröder-Devrient too ultimately became an enemy. At the commencement of his appointment she lent him a generous 1000 thalers, which Wagner used to settle debts in Paris and Magdeburg, and she bestowed lavish presents on Minna. The soprano's private life was a catalogue of entanglements and disorder brought about by her infatuation with one lover after another. In 1847 she married a certain Lieutenant von Döring of the Guards, having signed all her money over to him. He promptly squandered all of it and she left him after six months in a distressed state of mind and health. This affair, together with her jealousy of Wagner's niece Johanna, who was steadily ousting her from her old and cherished roles, led Schröder-Devrient to take legal action against the Kapellmeister in order to recover her loan.

The most significant friendship of these years was with the assistant conductor who joined the theatre shortly after Wagner, August Röckel.* His versatility and excellence as a musician may partly be explained by inheritance: he was the nephew of the worthy Hummel, the son of a Viennese tenor who sang Florestan in the 1806 version of *Fidelio*, and in addition brother-in-law of the composer Lortzing. Röckel himself was an ambitious composer and his efforts included an opera, *Farinelli*, to his own libretto. On meeting Wagner, these aspirations withered. *Mein Leben* informs us:

> On making a closer acquaintance with my completed operas and plans for new works, he declared to me that he felt it his vocation to play the part of spectator, to be my faithful helper and the interpreter of my new ideas and, so far as he was able, to remove entirely or at least relieve me from all the unpleasantness of my official position and of my dealings with the outside world. He wished, he said, to avoid placing himself in the ridiculous position of composing operas of his own while living on terms of close friendship with me.

Wagner had found exactly the sort of companion he needed all his life: someone who was willing to sacrifice mere personal interests in order to listen to, sympathize with, understand and help the greater creative mind. Röckel was no mere lap dog though; he possessed a wide-ranging intellect, a sure command of other languages and a political awareness which stimulated Wagner, and was to lead him on a collision course with the authorities.

Wagner's creative energy was astonishing, and his considerable achievements as a conductor in Dresden no less remarkable. The first outstanding landmark to follow his official appointment was a production on 5 March 1843 of Gluck's *Armide* in which Schröder-Devrient took part. The opera was magnificently staged and Wagner's skilful editing of tempo and dynamic markings together with the enthusiasm he imparted to the singers convinced the Dresdeners that not only had the right man been found for the post, but also a young musician of extraordinary creative and interpretative originality. A comparison must have been invited with Mendelssohn who conducted his *St Paul* at the Palm Sunday concert that year. Wagner sensed as before that there was an impenetrable barrier between himself and Mendelssohn, but he was struck favourably by the oratorio, which was not without influence on *Tannhäuser*.

During 1843 the Wagners moved house twice, on each occasion to more comfortable quarters, as might befit the status of a Kapellmeister. The second move in October was to a pleasant apartment at a rent of 220 thalers per year. The furniture was probably expensive as the autobiography tells us that 'everything was good and substantial, as is only right when a man of thirty settles down at last for the rest of his life'. Naturally payment was made by incurring debts elsewhere. A grand piano was obtained from Breitkopf und Härtel with a down-payment of 240 thalers; Messrs Breitkopf liquidated the long-awaited instalments and the interest accrued when they acquired the publication rights of *Lohengrin* in 1850. Wagner's greatest pride was a large and comprehensive library which he built up carefully and systematically. The expectation was that all this luxury would soon be paid for when other German theatres took up *Rienzi* and *The Flying Dutchman*. From Dresden he had received 300 thalers all told for *Rienzi* and, within a few weeks, another fee for *The Flying Dutchman*. Confident hopes that similar fees from all over Germany would soon materialize caused him to mortgage his future. In fact the two operas were slow in reaching other towns. *Rienzi* was heard only at Hamburg, Königsberg and Berlin and *The Flying Dutchman* at Cassel, Riga and Berlin during the remainder of the 1840s. Outside Dresden there was no vogue for Wagner's music until after Liszt's performance of *Lohengrin* at Weimar in 1850. The situation has no more poignant illustration than that of a debt of 150 thalers referred to in a letter to Pusinelli of December 1844. Wagner promises to pay off the sum by the following Easter. Pusinelli cancelled the debt in 1873.

The problem of what to do with Natalie was solved temporarily in April 1843 when she was sent from Paris to live with Minna's relatives in Zwickau. Natalie was slow and backward and her stay in France had not improved her. On her return to Germany an attempt was made to cultivate in her a few domestic talents – piano-playing, sketching and some knowledge of French and English – in the hope that she might become a governess, but the unfortunate girl was not equal to this and Wagner resignedly accepted her into his Dresden home in 1845 where she was able to help Minna with some of the housework. Natalie resented being told what to do by her supposed elder sister, and continual quarrels between mother and daughter resulted in a disturbed atmosphere hardly conducive to creative work.

Early in 1843 Wagner sold the performing rights of *The Flying Dutchman* to Cassel for 20 louis d'or (just over 100 thalers) and to Riga for only 15 louis d'or. We gain some idea of how little this was when we learn that the cost of his court uniform was about 100 thalers. And German theatres paid no royalties. He was reluctant to offer the scores of his two operas for publication until a number of theatres had adopted them and he could ask for a decent price. On approaching Breitkopf und Härtel in the summer of 1843 he found them willing to publish *The Flying Dutchman* but unwilling to pay any fee for it. Wagner informed them in a blunt but courteous letter of his opinion of this treatment of a young German artist and of his determination to withold his score until they were convinced of its proper worth.

A performance of *Don Giovanni* on 26 April 1843 failed to achieve success as the players, and Lipinski in particular, took exception to Wagner's novel ideas about tempo and interpretation. At a meeting with the management on 1 May to discuss the problem Wagner lost his temper. Next day he wrote to Lüttichau apologizing for his angry and vehement behaviour. He accused Lipinski of artistic dishonesty and deliberate provocation. Lipinski had admitted that in some respects the standard of performance of the older operas at Dresden had fallen into a slovenly distortion, yet when Wagner took radical steps to remodel the interpretation Lipinski stirred up an agitation against him and disputed his right to interfere with the established and traditional methods of performance. Wagner told Lüttichau that in future he would endeavour to forget this quarrel and hoped that work with Lipinski would be restored on a basis of mutual respect.

Later in May he was asked by the Vienna Court Opera to supply a work for their approaching season. He replied that he was about to compose *Tannhäuser* which was promised to Dresden but hoped that another work (*Lohengrin*) would be ready for the season of 1844–5. In the meantime he suggested that Vienna mount *Rienzi*, but nothing came of this, probably because the Austrian censor objected to the democratic politics inherent in the libretto.

On 7 June occurred a performance of one of the 'official' works Wagner was obliged to compose. This was a *Festgesang* for male chorus to celebrate the unveiling of a statue of the late Friedrich August I. For his trouble Wagner was rewarded with a gold snuff box. He had to conduct a contribution to this ceremony by Mendelssohn, and wrote to Minna in Teplitz, 'my chorus won victory over Mendelssohn's which was ineffective and unintelligible'. Apparently Mendelssohn had contrived a contrapuntal combination of an original melody and the Saxon National Anthem (to the same tune as *God save the Queen*). This puzzled the assembled throng who preferred Wagner's simple and direct song.

In addition to this piece Wagner was asked to write a work for a big choral festival in July. Between 14 May and 16 June he wrote *The Love Feast of the Apostles* which bears evidence of the speed of its composition. It was heard in the Dresden *Frauenkirche* on 6 July, performed by a chorus of 1200 male voices and an orchestra of 100. Forty singers were placed in the cupola of the church to create an effect of voices in the heights, not unlike those in the temple scenes of *Parsifal*. After a long *a cappella* passage the entrance of the orchestra to depict the descent of the Holy Spirit is most effective. But never again did Wagner write for such huge Berlioz-like forces, and in later years he had a very poor opinion of this work. Breitkopf considered it worthy of publication, however, and issued it in full score and vocal score late in 1844. It was dedicated to the widow of his revered teacher, Weinlig.

Another publisher was the cause of concern to Wagner when he was composing *The Love Feast*. On 15 May he printed a letter in the *Neue Zeitschrift für Musik* objecting to the publication of his song *Les Deux Grenadiers* by Schott. By a peculiarity of the German and French copyright laws, Schott was legally entitled to reprint Wagner's song without paying him any fee. The publisher threatened Wagner with a libel action, and the composer was compelled to apologize in the columns of the Leipzig journal on 19 June. He never forgave Schott for this slight.

In the third week of July Wagner joined Minna for a holiday at Teplitz. He made a start to the music of *Tannhäuser*, and pored over the *Deutsche Sagen* of the brothers Grimm, but work proceeded only fitfully and was interrupted by a visit to Prague to see his friend Johann Friedrich Kittl,* now director of the Prague Conservatoire. (The long story of the *Hohe Braut* libretto found a happy ending thanks to Kittl who set it to music as *Bianca und Giuseppe, oder die Franzosen vor Nizza*. His opera met with considerable success at its first performance in Prague, in February 1848; but in 1853 Wagner wrote to Breitkopf und Härtel who were about to publish the score and asked them not to print his name as the author.) In Prague in the summer of 1843 Wagner was pleased to find that Count Pachta's daughters, Jenny and Auguste, had both made favourable marriages. On his return to Dresden later in August, serious work began on *Tannhäuser*. The first act was completed on 27 January 1844.

Owing to Meyerbeer's continuing influence on Wagner's behalf, Berlin staged *The Flying Dutchman* at last, with Wagner conducting, on 7 January 1844. The Court Theatre had been destroyed by fire in the preceding August and therefore all Wagner's expectations of a large stage, sumptuous sets and excellent technical resources were not realized. His opera was performed in the smaller Playhouse, and the orchestra was considerably reduced in size. Although pleased with the public reaction and the individual performances Wagner was despondent at the unanimous hostility of the press: the antagonism of the powerful critic Rellstab spelt disaster in Berlin and, after one more performance in January and two late in February with Schröder-Devrient, the opera was dropped from the repertory for a quarter of a century. When the new Royal Opera House opened the management refused to buy the necessary new scenery for *The Flying Dutchman*. In Berlin Wagner paid court to Meyerbeer and spent some time with Mendelssohn who, as we learn from a letter to Minna, 'delighted me by coming on stage after the performance, embracing me and congratulating me very warmly'. Wagner wrote to him:

> I am really glad that you have a kindness for me. To have drawn a little nearer to you is for me the happiest incident of my whole Berlin expedition.

In *Mein Leben* the description of Mendelssohn's reaction to the opera is very different:

> He followed its progress with a pale face, and afterwards came and murmured to me in a weary tone of voice, 'Well, I should think you are satisfied now!' . . . .

I heard that he had responded with equal indifference to the earnest warmth of my allusions to his own music for the *Midsummer Night's Dream* . . .

One new disciple in Berlin was an amateur musician and poet, Karl Werder, Professor of Philology and Aesthetics at the university, who was a welcome friend to the composer on his future visits to the town. Unknown to him the composer of *The Flying Dutchman* adopted the name 'Professor Werder of Berlin' when he fled from the German police in 1849.

Liszt fulfilled his promise to Wagner and attended a performance of *Rienzi* in Dresden on 9 February 1844, and in Tichatschek's dressing room, during the intervals, Liszt assured Wagner that he would praise the work everywhere he went. *Rienzi* certainly brought fame to Wagner, but no fortune. In March he conducted its first performance outside Dresden – a somewhat tawdry production in Hamburg. The mercenary Hamburg director Julius Cornet was interested in nothing more than a quick success, and he even paid Wagner's modest fee in a series of tiny instalments. As if to compensate the composer of the spectacular grand opera he presented him with an intelligent grey parrot, Papo. Soon this bird brightened the Dresden household by whistling selections from *Rienzi*.

Wagner's niece, Johanna, then aged eighteen, made her debut in Dresden with considerable success. She was given a permanent contract with the theatre in July 1844 and her father, Albert Wagner, whose own career had reached stalemate, moved to Dresden to act as her manager. Albert disapproved of his younger brother's way with money, and Richard in turn quarrelled with him about Johanna's choice of roles which were frequently un-Wagnerian. One of Wagner's most foolhardy economic mistakes was his decision to publish his operas at his own expense, for this venture created problems that troubled him for over thirty years. He came to an arrangement with the court music dealer C. F. Meser who agreed to publish *Rienzi*, *The Flying Dutchman*, and later *Tannhäuser* in return for a ten per cent commission on sales. To provide the necessary capital Wagner borrowed from the oboist Hiebendahl, the actor Kriete and Dr Pusinelli. Schröder-Devrient offered to sell some of her investments to help the enterprise. Unfortunately when the work was well under way she found herself unable to oblige, as she had signed away her property to her lover. By late 1844 the first two operas appeared in an engraved piano arrangement and in full score prepared by an expensive lithographic process. Virtually nothing was recouped of the heavy costs. All the full scores sent to theatres were returned – in the case of Munich, unopened. The rejection of Wagner's work was partly due to the bad press reviews it had received but more significantly because his operas had gained a reputation for being expensive to mount, difficult to rehearse and awkward to cast – singers of Tichatschek's calibre were rare.

At five o'clock on the morning of 12 August 1844 Wagner, together with

300 singers and an orchestra of 120, embarked on a river boat bound for Pillnitz, country seat of the Saxon King. With characteristic enterprise Wagner had arranged an impromptu performance of a choral work designed to welcome the monarch on his return home from a successful visit to England. On this occasion his initiative exceeded the wishes of his superiors at the court. Lüttichau was enraged at Wagner taking into his own hands a project that only the Intendant himself should have arranged. Wagner saved the situation by allowing Reissiger to conduct, and the unexpected performance of the *Grüss seiner Treuen an Friedrich August den Geliebten*, with the composer singing among the tenors, delighted the King. As a result relations between Wagner and Lüttichau became more intimate and friendly for a time.

On a holiday in the country near Dresden Wagner completed the composition sketch of Act Two of *Tannhäuser* on 15 October, interrupting his work to attend the twentieth performance of *Rienzi* in Dresden on 20 September. The audience included Spontini, General Lwoff, composer of the Russian national anthem, and Meyerbeer, who was impressed by the enthusiasm aroused by the work and promised to help promote a production in Berlin. At the end of the year Wagner wrote a letter urging him to remember this promise and effusing over Meyerbeer's artistic 'mastery'.

Spontini was in Dresden to supervise the production of his opera *La Vestale*. The renowned old master of Parisian grand opera had much to teach Wagner but his visit was something of an exhausting trial. Exceedingly demanding in rehearsal, apt to make the most exacting and time-consuming requests of singers and orchestra, and accustomed to strict obedience in the fulfilment of his wishes, Spontini reminded Wagner of a haughty Spanish grandee. But he had a kindly, humorous side to his nature too and was able to receive with equanimity the relative failure of *La Vestale* in Dresden. He left the town in a state of childish excitement as he was about to receive decorations from both the Pope and the King of Denmark. Wagner probably heaved a sigh of relief. Spontini's visit resulted in one important reform at the theatre, however: his insistence on laying out the orchestra with an even distribution of strings and wind instruments was adopted as a permanent feature, instead of the old unsatisfactory grouping of strings on the one side and woodwind and brass on the other. The rivalry between Wagner's niece and Schröder-Devrient was increased with the performance of Spontini's opera in which the youthful Johanna appeared as a high priestess, and the ageing prima donna as a most unsuitable vestal virgin. Wagner himself made an arrangement of the Triumphal March from *La Vestale*.

In addition to his abundant creative work during the autumn of 1844 – Act Two of *Tannhäuser* was sketched by 29 December – Wagner energetically joined in a project to bring Weber's remains back from London to Dresden. This idea was originally proposed by Professor Löwe, founder and secretary of the Dresden Choral Society, and received the support of

Ferdinand Heine and Weber's son Max who was a student in London. Their aim was achieved despite the opposition of the King on religious grounds, and of Lüttichau, who feared that it would set a precedent for exhumations of former Dresdeners all over Europe. On 14 December the arrival of the remains was greeted by a torchlight procession and the performance of an arrangement by Wagner for eighty wind instruments and twenty drums of themes from *Euryanthe*. At the burial ceremony next day a male voice choir sang *Am Webers Grabe*, words and music by Wagner, and the young Kapellmeister delivered a magnificent oration which he had carefully memorized. In the course of his emotional speech he experienced the strange sensation of hearing and seeing himself speaking to the crowd as though he were carried away in a trance as a different person. At one point he embarrassed his listeners by pausing for quite a long time, expecting the other being to continue. Then he became aware that he was there to speak, not to listen, and the impressive tribute resumed.

Wagner considered that Marschner's operas were unjustly overlooked at Dresden and secured the first performance of his latest score, *Adolf von Nassau*, in January 1845. Wagner conducted and the composer was present in the audience. As a Leipzig student Wagner had been greatly affected by Marschner's earlier operas. Now he found the music superficial and the plot of *Adolf von Nassau* ridiculously contrived. After the premiere he felt as though he had given birth to a still-born child. Nonetheless the opening scene of the opera, Adolf's speech to his knights, influenced *Lohengrin* with its parallel scene in which Henry the Fowler addresses the nobles.

The great task of the early part of 1845 was the scoring of *Tannhäuser*, a huge labour which he completed on 13 April. The orchestral score was written on special paper prepared for lithography in order to save time and money. The Dresden management expressed a keen desire to perform it as soon as was practicable. They commissioned special scenery from Desplechin of Paris and spared no expense on the costumes. In the event, Lüttichau annoyed Wagner by cancelling the order for a new Hall of Song, and saving money by using a set from *Oberon*.

With the premiere arranged for the autumn, Wagner and Minna holidayed at Marienbad in July and August. Here the libretto of *Lohengrin* was sketched, after a study of the anonymous medieval poem in an edition by Guido Görres (Heidelberg, 1813). Further reading of the poems of Wolfram von Eschenbach and Gervinus' *History of German National Literature* (1826) resulted in a very detailed scenario for another opera, *Die Meistersinger von Nürnberg*. Again this sketch owes a debt to Hoffmann, whose story *Meister Martin der Küfner und seine Gesellen* contains the bare bones of Wagner's plot. It is difficult to realize that his stay at Marienbad was intended to be a rest cure: the doctors soon abandoned him as a hopeless patient. One visitor to Marienbad that summer introduced himself as an admirer of Wagner's *Rienzi* and *Flying Dutchman*. This was a twenty-year-old law student from Prague named Eduard Hanslick* to whom Wagner extended a friendly invitation to the *Tannhäuser* premiere. Hanslick was able to accept this invitation a year later and in the autumn of 1846 became Wagner's first champion in Vienna, where he divided his energies between studies and music criticism.

At its first performance, *Tannhäuser* was not an instant success but with repeated hearings it attained a popular following not unlike that for *Rienzi* and gained for Wagner his first really staunch disciples. Faults in production were corrected in time; the main problems on the evening of 19 October 1845 were those of casting. The role of the eponymous hero demanded a subtlety and intelligence that Tichatschek did not possess. The amply-proportioned Schröder-Devrient was hardly the ideal Venus. Johanna Wagner as Elizabeth fared much better. After a great deal of coaching, Anton Mitterwurzer as Wolfram convinced Wagner that there was some hope for training suitable singers for his works. The overriding factor was the inability of the cast as a whole to comprehend Wagner's declamatory vocal writing: they continued to think in terms of the traditional division between recitative and aria and failed to come to terms with his new style of continuous arioso. When Tichatschek became hoarse after the first night a dangerous myth began to circulate – that Wagner's music was fatal to the voice. This fallacious rumour was current for many years and the hostile press made capital out of it. For the second performance Lüttichau had agreed to provide a new set for the Hall of Song, and Tichatschek's voice was completely restored. But the theatre was almost empty. Wagner's new opera was a challenge to the public, and only gradually did the group of enthusiasts for his dramatic and musical intentions grow into a large body. In the audience on the first night was the beautiful and talented Marie Kalergis, who as the Countess Muchanoff* was to play an important part in Wagner's later career. She had attended *Tannhäuser* on Liszt's recommendation, and her reaction to it was typical of many. Apparently she was disillusioned by the poor production, perplexed by the performance and disappointed by the reception with which it met; yet it made a forceful impression on her which she was never to forget.

Without a successful performance in Berlin there was little chance that the rest of Germany would take notice of the work and Berlin had a unique advantage in that it paid royalties. So in December 1845 Wagner obtained leave to visit the Prussian capital. Küstner, the director, considered *Tannhäuser* 'too epic' for a production there and an attempt to dedicate the work to the King of Prussia failed, as the monarch only accepted the dedication of works already known to him. Meyerbeer was out of town but Frau Meyerbeer gave him a friendly welcome. Wagner sent his scores to Jenny Lind. They were returned unopened. Apart from a promise that *Rienzi* would be performed there in the following autumn, Wagner secured nothing of value from this visit to Berlin.

The poem of *Lohengrin* was complete by 27 November 1845. He read it to a group of friends who were much impressed, but failed to understand how it would work as an opera. Schumann was especially puzzled by it. Wagner was hopeful of interesting the King of Prussia in *Lohengrin* and considered returning to Berlin to read the libretto to him. He sought Meyerbeer's help once more with a view to obtaining a commission from the Prussian King. He knew that Dresden was interested in his new plan, but became more and more aware during 1846 that his artistic inclinations were isolating him from his colleagues in the provincial Opera. Karl Gutzkow* replaced Eduard Devrient as dramatic director in February. In the spheres of journalism, drama and poetry Gutzkow was recognized as a considerable talent. He loathed Wagner's music, found *Tannhäuser* undramatic and boring, disliked Johanna Wagner and was irritated by the composer's popular local following. Wagner found him totally unmusical and resented his interference in the operatic section of the theatre. Gutzkow sided with the anti-Wagnerian critics, who increased in number after a feeble performance of the *Tannhäuser* overture by Mendelssohn in Leipzig, a rendering which Hans von Bülow* described as 'an execution in more senses than one'. Leipzig viewed anything from Dresden with disdain and only too happily branded this overture as incomprehensible.

It is unfortunate that Wagner's potentially greatest act towards the Dresden theatre fell upon deaf ears. This was his report 'Concerning the Royal Orchestra' of March 1846. Whenever he turned his mind towards improving the standards of efficiency and quality of an artistic institution, Wagner spoke with common sense and conviction: his views may have been idealistic but they were not impractical. These are the main points he submitted to Lüttichau:

(1) There is an unfair discrepancy between the paltry fees paid to an overworked orchestra and the inordinately high sums given to individual singers who are generally less musical. This anomaly must be eradicated or standards will decline irreparably.

(2) The orchestra has become progressively overworked, resulting in damage to players' health and a decline in the quality of performance.

(3) Older players ought to be pensioned off, and the system of life appointments, which leads to slackness and complacency, abolished.

(4) A number of instruments in all departments should be replaced with modern ones.

(5) Work should be rationally distributed between the players. This would enable the better players to be reserved for more exacting works.

(6) Players' salaries have not kept pace with rising living standards, and should be brought up to date.

(7) The physical layout of the orchestra and the position of the conductor is bad. Smaller seats and metal music stands would mean that the players

were less cramped. Each player should have his own stand and should face the conductor.

(8) At least six orchestral concerts should be given in the winter months. This would enhance the knowledge of the repertoire of both players and audience. A suitable hall should be built for such concerts.

(9) The additional cost of these suggestions would be 3050 thalers per annum. (Wagner gives detailed statements of present and proposed numbers and running costs.) This sum would be well spent in view of the improved standards of performance, and could be offset by profits from the winter orchestral concerts.

(10) A proportion of the concert receipts should be used to establish a Benefit Fund for musicians in distress. The players would therefore be insuring themselves rather than being dependent on the management for charity.

As Ernest Newman concluded:

It would have been well for the Dresden theatre and for Dresden had the authorities listened to him and taken his advice; they would almost certainly have kept him for many more years and raised their city to the foremost place in German music. But no one in a placidly self-satisfied institution welcomes a reformer; and for the reformer to be so devastatingly right in every one of his criticisms and so unerringly practical in every one of his suggestions is merely an extra reason for suspecting and opposing him.

After waiting for a whole year, Wagner was informed that his proposals had been rejected.

These proposals coincided with a powerful demonstration of Wagner's ability to rejuvenate artistic life in the town. On Palm Sunday 1846 he conducted a memorable performance of Beethoven's Ninth and wrote various illuminating articles about this work which was still incomprehensible to most listeners. Beethoven, and in particular the choral finale of this symphony, responded well to Wagner's novel and perceptive interpretation. No German conductor before Wagner had so successfully explored the expressive qualities of late Beethoven. In the audience on that first Sunday in April were two young men whose destinies were to be closely linked with Wagner: Ludwig Schnorr von Carolsfeld* and Hans von Bülow.

Bülow's family had lived in Dresden since 1842. In July 1846 they were due to depart for Stuttgart. Before leaving Saxony Bülow was determined to meet the conductor and composer he had come to adore. He visited Wagner at Grossgraupa near Pillnitz where the composer holidayed for three months of the summer with Minna and Peps. Young Bülow's enthusiasm, a sign of an ardent support for his cause from a new generation, touched Wagner, and a correspondence between them ensued. From Grossgraupa Wagner journeyed to Leipzig and met Louis Spohr* for the first time at a dinner in Hermann Brockhaus's home. Despite his conservatism Spohr found much to admire in Wagner's work; he had already performed *The Flying Dutchman* at Cassel and now studied the libretto of *Lohengrin*. The score of the latter work was begun in earnest on Wagner's return to Dresden in August. He commenced with the last act, partly because the endings of both *The Flying Dutchman* and *Tannhäuser* had proved problematical (and had to be remodelled) and partly because friends had cast doubt upon the necessity of a tragic ending and he wished to establish this clearly as the only possible goal of the work.

On commencing his summer holiday of 1846 Wagner had written to Spohr revealing his feelings towards Lüttichau: 'I am very much obliged to my Herr General-Director for granting me permission to have nothing to do with him for a whole three months!' But on returning to Dresden he found it necessary to turn to Lüttichau and confess his financial plight. Despite borrowing widely from friends such as Pusinelli and Röckel, the mounting debt to his publisher Meser and the demands of creditors including Breitkopf und Härtel and Schröder-Devrient had placed him in an impossible position, which was rapidly becoming the talking-point of all Dresden. Lüttichau listened sympathetically to Wagner's appeal, interceded with the authorities and obtained for him a loan of 5000 thalers from the Theatre Pension Fund at five per cent interest, to be paid in ten annual instalments of 500 thalers. In return Wagner was to provide security in the form of a life-insurance policy, one-third of his salary and the publication rights of his three operas. Even this generous loan only settled his more urgent debts and it committed Wagner to years of economy and restraint.

The burden of financial care, the threat of a public scandal and the remorseless attacks of his critics contributed to a serious deterioration in Wagner's health which is easily overlooked in a summary of his energetic achievements of these years. His close friend Ferdinand Heine considered that he would not live long.

Liszt had attempted to interest the director of the Viennese Theater an der Wien in Wagner's works, but Vienna was to prove very slow in accepting Wagner. Ironically the very man who was to lead the campaign against Wagner in Vienna in later years was his staunchest supporter in the winter of 1846–7. Eduard Hanslick visited Wagner in September 1846, heard *Tannhäuser*, borrowed a score from Liszt and wrote a lengthy eleven-part analysis of the opera in the *Wiener Musikzeitung*.

That winter saw a first sketch for a drama about Friedrich Barbarossa, an epoch-making production of Gluck's *Iphigenia in Aulis*, the completion of Act Three of *Lohengrin* (5 March) and another Palm Sunday production of Beethoven's Ninth (28 March). Act One of *Lohengrin* was completed on 8 June and Act Two on 2 August 1847. With the completion of the Prelude on 29 August the opera was finished except for the orchestration.

The performance of Gluck's opera late in February was one of Wagner's greatest Dresden accomplishments as conductor, producer and arranger. Working from the original Paris score of *Iphigenia in Aulis*, he recast the music completely in an attempt to rid it of eighteenth-century conventions and anachronisms. Instrumental passages were recomposed, harmonies altered to heighten dramatic effect, the orchestration revised, vocal parts redistributed, new recitatives and a new aria inserted, and passages dovetailed to achieve forward movement. The text was revised and the plot altered – Gluck's happy ending was changed to a tragic one. The King was impressed with Wagner's devoted efforts for *Iphigenia* and stopped in the public promenade to congratulate him on the production.

Unknown to the Dresdeners who applauded his work, Wagner was gradually turning away from them. The rejection of his plans for the reform of the orchestra left him with few illusions as to the extent of his real influence. He withdrew into the world of his *Lohengrin*, avoided the company of his colleagues and adopted an attitude of indifference towards Lüttichau and Reissiger. In April 1847 circumstances forced him to find cheaper accommodation in the suburbs of the town, and his new apartment in the Marcolini Palace was a considerable walk from the theatre.

Wagner's contempt for the theatre was complete by the summer of 1847. In a letter to Lüttichau on 9 July he admits that he has avoided the Intendant out of sheer vexation and will no longer tolerate the interference of Gutzkow:

> This ill-disposed person, who destroys confidence everywhere through his intrigues and calumnies is preparing inevitable moral destruction of our whole enterprise, and is particularly troublesome to me, as I am openly, warmly and enthusiastically working for high ends and, without this added burden, have all too frequently had to see my efforts rewarded by misunderstanding and suspicion. . . . If outward circumstances had been more favourable I should have had no hesitation in asking His Majesty for my *complete discharge*.

On 1 August *Tannhäuser* was revived in Dresden with its changed ending. Despite an outward success Wagner despaired of the standard of performance. He wrote to Ferdinand Heine, 'I am so full of contempt for the theatre as it is at present that . . . my dearest wish is to be free of it altogether. . . . You may have heard already that some three weeks ago I completely broke with Lüttichau and from my side there can be no question of a reconciliation.'

To score a success in Berlin was now urgently necessary. *Rienzi* went into rehearsal there in September and Wagner conducted the first performance on 26 October. After weeks of excited and hopeful rehearsals the result was a depressing anticlimax. Wagner had pinned his hopes on the patronage of the King, but Friedrich Wilhelm IV did not attend and refused to receive Wagner in audience. The public's obvious appreciation of *Rienzi* was eclipsed by the hostility of the press, and much malicious capital was made by the journalists of Wagner's humorous reference in rehearsal to this opera as a 'sin of his youth'. Every sneer at Wagner's work was gleefully reprinted by his Dresden enemies. The only profit

from his two months in Berlin, a royalty payment for the three performances he had conducted, was swallowed up by debts he had incurred.
Wagner thought he had found an influential friend in the Countess Rossi
(formerly the singer Henriette Sontag) but this lady merely provided him
with a neat illustration of the prevailing Philistinism. What had appealed
to her so much when reading the poem of *Lohengrin*, she told him, was
that she could actually see the little fairies and elves dancing about in front
of her. In *Mein Leben* Wagner says that he felt as if cold water had been
suddenly poured down his back.

On 4 November 1847 Mendelssohn died and on 9 January 1848 Wagner
learned of the death of his mother, Johanna Geyer. The scoring of *Lohengrin* occupied him from 1 January until 28 April, and on its completion he
abandoned his mind to a surging torrent of new ideas, for an important
change had occurred in his life in the early months of the new year and his
growing friendship with Liszt was a significant factor in that change.
Over five years were to elapse before he embarked on the music of
another opera. Meanwhile every fibre of his being, every creative thought
and outward action was embraced in one overwhelming passion: Revolution.

above 1. The Battle of
Leipzig, 19 October
1813

right 2. Wagner's
birthplace in Leipzig

Above 3. Ludwig Geyer

Right 4. Wagner's
mother, Johanna
Rosine

Wagner's sister,
osalie

Wilhelmine
hröder-Devrient

7. Wagner in 1842; drawing by E. B. Kiet

8. Minna Wagner

9. Richard Wagner's mother

Left 10. Theodor Apel

Below 11. The Royal
Court Theatre,
Dresden; built 1837–4
destroyed by fire 1869
it was rebuilt to the
same design shortly
after and again
destroyed in World
War II

Opposite right 12.
Wagner's niece
Johanna, as Elizabeth
in the first
performance of
Tannhäuser, 1845

Opposite far right 13.
Joseph Tichatschek as
Tannhäuser,
1845

Opposite below 14.
Programmes for
Tannhäuser, 1845, and
Die Meistersinger, 186

RIOTS AT DRESDEN.—BARRICADE IN THE GROSSE FRAUEN STRASSE ATTACKED FROM THE NEUMARKT.

15. The Dresden Uprising, *Illustrated London News*, June 1849

16. Theodor Uhlig from a signed portrait-medallion Gustav Kietz

Five

Revolution

I am the ever-rejuvenating, ever-creating life! Where I am not is death! I am the dream, the comfort, the hope of the oppressed! I destroy what is, and wherever I go new life springs from the dead rocks. I come to you to smash all the chains which crush you, to redeem you from the embrace of death and breathe young life into your veins.

Wagner, *The Revolution*

FEBRUARY OF THE YEAR 1848, the month in which Marx and Engels issued the *Communist Manifesto*, saw Louis Philippe of France 'going out of the same door he came in by', as Czar Nicholas I sardonically observed. News of the Paris revolt and the fall of the Orléans monarchy reached Vienna by 1 March and in Hungary democratic laws were passed. Within a fortnight revolution broke out in Vienna and Prince Metternich fled the Austrian capital with a forged passport 'like a criminal'. Revolts in Venice, Parma and Berlin quickly followed and on the last day of March the German Vorparlament met in Frankfort. In May the Prussians suppressed the Polish insurrection in Warsaw, in Paris there was a Communist uprising, in Vienna a second revolt and the flight of the Emperor, and in Frankfort the Vorparlament was replaced by an elected National Assembly, an extremely talented body drawn from the professional middle class and including some of the most famous names in literature and scholarship. On 17 June Austrian forces suppressed a revolt in Prague and the anarchist agitator Bakunin fled from there to Dresden.

The political crisis coincided with Wagner's completion of the *Lohengrin* score, and the personal crisis with his Dresden superiors. Early in February Lüttichau conveyed to the King Wagner's request for a rise in salary and pointed out the composer's appalling debts and the fact that he had apparently been adversely affected by sudden success and the poor counsel of his friends. At the same time he praised Wagner's artistic achievements, notably his orchestral concerts and the *Iphigenia* production. The King replied by granting Wagner an extra 300 thalers, but did not spare him a severe criticism. It was made plain to him that if matters did not improve then he would be dismissed.

Clearly Dresden tried to help Wagner and had no real wish to lose him, but their help was not sufficient and Wagner turned to other means. His friendship with Liszt became closer when the pianist called at Dresden in March on his way to Weimar, where he was to settle permanently as Kapellmeister. They spent the evening at Schumann's house where there was general music-making. A discussion about the merits of Mendelssohn and Meyerbeer developed into a heated argument and Schumann became so upset at the opinions of Liszt and Wagner that he retired angrily to his bedroom. In June Wagner wrote to Liszt in his suitably grovelling style, begging him for 5000 thalers to pay off the debt to Meser. Liszt would then become the copyright owner of Wagner's three operas. Unfortunately his Weimar friend was not in a position to help him at that time. Nor was the firm of Breitkopf und Härtel willing to buy the works from Meser. The three operas in fact belonged to Pusinelli as surety against almost 6000 thalers he had loaned to the composer. Pusinelli was not prepared to pay even more for his enthusiasm, but generously waived his rights of ownership to the scores to enable Wagner to dispose of them advantageously. No one seemed to want them, however, and Meser was too lackadaisical in his efforts to distribute them over the years for any profits to appear.

Only in a totally transformed German society could Wagner see a possibility of realizing his ideals. Artistic reasons, therefore, rather than the political ones of his friend Röckel, led him into active participation in the Vaterlandsverein, an association founded in March 1848 to campaign for the establishment of democracy. There was inevitably a cross-fertilization between Röckel's revolutionary views and hatred for the perversity and pomposity of Court life and Wagner's conviction that in a new society the 'Folk', liberated from the domination of the ruling class, would find true expression in a new German culture. The prevailing fervour with which revolution, republicanism, socialism, communism and anarchism were discussed naturally captured much of Wagner's attention. He did not become a wholly political animal, though, for his revolutionary thoughts overflowed into creative projects and ideas for theatrical reform which he pursued with characteristic energy.

On 16 May he submitted a detailed *Plan for the Organization of a German National Theatre for the Kingdom of Saxony*, which displayed the same practical common sense and clarity that characterized the report on the royal orchestra of two years before. As with the orchestral report, the unwillingness of the Dresden authorities to consider Wagner's proposals set the seal on the destiny of their Kapellmeister. Once again, had they acted upon a few of his suggestions then he would probably not have thrown himself so wholeheartedly into the revolution. Fearing that events might shortly lead to the establishment of a popular government that would have no use for a bourgeois institution like the Court Theatre, Wagner proposed that it be re-established as a National Theatre directed by a committee of dramatists and composers. There should be a union of composers to elect the Kapellmeister and choose the works for performance which must be fewer in number but better in quality. The King ought to remain head of this national enterprise but the actual director should no longer be a Court official without real qualifications for the post. This part of his thoroughly worked-out plan, which also recommended reformation of Dresden church music, regular orchestral concerts and the establishment of a school of music and theatre, led Wagner to avoid consulting Lüttichau and instead he approached the Minister of Education, Ludwig von der Pfordten.* Pfordten, who was to play a decisive role later in Wagner's Munich days, was not particularly interested in any ideas for reform. Martin Oberländer, Minister of the Interior, was more responsive and advised Wagner to approach the Chamber of Deputies. The politicians proved totally indifferent to his plan and the only effect it had was to alienate Lüttichau who saw in it an attack on everything he represented.

Wagner's interest in the efforts of the Frankfort Assembly to draw up a plan for the unification of Germany is shown in a letter of 19 May to one of the Saxon representatives. In the following month he joined the revolutionary Communal Guard and launched into print with two revolutionary poems and an article. *Gruss aus Sachsen an die Wiener* (Greeting from Saxony to the Viennese) was a poetic tribute to the Austrians who had just forced their Emperor to flee, and an incitement to the Saxons to follow their example and draw the sword. *Die alte Kampf ist's gegen Osten* (The old fight is against the East) called for a great crusade against reactionary Russia. The article *What relationship do republican endeavours bear to the monarchy?* appeared in the Dresden *Anzeiger* under the signature 'A member of the Vaterlandsverein', and was read to that body by its author on 17 June. Wagner looks forward (after the annihilation of the ruling class) to a kind of Saxon Utopia with a people's army, universal suffrage, a single chamber, a new economy, free trade and the spreading of German greatness and goodness by colonies throughout the world. The Folk are to be led by their King in a rather odd compromise between monarchy and republicanism. Wagner conveyed these views to the Vaterlandsverein with tremendous enthusiasm and created such a stir that a performance of *Rienzi* two days later was cancelled for fear of demonstrations.

Although Lüttichau was fully aware that Wagner was playing a dangerous game he showed a commendable degree of indulgence and tolerance. In a letter clarifying his views on the monarchy Wagner expresses a regret that his opinions have been widely misrepresented and begs Lüttichau for two weeks' leave of absence on account of a gastric complaint. He has promised his wife that he will take no further personal part in politics. Lüttichau complied with his request for leave and Wagner wrote a hearty letter of thanks. Asking Reissiger to take on his duties, Wagner described himself as 'an incurably sick man who is simply unavailable'.

Instead of seeking a cure, the 'incurably sick man' headed directly for Vienna – hot-bed of revolutionary activity! On the way he spent an evening at Breslau discussing politics with Johann Theodor Mosewius and examining that scholar's collection of unpublished J. S. Bach cantatas. (In January Wagner had conducted Bach's motet *Singet dem Herrn* in Dresden.) In the new democratic atmosphere of Vienna Wagner hoped that a people's theatre might be founded and he discussed the possibility of becoming manager of the Kärntnertor Theatre. He contacted the journalist and author Friedrich Uhl who introduced him to sympathetic political circles, and the composer and critic Alfred Julius Becher who was to be executed for revolutionary activities before the year was out. On the first day of August the Leipzig *Signale* reprinted a report from a Vienna newspaper of 20 July concerning the interesting composer Richard Wagner and his comprehensive plans for reorganizing the Vienna theatres. Lüttichau must have been painfully conscious of his Kapellmeister's duplicity and on Wagner's return their relations became even more strained, particularly as Wagner had to confess that his financial situation was now worse. Lüttichau told the King that Wagner appeared to be incapable of fulfilling his obligations and raised the possibility of his dismissal. Wagner called at Weimar in another attempt to secure a loan from Liszt; he found his friend very sympathetic but unable to provide such a large sum of money.

Apart from an arrangement of Palestrina's *Stabat Mater* (for a concert on 8 March), creative work in 1848 was devoted entirely to literary projects during the summer and autumn. The revolutionary turn in his outward affairs is reflected in these writings which enter a new realm of speculative philosophy. He extended the 1846 sketch for a drama about Friedrich Barbarossa but soon abandoned this historical subject and explored the possibility of myth, with its potential for crystallizing the dramatic essence of human archetypes. Wagner's political views are inherent in the *Friedrich Barbarossa* sketch of 1848: his concern with the problem of property and his image of the King as ruler of a benevolent republic. The lengthy essay *The Wibelungs* is subtitled *World history as revealed in Saga*. Wagner's view of world history is extremely confused and clouded; much of the essay reflects on his own social, political and financial concerns and at the same time he tries to come to terms with the complex mass of muddled fact and fiction, legend and history absorbed in his recent reading. His own hatred of the problems caused by money led him to consider the idea of the Hoard as a symbol of all that was evil in politics, economics and power. For Wagner, the legendary Nibelung's Hoard was present in the modern world in the worship of gold and property which enslaved the ordinary man and corrupted the aristocracy. He identified the historical Wibelungs with the legendary Nibelungs. He saw the historical Friedrich as a rebirth of the pagan Siegfried, a god-like figure of light capable of redeeming the evil Hoard. Siegfried in turn was identified with Christ and the spiritual aspect of the Nibelung Hoard with the mystical Holy Grail.

There emerged from all this confusion an essay called *The Nibelung Myth as a sketch for a Drama* which contained the essence of the *Ring* story as we know it today. The Nibelung sketch was distilled from many sources including Karl Lachmann's edition of the *Nibelungenlied*, Ludwig Ettmüller's translation of the *Edda*, Grimm's *Deutsche Sagen* and *Deutsche Mythologie*, von der Hagen's version of *The Volsunga-Saga* and *The Wilkina and Niflunga-Saga*, Simrock's six-volume edition of the *Deutsches Helden-buch*, Mohnike's translation of the *Heimskringla* and Mone's writings on Teutonic sagas. Almost certainly Wagner was influenced by an essay of Friedrich Theodor Vischer, *Suggestions for an Opera*, which appeared in 1844, and was a call for a new style of heroic opera for which the *Nibelungenlied* would be the ideal source. Wagner was not the first person to use the Nibelung subject as a basis for drama. In 1810 Friedrich de la Motte Fouqué (the author of *Undine*) treated the Sigurd story in his *Der Held des Nordens*. In 1828 appeared E. B. S. Raupach's play *Der Nibelungen Hort*, and in 1837 an article by A. W. F. von Zuccalmaglio in the *Neue Zeitschrift für Musik* recommended the Siegfried myth for musical treat-ment. Both Schumann and Mendelssohn considered the Nibelung legend as an operatic subject and in 1854 Heinrich Dorn's opera *Die Nibelungen* was staged in Berlin. Wagner's old hatred of Dorn increased at the appearance of this opera and he also bore a life-long grudge against Friedrich Hebbel whose play *Die Nibelungen* was a highly successful, well-written trilogy (1855–62).

The sketch of October 1848 was the first stage of a mighty creation unparalleled in the history of music. The history of the *Ring* text is a complex tale of amendments and revisions. Between 12 and 24 November Wagner wrote the poem of a grand heroic opera in three acts, *Siegfrieds Tod* which was in essence the fourth part of the present *Ring* cycle, *Götterdämmerung*. He read it to a somewhat bemused group of friends including Bülow, Fischer, Ferdinand Heine and his son Wilhelm, Gustav Kietz, Karl Ritter* and Semper. In December a fair copy was made with some amendments to the scenic directions, but in 1849 the entire poem was thoroughly revised. The distinguishing feature of Wagner's poem is his use of Stabreim, an alliterative verse form derived from Old Germanic poetry. Another long and extremely detailed sketch for a drama followed hard on the heels of *Siegfrieds Tod* and was complete by the end of 1848. This was *Jesus of Nazareth*, in which the hero is portrayed as a social revolutionary.

On 22 September the finale of Act One of *Lohengrin* was included in a concert celebrating the tri-centenary of the Dresden Kapelle, but the fragment made little intelligible impression: Reissiger received a decoration on this occasion but Wagner was passed over. Two days later occurred a *Tannhäuser* performance to which Wagner had hoped

Liszt might come. Liszt could not leave Weimar but sent his mistress, Princess Carolyne Sayn-Wittgenstein.* In November Liszt performed the *Tannhäuser* overture in Weimar and was greatly impressed by it.

Röckel, who had recently founded a radical paper, the *Volksblätter*, was dismissed from his post at the theatre at the end of September because of his avowed commitment to revolutionary activity. Wagner was by then totally disillusioned with the immediate prospects for reform in the theatre. He found relief for his mental state in the *Siegfried* project and a gradual move towards more practical involvement in politics. In mid October he supplied an anonymous article for the *Volksblätter*, *Germany and her Princes*, which indicates his lessening respect for the monarchy. The decision by the Dresden management, late in the year, that they would not produce *Lohengrin*, was the last straw for Wagner: he viewed it as a detestable breach of faith and a deliberate act of revenge. No doubt the theatre committee had other reasons for rejecting his opera – above all the unsettled revolutionary atmosphere which was not conducive to presenting modern works, especially of national character such as *Lohengrin* – but Wagner saw none of that, declared that he would dissociate himself from any further decisions of the management and resolved to dedicate himself to the ideals of outright revolution.

Three articles of January 1849 dwelt on the urgent necessity for theatrical reform. The first was a review of Eduard Devrient's third volume of a history of the German stage and, although Wagner's call for a theatre of the people was couched in fairly gentle language, it was rejected by the Augsburg *Allgemeine Zeitung*. Writing anonymously in the Dresden *Anzeiger* on 16 January Wagner criticizes the system that allows courtiers who are totally ignorant of art to become theatrical managers when they would be more at home in their former occupations such as masters of the hounds. This was a pointed attack on the former Master of the Royal Forests, Baron von Lüttichau. Wagner published this article at his own expense together with a more radical sequel which developed the same theme; calling for a complete application of democratic ideals to the theatre, it created a sensation in the town. A greater stir occurred early in February when the King dismissed the liberal minister Oberländer and replaced him with the reactionary Count von Buest.

Meanwhile in Weimar Liszt was planning a production of *Tannhäuser* and informed Wagner that he was studying the score with ever-increasing sympathy and admiration. It was his hope that the composer would attend the final rehearsal and first performance (indeed the first performance outside Dresden) on 16 February, but Lüttichau refused to grant Wagner a leave of absence until May. On 20 February Wagner thanked Liszt for his efforts on behalf of *Tannhäuser* which had deeply moved him. Were it not for the attitude of his 'tormentor' he would have been there. Liszt replied:

I owe so much to your bold and lofty genius, to the fiery and magnificent pages of your *Tannhäuser*, that I feel quite awkward in accepting the gratitude you are kind enough to express with regard to the two performances I had the honour and happiness to conduct. . . . Once for all, number me in future amongst your most zealous and devoted admirers; far or near, count on me and dispose of me.

In writing these lines Liszt could hardly have imagined just how useful he was to be to Wagner within a very short time. Wagner was greatly flattered at Liszt's suggestion that he make piano transcriptions of the overture and *O du mein holder Abendstern* scene. He wrote to Weimar, on 1 March: 'We are getting on nicely together. If the world belonged to us, I believe we should do something to give pleasure to the people living in it!'

Four days prior to the Weimar *Tannhäuser* Wagner attempted to start an agitation among his players. Addressing the Orchestral Players' Union he explained that all his ideas for improving conditions had been rejected and that it was now time for them to take matters into their own hands. Hearing of this, Lüttichau was furious, summoned Wagner and threatened to dismiss him. Wagner replied that he would gladly resign were it not for his wife and his 'domestic circumstances', by which he meant his debts. In March he requested permission to leave the Communal Guard, which may have been a diplomatic move designed to appease both Lüttichau and Minna. His avowed excuse was on the grounds of health. Minna viewed his political activities with the wildest alarm and she was sorely troubled by the obvious breach between Wagner and the management. During the years of his secure employment at Dresden their marriage was generally stable and happy. The early flame of physical love had now faded but they had settled into a close and contented companionship. Minna felt quite at home in her comfortable niche as wife of the Kapellmeister and was unable to comprehend her husband's apparently reckless and suicidal behaviour towards the Court. His artistic evolution from *Rienzi* to *Lohengrin* and the nature of the *Siegfried* plan now preoccuping him were beyond her understanding, nor is it likely that he ever discussed his inner ideas with her. She could only view his latest activities with puzzled dismay. Outbursts of anger and irritation became frequent in the last Dresden months, but through it all Wagner still desperately needed the consolation that Minna could provide.

Two poems of late March 1849 express the bitterness of Wagner's frustration with the State. *An einen Staatsanwalt* (To a State attorney) pours contempt on a representative of that egoistic monster, the State. *Die Noth*[1] is a vicious and obscene vision of Want as an avenging goddess kindling a fire that will reduce cities to skeletons and destroy the enslaving powers. On 8 April Wagner published an anonymous article in the

---

[1] *Noth* cannot be precisely rendered into English. It means need or want in times of misery, trouble and distress. Siegfried destroys the old world-order with his sword *Nothung*.

Richard Wagner

Volksblätter, *The Revolution*: a passionate, effusive prose-poem glorifying the goddess Revolution in an unrestrained torrent of fanatical verbiage. It was deliberately inflammatory and almost certainly the identity of the author would have been common knowledge.

Wagner's last concert in Dresden, on 1 April, was his third Palm Sunday presentation of Beethoven's Ninth. At the end of the public rehearsal Bakunin stepped forward from the audience, shook Wagner's hand and said in a voice loud enough for all to hear, that if all the music ever written were lost in the coming world-conflagration, they must pledge themselves to rescue this symphony, even at the peril of their lives. Apart from this Bakunin had little time for Wagner, the dreamer of operatic reforms. But Wagner was fascinated by the exuberant Russian anarchist and his association with him attracted the attention of the police spies who watched Bakunin's every move, knowing that he intended not just to preach his gospel of fire and destruction in Dresden, but to carry it out.

On 30 April the Chamber of Deputies was dissolved – marking the beginning of a fierce reaction and amid the wildest rumours of successful revolts elsewhere in Germany. Röckel, who had hitherto enjoyed immunity as a member of the Chamber, was forced to flee to Bohemia and Wagner stepped in as guardian of his family and editor of the *Volksblätter*. Röckel's aim was to persuade the Bohemian revolutionaries to join forces with those in Saxony and prepare for a rising throughout Germany, planned for 9 May. Wagner's participation in the Dresden revolt, and the resulting charges made against him may be summarized in brief: he was intimate with the leaders of the rising, Bakunin, Heubner* and Röckel; he attended meetings of revolutionary conspirators, some held in his own garden; he took an active part in arming the people; he ordered the manufacture of hand grenades; he was a party to Röckel's attempt to find support in Prague; he ran the *Volksblätter* after Röckel's flight; he obtained guns from Tichatschek's house; he attempted to seduce Saxon troops from their duty, and therefore committed treason; and he was seen to be present at various strategic points – at the Town Hall during the election of the provisional government, on the tower of the Kreuzkirche and in the company of revolutionary reinforcements from nearby towns.

Thursday 3 May saw the rejection by the King of the demands of the Democrats, and the government ordered the Communal Guard to disband. In a mood of intense excitement a meeting of the Vaterlandsverein that afternoon decided to offer armed resistance to the authorities. On leaving the meeting Wagner heard church bells signalling the start of the revolt. The people had attacked the town arsenal and there were several casualties. Intoxicated with delight at the arrival of this long-awaited moment Wagner ran to Tichatschek's house, knowing the tenor to be away on tour, and persuaded his startled wife to surrender her husband's shotguns. In the Altmarkt he observed a distressed Schröder-Devrient addressing the crowd from a first-floor window. For the remainder of the day he followed the mob all around the town and explored the barricades before returning home to the suburbs. That night the King and his Court fled by boat to the fortress of Königstein, and Röckel, learning that the revolution had come unexpectedly early, set out from Prague to Dresden.

For the next six days Wagner ensured he was never far from the centre of things and, although he tried to underestimate his commitment to the uprising in later years, the very detail of the account of it given in *Mein Leben* shows that he was close to the ringleaders. On the second day of the revolt it became known that Prussian forces were advancing on Dresden. The rebels at first hoped vainly that the King would unite with his people against the Prussian invaders and there was a general belief that the Saxon troops were secretly on the side of the uprising. A provisional government was formed, led by Heubner, Karl Todt (a Privy Councillor) and S. E. Tschirner (an advocate). Wagner's contribution to their policies was to order the *Volksblätter* printer to produce a quantity of leaflets addressed to the Saxon troops, reading 'ARE YOU WITH US AGAINST FOREIGN TROOPS?' He also ordered Semper to supervise the construction of the barricades. Much of Friday 4 May he spent with Bakunin, who soon despised the Saxons for their amateurish efforts at revolution. They had every opportunity to consolidate the position they had won, to seize the arsenal before government troops were reinforced, and to utilize Polish soldiers in the town. Instead they wasted time attempting to organize themselves in a suitably 'parliamentary' fashion. Bakunin also scorned the Communal Guard and the merchants of the town, many of whom actively opposed the insurgents.

During the evening of Saturday 5 the first Prussian troops reached Dresden and by the very early hours of Sunday fighting was widespread in the town. Wagner ascended the tower of the Kreuzkirche which was utilized by the rebels as an excellent observation post. The provisional government had rather belatedly called on the Polish troops to help them and Wagner observed that the Prussian forces were kept at bay for a time while food and reinforcements reached the rebels from the nearby countryside. He noted the placement and movement of the fighting from his vantage point and threw down messages tied to stones which conveyed information to Heubner and Bakunin at the Town Hall. Meanwhile Wagner's tower was under continual fire from Prussian troops in the tower of the Frauenkirche. If we are to believe *Mein Leben*, he spent the night of Sunday discussing philosophy and religion with fellow revolutionaries while under this bombardment. At sunrise he viewed an impressive column of rebel reinforcements, mainly miners and other workers from the Erzgebirge, singing the Marseillaise as they entered the town. The old opera house where Wagner had recently conducted Beethoven's Ninth was burnt down to protect the neighbouring barricades. As he was unarmed and had no wish to wield a gun himself, Wagner felt he was only in the way at the Kreuzkirche and decided to return home to his anxious wife, who implored him to stay with her.

The very next day (Tuesday 8) he was back at the Town Hall again, having met Röckel on the way there. Wagner agreed to conduct a troop of several hundred students to the Town Hall, and left Röckel to continue issuing orders. They did not meet again for thirteen years. That night Röckel was taken prisoner by Saxon troops and on his person was found a letter from Wagner, sent to him in Prague on 2 May. The letter was to prove the most important piece of evidence against Wagner, as it showed clearly that he was closely involved with the revolutionary leaders.

Despite the reinforcements things began to look black in Dresden, and Wagner decided to take Minna to safety to Chemnitz[1] where his sister Klara lived. He set out with Peps; she was to follow him with Papo. One of the many apochryphal stories about Wagner and the revolution tells us that before leaving for Chemnitz he returned to the town centre and found that the Prussians had shot a girl of eighteen on the barricades. Leaping upon a cart he shouted, 'Men! Will you see your wives and daughters fall in the cause of our beloved country and not avenge their cowardly murder? All who have hearts, all who have the blood and spirit of their forefathers and love their country, follow me, and death to the tyrant!' He is then supposed to have led the crowd, brandishing a musket, and come upon a small, isolated group of Prussians, who surrendered as prisoners. Several untrue accounts of his activities gained circulation and damaged his reputation for years to come. He is said to have marched with a gun on his shoulder; to have ordered lead to be stripped from the roofs for the casting of bullets; to have been responsible for burning down the old opera house; and to have attempted to obtain chemicals and spirits in order to set fire to the royal palace.

Wagner met up with Minna on the way to Chemnitz but their carriage was stopped at Oederan by leaders of the Chemnitz Communal Guard which was marching to Dresden, spurred on by 1400 volunteers. Wagner was interrogated and then arrested as a suspicious fugitive. He was released only when he promised to return to the capital as soon as he had accompanied his wife to Chemnitz. To Minna's horror he left her in the care of his family and once more headed for the centre of the revolt. He found Dresden in the grip of house-to-house fighting and the men at the Town Hall gloomy and fatigued after six sleepless nights. Wagner told them that he had passed hundreds of volunteers in Freiberg, so he was immediately despatched there with the lawyer Marschall von Bieberstein to summon these men instantly to Dresden. They arrived at Freiberg at four in the morning of Wednesday 9 May, persuaded the forces there to requisition every horse and cart they could find and supervised their departure for Dresden. Leaving Marschall Wagner took a special coach

---

[1] Now Karl-Marx-Stadt, GDR.

and set off for Dresden himself. He fell sound asleep and was only awakened by the noise of violent shouting. Looking out, he was astonished to see the road filled with armed revolutionaries marching *away* from Dresden. By nine o'clock the Saxon and Prussian troops had successfully crushed the rebellion.

Wagner sprang out of his coach and ran to find the carriage conveying Heubner and Bakunin to Freiberg. He joined them and took part in a conference on arrival at the town early in the afternoon. They adopted Wagner's suggestion that they should retreat to Chemnitz and re-establish the provisional government there. After a short sleep, sharing a sofa with the bulky Bakunin, Wagner emerged to find Heubner organizing the chaotic horde of tired and hungry men. Longing to be away from all the confusion Wagner attempted to leave by coach for Chemnitz but found the road impassable on account of the columns of men; he tried to find Heubner and Bakunin once more but failed to locate them. Eventually his coach was able to depart and, reaching Chemnitz late that night, he slept at the first inn he could find. At five o'clock next morning he rose and walked to his relatives' house. Later in the day he learned from his brother-in-law Heinrich Wolfram that Heubner and Bakunin had arrived in Chemnitz before him and had lodged at a different inn, where they had been betrayed and removed to prison at Altenburg under strong military guard.

Only by the narrowest twist of good fortune did Wagner escape their fate. Heubner, Bakunin and Röckel were condemned to death, the sentences being commuted to life imprisonment. Heubner in fact served ten years and Röckel thirteen. Bakunin was sent to Siberia but escaped to London in 1861. In her diary for Thursday 10 May, Clara Schumann recorded the fate of the rebels in Dresden:

We heard of the awful atrocities committed by the troops; they shot down every insurgent they could find, and our landlady told us later that her brother, who owns the *Goldner Hirsch* in the Scheffelgasse was made to stand and watch while the soldiers shot one after another twenty-six students they found in a room there. Then it is said they hurled men into the street by the dozen from the third and fourth floors. It is horrible to have to go through these things! This is how men have to fight for their little bit of freedom! When will the time come when all men have equal rights?

Wolfram smuggled Wagner out of Chemnitz under the cover of darkness and lent him enough money to reach Weimar. Even the coachman was unaware that he had an extra passenger.

Liszt had expected the Royal Kapellmeister of Dresden to arrive in Weimar during May for the third performance of his *Tannhäuser*, but he had not counted on harbouring a political refugee. On 17 May, four days after his arrival, Wagner wrote to his friend Eduard Devrient in Dresden. It is clear from this very long letter that Wagner was attempting to justify his recent behaviour and in the detailed account he gives of his activities in the week of the revolution he is careful to make it clear that he was not in any sense a real revolutionary:

> I followed the rising at first with full sympathy, on the two middle days with exasperation, and on the last two days with the most intense excitement and curiosity, but at no time did I take active part either by deeds or public speaking and I never had any official standing under the provisional government.

He is anxious that Devrient should find out whether there is a legal case against him and hopes that the present storm will soon pass so that he will appear less politically compromised than he does at the moment. In the meantime he intends to request leave of absence to supervise productions of his operas in London and Paris, a scheme suggested to him by Liszt. To Minna he wrote indicating his conviction that he was perfectly safe in Weimar and that sudden legal action against him was impossible. He clearly had no idea of the seriousness of his offences. On 15 May the police visited Minna in Dresden and warned her that her husband faced grave charges. A warrant for his arrest was issued four days later. He was liable to be charged with treason, which carried the death penalty: there was plenty of evidence against him, including the letter found on Röckel, and there were plenty of witnesses ready to vouch for his involvement, including a local brass founder from whom Wagner had ordered hand grenades.

An escape from Germany was now imperative but Wagner was determined to see Minna before he left. In Weimar he had attended a rehearsal of *Tannhäuser* (from a concealed position in a box) and was delighted with Liszt's sympathetic interpretation. He was presented to the Grand Duchess who took a friendly, if rather curious, interest in him. To attend the public performance of his opera was, however, not possible; and after the issue of the warrant the Weimar Court could no longer harbour him in safety. Therefore, borrowing sixty thalers from Liszt and posing as Professor Werder of Berlin, he left for Magdala (near Jena) on 19 May and Minna joined him there three days later. They travelled separately to Jena and rendezvoused with Liszt and a friend, Professor Widmann, who gave Wagner his out-of-date passport. Liszt's advice was that Wagner should go to Paris, but by a route unlikely to be closely scrutinized by the police, through Bavaria and Switzerland. On the evening of Thursday 24 he bade Minna and the good Liszt an emotional farewell and reached Coburg by nightfall of the following day. The long journey south took him to Lindau on the Bodensee (Lake Constance) by the evening of Sunday 27, where he spent a troubled night convinced that the officials would query his passport or that his efforts to disguise his strong Saxon accent – Widmann's passport was Swabian – would lead to interrogation. The following morning an amiable official created no such problems and Wagner joyfully stepped aboard the steamer bound for Rorschach in

Switzerland. Eleven long years were to pass before he returned to his native Germany.

Proceeding to Zurich he met an old friend from Würtzburg, Alexander Müller, a piano teacher and choral conductor, with whose family he spent two nights. He adored Switzerland with its glorious scenery and was pleased to find that he was already well known as a composer in Zurich: both *Rienzi* and *The Flying Dutchman* had been played there in concert versions, and *Tannhäuser* was planned. Müller arranged a passport and Wagner reached Paris on the morning of 2 June. Gaetano Belloni, Liszt's former secretary, was at Wagner's disposal and gave him the benefit of his inside knowledge of Parisian musical life. One of Belloni's ideas was to commission Gustave Vaez, a translator and librettist, to turn one of Wagner's prose sketches into a grand opera which might interest the Opéra management. One day Wagner called at Schlesinger's music shop and discovered Meyerbeer there. On hearing Wagner's voice Meyerbeer remained hidden behind an office screen but Wagner led him out and found him to be acutely embarrassed and unwilling to converse. As an official of the Royal Prussian Court, Meyerbeer had no desire to be seen in the company of the notorious Dresden fugitive.

Paris was unbearably hot and an epidemic of cholera was claiming hundreds of lives each day. To Minna Wagner described the city as a 'great, atrocious, noisy and expensive prison'. His sojourn there had been largely to appease Liszt and he had no real hope of a commission from the Opéra. Instead his thoughts turned to friendly, wealthy, spacious Zurich and he wrote to Minna proposing that she join him in Switzerland. They will live tranquilly, surrounded by the most splendid scenery; she will grow healthier and he will have the peace necessary for creative work. On 8 June Wagner escaped from cholera-ridden Paris to Reuil, where he was near Belloni. Within a fortnight he was back in Zurich, staying once more with Müller.

Minna had no wish to forsake Dresden for what she regarded as the provincial outpost of Zurich, and suggested that all communications between herself and Wagner cease. On 10 July Wagner wrote to Natalie and begged her to persuade Minna to return to him. He told her that for the present the Müllers were willing to accommodate them both, and there was room for Natalie too. The practical Minna wrote to him a week later declaring her willingness to join him in Zurich:

> I hope you will understand, my dear Richard, that in coming to you I make *no slight sacrifice*. What sort of future do I face? What have you to offer me? Almost two years may elapse before you, by a stroke of luck, may count on some income, and depending on the good will of one's friends only is a dreary existence for a wife. . . . I have no wish to dampen your courage; but to venture once again into the unknown, to court worries and misery in a foreign country, for this *my* courage is not enough. I have lost faith in your beautiful promises, and there is no longer any happiness for me on this earth!

Richard Wagner

It was painful for Minna to turn her back on her many friends and relatives in Saxony but, selling all their household goods and with a hundred thalers provided by Liszt, she travelled to Zurich in the last days of August. She was now forty, her heart condition was well developed, she had aged prematurely and she faced a future of financial uncertainty with fear and foreboding.

Wagner on the other hand felt reborn – a new energy and elation replaced the discontent and drudgery of Dresden. In July he wrote the lengthy essay *Art and Revolution* in fourteen days, and late in November completed another tract, *The Art-Work of the Future*, written in eight weeks. Both articles were printed by the radical Leipzig publisher Otto Wigand, and in February 1850 the *Deutsche Monatsschrift* published a third, *Art and Climate*. Often miscalled Wagner's 'theories', these writings were more accurately rationalizations, justifications and analyses of the confused and excited mass of creative and speculative thought that surged through his mind. They clarified his attitude to the relations between art and society. To the modern reader they are anything but clear: Wagner's sense of history is bewildering and his prose style dense and convoluted. His principal thesis is that European society must be regenerated before true art can exist. *Art and Revolution* examines the concept of the *Gesamtkunstwerk*, the complete all-embracing art-work, and its relation to society. The drama of ancient Greece was not just the theatre but a combination of music, singing, dancing, poetry, mime, drama and visual effects. Only a healthy and harmonious society could produce such an art in which all the elements mutually blend. In Germany only the well-to-do patronize the theatre and they regard it as an amusement or a pleasant distraction. In ancient Athens the entire community participated in the drama and the theatre became a universal religious experience. The disintegration of the Greek drama led to the various art forms pursuing their own courses. Now the time is ripe for them to harmonize once more. The Folk will be the true creators of the new universal art-work which will be a rebirth, not of the substance, but of the spirit of Greek drama. Revolution is the prelude to the reform of society necessary for the production of the composite work of art. To his friend Uhlig in Dresden he wrote:

> The art-work cannot be created now, it can only be prepared for, and that by revolution, by the destruction and overthrow of all the things which deserve destruction and overthrow. That is our work and men other than we will be the first truly creative artists. . . . Any work I may write for Paris and produce there, can be only an incident in the revolution, a sign affirming destruction. Destruction alone is now necessary . . .

By January 1850 Wagner had sketched the text for the opera he hoped Belloni and Vaez would help him produce in Paris, though nothing less suited to French taste could be imagined than the thoroughly Teutonic

Wieland der Schmied. Many symbols in this sketch reappear in the *Ring*, *Tristan* and *Parsifal*, including the swan, the ring of power, the spear wound and the Valkyries. Wieland, tricked, impoverished and crippled by the world is an image of Wagner, and Schwanhilde the heroine, his inspiration – a muse who enables him to overcome his frustrations, escape from his fetters and soar towards the ideal. Wagner never composed *Wieland der Schmied* but tried unsuccessfully to interest Liszt, and later Berlioz and Weissheimer in the idea.[1]

Minna was anxious for Wagner to return to Paris. Upon her arrival in Zurich with Natalie, Peps and Papo they had found fairly humble lodgings. She had brought many of his manuscripts but not his library: all his precious books were in the hands of Heinrich Brockhaus* as security for a loan of 1500 marks, and he never saw them again.[2] Liszt had kept his full scores for safety and sent them to Zurich late in July 1849, parting with *Lohengrin* most reluctantly as he had formed a special admiration for it. He also sent Wagner as much money as he could but his own resources at Weimar were limited; he had three children in Paris to support and the Princess Wittgenstein had been forced to surrender most of her fortune to the Czarist authorities after her elopement with Liszt. But in every other conceivable way Liszt offered practical help. It was natural that he should view Paris, the cradle of his own success, as the hub of the artistic world and urge Wagner to concentrate his efforts there. On 18 May the Paris *Journal des Débats* had published a long article by Liszt in praise of *Tannhäuser*. He had as yet no notion that Wagner's theatrical ideals were far and away removed from the commercial battlefield of the Opéra, and he hoped that all revolutionary ardour had subsided in Wagner, who had written to him on 5 June, 'I promise you to leave politics alone as much as possible, and therefore will not compromise you or anyone else'. Liszt did not understand his new friend but his suggestions were well meant and intended to help him earn some money. He proposed that Wagner write a popular volume of songs, or concoct an oratorio text from Byron's *Heaven and Earth*, or arrange more Gluck operas.

Another beneficent friend was Frau Julie Ritter* of Dresden. She and her son Karl had become ardent enthusiasts for Wagner's cause and although she had hardly come to know him well during his time as Kapellmeister she was to provide him with a regular income throughout his Swiss exile. Wagner wished there were more people like her. He wrote to Ferdinand Heine in November 1849, 'They should see in me not a person in need of help, but an artist and an art trend which they want to preserve for the future and not allow to perish.'

It delighted Minna that Wagner's first concert in Zurich, a performance

---

[1] An opera based on Wagner's sketch by Kurt Hoesel was produced in Berlin in 1913, without success.
[2] They were presented to the Wagner Foundation in Bayreuth in November 1974.

of Beethoven's Seventh Symphony on 15 January 1850, astonished the audience. They had never heard an interpretation of such dynamic conviction. His wife was even more pleased when Wagner left for Paris two weeks later, subduing for the moment his detestation of all things French. Minna would have been less happy had she known that in Paris Wieland was to meet his Schwanhilde.

There had been a plan to perform the *Tannhäuser* overture in Paris but as the parts had not arrived in time the idea was abandoned for that season. Belloni was out of town and the enemy Meyerbeer was being fêted at the Opéra. There was nothing for Wagner to do in Paris except mull over his *Wieland* sketch. He was depressed, sleepless, racked by rheumatism and feeling resentful towards Minna for forcing him to Paris. 'Deliverance from this hell is all I wish for,' he wrote to her on 2 March.

His deliverer came in the person of Jessie Laussot, a young Englishwoman married to a Bordeaux wine merchant. As Jessie Taylor, a girl of sixteen, she had attended the first performance of *Tannhäuser* and had called on Wagner in Dresden in 1848. A close friend of the Ritters, she seems to have made little impression on him at that time. From Paris on 6 February 1850 Wagner wrote to Liszt informing him of 'a beautiful occurrence which has recently delighted me'. Julie Ritter has told him 'in a delicate fashion' that Jessie Laussot was prepared to join her in providing him with 'a not inconsiderable sum of money'. The proposed sum from these two ladies amounted to a comfortable yearly pension which would dispose of his need to work in Paris and make possible his higher aims. Proud, bourgeois Minna hated the idea of their living on the charity of friends, so Wagner broached the matter carefully in a letter to her of 2 March:

> No one could possibly act more kindly, more nobly, more delicately than our friend Mme Laussot! I should have thought, dear wife, that it would have really uplifted you to see what a deep impression your husband's work can make on wholesome, unperverted noble hearts; to see that he is able to influence them to make such sacrifices because of their warm sympathy!

He had Kietz do a portrait of him and sent it as a gift to Jessie. The Laussots then invited him to stay with them in Bordeaux. Before leaving, he wrote to Minna, on 13 March:

> Will you be cross with me if I tell you that I have suddenly decided at last to accept the very pressing and cordial invitations of my friends in Bordeaux – they have even sent me my travelling expenses – and that I accordingly set out tomorrow morning for Bordeaux? You see, I am utterly useless here now and am simply wearing myself out in worry and fruitless endeavours.

Minna was indeed very cross. She considered the visit to Bordeaux a mere pleasure trip while she was left to struggle on in Zurich and, among other things, find a new apartment. (In April she found lodgings by the Lake of Zurich.)

Revolution

In Bordeaux Wagner felt as if he had been transported to heaven. The Laussots were devoted to him, Jessie full of sympathy and encouragement for his ideas; her wealthy mother Mrs Taylor (a Scottish widow) and her German-speaking husband could not have been more friendly. He wrote of his euphoria to Minna, at the same time admitting that he had no wish to forsake Switzerland for Bordeaux. 'To lead a happy, undisturbed life with you, dear Minna, in that glorious fresh Alpine world is the highest bliss I can desire.' He knew that Minna had no real understanding of him, that she still bitterly resented his reckless behaviour in Dresden and that she disapproved of his visit to Bordeaux. Jessie seemed to provide everything that Minna lacked – beauty, understanding and musical talent. Furthermore he soon discovered that her marriage to Eugène Laussot was not a happy one. Eugène had formerly been the lover of her mother, Ann Taylor, who had saved him from bankruptcy and presented him with her daughter. Before Wagner returned to Paris he and Jessie discussed the idea of escaping together from their unhappy marriages and travelling to Greece or somewhere further east to start a new life together.

After his departure Jessie wrote a polite and friendly note to Minna explaining her pleasure at being able to help Wagner. At the foot of this letter Minna scrawled (possibly at some later date), 'false, treacherous creature'. In order to avoid his wife Wagner took secret lodgings in Montmorency but addressed his letters to her from Paris. On 16 April he wrote to tell her of his decision to separate from her and proposed that she receive one half of his yearly allowance. Although in *Mein Leben* Wagner claimed that he did not bid a final farewell to his wife, his letter ends:

> Farewell! Farewell! My wife! My old, dear companion in misfortune! Oh, if you could only have shared the joys which I draw from *my great faith*, how happy you would have been with me despite all privation! It was not granted to me to reward you in this way! May I now succeed – through the separation – in reconciling you to your life, in bringing you peace and comfort! Farewell! Farewell! For two weeks I have wept a thousand bitter tears over this distressing separation! But it must be! Every hesitation would be a fatal weakness! Fatal for you and me! Farewell! Farewell! My good Minna! Farewell! Think only of the happiest hours we spent together; then you will be happy in remembering me, just as I will think of you only with nostalgia and love after this separation! Farewell! Farewell! For the last time I kiss you fervently!

The following day he wrote to her again in reply to a letter in which she angrily rebuked him and addressed him with the formal 'Sie'. He pointedly uses the intimate 'du' and says that the tone of her letter has left him with no further illusions concerning the impossibility of living with her again.

The contents of these two letters were more than Minna had bargained for. She had not counted on his determination to bid her such a firm farewell. Although he had not mentioned Jessie in his letters she was almost certainly convinced that his attitude had been formed by the association with her. Alarmed, she sought the help of his closest friends in Zurich and, armed with a letter from them urging him to return there, she set out for Paris to find her husband. Forewarned of her journey, Wagner found a secluded hiding place in the city and avoided her. He confided in Kietz and asked the bewildered painter to keep his movements secret. To Liszt he wrote on 21 April:

> Decisive events have just been happening in my life; the last fetters which bound me to a world in which I must speedily have gone under, not only spiritually but physically, have fallen away. I have lost my health, my nerves are shattered through the ceaseless constraint imposed on me by my immediate environment. I am provided for and you shall hear from me from time to time.

Some days later Wagner left Paris, took a train to Clermont-Tonnere and travelled on to Geneva. From there he wrote to Minna and Kietz on 4 May announcing his intention to go to Marseilles and take a boat to Malta. He would then sail to Greece and Asia Minor.

In the Burrell Collection there is a draft of a long and bitter letter from Minna to Wagner, dated 8 May. Its tone of rancour and reproach epitomizes all that he wished to escape from. During the second week of May Karl Ritter joined Wagner at Villeneuve on the Lake of Geneva. For a few days all was tranquil until a wildly excited letter arrived from Jessie informing him that she had confided in her mother who had in turn told Eugène of their plan to escape. Her husband was now anxious to put a bullet through Wagner's body. Worse still, Jessie now refused to join him. At once Wagner wrote to Eugène and left for Bordeaux – a journey of three days – apparently with the intention of informing the aggrieved husband that he had no right to stand in the way of a wife who did not love him. Learning of Wagner's journey Eugène took his family away from Bordeaux and requested the police there to deal with the unwanted visitor. All Wagner was able to do was leave a letter for Jessie at their house and return to Switzerland disappointed and annoyed.

Julie Ritter and her daughter Emilie joined him to celebrate his birthday in Villeneuve after which he spent a few days exploring the canton of Valais with Karl. He wrote to Frau Ritter from Zermatt on 9 June in great anguish of mind, lamenting for Jessie and feeling that he was 'neither dead nor living'. He still hoped that after a year he would see Jessie again. But Mrs Taylor and her daughter had been corresponding with Minna and had begun to view Wagner and his plans for elopement in a very unpleasant light. In a letter of 26–27 June Wagner told Julie Ritter that Karl had heard from Jessie that she had broken completely from the past and would burn any letters received from Wagner without reading them. In Wagner's eyes she had committed an unpardonable crime: she had failed to believe in him. He now regarded her as a weak and pitiable creature, unworthy of his love. In his Autobiography Wagner deliberately underestimated the importance of this affair and his more pious biographers attempted to ignore it altogether. Its true complexion is gauged however from his letter of late June to Frau Ritter: 'I have to place in your hands the testament of a love of which I shall never be ashamed, and which, though now corporeally dead, may perhaps be a source of glad remembrance and emotion to me till my life's end.' Five years later he was still greatly excited to hear news about Jessie from Liszt and admitted the profound effect the 'catastrophe' had had upon him. While she continued in her unhappy liaison with Eugène, which was to break up within a few years, he wrote a lengthy letter to Minna blandly explaining away his recent behaviour and expressing astonishment that she could regard it with jealousy. Ascertaining that she was prepared to accept him and forget the idea of separation, he arrived at the little house christened 'Villa Rienzi' on 3 July. His flight to the east was forgotten and he set about the task which had preoccupied his thoughts even in the recent turbulent months – the creation of *Siegfried*.

Six

Swiss Refuge

Mine is a highly susceptible, intense, voracious yet uncommonly sensitive and fastidious sensuality, which must somehow or other be flattered if my mind is to accomplish the agonizing labour of calling a non-existent world into being.

Wagner to Liszt, January 1854.

WAGNER RETURNED TO ZURICH with Karl Ritter who lodged in an upstairs room of their little house by the Lake. Karl was a somewhat moody boy with more ambition than talent and cynics might suppose that Wagner tolerated him solely on account of the pension from his mother. However, Wagner valued Karl's companionship. He fulfilled a role that had been intended for Jessie and was later to be played by other sympathetic young men: Ludwig II, Nietzsche* and Paul Joukowsky.* 'I can create nothing when I have no one to whom I can and may impart it,' Wagner wrote to Karl in April 1852. Apart from the solitude he needed during the actual hours of composition, he could not bear to be left alone and without an audience. Always an exhibitionist, he sought out those who were willing to listen to him. He needed Minna to provide him with domestic comforts but in addition he craved for an ever-present circle of intellectual admirers. As soon as the text of a drama was complete, a group of friends would be summoned and it would be read to them. At such gatherings he displayed his considerable talents as an actor and proved a wonderfully expressive and skilful reader, apparently losing every trace of his native Saxon accent. But if he were not the sole centre of attention then he would exhibit symptoms of childish rage. He demanded so much from his friends that very few of them could stand the pace. Despite this, his extraordinary personal magnetism ensured that he never wanted for congenial company.

Switzerland at that time harboured many artists and writers who were, like Wagner, political refugees. Some of them were fugitives from Dresden, including Hermann Köchly (former member of the Saxon provisional government, appointed Professor of Classical Philology in Zurich in 1851), Adolph Kolatschek (editor of the Stuttgart *Deutsche Monatsschrift* to which Wagner contributed) and Gottfried Semper (the architect, appointed a professor at the Zurich Polytechnic in 1855). In 1851 Wagner met one of the more notorious of the failed revolutionaries, the poet Georg Herwegh* who has been blamed for sharing (and encouraging) Wagner's fondness for the luxuries of life. Wagner's activities were kept under close surveillance by the police but he consolidated his position in Zurich by making friends with officials of the Swiss republic, notably Jacob Sulzer (a cantonal secretary) and Franz Hagenbuch (second State official of the canton). Both these young men were highly cultured, both stood financial security for Wagner's residence in their country and Sulzer in particular shared with Wagner his cigars, the produce of his vineyard and his interest in Hegelian philosophy. The standpoint and style of Wagner's prose works of this period owed something to the philosophy of Ludwig Feuerbach* and his attraction to Feuerbach's writings was reawakened by Wilhelm Baumgartner, a local piano teacher and composer. *The Art-Work of the Future* first appeared with an introductory letter to Feuerbach, beginning: 'To no one but you, my dear sir, can I dedicate this work, for with it I give you back your own property.'

Ludwig Ettmüller, the distinguished authority on Teutonic sagas (Wagner called him 'Eddamüller') was living in Zurich and helped in the shaping of details of the *Ring*. The composer Franz Abt* was the resident conductor in the town and had shown considerable interest in Wagner's operas, but when Wagner himself conducted in Zurich, Abt became painfully conscious that he was faced by a formidable rival. The wheels of provincial musical politics inevitably began to turn and many people hoped that Wagner would replace Abt as conductor of the Allgemeine Musikgesellschaft. The former Dresden Kapellmeister had no wish to usurp Abt's position and refused to accept the post when Abt left for Brunswick in 1852. Alexander Müller was then appointed conductor. The local choral society conductor, Ignaz Heim, befriended Wagner who was in turn captivated by the charms of his wife, Emilie. Minna kept a jealous eye on this lady and on the wife of another of Wagner's companions, the lawyer Bernard Spyri.[1] Spyri edited the *Eidgenössiche Zeitung*, another journal to which the composer contributed. That a coterie of female admirers grew around him was perhaps inevitable. Eliza Wille displayed a generous sympathy towards Wagner that was not shared by her husband François, a wealthy former newspaper editor from Hamburg. In October 1850 Otto Wesendonck, a rich partner in a New York silk company, arrived in Zurich and settled there in the following year with his young wife Mathilde. The exact nature of Wagner's relationship with Mathilde, then in her early twenties, remains obscure despite the wealth of letters and other documents testifying to the bond of attraction and heartfelt sympathy that existed between them. In the manuscript of the first act of *Die Walküre* there are many cryptic references to the woman who played Sieglinde to Wagner's Siegmund. Otto proved a congenial

---

[1] This was Johanna Spyri, author of *Heidi*.

and understanding Hunding and helped Wagner in countless material ways. Another member of Wagner's circle was the poet and novelist Gottfried Keller, who returned from Germany to his native Zurich in 1855.

While at Villeneuve, immediately prior to the crisis with Jessie, Wagner wrote a short preface to *Siegfrieds Tod*. He attempted to publish the poem but Wigand rejected it on account of Wagner's current affectation for Latin rather than German script and his insistence on small letters rather than capitals for all nouns except proper names. That he intended to compose the music immediately is shown by a composition sketch dated 12 August 1850, consisting of a draft of the Norns scene and twenty lines of the Brünnhilde and Siegfried scene (the prologue to Act One of the present *Götterdämmerung*). The abandonment of this task indicates that Wagner realized he had yet to develop a suitable musical language for the *Siegfried* saga. The style of *Lohengrin* pervades the sketch of August 1850 although one or two leitmotifs of the later *Ring* music are foreshadowed, such as the Treaty and Ride of the Valkyries themes.

His most notorious essay, *Judaism in Music*, was completed on 24 August. It appeared in the *Neue Zeitschrift für Musik* in September signed K. Freigedank (Freethinker) but the author's identity was not a secret for long. In *Art and Revolution* Wagner had attacked Christianity as a force that had degraded man and stifled art. Only by expressing the fullest consciousness of his cultural heritage, the deepest feelings, hopes and conflicts of his own native people could the modern artist attain true greatness. Jews, Wagner argued, could not do this in European society because they had no part in its cultural heritage. He saw clearly (and correctly) that the Jewish composers of the earlier nineteenth century were representatives of a newly emancipated people. They had the talent to imitate the forms and styles of European music with considerable success – witness the grand operas of Meyerbeer and Halévy (both Jews) which virtually monopolized the Parisian repertoire. Wagner considered that 'Mendelssohn has shown us that a Jew may have the amplest store of specific talents, may possess the finest and most varied culture, the highest, most impeccable integrity – yet is not capable, not even once, of producing in us that deep, that heart-searching effect which we expect from art.' Wagner was the first to speculate on a new phenomenon – the Jewish composer. He felt that composers like Meyerbeer and Mendelssohn could only imitate the more obvious, shallow, surface characteristics of Western art and could never penetrate its depths or reveal anything of greatness. What Wagner failed to realize as significant was that composers like Mendelssohn, Meyerbeer and Halévy were only the *first* musical ambassadors of a recently emancipated people. They had indeed turned their backs on their own hereditary culture and had, with considerable speed and skill, adapted their talents to the fashionable culture of the day. Wagner can be forgiven for failing to foresee figures like Mahler and

Schoenberg (ironically two of his most ardent champions). What is disturbing in *Judaism in Music* is the thesis that Jews can *never* become the equals of European composers; that they will always be borrowers who utter their thoughts in a foreign tongue. Worse than his inability to see contemporary Jewish culture as passing through a transitional period is the anti-Semitism that is clearly at the core of Wagner's speculations. Admittedly his anti-Semitism is nothing like so vehement and hysterical as in his later essays, but it was sufficiently evident to cause a furore throughout Europe at the very time that Wagner's reputation as a composer was becoming established widely. The good and bad in Wagner, his greatness and his baseness, were from that time inseparable. No sooner had his niche in the temple of fame been chiselled out than it was sullied by this unworthy slur upon a whole people.

The editor of the *Neue Zeitschrift*, Franz Brendel, was a professor of musical history at the Leipzig Conservatoire. As a result of Wagner's article, every one of his fellow professors (including Joachim, Ferdinand David, Julius Rietz and Moscheles) called for his resignation. Wagner's writings, far more than his operas, succeeded within a few years in dividing the musical world into two fronts: the press of England, France, Germany and Austria was arrayed against Wagner and his supporters who were viewed as a serious challenge to the dilletante musical criticism of the past. It was, and it remains today, unfortunate that so much of the controversy about Wagner stemmed from his own personal prejudices. These were neatly outlined in a letter to Liszt of April 1851:

> I have cherished a long-repressed resentment about this Jew business, and the grudge is as necessary to my nature as gall is to the blood. An incentive came when their accursed scribblings annoyed me intensely, so at last I let fly. It seems I have struck home alarmingly, and that is as I would have it, for I really only wanted to give them just such a fright. That they will remain our masters is as certain as the fact that, not our princes, but our bankers and the Philistines are our lords now. My attitude towards Meyerbeer is now a peculiar one. I do not hate him, he is infinitely repugnant to me. This everlastingly amiable, complaisant fellow reminds me of the most muddy, I might almost say the most degraded period of my life, when he used to make a show of protecting me. It was the period of intrigues and back-stairs, when we are made fools of by patrons for whom we inwardly care not a rap.

During the summer of 1850 Liszt and the Weimar theatre were busily preparing for the premiere of *Lohengrin* which took place on 28 August: a production not great in itself, but of vital significance for Wagner's career. *Lohengrin* was a tall order for the tiny and inadequate Weimar orchestra and Liszt was bitterly disappointed with the standard of the scenery and costumes, despite the outlay of an unprecendented 2000 thalers. But the first performance of the opera with such meagre resources had one all-important result – it exploded the myth that Wagner could only be handled by large theatres. Other provincial companies were soon clamouring to join in the suddenly successful venture of performing Wagner. Liszt established himself as a front runner in the game of presenting new music and he drew the attention of the musical world to the little Weimar court. Wagner had hoped to attend the premiere but this was out of the question; instead he took a few day's holiday with Minna to Lucerne, taking advantage of the gift of 100 thalers from the Grand Duke of Weimar (who sent it anonymously through Liszt). There he listened in imagination to the performance several hundred miles away in forbidden Germany. He was afterwards upset to learn that the opera had taken over an hour longer than he had anticipated and blamed Liszt for dragging the tempi, although later he discovered that this was not the case, and that Liszt had paid the most careful attention to musical details. The fault, Wagner assumed, was probably with the singers, who slowed down what they considered to be the 'recitative' passages and had no notion of their dramatic unity and coherence.

For some time Wagner considered writing *Siegfrieds Tod* for Weimar and hoped that Liszt would secure a suitable advance from the Grand Duke, but in the wake of the Weimar *Lohengrin* he seems to have reconsidered that idea and to have hit upon a more radical one. In letters to Kietz and Uhlig of 14 and 20 September he outlined for the first time a plan for a series of festival performances: the germ of an idea that came to fruition with the first *Ring* cycle at Bayreuth, twenty-six years later. Convinced that any production at an established court theatre would fall far short of his ideal, he envisaged the construction of a wooden theatre outside Zurich, built to his own plans, where the finest singers and instrumentalists from Germany would gather for a few weeks in the summer, and invitations would be extended to all those friends interested in his works, who would be admitted to the performances free of charge. 'After this the theatre would be torn down, and the thing would come to an end.' Yet even this plan would require a lot of money, and with an eye to completing *Siegfrieds Tod* Wagner continued to sound out Liszt as to the possibility of obtaining the means for subsistence from the Weimar court. In October he told Liszt that, rather than do battle with his 'deadly enemy – Winter', he would wait until the spring of 1851 before beginning work on *Siegfried* and would complete his score in the summer.

Meanwhile he turned again to prose writing and between October and February worked at a huge tract, *Opera and Drama*. He was, as he told Liszt on 25 November 1850, clearing his mind for creative work:

> Between the musical composition of my *Lohengrin* and that of my *Siegfried*, there lies for me a world of storm but also – I know it – of fruitfulness. I had to turn over in my mind a whole past lifetime, to bring its darkling things to the clear light of consciousness, to master the reflections aroused in me by dwelling on them – by closest investigation of their meaning – so that I might once again throw myself, with clear and happy consciousness, into the beautiful *un*consciousness of artistic creation.

Opera and Drama dwells at great length on his artistic desires and intuitions and presents them as clearly defined goals. He traces the history of the art of drama from Greek tragedy, through medieval Romance to the achievements of Shakespeare and Racine; then that of recent opera – Gluck, Mozart, Rossini, Weber and finally Meyerbeer whose work is represented as the nadir of the art, a shallow sacrifice of every ideal for mere 'effect'. Meyerbeer is utterly superficial and always follows the latest trend 'like the starling who follows the ploughshare down the field and merrily picks up the earthworm just uncovered in the furrow'.

Wagner considered myth to be the ideal vehicle for the poet because it had its roots in the Folk and contained eternal truth. It had the power to lift the innermost essence of the Folk above the ordinary human plane and could portray the urges and aspirations of mankind in a condensed and strengthened form. For example 'today we need only to expound faithfully the myth of Oedipus according to its innermost essence, and we gain an intelligible picture of the whole history of mankind from the beginnings of society to the inevitable downfall of the state.' Wagner contended that the speech of modern daily life was not suitable for mythic drama. A new, concise and vigorous art-speech, full of serious expression, had to be created. For this, Stabreim was ideal and its constant alliteration would serve to unify the expression. After establishing the idea that 'music cannot think – but she can materialize thoughts', Wagner outlines a system of musical motifs that would both unify the drama and be capable of foreboding an emotion not yet defined in words. Throughout *Opera and Drama* he stresses that it is the poet who dictates to the musician and not *vice versa*. The function of the music is to interpret the text. The modern orchestra, with its many varied tone-colours, is ideal for the task of commentary and elaboration and would fulfil the function of the traditional chorus. In fact, both in practice and in his later prose writings, Wagner consistently ignored his theory of the sovereignty of words over music. Despite *Opera and Drama* he never really departed from the stance taken in his Paris writings for Schlesinger where the primacy of music is accepted and, like Gluck, he wrote his best music when he ignored or forgot his own speculations about this vexed question. The contradictions between this essay and later writings such as *Zukunfstmusik* or *Beethoven* are reminiscent of the perplexing dilemma of the Countess in Strauss's *Capriccio* in having to choose between the dictum 'prima la musica e poi le parole' or alternatively, 'prima le parole, doppo la musica'. It is in the later operas themselves that Wagner provides the answer beyond all doubt.

Much of Wagner's polemic in *Opera and Drama* was directed against the abuses and excesses of grand opera as exemplified in Meyerbeer's settings of Scribe's tailor-made, action-filled libretti. In contrast to the restless extravagance of 'historical' opera, Wagner's mythic variety would concentrate on a smaller number of characters and a limited number of powerful dramatic images. Ensembles, from duets to choruses, were to be replaced with monologue and the underlying, rich unity of the orchestral web of motifs.

A stoical group of friends attended a reading of *Opera and Drama* in twelve instalments during February and March 1851. In January Wagner had written an article, *Recollections of Spontini*, in which he paid tribute to the integrity and lofty dramatic aims of the composer who died on the 14th of that month. In praising Spontini, he grasped the opportunity once more to denigrate the frivolity of Rossini and the charlatanism of Meyerbeer. During the winter of 1850–1 Wagner found himself drawn reluctantly into the musical life of Zurich. The opera management was anxious to secure his valued services as a conductor but Wagner was equally determined never again to commit himself to a regular conducting post. Instead he somewhat rashly recommended Karl Ritter as musical director and gave a personal guarantee of his capabilities. Despite Wagner's supervision and the incentive of a fine salary of 100 thalers per month, Ritter proved hopelessly inadequate during the rehearsals of the first offering of the season, *Der Freischütz*. To make amends, Wagner was obliged to conduct the work himself on 4 October. During that month Hans von Bülow arrived in Zurich and Wagner, who formed a high opinion of the young man's musical potential, arranged for him to take charge of the Zurich repertoire. He conducted four works in the latter part of 1850, but the public soon began to make it clear that they wanted Wagner, and not one of his protégés. The members of the opera also found Bülow's abrasive and demanding nature unpalatable on account of his extreme youth. He was compelled to resign in December and left for a post at St Gallen, where Ritter was also appointed as chorus-master, but conditions there were appalling and Bülow soon quarrelled with the director. Disillusioned, he left for Weimar at Easter 1851, to resume piano studies with Liszt. Ritter soon abandoned his hopes of a conducting career.

While Bülow was in Zurich, Wagner, in true fashion, began to form ideas for the improvement of musical life there. It soon transpired, however, that although he was welcome as a box-office attraction, his radical ideas on theatrical reform and on raising conditions and general standards were not so acceptable. In addition to *Freischütz*, Wagner conducted *La Dame Blanche*, *Norma*, *The Magic Flute*, *Fidelio* and *Don Giovanni*. His work was greatly appreciated but the fact that enthusiasm did not extend to his practical and sensible suggestions for a general reorganization, led Wagner to avoid further contact with the theatre. He had no desire to return to the dreariness of a Dresden-like routine, but mustered a little more enthusiasm for conducting the occasional orchestral concert in Zurich. His concerts of the Zurich years were mainly of Beethoven symphonies and overtures, for which he provided explanatory programmes, together with his own operatic overtures for which he wrote similar notes.

Swiss Refuge

Wagner's appeal for the rational organization of *A Theatre in Zurich* was published in the *Neue Zeitschrift für Musik* in the summer of 1851, but for some months prior to this his thoughts turned more to Weimar, and in particular to the possibility of economic help from there. In a letter to Liszt of 9 March he asked his friend to consider arranging some form of financial security for him. Without this there can be no cheer for him as his wife has no understanding of his inner self: 'I am spiritually a stranger to her.' The incident of the death of Papo the parrot in the previous month was of the nature of a crisis in Wagner's relationship with Minna. Such pets were indispensable to their union, and another parrot, Jacquot, was soon found to fill Papo's place. In response to Wagner's letter, Liszt sent him 100 thalers and the manuscript of his essay in praise of *Lohengrin and Tannhäuser*. This tribute to Wagner was published in French and German and was an expanded version of an article by Liszt that appeared in the Paris *Journal des Débats* shortly after Wagner's flight from Dresden in 1849. Moreover, Liszt negotiated with the Weimar management for a commission for *Siegfrieds Tod*. On 3 May 1851 they offered Wagner 500 thalers for the work, to be paid in instalments, and hoped that the score would be delivered to them by July 1852. Just at that time Wagner had come to the conclusion that he would not write *Siegfrieds Tod* as neither the singers nor the public for it existed. Instead he planned a preliminary drama, *Young Siegfried*, which would depict the youthful hero setting out to learn fear, winning the Nibelung's treasure from the dragon, and awakening the warrior-maiden Brünnhilde from her magic sleep. He saw *Young Siegfried* as a lighter work, much more suited to Weimar's size and taste. The prose sketch of *Der Junge Siegfried* was made between 28 May and 1 June, and the poem was complete by 24 June.

On 25 June Breitkopf und Härtel informed an astonished and delighted Wagner of their decision to publish the full score of *Lohengrin*. He was full of boisterous enthusiasm for life when he set out to meet Uhlig, his devoted friend and champion from Dresden, one week later. Armed with his poem of *Young Siegfried* Wagner first walked to St Gallen, via Rapperswil, Utznach, the Ricken Pass and Lichtenstein. Ritter welcomed him in St Gallen and together they proceeded to Rohrschach to find Uhlig. In the two years since Wagner had left Dresden, Uhlig had been steadily weakened by consumption and on seeing his wasted state Wagner hesitated to continue with their original plan of walking back to Zurich by a strenuous route over the Santis peak. But Uhlig insisted on carrying out the climb, protesting that the exercise and the fresh air could only do him good. Wagner too welcomed the exhilaration of the mountain scenery after his months of writing and study. During the precipitous ascent, which held no terrors for Wagner who had an excellent head for heights, Karl Ritter became dizzy and insensible with fear. Realizing that the descent would prove yet more dangerous, Wagner saw his folly in having persuaded Karl to share in their perilous adventure. To avert the possibility of a fatal accident, Wagner and Uhlig succeeded in reaching the hut of a mountain guide where they left Karl to be taken home by a safer route. The two stronger characters then continued their wild trek towards Zurich where, after some anxious days, they were relieved by the arrival of Karl, safe and well.

Learning that his friends planned further mountaineering, Karl diplomatically escaped back to St Gallen. At the end of July, Wagner and Uhlig embarked on an energetic exploration of Switzerland's dramatic terrain, the high mountain passes, valleys and lakes of the William Tell country. It was a blissfully happy holiday for Uhlig but, sadly, his last meeting with his hero and former Kapellmeister: he died on 3 January 1853.

On his return to Zurich Wagner wrote an extensive account of his artistic development, *A Communication to my Friends*, which Breitkopf agreed to publish as the preface to an edition of the texts of *The Flying Dutchman*, *Tannhäuser* and *Lohengrin*. Before the *Communication* was issued in December 1851, Wagner added a final section announcing a bold scheme for 'a special festival at some future time' which would be produced 'in the course of three days and a preliminary evening'. During November he had conceived the final shape of the *Ring* idea. As *Young Siegfried* prepared the audience for the events of *Siegfried's Death*, *Die Walküre* (dealing with the ill-starred love of Siegfried's parents, Siegmund and Sieglinde and the involvement of Wotan and Brünnhilde with that love) would give the whole presentation of the myth a greater clarity, depth and breadth. The three principal parts of the drama, *The Valkyrie*, *Young Siegfried* (later simply called *Siegfried*) and *Siegfried's Death* (later called *Götterdämmerung*) were in turn to be preceded by a 'great drama' *The Theft of the Rhinegold* (later called *Das Rheingold*). This would deal with the theft of the gold, the creation of the ring and Alberich's curse upon it.

Wagner formed this plan for the Nibelung Saga, and made prose sketches for *Rheingold* and *Walküre*, during November at Albisbrunn, where he was undergoing an arduous water-cure. This treatment had been enthusiastically advocated by Uhlig, who introduced Wagner to the writings of J. H. Rausse. Rausse repudiated the science of medicine as pure quackery and dismissed all its drugs and remedies as poison. Only the simple, refreshing treatment of water could purify the system. During the Swiss years Wagner was rarely in good health and his addiction to crank 'cures' in all probability exacerbated the minor ailments from which he suffered. In the spring of 1851 he tried to alleviate an attack of shingles by submitting himself to a course of sulphur baths, but this unpleasant treatment resulted in a series of irritations and a prolonged lassitude and depression. He began to take cold baths every morning and to drink cold water in bed in the belief that only a rigorous hydropathic treatment would expel the poisons from his body. On 16 September, a few days after moving to a new flat, he commenced a ten-week stay at Albisbrunn. In *Mein Leben* he described the horrors of this aquatic hell:

> Early at five o'clock in the morning I was wrapped up and kept in a state of perspiration for several hours; after that I was plunged into an icy cold bath at a temperature of only four degrees; then I was made to take a brisk walk to restore my circulation in the chilly air of late autumn. In addition I was kept on a water diet; no wine, coffee or tea was allowed; and this regime, in the dismal company of nothing but incurables, with dull evenings only enlivened by desperate attempts at games of whist, and the prohibition of all intellectual occupation, resulted in irritability and overwrought nerves.

He found some compensation in the company of two friends whom he persuaded to join him at the establishment: Karl Ritter and Hermann Müller, a former lover of Schröder-Devrient. Poor Karl became quite miserable after a mere day or two of the torturous treatment at Albisbrunn. Before long he discovered a confectioner's shop in the neighbourhood and found relief from the enforced diet of dry bread and water by procuring cheap pastry on the sly.

Karl's mother, Julie Ritter, wrote to Wagner at Albisbrunn, with the excellent tidings that she had recently inherited a considerable sum of money and was in a position to guarantee him a regular annual income of 800 thalers. With the promise of such a sum, he no longer felt that the *Siegfried* plan for Weimar was necessary, and turned his thoughts to the bolder scheme of a Nibelung drama in four parts. On 20 November he sent Liszt a lengthy explanation of his latest conception of the work and, thanks to Karl Ritter, was able to return to Weimar the 200 thalers he had already received for the commission. Three days later he left Albisbrunn weak, emaciated, feverish and with a general aggravation of the various symptoms that had originally prompted his visit there. Nonetheless, his stubborn belief in the value of water therapy persisted to such an extent that he quarrelled bitterly with Sulzer and Herwegh who denounced it and refused to adopt Wagner's practice of cold baths and abstinence from alcohol. To his friends, Wagner's pale, excitable, sleepless condition was clear evidence of the folly of his convictions. The tenacity and obstinacy with which he clung to his delusions was incomprehensible to them.

Liszt's reaction to Wagner's withdrawal from the Weimar *Siegfried* plan was characteristically generous. Reading between the lines of his letter of 1 December, there is a hint of relief that responsibility for the new work will not fall upon his shoulders. At the same time, and throughout the ensuing correspondence, he offered Wagner every encouragement in the pursuit of his 'extraordinary goal': 'Your programme should be like the direction given by the Chapter of Seville to the architect of the new cathedral – "Build us such a temple that future generations will be obliged to say that the Chapter was mad to undertake anything so extraordinary".' In producing *Lohengrin* and *Tannhäuser* at Weimar, Liszt had become aware of both the inadequacies and the potentialities of the small court theatre. He had the greatest sympathy for Wagner's music, and even if he had not yet fully comprehended Wagner's ambitions as a dramatist, he realized that, with the correct understanding and support, Wagner would create something of monumental importance. In the meantime he turned his energies to his own very different problem of reforming conditions at Weimar and creating there a platform for new music. His first important task was a production of *Benvenuto Cellini* by Berlioz, in March 1852, an undertaking with which Wagner had little sympathy as he was aware of the opera's serious dramatic weaknesses.

It was not to Liszt, but to Uhlig that Wagner confided his real hopes for the future. In a letter of 12 November 1851 which outlines the four-part *Ring* plan, he revealed that his radical views had not changed in the past few years. His new work will only be possible after the revolution and will reveal to society the meaning and noble purpose of a new epoch in world history. *Opera and Drama* was published that month and was significantly regarded more as a political tract than an essay on aesthetics. On leaving Albisbrunn, his first desire was to complete the poems of *Rheingold* and *Walküre*, but continuing depression and ill-health together with a commitment to various concerts in Zurich prevented this during the winter. In addition he was shocked and disillusioned by Napoleon III's *coup d'état* of 2 December. He presumed that Europe was rushing headlong to its doom and told Kietz that he considered that America provided the only hope for the fulfilment of his dreams, and his Nibelung drama would first be performed on the banks of the Mississippi: 'My entire politics consists of nothing but the bloodiest hatred for our whole civilization, contempt for all things deriving from it, and a longing for nature.'

Apart from another foray into print, *On Musical Criticism* (*Neue Zeitschrift für Musik*) first published in February 1852 and later issued as a pamphlet, the early part of the new year was spent in gloomy brooding. On 12 January he confessed to Uhlig that his water cure was followed out too rigorously and the result had been a fresh exasperation of the nerves. He had lost every one of his illusions about the world, his plans for reform in Zurich had failed, no one had true sympathy for his ideals and he would be happy to die. His malady was worse than Beethoven's deafness for he no longer lived in his epoch. But one month later Uhlig learned that his friend was not entirely without admirers:

> Some new acquaintances have forced themselves on me: the men are highly indifferent to me, the women less so. A rich young merchant, Wesendonck . . . settled in Zurich some time ago, and in great luxury. His wife is very pretty and seems to have caught some enthusiasm for me after having read the preface to the three operatic poems. Thus it is with some Swiss families of the aristocracy here (I refer only to the women, for the men are horrible).

Mathilde Wesendonck was present at an impressive performance of the

Tannhäuser overture, under Wagner, on 16 March. It was the most over-whelming experience of her young life and largely due to her influence and enthusiasm *The Flying Dutchman* was produced with slender resources in Zurich, on four evenings between 25 April and 2 May. These performances were an improvement on the Dresden production and Wagner took the opportunity to reduce the somewhat raucous orchestration of the original score and to alter the endings of the overture and the final scene.

As spring approached, the dark thoughts and doubts of the winter gave way to creative activity. The prose sketch of *Rheingold* was amplified between 23 and 31 March and that of *Die Walküre* between 17 and 26 May. Encouraging news came from Liszt who continued to promote Wagner's work in Germany. Early in 1848 Wagner had sent him the score of his *Faust Overture* with a note explaining 'that it does not please me any longer'. Liszt conducted the overture at Weimar on 11 May 1852 and urged Wagner to revise it and expand the lyrical idea associated with Gretchen. This Wagner felt unable to do without remodelling the whole work, but he returned to Liszt's suggestion at a later date. At a two-day festival under his direction at Ballenstadt (22–23 June) Liszt included a number of Wagner extracts. From May until early July Wagner and Minna stayed at the Pension Rinderknecht, where he tried another cure – a somewhat gentler treatment devised by Dr Karl Lindemann of Paris, which Hermann Müller had recommended. Here the baths were tepid rather than ice-cold and the occasional glass of wine was allowed. More importantly, intellectual work was not discouraged and by the first day of July the poem of *Die Walküre* was complete. Instead of resting quietly, Wagner once more made the mistake of setting out on a vigorous walking holiday, roaming over peaks and glaciers with 'an energy that matched any Alpine guide'. Reaching Lake Maggiore in Italy, he sailed to the Borromean Islands and wrote to Otto Wesendonck that he was smoking 'the first of your god-like cigars'. Next day, 21 July, he arrived in Lugano feeling lonely and exhausted. He telegraphed to Minna requesting her to join him, which she did without delay, and she was followed shortly by Herwegh and François Wille. Together they visited the Borromean Islands and then Wagner and Minna returned to Zurich by a circuitous, scenic route through Switzerland.

Once home, he was preoccupied with what he himself termed the 'hailstorm' of requests from German theatres to perform *Tannhäuser*. It was mainly the smaller theatres that showed interest in his work, and so the apparent change of fortune was artistic rather than financial, as the standard practice was to pay the composer one small lump sum for the entire run – an amount far smaller than that which a good singer could expect for one single performance. At Schwerin, Wiesbaden, Würzburg, Breslau and other small towns *Tannhäuser* became a popular repertory piece, and it was even revived in Dresden. Düsseldorf, Frankfort, Hamburg,

Riga and Rudolstadt all expressed interest in it. Leipzig, which had hitherto given scant attention to its notorious son, gave twenty performances of *Tannhäuser* in 1853. At Munich the conductor Franz Lachner* and the Intendant Franz Dingelstedt* displayed an interest in mounting the opera but there was a public outcry against performing any work by the 'red republican' Richard Wagner. The Minister-President, Baron von der Pfordten, advised the Bavarian King to reject the work. Prestigious Berlin also sought to perform *Tannhäuser* and, despite his unpleasant recollections of the town and his low opinion of the conductors Wilhelm Taubert and Heinrich Dorn, Wagner saw the advantages of a production there. As he was unable to attend in person, his principal concern was that some trustworthy friend should supervise a Berlin production to ensure that the composer's intentions were properly carried out. Liszt was chosen for this task and expressed willingness, but the director of the Berlin Court Theatre, Botho von Hülsen,* saw the proposed intervention of Liszt as an affront to his own conductors. Lengthy negotiations failed to solve the problem and merely stirred up feelings of ill will on either side – and Wagner's score was returned to him in February 1853 without so much as an accompanying note. Hülsen's dislike of Wagner can be explained by the fact that he was formerly an officer of the Prussian army and had participated in the suppression of the Dresden revolt.

There were two important consequences of the 'hailstorm' of interest in Wagner's earlier work. Characteristically it led him to spend lavishly on the furnishing of his Zurich apartment in the expectation that fees would shortly be pouring in from all over Germany. As ever, Wagner's optimism raced ahead of his common sense and, when the demands from German theatres began to grow scarce, he was left heavily in debt. Secondly, he became more and more frustrated at not being able to attend the German performances of his work; he knew that without his presence his operas would be misrepresented and misunderstood. In his Zurich exile he was impotent and increasingly tortured by homesickness. On returning from Italy in August 1852 he wrote a brochure, *On the Performing of 'Tannhäuser'* and had two hundred copies printed and sent to German theatres, at his own expense. Its purpose was to clarify his artistic intentions, outline the minimum forces required, and explain the dramatic structure and the required demands for singers, conductors and producers. In *Mein Leben* Wagner admitted that he had never heard of a single person who had either read this pamphlet or taken any notice of it. Twelve years later he found a number of copies in the Munich theatre archive: the pages remained uncut. At the end of 1852 he wrote a similar essay, *Remarks on performing 'The Flying Dutchman'*.

The poem of *Rheingold* was written between 15 September and 3 November, and the texts of *Siegfried* and *Götterdämmerung* then revised. By 17 December the libretto of the entire cycle was complete (although there were textual revisions of the last two dramas in 1856). A few days later he read all four dramas to a small group of friends at the Wille's country house, Mariafeld. In January 1853 *Der Ring des Nibelungen* was published privately in Zurich and fifty copies of this *edition de luxe* sent to friends. A large gathering was invited to the Hotel Bauer au Lac, Zurich, on 16 February and on the three succeeding evenings, to hear Wagner read his monumental saga. He declaimed his lines magnificently and was pleased with the attentive response of the audience. Those friends honoured by the gift of the *Ring* poem were also polite and discreet in their praise, but before long Wagner bitterly regretted the distribution of his text. He realized that his drama was regarded as a wildly ambitious extravaganza, an imaginative caprice whose very scope and boldness bewildered anyone who tried to imagine what sort of music would be provided for it. In issuing the poem long before the music was conceived it was inevitable that it would be judged purely as a piece of literature – and the verdict was unfavourable. Wagner felt that only Uhlig would truly have understood it, but the opening days of the year had been darkened by the news of his death. To Liszt he poured out his woes and expressed his longing to return to Germany. In letter after letter he complained of his ill-health and spiritual loneliness, confessing on 30 March:

> The truth is that I reached my thirty-fifth year before realizing that *up till then I had not lived at all*. It was my art that first revealed to me what a wretched life, barren of love and joy, I have lived up to now. What will you say when I tell you that I have never yet enjoyed the true happiness of love? Now I drag out my life between deprivation and a resigned submission to a restricted, petty environment in which I am understood less and less every day!

Liszt realized that the root cause of Wagner's anguish was his inability to commence the music of the *Ring*. In the previous autumn he dissuaded Wagner from a plan to present *Tannhäuser* in a French translation at the Paris Opéra. Belloni had encouraged this idea and Wagner longed to take the opportunity of beating Meyerbeer on his home ground. His niece Johanna could be utilized and thus fulfil a task far nobler than that of starring in Meyerbeer's works. Wagner was disgusted that Johanna 'should have been obliged to sell herself to that avaricious Jew. She might well have found nobler employment for her youthful powers than to sacrifice herself to that rotting carcase' (letter to Johanna's sister Francisca Wagner). Liszt reasoned that a work so German as *Tannhäuser* was unthinkable for Paris: 'Write your *Nibelungen*, and care about nothing else. All other things will arrange themselves of their own accord when the time comes.'

One oasis of happiness in the desert of pessimism that constituted the first half of 1853 was an expensive but highly successful three-day Wagner festival in Zurich. On the evenings of 18, 20 and 22 May excerpts from his operas, ranging from *Rienzi* to *Lohengrin*, were given by a group of singers and instrumentalists recruited from far and near. The venture created considerable publicity in Germany. In Vienna Johann Strauss II was already including Wagner extracts in his concerts. During the year the composer Joachim Raff* was engaged upon a study, *Die Wagnerfrage* (*The Wagner Question*, published 1854). In the French press the topic of Wagner had recently created much agitation. The great Wagner debate had begun and his name was eagerly discussed both by those who hailed him as a prophet of the art of the future and by those who were merely irritated by this thorn in the side of the musical establishment. The little Zurich festival made a loss of 1190 francs which was borne by eight or nine supporters, one of whom was Otto Wesendonck.

Mathilde Wesendonck inspired the only compositions from Wagner's pen between *Lohengrin* and *Rheingold*. On 20 June Wagner sent to Otto an Album Sonata in A flat major for piano, dedicated to Frau Wesendonck. A Polka in G major, also inscribed to her, belongs to this year. In 1854 another trifle, the *Züricher Vielliebchen-Walzer*, was dedicated to Mathilde's sister by 'Richard der Walzermacher'. The sonata is the most considerable of these piano works, consisting of an extensive single movement.

Whatever happiness had been aroused in Wagner by the May festival venture, or by his removal in the previous month to a more pleasant and sunny adjacent flat, was promptly reversed in June by the news from Saxony that there could be no question of an amnesty for him. From Dresden the police circulated a portrait of the former Kapellmeister and prominent revolutionary in order to facilitate his immediate arrest if he attempted to re-enter Germany. Fortunately, Wagner's resultant depression was dispelled during the first ten days of July by the presence of Liszt in Zurich. Liszt told the Princess Wittgenstein that:

> Wagner was waiting to meet me at the post-house. We almost choked one another with embraces. Sometimes he has a kind of eaglet's cry in his voice. He wept and laughed and stormed with joy at seeing me again for at least a quarter of an hour. . . . Twenty times during the day he fell upon my neck – then rolled on the ground stroking his dog Peps and talking nonsense to it turn by turn – reviling the Jews, with him a generic term of very wide meaning. In a word, a grand and grandissimo nature, something like a Vesuvius letting off fireworks, emitting sheaves of flame and bouquets of roses and lilacs.

Wagner read the *Ring* poem 'with astonishing energy and intelligence of accent' and Liszt in turn played his friend a number of his latest piano pieces and symphonic poems. Together with Herwegh they spent a few days exploring the Tell country in the vicinity of Lake Lucerne. Liszt was surprised at the elegance and luxury of Wagner's surroundings and informed the Princess that it must take two or three times the amount of Frau Ritter's pension to live in such style. It appears that in order to create a conducive atmosphere for composition Wagner felt compelled to sur-round himself with every conceivable, lavish domestic luxury, regardless of reckless expense. He told Liszt, 'I cannot live like a dog, I cannot bed in straw or satisfy my soul with gin.' And Eliza Wille recalled a statement he made while staying at Mariafeld in 1864:

> I am a different kind of organism, I have hyper-sensitive nerves, I must have beauty, splendour and light. The world ought to give me what I need! I cannot live the wretched life of a town organist like your Meister Bach! Is it such a shocking demand, if I believe that I am due the little bit of luxury I enjoy? I, who have so much enjoyment to give to the world and to thousands of people!

During his stay with Wagner in July 1853 Liszt also became aware of his friend's need to dominate, of his inability to accept argument or opposition. To disagree with Wagner was a mistake. In later years the expression of a mere difference of opinion was sufficient to drive him from the room in a rage. Herwegh's wife, Emma (a close friend of Minna) dismissed him as 'this pocket-size edition of a man, this folio of vanity, heartlessness and egoism'. When Wagner approached his niece Johanna for a loan during 1853, her father Albert wrote to his brother:

> I am used to seeing you respect people only *if* and *as long as* they can be of use to you. A person no longer exists for you when their usefulness is over. You know nothing of gratitude for the past: all that is merely an infernal obligation! It has always been so – towards Brockhaus, the King, Lüttichau, Pusinelli, Tichatschek and everyone else who had helped you in one way or another. Whilst I greatly love and esteem your talent, it is just the opposite with regard to your character. Since your last letter the first sign of life you give Johanna is – lend me a thousand thalers! A mere trifle!

Liszt was aware of his friend's potential as much as he realized his character to be that of a Narcissus: a vainglorious, self-centred exhibitionist who would turn from flattery to pugnacious ingratitude as swiftly as the mere twist of a weathercock. And Liszt, despite all the tests and trials to which their friendship would be put, would have concurred with the verdict of Heinrich Porges* who wrote after Wagner's death:

> Such demoniac personalities cannot be judged by ordinary standards. They are egoists of the first water, and must be so, or they could never fulfil their mission.

When Liszt left Zurich, Wagner sank into despondency once more. Despite their rejection of his plans for a reorganization of musical life in Zurich, the musicians there were keen to honour their exiled guest. Wagner was not unmoved by a torchlight procession and serenade, and the presentation of a Diploma of Honour, shortly after Liszt's departure, but such friendly exhibitions of goodwill were not enough to cure his spiritual loneliness and gloom. He felt ill at ease, restless and mentally exhausted. On 14 July, the day after the local singers and orchestral players had paid their tribute to him, he left to try another water cure, this time at St Moritz in the Upper Engardine, accompanied by Herwegh. Predictably, the treatment merely aggravated his condition and an attempt at mountaineering fatigued him considerably. He returned home on 10 August to an irritable Minna, peeved at his excursions with the womanizing wastrel Herwegh. A fortnight later Wagner set out once again, to seek fresh scenery and the correct mood for creative work: Italy was his destination and he travelled via Geneva and Turin to Genoa. There he found himself weak, listless and tormented by frustration at his inability to settle down to composition. He contracted dysentery which worsened during a voyage to Spezia, and he was further weakened by sea-sickness. In Spezia he staggered to the nearest hotel which was in a noisy, narrow street and spent a feverish, sleepless night. After a long, exhausting walk the following morning he experienced the famous trance-condition so vividly described in *Mein Leben*:

> Returning in the afternoon, I stretched myself, dead tired, on a hard couch, awaiting the long-desired hour of sleep. It did not come; but I fell into a kind of somnolent state, in which I suddenly felt as though I were sinking in swiftly flowing water. The rushing sound took a musical shape in my brain as the chord of E flat major, which continually re-echoed in broken shapes; these broken chords seemed to form melodic figures of increasing motion, yet the pure triad of E flat major never changed, but seemed by its continuity to impart infinite significance to the element in which I was sinking. I awoke from my doze in sudden terror, feeling as if the waves were rushing high above my head. I at once recognized that the orchestral prelude to the *Rheingold*, which must have been latent within me for a long time, though I had been unable to give it definite form, had at last been revealed to me. I quickly realized the essence of my own nature; the stream of life was not to flow to me from without, but from within.

It has been speculated that this description, written many years later and after Wagner had become familiar with Schopenhauer's theories about the connection between creativity and the dream state, is somewhat over-fanciful. But there is no real cause to doubt that Wagner suddenly realized how to harness the thematic elements that had been vaguely present in his mind for many months, and that the shape of the E flat major prelude did come to him in this dramatic and powerful way. Stravinsky spoke of similar experiences in connection with *The Rite of Spring*, parts of which were shaping in his mind long before he had any notion of how to commit them to paper.

From Spezia Wagner telegraphed Minna, informing her of his decision to commence work on the *Ring* music without delay, and asking that his study be prepared for the task. On reaching Genoa he felt so much better that for a moment he was tempted to revert to his original plan and enjoy the exquisite Italian countryside. At once his symptoms returned – and he concluded that his recent spell of good health was due, not to the delights of Italy, but to his resolve to take up work again. Without further delay he turned his back on the south and headed over the St Gotthard pass to Zurich, arriving home on 10 September.

Minna was taking the waters at Baden am Stein and Wagner found himself still too unsettled to work. He was due to meet Liszt at Basel in October and decided to postpone composition of *Rheingold* until then. In the meantime he added to his excitability and restlessness by bathing at the hot springs of Baden. At Basel Liszt was surrounded by a circle of young and talented admirers: Bülow, Joachim, Peter Cornelius,* Richard Pohl,* Dionys Pruckner* and Eduard Remenyi* collectively serenaded Wagner at his hotel on 6 October. An evening of great conviviality ensued and the next day the Princess Wittgenstein arrived with her fifteen-year-old daughter Marie. Marie von Sayn-Wittgenstein* enchanted Wagner and was the inspiration for Freia's music in *Rheingold*. Liszt and the Wittgensteins left for Paris on 9 October and Wagner decided to accompany them. He read his *Ring* poem aloud once more and recited it to an exceedingly bemused Berlioz. The current success of Meyerbeer's *Robert the Devil* in the French capital had an adverse effect on Wagner's health, but his spirits were restored by a revealing performance of Beethoven's C sharp minor quartet. The essential purpose of Liszt's Paris visit was to see his children, the offspring of his liaison with Countess Marie d'Agoult,* who were in the care of a governess and who had last met their father eight years previously. Wagner was introduced to his son Daniel, and his daughters Blandine and Cosima, the latter then sixteen years old. Liszt felt very much at home among the social élite of Paris, while Wagner found the city as uncongenial as ever and suffered from recurrent headaches and a sense of isolation. With the aid of funds from Sulzer, he persuaded Minna to join him for a holiday and together they visited their old friends Kietz and Anders. The Wesendoncks were also in Paris at the time. Towards the end of October he left Paris 'tired out, restless and exceedingly fretful, without the least understanding why I had spent so much money there'.

The music of *Das Rheingold* was begun in Zurich on 1 November. As soon as he was at work Wagner noticed a general improvement in his health. Despite an interruption of ten days owing to a feverish cold, the composition sketch of the work was complete by 14 January 1854. The following day Wagner wrote a candid letter to Liszt in which he confessed the dual cause of his 'long-nourished, long-imprisoned wretchedness' – lack of love, and lack of cash. 'Not a year of my life has passed recently without bringing me *once* to the very verge of a decision to make an end of my life. . . . A too hasty marriage with a woman, estimable but totally unsuited to me, has made me an outlaw for life.' In a reference to his thirty-sixth year he admits obliquely that it was through Jessie Laussot that he realized the emptiness of his heart. Now he is doomed to love 'unhappily' – an allusion to his growing passion for Mathilde Wesendonck. Turning to that other root evil, money, he tells Liszt, 'You must help me now! Things are bad – very bad with me . . . Härtels have been very open-handed [with an advance for *Lohengrin*] but what's the use of hundreds to me when I need thousands?'

His financial plight was mainly the result of lavish spending on furnishings on the one hand and the demands of former creditors in Dresden on the other. He was faced with urgent bills from the various Zurich firms that had helped him feather his nest with fine carpets, silk curtains, beautiful furniture, chandeliers and other simple necessities for his work. Wagner had more or less abandoned the entangled remains of his publishing venture with Meser in Dresden, where the principal creditors were Pusinelli, Kriete and Hiebendahl. In September 1853 they were assigned all 'literary rights' in the three operas published by Meser. In 1855 Karl Ritter paid Hiebendahl the 400 thalers he was owed, and this amount was deducted from Julie Ritter's pension for Wagner of 800 thalers. After Meser's death, in 1856, Kriete threatened to sue Wagner for his 1200 thaler loan plus interest accrued over twelve years. In vain Wagner tried to save the situation by persuading Pusinelli to buy the owner's rights to the works. He pointed out that the cause of the problem was Meser's complete failure to find a market for the scores; now that the operas were in demand, surely Pusinelli could 'think in large terms' and invest in the future. But Pusinelli and Kriete had no such faith. Instead they appointed a music dealer, Hermann Müller, to manage the hopeless enterprise. Thoroughly disillusioned and exasperated with the project, they sold all their interests in it to Müller in 1859, for a mere 3000 thalers. Pusinelli alone lost about 10,000 thalers and, in addition, it fell to his lot to appease many of Wagner's other Dresden creditors.

During 1854 *Tannhäuser* reached Austria (Graz, January) and Bohemia (Prague, October), but the year began badly with a disastrous performance of *Lohengrin* at Leipzig, on 7 January. The fiasco resulted in a great deal of bad publicity for Wagner.

The winter season of six orchestral concerts in Zurich involved Wagner in much guest conducting. The generous sacrifice he made of his time to assist the local musical society is easily overlooked. His suggestions for reforming musical life in the town also cost him much time and energy. In all he prepared three painstakingly detailed plans for the improvement and co-ordination of the orchestral and operatic performances. For a concert on 7 March 1854 he prepared a concert ending for Gluck's overture to *Iphigenia in Aulis* which is in standard use today. (He published a letter on the subject of this overture in the *Neue Zeitschrift für Musik*, on 1 July.) The Zurich theatre director, Löwe, died in August 1853 after a shooting accident which occurred during a performance of *Uncle Tom's Cabin* in Baden. His widow was forced to abandon her attempt at maintaining the company at the end of the following January. Wagner conducted two concerts in March 1854, in aid of the orchestral players who had suffered considerable hardship at the closure of the theatre.

The orchestral sketch of *Rheingold* was completed on 28 May and the full orchestral score was prepared during the summer and finished on 26 September. This three-fold method of working – composition sketch, orchestral sketch and final fair copy of the full score – was thereafter Wagner's standard method of composition. The first sketch of the *Walküre* music is dated 28 June and the huge three-act drama was completed in composition sketch within six months, by 27 December 1854. The peace of mind required for this task was achieved by the liquidation of Wagner's most pressing debts by Sulzer and Otto Wesendonck. Mathilde also aided the composer with the gift of 'a golden pen, of indestructible writing power'; she was constantly present in his mind during the writing of the first act.

A major interruption to work on the score occurred in July when Wagner had to fulfil a promise to conduct Beethoven's Seventh Symphony at a festival in Sitten (Sion), capital of the Valais canton. During the week before this, he stayed with Karl Ritter at Colonnes, near Montreux. Karl had for some time been enjoying a love affair with a young actor in Stuttgart. To Wagner's surprise he had now married a girl from Dresden; an arrangement which, Wagner thought, was not likely to last long. Indeed Karl was showing far more interest in Baron Robert von Hornstein,* a dilettante composer and Wagner enthusiast who travelled with them to Sitten on 8 July. The festival was very badly organized and Wagner became angry when he saw the scanty orchestra and heard the poor acoustic of the church intended for the performance. He returned to his hotel depressed and disappointed at having been distracted from his *Walküre* work to attend such an inartistic enterprise. Hornstein and Ritter then committed the inexcusable offence of laughing at the whole affair. Assuming that their irrepressible merriment was at his expense, Wagner packed his bags and left without another word, leaving an explanatory note for the festival director. After visiting Geneva and Lausanne for a few days, he returned to Montreux and restored relations with his two young friends. After a few days Hornstein accompanied Wagner on foot as far as Lausanne. Wagner then continued alone from Berne to Lucerne and on to Seelisberg where Minna, now sorely troubled by her heart condition, was taking a sour-milk cure. Like a dutiful husband he remained with her for a week or so, finding compensation in the wild countryside nearby. It was 3 August before he returned to Zurich and the task of completing Act One.

It was now Minna's turn to travel, and in the last week of August she departed for Germany – her first visit since she joined Wagner in exile five years before. Ostensibly her journey was for reasons of health and to enable her to see her family in Dresden, but she also carried out two important missions on her husband's behalf: an attempt to petition the King of Saxony for an amnesty and a visit to Hülsen of the Berlin Court Opera to secure a performance of *Tannhäuser*. Both strategies failed.

Minna called at Weimar and obtained a letter from the Grand Duke in support of an amnesty for Wagner, but Friedrich August II of Saxony had recently been succeeded by his sterner brother Johann and a decision about the matter was deferred until three months after his accession to the throne. When the official reply did reach Zurich in December, it was couched in uncompromising language: there was no possibility of a pardon until the fugitive had returned and submitted himself to justice. The attempt to mount *Tannhäuser* in Berlin had reached a similar point of stalemate. Minna approached Hülsen with the suggestion that Wagner himself might gain permission to attend the rehearsals in Berlin and this would remove the necessity of Liszt's presence – the principal obstacle to further progress at the time – but Hülsen had no authority to act upon this suggestion, and Liszt would not withdraw from his original promise to Wagner. Minna's efforts on Wagner's behalf show how devoted she remained to his well-being and future hopes, although she had no understanding whatsoever of his aspirations for the Nibelung plan. Naturally he valued her help and remained grateful for her provision of domestic comfort and her devoted concern. In turn he was anxious about her own happiness and health. Inwardly, however, she was a total stranger to him. The relationship of Richard and Minna is mirrored in that of Wotan and Fricka, as expounded by Wagner in a letter to Röckel, 25 January 1854:

> The strong chain which binds these two, forged from love's instinctive error in seeking to prolong itself beyond the inevitable laws of change, in maintaining mutual dependence in opposition to the law of eternal renewal and change in the world of phenomena – brings both of them to a state of mutual torment and lovelessness. The whole course of the drama shows the necessity of recognizing and yielding to the multiplicity, and the changeableness, the many-sidedness, the eternal newness of reality and of life.

That summer of 1854 provided much to depress Wagner's thoughts – an awareness of the growing spiritual estrangement from Minna, of the unattainable Mathilde whom he really loved; the impossibility of financing his *Ring* project, the lack of response to his ideals in Zurich, his banishment from Germany – apparently forever. Once more his health declined and he contemplated suicide. In the autumn, Herwegh introduced him to the writings of a man whose pessimism matched Wagner's own – Arthur Schopenhauer.*

Schopenhauer's *The World as Will and Idea* had appeared in 1819, but was virtually ignored until brought to the attention of the literary and artistic world by an Englishman, John Oxenford, in the *Westminster and Foreign Quarterly Review* of April 1853. During the long years of his neglect the philosopher had become a recluse and was derided as a madman. Schopenhauer's greatest gift to Wagner was to provide him with a key to a new and fuller understanding of his own work. Wagner never absorbed more of Schopenhauer than he chose to. The 'prince of pessimism' saw man as 'in essence, a wild, horrifying beast'. But Wagner always regarded true human nature as good, or at any rate capable of redemption. Nor did he follow Schopenhauer's precepts for the good man – poverty, fasting, chastity and self-torture. The philosopher himself belied his own principles. In Bertrand Russell's words:[1]

> He habitually dined well, at a good restaurant; he had many trivial love-affairs, which were sensual but not passionate; he was exceedingly quarrelsome and unusually avaricious. . . . It is hard to find in his life evidences of any virtue except kindness to animals which he carried to the point of objecting to vivisection in the interests of science. In all other respects he was completely selfish.

(That could almost be a description of Wagner.) Schopenhauer's theory of the negation of the will to live was nothing new to the creator of Wotan whose very tragedy was to will his own destruction. No gaps in Wagner's artistic nature were filled by Schopenhauer – the *Ring* text had been completed two years before. Much of Schopenhauer's thought directly contradicted Wagner's own writings: the revolutionary optimism of Wagner's prose writing seemed an odd bedfellow for Schopenhauer's pessimism. Wagner's view that music required an object – the text of a drama – to which it lent expression was at odds with Schopenhauer's thesis that music is a direct manifestation of the Will.

What then was the importance of Schopenhauer to Wagner? In *The World as Will and Idea* Wagner found a reinforcement of his own recent pessimism; and he found reasons and arguments that clarified and strengthened his own emotions and intuitions. The attitudes expressed in the *Ring* now became conscious formulas. He discovered that he had been a Schopenhauerian without knowing it. On 16 December he told Liszt:

> Apart from my – slow – progress with my music, my sole preoccupation now is with a man who – if only through his writings – has come to me in my loneliness like a gift from heaven. This is Arthur Schopenhauer, the greatest philosopher since Kant, whose ideas – as he himself puts it – he has completed by thinking them through to a logical conclusion. . . . His central conception, the ultimate negation of the will to live, is terribly stern, but it is the only salvation. Of course the idea was not new to me, and no one can conceive it at all in whom it does not already exist; but this philosopher is the first to awaken me to fuller consciousness of it.

Through Schopenhauer Wagner understood his long-cherished desire to escape from the hatefulness of reality. He had changed from the political optimism of 1849 to a state of spiritual resignation. Schopenhauer reinforced this mood and enabled him to transform his inner feelings into creative action. In the same letter to Liszt he announced:

> As I have never in my life enjoyed the true happiness of love I will erect a memorial to this most lovely of all dreams, in which from beginning to end this

---

[1] *History of Western Philosophy*, London 1946.

love shall for once be truly and utterly satisfied. I have sketched a *Tristan and Isolde* in my mind . . .

He had known the story of Tristan for many years: Schopenhauer showed him its possibilities.

Long before he read Schopenhauer, Wagner's conception of the *Ring* had changed from optimism to pessimism. In his first sketch of 1848 Brünnhilde, after restoring the Ring to the Rhinemaidens, declares Alberich and the Nibelungs to be free once more, and Wotan alone to be ruler of all. To Wotan she sends Siegfried as a pledge of the Gods' eternal might. But by 1851 this ending to the drama was radically altered, and indeed the entire message became the annihilation of the Gods through Wotan's willing of that end: not as previously the eternal establishment of the power of the Gods. At the close of *Götterdämmerung* – that very title is significant in Wagner's changing conception of his drama – Brünnhilde speaks of the great ending of the Gods: Valhalla is consumed by flames and the Gods are redeemed in their downfall from the curse of the Ring by the deeds and the death of Siegfried. She does not refer to Alberich who, significantly, is not destroyed. On 25 January 1854 Wagner sent August Röckel a commentary on the meaning of the *Ring* poem. These were the thoughts of a mind ripe for Schopenhauer's theories:

> Instead of the words 'a dark day dawns for the Gods. Thy glorious race shall yet end in shame, unless thou surrender the Ring!', I shall now have Erda say only 'All that is – has an end. A dark day dawns for the Gods. I counsel thee, shun the Ring!' – We must all learn to *die*, and to *die* in the fullest sense of the word; dread of the end is the source of all lovelessness and it arises only where love has already faded.

Röckel had failed to understand why, if the gold had been returned to the Rhine, the Gods nevertheless had to perish. Wagner answers this with an involved tangle of words which suggests that he himself was at a loss to explain his idea in prose or verse. The gist of his reply is that all will become clear to the listener through *feeling* – through the music.

Wagner never solved the problem of how to express in words the idea that the world was doomed to outer destruction and yet would be redeemed in essence by the power of love. In musical terms he was to convey his idea magnificently in the final scene of *Götterdämmerung* but the closing words of the text – the ethical crux of the drama – presented him with a task he was not able to resolve coherently. In 1856 he made a sketch for another ending and in August of that year wrote again to Röckel, explaining that in all his works from *The Flying Dutchman* onward the poetic motive 'is to be sought in the sublime tragedy of renunciation, the deliberate, reasoned, ultimately necessary negation of the will, in which alone is redemption possible'. While he expressed this theme intuitively in his works, his conscious intellect was at the same time in direct opposition. When forming his Nibelung drama he was full of ideas about a new optimistic world, based on Hellenic principles. With that end in view he moulded the character of Siegfried, intending to represent an existence free from pain:

> And all the time I scarcely noticed that in the execution, indeed in the very basis of my design, I was unconsciously following a wholly different, infinitely deeper intuition and, instead of discerning a phase in the development of the world, I had grasped the very essence of the universe itself in all its conceivable phases, and had realized its nothingness; thus it was natural that, as I was faithful to my living intuitions and not to my abstract concepts, something emerged quite different from what I had actually proposed. But I remember that I determined to make my original purpose clear, by force as it were, in one single passage – Brünnhilde's somewhat tendentious final invocation to the bystanders to look away from the evil thing, property, to the only satisfying thing, love – without (unfortunately!) making quite clear what the nature of that 'love' is, which in the development of the myth we have seen as an utterly devastating force. In this one passage, then, I was blinded by the interposition of my *intellectual* intentions. Well, strangely enough, this passage was always a torture to me, and it required a complete revolution in my rational concepts, ultimately brought about by Schopenhauer, to show me the reason for my trouble and to give my poem a fitting keystone in keeping with the idea of the drama which consists in the simple and sincere recognition of the true nature of things, free from any attempt to preach a particular doctrine.

Wagner the intuitive artist always had difficulty in explaining his instincts in terms of pure reason.

It was Karl Ritter who reminded him of the Tristan subject by submitting a sketch of his own for Wagner's criticism. On returning from a walk one day, Wagner jotted down a concise outline of a three-act drama and then placed it aside while he continued work on *Walküre*. This first sketch contained an episode which was later discarded but which illustrates Wagner's habit of embracing more than one legendary theme at a time: the pilgrim Parzival visits Tristan's deathbed during his search for the Holy Grail. The idea behind the introduction of this apparently foreign element was to link Tristan the man of longing with Parzival the man of renunciation. Tristan's question as to what can ever allay the unsatisfied longing of life is answered by the mysterious melody of Parzival.

During the winter of 1854–5 Wagner involved himself for the last time with the season of orchestral concerts in Zurich. Six performances of *Tannhäuser* were given in the town, to great acclaim. On 23 January he conducted a performance of the *Faust Overture*, newly revised. To Liszt he explained that his aim was to remove some of the crudities of the earlier version and to develop the portrait of Faust along broader lines. He was not able to include any mention of Gretchen – that would have involved composing an entirely different work. With due modesty he confessed that his overture would look very insignificant beside his friend's *Faust Symphony*. That very month Liszt startled Wagner by publishing a somewhat fulsome article on *Das Rheingold* in the *Neue Zeitschrift für Musik*, although Wagner's intention in sending him the full score in the previous autumn was that it should be for private perusal. In committing this 'indiscretion', as he called it, Liszt's motives were good – to bring Wagner's activities to the notice of the musical world. Wagner politely acknowledged this display of Liszt's 'increasing sympathy' with him, but observed that the article merely confirmed the popular prejudice against his plan by stressing the colossal size of the three dramas yet to be completed. At that stage there was little or nothing in the way of propaganda that Liszt could do for his friend. His greatest service to Wagner during the 1850s was as a composer, and the exile in Zurich took the keenest interest in the scores of Liszt's Weimar years. It was the most fruitful period of their artistic friendship. Wagner could write to Liszt, 'When I compose and orchestrate, I always think only of you.' The opening theme of Liszt's *Faust Symphony* has a famous parallel in the last scene of *Walküre* Act Two, when Sieglinde awakes just prior to the battle of Siegmund and Hunding. But far more significant, if less easy to illustrate specifically, was Wagner's indebtedness to the harmonic innovations in Liszt's work. During the maturing of *Tristan* Wagner immersed himself in reading Liszt's scores and when composing Act Two of that work he listened daily to Liszt's piano music played by Karl Tausig.* Wagner's expression of his debt in letters to Liszt might well be dismissed as the idle flattery of an opportunist expecting another handsome loan, were it not for a revealing letter to Bülow of October 1859. In an article on *Tristan* Richard Pohl had been indiscreet enough to refer to the influence of Liszt. Wagner commented:

There are many matters concerning which we are quite frank among ourselves (for example that since my acquaintance with Liszt's compositions my treatment of harmony has become very different to what it was formerly), but it is indiscreet, to say the least, of friend Pohl to babble this secret to the whole world.

On Christmas Eve 1854 the committee of the London Philharmonic Society met to decide upon a guest conductor for their forthcoming season. Spohr had declined an invitation and Michael Costa had recently and abruptly resigned the post. Berlioz was approached, but he had been engaged by the rival New Philharmonic Society. It was therefore all the more important that the 'old' society secure an international figure of some rank. Wagner's name was proposed by the orchestra's leader Prosper Sainton* who had been introduced to his prose works by his perceptive friend and house-mate, the German Charles Lüders. Wagner's reaction to the Society's letter was to express cautious interest and a hope that the minor items in the programmes would be taken by an assistant conductor. Most importantly, he stressed the necessity of a sufficient number of rehearsals to ensure the standard of performance he considered essential. The prospect of a fee of £200 for the eight concerts was the principal attraction of the London venture, and although he no longer had the slightest enthusiasm for pursuing the career of a conductor, the opportunity of conducting a fine orchestra in extracts from his own works was attractive. He made inquiries among friends, including Liszt, as to the wisdom of a London visit, and wrote to Ferdinand Praeger,* the London correspondent of the Leipzig *Neue Zeitschrift*, whose name had been given to Wagner by Röckel's father. Praeger, a German who had lived for twenty years in the English capital as a teacher of music, was one day to write the most notoriously inaccurate book about the composer, *Wagner as I knew him* (published 1892; the German edition of the book was withdrawn from circulation within a year when Houston Stewart Chamberlain exposed its countless falsehoods). In this extraordinary memoir, Praeger portrayed himself as one of Wagner's most prominent early advocates and grossly exaggerated the extent of his friendship with him. In fact their relationship was slight and, on making his acquaintance, Wagner showed every desire to keep it that way. On 17 January he was visited in Zurich by the treasurer of the Philharmonic Society, George Anderson, and Wagner rewarded him for his long journey (and delighted Minna, too) by accepting the engagement.

After spending a few days in Paris he arrived in London on 4 March. Zurich had been in great excitement as a result of the recent *Tannhäuser* performances. In contrast, London was to prove a bitter disappointment. His first act was to seek out Praeger who became Wagner's guide and interpreter. On the following day he secured rooms at 22 Portland Terrace, Regent's Park. The proximity of the park and the loan of a grand piano from Erard (through Liszt's good offices) combined to make his residence attractive, but the one great disadvantage was the distance from the north side of Regent's Park to the concert rooms in Hanover Square. The resultant cab fares, together with his rent, formal dress, his meals and the general high cost of living in London considerably reduced the enchantment of the £200 fee.

He was virtually unknown as a composer in London and (except for the occasional rare soul) totally misunderstood as a writer. His contempt for Meyerbeer and Mendelssohn was common knowledge – and Mendelssohn was the musical idol of the English public. His friendship with Liszt, then vaguely dismissed as a flirtatious showman of the keyboard, did not enhance his reputation. The unfortunate Praeger contributed an article to an American paper praising Wagner as an 'ultra-red republican in music' and relishing the effect he would have on 'classical, staid, sober, proper, exclusive, conservative London'. James Davison, the highly influential music critic of *The Times* and prominent adherent of the Mendelssohn cause, took pleasure in reprinting Praeger's words in his own journal, *The Musical World*. Weeks before Wagner's arrival in London Davison began a campaign against him. It was customary to pay a duty call on critics, to flatter them and even to offer small gifts. This Wagner flatly refused to do, with the result that his attitude from the start was construed by the critics to be arrogant and stubborn, if not downright hostile. When the attacks came Wagner wrote to Otto Wesendonck describing the London press as 'a rabble of Jews': 'Mendelssohn is to the English exactly what Jehovah is to the Jews. And Jehovah's wrath now strikes me, an unbeliever.' In order to show his contempt for Mendelssohn's *Italian* Symphony he conducted it while wearing his kid gloves, and then removed them to commence Weber's *Euryanthe* overture.

The concert programmes were long and arduous. The allotted rehearsal time was grossly insufficient and inevitably curtailed because of the need to translate all Wagner's instructions into English. In eight programmes Wagner conducted all the Beethoven symphonies from the *Eroica* onwards, Beethoven's Violin Concerto, Second Piano Concerto and *Leonora* Overture No. 3; five Weber overtures; two Mozart symphonies and the *Magic Flute* overture; a Haydn symphony; two Mendelssohn symphonies, his Violin Concerto and overtures *The Hebrides* and *A Midsummer Night's Dream*; three works by Spohr; George Onslow's overture, *L'Alcalde de la Vega*; two overtures by Cherubini; and concertos by Chopin and Hummel. The *Tannhäuser* overture received two performances and one concert included instrumental extracts from *Lohengrin*. In addition it fell to Wagner's lot to conduct some British scores – Alexander Macfarren's *Chevy Chase* overture and a Symphony in G minor by Cipriani Potter. Wagner found Macfarren a 'turgid, dour Scotsman', but liked the amiable and exceedingly modest Potter. Most of the trifling items that filled out these lengthy programmes were taken care of by others, but Wagner was astounded at the ability of the audience to give their undivided attention to a trivial vocal duet immediately after a Beethoven symphony, and to accord it just as much applause! The orchestra he found fairly satisfactory but entrenched in bad habits. They consistently played *mezzo forte*: any dramatic dynamic contrast was foreign to them, and too much expression was regarded as not quite proper.

Choice of tempo was the most serious problem. The players were used to the methods of Mendelssohn and Costa who conducted every movement of a work at a brisk pace (largely in an effort to conceal poor playing and intonation) and the critics presumed Wagner to be in error when he made very clear distinctions between fast movements and slow. They dismissed his sense of rubato as uncertainty of beat and his accentuation of the dramatic contours of a movement was thought to be an unnatural liberty. No doubt many aspects of the performances were bad enough to merit some of the adverse criticism, chiefly owing to the lack of rehearsal time and Wagner's consequent failure to make his intentions sufficiently clear to the orchestra.

Wagner's discontent in London is revealed in his letters to his wife and to Otto Wesendonck. On 16 May he wrote to Liszt:

I am living here like a damned soul in hell! I did not think I should ever again be obliged to sink so low! I cannot describe how wretched I am in having to put up with conditions so utterly repugnant to me, and I realize it was no less than a sin and a crime to accept this London invitation which must, even at the best, have led me far out of my true path.

He had intended to complete the scoring of *Walküre* in London, but work proceeded only fitfully. He was embittered by the distractions from his task and unhappy at the long separation from Mathilde. Had his efforts been appreciably successful then matters might have seemed different, but he could find no compensation in the musical life of London. The English addiction to oratorios particularly puzzled him.

Four hours they sit in Exeter Hall, listening to one fugue after another in perfect confidence that they have done a good deed for which they will be rewarded in heaven, where they will hear nothing but the most beautiful Italian arias. It was this earnest fervour in the English public that Mendelssohn understood so well . . .

(Letter to Otto, 5 April)

He informed Mathilde that his sole delight was in reading Buddhist literature and that each day before work he would read a canto from Dante's *Inferno*: 'its horrors accompany me as I work on Act Two of *Die Walküre*. Fricka has just departed and Wotan is to pour forth his terrible woe.'

He made but one visit to Covent Garden and heard a 'somewhat grotesque' *Fidelio* given by 'unclean Germans and voiceless Italians'. He sampled Shakespeare at the Marylebone and Haymarket Theatres, Schiller at the City of London Theatre and vaudeville at the Olympic Theatre. The most amusing distraction was found at the Adelphi Theatre – a grand pantomime which embraced Mother Goose, Little Red Riding Hood and Cinderella. This, says *Mein Leben*, gave him 'a very good notion of the imaginative fare in which the English people can find amusement'. Apart from the congenial friendship of Sainton and Lüders, Wagner found sympathetic company in the person of Karl Klindworth,* a former pupil of Liszt who had settled in London. Klindworth played Wagner Liszt's new Piano Sonata in B minor and began to make a piano score of *Walküre*. Semper was in London at that time, and Wagner was delighted to meet another former Dresden friend, Hermann Franck, who had come to live in Brighton. Franck, who shared Wagner's enthusiasm for Schopenhauer, met his end later in the year in a domestic tragedy. He strangled his son at his Brighton home after a dispute over the boy's desire to join the British navy, and then threw himself out of a window. Another European exile, Malwida von Meysenbug* became one of Wagner's foremost lifelong champions. The prolific English composer John Lodge Ellerton also declared adherence to Wagner. Other acquaintances proved awkward. Herr Beneke, a merchant friend of Otto Wesendonck, revealed himself as a staunch admirer and former friend of Mendelssohn and regaled Wagner 'with descriptions of the generous character of the deceased'. Relations were friendly with the secretary of the Philharmonic Society, George Hogarth, but for one exceedingly embarrassing encounter. On calling at Hogarth's home before leaving London Wagner found Meyerbeer there. The worthy secretary found his powers of diplomacy stretched to the limit as the two great men greeted each other in cold silence. After Berlioz arrived in June Wagner saw a good deal of him and their relations were never friendlier. There is irony in the prospect of these two composers drawn independently to London to eke out a miserable conductor's life (Berlioz playing Toscanini to Wagner's Furtwängler, as David Cairns wittily commented on their rivalry). Despite their cordiality they remained poles apart in musical and philosophical matters.

The most distinguished meeting of Wagner's four-month stay occurred on the evening of his seventh concert, 11 June. Queen Victoria and Prince Albert attended, and received Wagner during the interval. The Queen wrote in her journal:

> He conducted in a peculiar way, taking Mozart's and Beethoven's Symphonies in quite a different time to what one is accustomed. His own overture to 'Tannhäuser' is a wonderful composition, quite overpowering, so grand, in parts wild, striking and descriptive. We spoke to him afterwards. He is short, very quiet, wears spectacles and has a very finely shaped forehead, a hooked nose and projecting chin.

Wagner told Minna that the Queen was '*not* fat but very short and not at all pretty, with, I am sorry to say, rather a red nose'. She had proved uncommonly friendly, had inquired after Minna, the parrot and the dog, and expressed a hope that one of his operas might be given by the Italian troupe at Covent Garden! What particularly impressed Wagner was that the Queen of England should receive with unembarrassed friendliness a man regarded in his own country as a dangerous political criminal.

Two weeks later Wagner conducted his final concert and was home in Zurich on the last day of June. London had been a bitter and humiliating failure, both artistically and financially. A painful skin complaint, erysipelas, attacked him periodically over the next twelve months and further hampered work on the full score of *Walküre*. For a while he considered an offer of a conducting engagement in America but was afraid of a repetition of the London disaster and of being unable to complete the *Ring*. On 11 July, the day after their little dog Peps died, a despondent Richard and Minna went to Seelisberg; she for a whey cure, he to work fitfully at his scoring. The weather was wet and dismal; thoughts of Buddhism and the *Tristan* idea filled Wagner's mind.

From Zurich, early in October, he sent the fair copy of Acts One and Two of *Die Walküre* to Liszt. The score of Act Three was completed on 23 March 1856. Meanwhile two significant productions of *Tannhäuser* had occurred. Munich heard the work for the first time, under Franz Lachner, on 12 August 1855, all objections and delays having been overcome. On hearing of its success, Wagner wrote a letter of thanks to Lachner, praising him for his hard work and diligent effort and for his friendship and sympathy. In *Mein Leben* all the references to Lachner are disparaging and Wagner had described him to Liszt in a letter of 2 May 1854, as 'an utter ass and knave'. Wagner clearly loathed him but was quick to exhibit oily flattery whenever it appeared that the honest Munich conductor was being of use to him. Berlin at last gave *Tannhäuser* on 7 January 1856, under Heinrich Dorn (another recipient of Wagner's contempt) and with Johanna Wagner as a superb Elizabeth. Wagner's musical intentions were not entirely understood despite the presence of Bülow and of Liszt, who, having made his peace with Hülsen, attended a couple of piano rehearsals. The costumes and scenery, however, were of unparalleled splendour and the opera was a considerable success with the public. Most important for Wagner were the royalties Berlin paid of 300 francs per performance. The work was given about forty times in the ensuing two years.

The result of Wagner's studies of Buddhism was a sketch for a drama *Die Sieger* (The Victors), dated 16 May 1856. Until the last years of his life Wagner intended to cast a drama from this tale of the Buddha's last days on earth, of love, self-denial and redemption. He frequently returned to the subject but it proceeded no further. Elements of *Die Sieger* found their way into *Tristan* and *Parsifal* (and according to Glasenapp into *Siegfried*, e.g. the Act Three motif known as 'World Inheritance').

Tichatschek came to see his old friend in Zurich at the end of May and, although Wagner was suffering acutely from erysipelas, they visited Lake Lucerne together. He learned from Tichatschek of a rising star among tenors – Ludwig Schnorr von Carolsfeld. With the aid of 1000 francs gifted by the ever-faithful and open-handed Liszt, Wagner was able to stay for two months at Mornex on Mont Salève and take a cure for his erysipelas. In Dr Vaillant he found at last a physician wise enough to diagnose and treat his condition as a nervous malady. When he left Mornex on 15 August, after a stay of over two months, he was cured and his erysipelas disappeared until the last years of his life. While there he had rested with his dog Fips, a good-natured spaniel presented to him by the Wesendoncks as a successor to Peps, as his only companion. Wagner's reading at Mornex included Byron, Walter Scott's novels and the recently issued symphonic poems of Liszt. The one thought that tortured him was the separation from Mathilde – but he was not anxious to hurry back to Zurich where problems and quarrels with Natalie had once more soured the household atmosphere. From Mornex he went to Lausanne and stayed some days with Karl Ritter and his wife.

Minna's sister Klara had arrived in Zurich and her presence brought a lull in the constant nagging of Minna and Natalie. Wagner began the music of *Siegfried* on 22 September, but soon another irritation arose. By an uncomfortable coincidence there was a new tenant in the house opposite to Wagner's, who, just as composition of the act that deals so much with smithying began, revealed himself to be a tinsmith. This good man's constant banging and hammering indirectly gave rise to a melody in the score, but soon an arrangement was made whereby the tinsmith agreed not to work on the mornings when Wagner was composing. On 11 October, the full score of Act One was commenced.

Two days later Liszt arrived – ill, irritable and inclined to be quarrelsome – to be followed by Princess Carolyne in voluble high spirits and domineering mood. Things began badly when Liszt lost his temper with the testy and tactless Karl Ritter. When Wagner intervened diplomatically in an attempt to avoid a showdown Karl turned on him and then left the house in a tearful rage. Julie Ritter heard her son's account of the incident and wrote a reproachful letter to Wagner, who replied with dignity and renounced the pension which had been his lifeline for five years. After the storm blew over, Frau Ritter's friendship (and the contents of her purse) were restored, but Wagner did not see Karl for almost two years.

Liszt and the Princess remained in Zurich for six weeks. The noise, fuss and excitement constantly engendered by Carolyne Wittgenstein irritated Wagner. He disliked her principally because she clearly had no time to listen to his own monologues and dogmatic ideas. Beneath her surface of restless vitality there lay an uncomfortably sharp intellect. Wagner had by now discerned that she also concealed a shrewd and scheming mind that had the sinister ambition of wishing to sunder his friendship with Liszt. The influence of her pompous and flowery notions upon Liszt's music and artistic ideas he viewed with dismay. In turn, she saw Wagner as a threat to Liszt's finances and as a dangerous rival to his originality as a composer. That Wagner might borrow ideas from Liszt for those Teutonic dramas with which she had such scant sympathy was an idea that obsessed her. Her championship of Berlioz and in particular her vital role in encouraging his opera *The Trojans* was a direct attempt to counter Wagner's ambitions. Her hope was that *The Trojans* would rival if not eclipse *The Nibelung's Ring*.

When Liszt felt better and when the Princess left them in peace, the two friends enjoyed perusing each other's scores. Wagner sang *Die Walküre* to Liszt's accompaniment, and Liszt played through his *Dante* Symphony which was dedicated to Wagner. The somewhat grandiose and bombastic coda to the symphony disappointed the dedicatee and he strongly urged Liszt to end the work with the Magnificat and its 'hint of a soft, shimmering Paradise'. Liszt agreed apparently and admitted that the noisy ending was the Princess's idea. When the work was published, however, the pompous ending remained unchanged. Carolyne had won the day. Wagner did not venture any criticism of his friend's paramour, but during this visit he did discuss with Liszt his own domestic problems, including a full explanation of the Jessie Laussot affair of six years before, and probably some confession of his feelings regarding Mathilde. On 23 November the two men gave a concert in St Gallen: Liszt conducted his *Orpheus* and *Les Préludes*, and Wagner the *Eroica*. The visitors then left for Munich and Wagner committed his recent impressions of Liszt's work to paper in an article *On Franz Liszt's Symphonic Poems*. In this he praised Liszt's music as a wonderfully expressive language, presenting the essence of things and ideas in a way that ordinary language cannot. This Schopenhauerian tribute delighted Liszt but when the article appeared in print (*Neue Zeitschrift für Musik*, 10 April 1857) it was altered and amended by the Princess. Wagner countered this sensibly by arranging for his original to be published in a Vienna journal.

Work on *Siegfried* was interrupted by another caller. In March 1857 the Brazilian ambassador to Leipzig presented himself unexpectedly in Zurich with a request from the Emperor Dom Pedro II. An astonished Wagner learned that His Imperial Majesty was greatly interested in his work and desired him to go to Rio de Janeiro. He sent luxuriously bound scores of *The Flying Dutchman*, *Tannhäuser* and *Lohengrin* to Brazil and then heard nothing more. For a while Wagner assumed he had been the victim of a practical joker. It was not until 1876 that he learned of Dom Pedro's genuine interest in his work, when the Emperor arrived in Bayreuth for the first festival. On that occasion the great man was asked to sign the hotel's visitors' book and wrote under the column headed 'occupation' one modest word – 'Emperor'.

For some time Wagner had been anxious to find a quieter, more secluded house in which to live and work. Recently the Wesendoncks had been engaged in building a magnificent villa on the 'Green Hill' overlooking the lake of Zurich. In the extensive grounds was a small country house which Otto proposed should be Wagner's for life. The advantages were overwhelming, not least the enchanting prospect of living only yards from Mathilde. It would be, in her own words, 'a true refuge ('Asyl') of peace and friendship'. His Muse would virtually be at his side: gone would be the need for those somewhat awkward visits to her each day in the late afternoon. With Mathilde to share in his creations and Minna to keep the little 'Asyl' trim and tidy Wagner envisaged a lifelong refuge of undisturbed bliss and contentment. He settled there on 28 April and the Wesendoncks moved to their residence on the Green Hill four months later. As administrator of Wagner's business affairs Otto had recently received 2000 francs. It was agreed that he should retain this sum in lieu of two years' rent. This allowed Wagner to feel financially independent of his neighbour and benefactor. Very soon, though, the expense of the removal, costly alterations to the house and the inevitable lavish furnishings returned Wagner to insolvency and he accepted gratefully Julie Ritter's offer to restore her pension.

When Wagner entered the 'Asyl', Act One of *Siegfried* was complete in full score. By 27 June the sketch of Act Two had reached Siegfried's words 'Dass der mein Vater nicht ist', beneath which Wagner wrote, 'When shall we see each other again?'. The next day he wrote to Liszt and referred to the recent refusal of Breitkopf und Härtel to consider publishing the *Ring* scores:

> I shall trouble no more about Härtel, as I have at last decided to abandon my obstinate attempt to complete my *Nibelungen*. I have led my young Siegfried into the lovely forest solitude; there I have left him under a linden tree and have bidden him farewell with tears from the depths of my heart; he is better there than elsewhere. – If I am ever to take up the work again, it must either be made very easy for me or I must be enabled to *give* my work personally to the world in the fullest sense of the term.

Rather than leave Siegfried in the forest Wagner spent the month of July completing the composition sketch of the second act, and he finished the orchestral sketch on 9 August. He did not return to the *Ring* for over seven years.

The publisher's lack of interest in the *Ring* scores was not the most significant reason for the abandonment of *Siegfried*, although the total lack of patronage for his vast project was a weighty factor in Wagner's decision. He was once more absorbed by the thought of his spiritual loneliness. The move to the 'Asyl' was an outward sign of his inner desire for a mystical withdrawal from the world. He was physically and mentally weary of a task that had preoccupied him since 1848. Each year had shown him that the work was a far larger and more arduous undertaking than he had foreseen, and before him lay the gigantic effort of setting the final act of *Siegfried* and the whole of the final drama *Götterdämmerung*. Intuitively he turned away from that daunting reality to consider subjects that harmonized with his world-weary state: Schopenhauer, Buddhism, the Tristan idea and the consoling sympathy of Mathilde. Wagner ran his outward life with a ruthless impracticality. He followed his inner urgings with an equally steadfast and reckless determination. The public would not now have to wait for the *Ring*. He would present them with something very different.

Seven

The Child of Sorrow

In sorrow came I hither, in sorrow did I bring forth, and in sorrow has your first feast day gone. And as by sorrow you came into the world, your name shall be called Tristan; that is the child of sorrow.

Tristan and Iseult

As Thomas Mann observed, when Wagner set out with the best intentions to write something tuneful, lyrical, singable, easy, approachable, Italianate and with a small cast, the result was *Tristan und Isolde*. This work, to borrow Nietzsche's phrase, was the *ne plus ultra* of Wagnerism. With characteristic optimism the composer confidently assured Liszt in June 1857 that the opera would be produced one year hence in Strassburg with the singers Albert Niemann* and Luise Meyer-Dustmann.* It cannot have escaped him that that town was a singularly appropriate choice in that Wagner's principal source for *Tristan* was a modern German version of the medieval tale of Gottfried von Strassburg. In addition, he told Liszt, he considered having the work translated into Italian and performed at Rio de Janeiro under the patronage of the Brazilian Emperor. By January 1858 his hopes for a production were fixed on Karlsruhe, where Eduard Devrient was director, and he offered the publisher Härtel

> a work more practicable and easier for theatrical production than any of my earlier operas. Instead of attaching difficult conditions to its circulation, my idea this time is to make things attractive and easy. The warm interest of my subject, its happy adaptation to a melodious flow in musical treatment, the effective leading roles, which should rapidly take their place among the most inviting parts open to our sopranos and tenors – all this satisfies me that. . . . I have gone the right way to achieve a remarkable popular success.

Indeed the demands made upon scenic designers in *Tristan* present none of the problems of the *Ring*, but the vocal parts are of daunting and unprecedented difficulty. Above all the extremely chromatic harmony of *Tristan* gave to Western culture a new concept of musical language, expression and tonality. Its contemporary impact, its influence on the development of music, the powerful spell it exerted on literature and the

149

visual arts, even its effects upon human thought and behaviour, were of an order achieved by few other single works in the history of art. The surprise is not that theatre after theatre rejected it as unperformable, but that it was produced, in Munich, as early as 1865.

During the summer of 1857 there were many visitors to the 'Asyl' including the composer Robert Franz, the writer and critic Richard Pohl, Praeger from London and Eduard Röckel, the revolutionary's brother. The previous Easter (according to *Mein Leben*) Wagner had sketched a three-act drama, *Parsifal*.[1] As with the *Meistersinger* scenario of 1845, which was conceived just before that of *Lohengrin* and then laid aside while the latter work claimed his full attention, the 1857 *Parsifal* draft was temporarily discarded from his mind while he preoccupied himself with the working-out of *Tristan*. The prose sketch of *Tristan* was begun on 28 August and the poem was complete by 18 September. This task coincided exactly with the visit to the 'Asyl' of Hans von Bülow and Liszt's nineteen-year-old daughter Cosima who had been married on 18 August. That Bülow should choose to bring his wife to Wagner for their honeymoon is significant. That he should arrive at the moment of *Tristan's* conception is doubly so, for that drama was to be inextricably linked with his own sad fate.

Wagner's interest in Hans dated from 1846 and since that time he had been closely attached to his young admirer. He encouraged the boy's activities as conductor, pianist and composer, and was instrumental in deflecting the antagonism of Bülow's parents towards their son's choice of a musical career. The boy's final choice of such a career was the direct result of his being overwhelmed by the Weimar *Lohengrin* of 1850, and he promptly abandoned his pursuit of law. After his period of conducting in Switzerland (referred to in the previous chapter) and a period of study with Liszt, he embarked on his first concert tour in 1853 playing at Vienna, Pest, Dresden, Karlsruhe, Bremen, Hamburg and Berlin. In 1855 he became principal professor of piano at the Stern Conservatoire in Berlin, was active as a critic and received great acclaim on his tours both as conductor and pianist.

Cosima's childhood and her marriage to Bülow afforded her little happiness. After Liszt's separation from Marie d'Agoult, the three children were placed in the care of Liszt's mother in Paris. In 1850, when Cosima was not quite thirteen, the Princess Wittgenstein persuaded Liszt to hand the children over to her own governess from St Petersburg, Madame Patersi, a tyrannical septuagenarian who travelled to Paris and at once submitted them to her strict regime. This background, lacking the love and the normal joys of childhood explains much of Cosima's later personality. She was ever-conscious of being Liszt's bastard child and

---

[1] He did not decide on the spelling 'Parsifal' until 1877, and until then also referred to ·'Parzival' and 'Percival'.

spent much of her life attempting to create a mask of frigid respectability which deceived few people. Her maternal grandmother had a Jewish father and so all her life Cosima sheltered behind a defensive attitude of vicious anti-Semitism; hatred of the Jews was one thing she had in common with Bülow, and Wagner's anti-Semitic views merely nurtured an already present venom. The victim of Madame Patersi's domination was a creature desperately in need of love. Both her mother and Carolyne Wittgenstein were strong personalities who greatly influenced her young mind; both of these women devoted their exceptional energies and keen intellects to the task of shaping Liszt's artistic life. Cosima determined to do the same with Bülow: to encourage and guide him as a creative artist. As the years of her marriage unfolded she began to face the bitter disappointment that in Hans there was no composer of the stature of her father or of Wagner waiting to be drawn forth. All her efforts merely resulted in an accentuation of the neurotic side of his personality. In her diary for 8 January 1869 there is this confession:

> It was a great misunderstanding that united us in matrimony; I still feel the same for him as I did twelve years ago: great sympathy for his destiny, delight in his gifts both of mind and heart, a real esteem for his character, together with complete incompatibility of disposition. In the very first year of my marriage I was in such despair at our misunderstandings that I wanted to die.

She appears to have been none too attracted to Wagner during that first year. He read each act of the *Tristan* poem to them as it was completed. Bülow was commissioned to arrange the vocal score of the work and in the meantime he was able to entertain the company with skilful piano renditions of the *Ring* music. *Mein Leben* informs us that 'Cosima listened silently with her head bowed; if pressed for an expression of opinion, she began to cry'. Gathered there together in the 'Asyl' were the three women most closely involved with Wagner's destiny: Minna, Mathilde and Cosima. Bülow's young wife felt sorry for Minna and upset by the continual quarrelling between her and Wagner. Mathilde did not appeal to Cosima, who frowned upon her relationship with Wagner. Whatever her impression of his music during the three-week visit of 1857, Cosima, clinging desperately to her bourgeois pose, thought Wagner the man to be nothing but self-centred and rather vulgar.

The prelude to *Tristan* was composed on 1 October; Act One was sketched by the last day of December and completed in orchestral sketch on 13 January 1858. By then Breitkopf und Härtel had shown remarkable confidence in Wagner by agreeing to publish the orchestral score, the libretto and Bülow's piano score. Between November 1857 and 1 May 1858 Wagner composed five songs for voice and piano to poems by Mathilde, now known as the *Wesendonck Lieder*. Two of the songs, *Im Treibhaus* and *Träume* were sketches for *Tristan*, and another, *Stehe still!* is imbued with the spirit of that work and with the secret passion of Richard and Mathilde:

> Dass in selig süssem Vergessen
> ich mög alle Wonnen ermessen!
> Wenn Aug in Auge wonnig trinken
> Seelen ganz in Seele versinken.
> (Then in blissful, sweet forgetfulness I may measure all delights!
> When eye drinks eye in bliss, soul drowns completely in soul).

Wagner orchestrated *Träume* and had it played outside the Wesendonck villa on Mathilde's birthday, 23 December. (The other songs were later orchestrated by Felix Mottl.*)

The feelings of the good-natured Otto and the long-suffering Minna concerning the tender exchanges between their respective spouses became clearly revealed in the new year. It would appear that Wagner had the effrontery to object to Otto's presence in his own villa and had become impatient with his intrusion during the evening conversations. This crisis on the Green Hill was serious enough for Wagner to leave for Paris on 14 January and remain there on the pretext of investigating his publishing rights, while the atmosphere at Zurich cooled down. He secured funds for the trip by borrowing from Liszt, Semper and Müller. At the same time he sent a begging letter to Praeger. Passing through Strassburg on the 15th, he was surprised to notice a poster advertising a performance of the *Tannhäuser* overture: he attended what proved to be an excellent performance, was recognized and treated to an ovation from the orchestra. Not for the only time in his life, Fate narrowly spared Wagner what could have been a dangerous plight. He had intended to stay in Paris at a hotel in the Rue Le Pelletier. At that hotel on 14 January Orsini had been arrested following his famous assassination attempt on Napoleon III. Had the police found the infamous revolutionary criminal Richard Wagner there, then the consequences might have been very serious.

In Paris he contacted Cosima's sister, Blandine, and her husband Emile Ollivier,* an eminent lawyer who advised Wagner concerning the safeguarding of his copyrights in France. He also sought out Berlioz who read to him the libretto of *The Trojans*. This, as Wagner told Bülow, was the final proof of their incompatibility:

> As he read it to me I was seized with horror, which made me wish that I might never meet Berlioz again. . . . To see him sitting there, brooding over the fate of this unspeakable absurdity, as if the salvation of the world and his own soul depended on it, is really too much for me.

The remainder of the Paris stay Wagner spent socializing, reading Calderón and investigating the possibility of a *Tannhäuser* production, either at the Opéra or at the Théâtre-Lyrique. No such opening for the work appeared likely but the overture was performed on 29 January and Wagner assisted at the rehearsal. He met the widows of Spontini and Hérold and also Madame Erard who presented him with a not inconsiderable prize – a magnificent Erard grand piano worth 5000 francs. This gift more than justified his expedition and he returned to Zurich on 5 February, after a short visit to Kietz at Epernay, in much higher spirits.

The full score of *Tristan* Act One was finished early in April, just as the extraordinary domestic arrangement on the Green Hill veered towards catastrophe. Little notes would pass daily to and from each household and most mornings Mathilde would visit Wagner at the 'Asyl'. On the morning of 7 April Minna stopped a servant who was conveying a roll of music from the 'Asyl' to the Wesendonck villa. It was the first composition sketch of the *Tristan* prelude which Wagner had decided to present to Mathilde in celebration of the completion of Act One. Inside was a letter which Minna opened and read. For some months Minna's dislike of the attractive twenty-nine-year-old Mathilde had increased and she now sought evidence to prove that she was no more than a common seductress. Every day Minna had felt good cause to be humiliated and insulted by that intelligent young woman who had won her husband's every confidence. She was now aware that her own physical beauty had faded completely, she suffered from insomnia and was seeking relief in opium and other drugs in a vain attempt to arrest the progress of her incurable heart disease. Worst of all, she was aware of her total inability to enter into her husband's realm of thinking. Since the Dresden years she had played no part in understanding, discussing or sharing his creative aims. Night after night in the Wesendonck's drawing room she sat, invited but unheeded, while Wagner and a circle of the devout would converse interminably about Schopenhauer, Buddhism, intellectual abstractions and the philosophical basis of art. Each morning that followed, Mathilde would flaunt herself at the 'Asyl' ignoring Minna or perhaps making a few condescending remarks before ascending to Wagner's study to delight in those pointless and obscure aberrations of his mind, the *Ring* and *Tristan*. To Mathilde and Wagner, their relationship was on a lofty, ideal plane; an innocent partnership between two souls who felt the need to withdraw from the harsh reality of life into mystical communion. She was, in her own words, 'a blank page' upon which he could write. For him, she was the ideal listener, a necessary mirror of his intimate inner thoughts. Significantly she mirrored *his* ideals and not vice versa. At no time did she 'inspire' or influence his work – but her interest and passionate response were vital for him. To Minna, that was incomprehensible. Given that the strain of long illness had made her especially susceptible to jealously, her attitude is perfectly understandable. The fact that Mathilde was married to a good husband and had two children, simply made her 'crime' worse in Minna's bourgeois eyes.

The intercepted letter was headed 'Morning Confession'. It began as an apology from Wagner for his irritation and anger with a guest of the Wesendoncks whom he had found dull and boring, and whose presence had prevented him from seeing her two days before. But when it was morning he felt reasonable again and 'from the depth of my heart could pray to my angel; and this prayer is love! Love! My soul rejoices deeply in this love, the source of my redemption!' All through the previous day he had been melancholy at being parted from her, to such an extent that he could not work. The letter then continues, for more than half its length, with a discussion of Goethe's *Faust*, and then concludes:

> What nonsense I am talking! Is it the pleasure of speaking alone, or the joy of speaking to you? Yes to you![1] But when I look into your eyes, then I simply cannot speak any more; then everything I might have to say simply seems as nothing! When this marvellous, holy glance rests upon me then everything becomes so indisputably true to me, I am so sure of myself, and I submerge myself within it. Then there is no longer any object or subject; then everything is one, united, deep, infinite harmony! Oh, that is peace, and in that peace the highest, most perfect life! O fool, who would seek to win the world and peace from without! How blind the one who would not recognize your glance and find his soul there! Only inside, within, only in the depths does salvation dwell! – I can only speak and understand myself when I do not see you, or when I may not see you. –
>
> Be good to me, and forgive my childishness of yesterday: you were quite right to call it that! –
>
> The weather appears to be mild. Today I will come to the garden, as soon as I see you; I hope I may be with you for a moment, undisturbed! –
>
> Take my whole soul as a morning greeting! –

This Tristanesque day dream, this outpouring of Schopenhauerian resignation, this confession that absence alone can bring true understanding of their love, was for Minna the evidence of a sordid affair. She burst into Wagner's room and confronted him with the letter. He tried to calm her, and then, according to *Mein Leben*, 'told her peremptorily to keep quiet and not to be guilty of any blunder either of judgement or in action'. Minna, however, went straight to her 'rival' with the letter and told her, 'If I were an ordinary woman I would show this to your husband'. The 'peace and happiness' of the 'Asyl' was shattered. Mathilde had nothing to hide from Otto, who had long known of her special relationship with Wagner, and she told him of the incident. What distressed the Wesendoncks most was that Minna's action had transformed the delicately veiled liaison on the Green Hill into an open and sordid wrangle. Wagner blamed Minna's absurd foolishness on her heart condition and suggested she take a cure. A few days later he accompanied her to Brestenberg, a recommended health resort, where she remained for three months. Wagging tongues in Zurich soon began to discuss the scandal. Mathilde

---

[1] Throughout the letter Wagner uses the intimate 'du'.

reproved Wagner for having allowed his wife to take such a view of the matter and all intercourse between the two homes was broken off. The Wesendoncks decided to leave for a holdiday of several weeks in Italy. Wagner too would have liked to escape from the claustrophobic atmosphere at the 'Asyl' but could not do so as he expected a number of visitors including Tichatschek. His most welcome guest was the young pianist Karl Tausig, a Polish Jew for whom Wagner felt great affection. Tausig put the new Erard to excellent use by playing the music of his teacher, Liszt. The boy also functioned as a messenger between the 'Asyl' and the Wesendonck villa upon their return on 1 June. Act Two of *Tristan* was composed between 4 May and 1 July.

Wagner made several visits to Minna at Brestenberg, and wrote to her regularly, urging her to cease her suspicious brooding: his letters are firm, but kind and sensible; he was clearly very concerned about her health. He hoped fervently that on her return a happier life would be resumed but, from the moment of her arrival, matters became steadily worse. Wagner had gone to collect her at Brestenberg on 15 July, and in his absence a servant had erected a floral arch as a greeting to the mistress of the house upon her return. With an air of smug triumph Minna demanded that this decoration remain displayed for several days so that Mathilde would see that she had not come home in humiliation. As she expected this crude gesture succeeded in insulting and angering Frau Wesendonck. Tichatschek took his leave and the Bülows, who had been some days in Zurich, now occupied the guest room. They had hardly entered the house when they witnessed a dreadful row between Minna and Wagner. A sad and trying month passed by in which several visitors, including Lachner from Munich, Klindworth from London and Cosima's mother the Countess d'Agoult became painfully aware of the domestic crisis. The one visitor Wagner would gladly have confided in – Liszt – did not come. On 4 August Wagner wrote to him, 'I leave Zurich on the 15th, never to return there. My wife will go a little later to Germany.' He postponed his departure until the day after the Bülows left the 'Asyl'. Hans wept as he took his leave on the 16th, and we learn from Wagner's letter to Mathilde of 4 September that

> Cosima was in a strangely excited state, which showed itself especially in convulsively passionate tenderness towards me. At our parting the next day, she fell at my feet and covered my hands with tears and kisses: astonished and alarmed, I gazed into this mystery without being able to find the key to it.

Cosima might well have appeared 'strangely excited'. According to the same letter from Wagner to Mathilde, Karl Ritter had told him of a dramatic incident at Lake Geneva: Cosima had begged him to kill her and had only been prevented from throwing herself from a boat into the lake when she realized that Karl, equally unhappy in his own marriage, was determined to follow her.

Wagner spent a week or so in Geneva and wrote several times from there to Minna. Their respective feelings are best conveyed in their own words. He wrote on 19 August:

> You reproach me and see only your own misfortunes. I am more just. I reproach no one – truly, not even you. A great deal was required of you – *too* much considering your terrible ill-health. So let us now part in peace, reconciled, each going his and her own way for a time in search of composure and renewed vitality. For me at present, solitude and withdrawal from all company is a vital necessity. . . . My many wounds are bleeding, and heartfelt anxiety for you is not the least of these. Furthermore, I feel the urgent need to balance the accounts of a whole lifetime. I must clear my mind about much that has moved me intensely of late, and above all I must consider how to find peace and quiet in the future to complete such works as I may be destined to give to the world.

And from her letter of 24 August:

> I was pleased to see in your letter that you miss the little dog; there is still a spark of feeling left in you for us poor creatures. I'm convinced that it won't be long before you'll be yearning for your comfortable, pleasant home life . . . even for me who may no longer be living, but that doesn't matter; but later you'll curse yourself for having broken away from everything and cast your faithful wife from you so wilfully.

From Geneva he sent some little presents for her birthday, and on the journey to Venice sent her no less than five telegams in addition to letters. Nothing, it seems, would console or calm her. Later Wagner was disgusted to learn that, in disposing of their household goods, she had advertised in the daily paper that they were to be sold cheaply owing to sudden departure. This encouraged gossip in the town and further embarrassed the Wesendoncks. The Erard piano was saved and later sent to Venice. Before leaving for Dresden, Minna despatched a bitter letter to Mathilde accusing her of having broken her marriage after twenty-two years: 'May this noble deed contribute to your peace of mind, to your happiness.'

Karl Ritter had also separated from his wife and he accompanied Wagner to Italy. Arriving in Venice on 29 August, the composer rented a large quiet room with adjoining bedroom in the Palazzo Giustiniani by the Grand Canal. He immediately had the grey walls of the room draped with inexpensive, dark red hangings, and matching portières over the doors. Throughout the seven-month stay in Venice he was comfortable, undisturbed and on the whole happy. An attack of dysentery during the first weeks delayed work and later he suffered from a painful abscess in the leg, but otherwise conditions for creativity were ideal and, separated from Mathilde, he immersed himself in Tristan's sorrow and his anguish for Isolde. Mathilde and Richard did not communicate by letter during his Italian sojourn, but each of them kept a diary which was intended to be read by the other at a later date. In his Venice Diary Wagner left for posterity a remarkable testament of his exalted love for Mathilde. The 'letters' are passionate prose-poems, idolizing his Muse and full of mystical references to Buddhism, Schopenhauer and Calderón. Significantly, as *Tristan* neared completion, the tone of the letters became less passionate, the intimate 'du' was replaced by the formal 'Sie', and by the time of his return from Italy Mathilde had once more become the conventional and friendly admirer of earlier years. At that time too the letters to Minna began to emphasize his desire for a reunion. The dream was over.

To survive financially in Venice presented a number of problems. Julie Ritter came to his aid; otherwise the occasional theatre royalty was all he could depend on without once more begging from friends. The first major production of Wagner in Vienna occurred on 18 August 1858 with a first-rate performance of *Lohengrin*. The progress of Wagner's music in Vienna was in no small way due to the efforts of Johann Strauss II whose inclusion of orchestral extracts from the operas brought them to the attention of a large audience. In November 1856 the Gesellschaft der Musikfreunde gave the *Faust Overture* which was attacked by the critic Hanslick, the former champion of *Tannhäuser* but by that time a foe of Wagner; he was already wearing the aesthetic blinkers that gave the hallmark to his later writings when he had reached the giddy heights of musical lawgiver in Vienna.[1] The Court Theatre remained closed to Wagner, but in August 1857 the suburban Thalia Theatre gave *Tannhäuser*, and although the presentation was ill-equipped and vocally disastrous the work had a long and popular run. The Court Theatre could no longer resist the demands for a Wagner production and it was there that *Lohengrin* was mounted a year later. *Tannhäuser* followed in November 1859 and *The Flying Dutchman* in December 1860. *Lohengrin* was sumptuously mounted, magnificently sung, and excellently played under the baton of Heinrich Esser.* Hanslick thought the work musically barren and fanatically tuneless; he also objected to the mythological subject. 'The true opera of the future is historical,' he declared and, in addition, Wagner 'is neither a great musician nor a great poet.' But the critic's voice did not prevail against the overwhelming enthusiasm of the Viennese public. Wagner wrote warmly to Esser when reports of the quality and beauty of the performance reached him in Venice.

He sorely needed the royalties. Munich had added *Lohengrin* to their repertory in February, but had rejected *Rienzi*. Weimar was expected to mount *Rienzi* but the new Intendant, Dingelstedt (formerly of Munich)

---

[1] Later in this book the pros and cons of Hanslick's attitude to Wagner will be discussed. His writings provide a valuable insight into nineteenth-century critical attitudes. The reader is referred to the excellent introductory selection by Henry Pleasants (see Bibliography). But (without endorsing the excessive contempt for Hanslick of earlier writers on Wagner) I have concluded from a careful study of his polished prose that his principal virtue, that of stubborn consistency, hardly compensates for the narrow prejudice of his musically stagnant mind.

was slow to offer any fee. On 5 December Wagner wrote to Liszt explaining that his sole interest in the fate of his early opera was the continuing hope that he would earn the occasional fee from it. To Sulzer he complained that the unpredictable profits from his operas had something of the character of lottery winnings. At Christmas Liszt wrote to express his delight upon seeing the proofs of *Tristan* Act One. He also mentioned that Ernst II, Duke of Saxe-Coburg-Gotha, a dilettante composer, desired to dedicate his latest opera to Wagner, and in Liszt's view it would be tactful to accept the offer. This enraged Wagner. Instead of indulging in petty, meaningless gestures, this duke could be sending him sufficient funds for the completion of *Tristan*. He gave vent to his fury in a letter to Liszt on the last day of 1858. He could no longer care a curse for Grand Dukes, theatres, even his own operas: all he needs is money. He considers Liszt's letter tiresome and pathetic. Instead let him send his *Dante Symphony* or *'Gran' Mass*, or better still, 'Money, money! – it matters not how or whence! *Tristan* will pay for all!' Although this outburst is couched in terms of grim humour, Wagner chose the wrong moment to take such a tone with his friend. Liszt had just experienced a major crisis in his career – a demonstration against him at Weimar which led to his resignation. He had suffered critical attacks from every direction and his private life was the cause of additional strain and worry, so he was in no mood to find patience for Wagner's ugly humour. That Wagner realized his words may have been rash and wounding is clear from another letter to Liszt three days later. In calmer tones he explains his urgent need for the security of a regular income of 2–3000 thalers per annum. If Liszt took the initiative then perhaps a number of the German princes could be persuaded to guarantee him this sum collectively. Before Liszt received this letter he replied to Wagner's of 31 December:

> In order not to expose myself again to the danger of boring you with a pathetic, serious way of speaking, I am returning the first act of *Tristan* to Härtel, and requesting the favour of not making the acquaintance of the remainder until it is published. As the *Dante Symphony* and the Mass are not valid as bank stock, it would be superfluous to send them to Venice. In my opinion it is equally superfluous to receive in future any more telegrams of distress or wounding letters from there.

Wagner wrote again on 7 January, insisting that his outburst had been aimed at the world in general and not at Liszt in particular. He now sees that Liszt too is suffering and hopes that this letter will end the misunderstanding. Liszt eventually responded on 17 February with a letter that re-established his sympathy, and the flow of correspondence continued in its former amicable vein. But the brief quarrel at the turn of the year, although healed, marked the beginning of a new chapter in the relationship between the two men; and the coming decade was to place the greatest strain on their friendship. Liszt's withdrawal from Weimar, and to a great extent from the world of practical music-making, had the result that he was no longer able to be of use to Wagner. His dream of Weimar as a great musical centre was never to be realized. Personal grief, including the death of his son Daniel in 1859, drove him towards the solace of his Church. In his Testament, drawn up on 14 September 1860, he wrote:

There is in contemporary art one name that is already glorious and will be more and more so: Richard Wagner. His genius has been a torch to me; I have followed it, and my friendship for Wagner has retained all the character of a noble passion. At one time (ten years ago), I dreamed of a new epoch for Weimar comparable to that of Karl Augustus, an epoch of which Wagner and I were to be the coryphaei, as Goethe and Schiller once were.

One more attempt by Wagner to raise funds while in Venice was another approach to Breitkopf und Härtel about the *Ring* scores. They continued to refuse him an advance, and began to stress their anxiety about the slow progress of *Tristan*. The text of the work was published in an edition of 2000 copies, in December 1858. One copy was sent to Schopenhauer, but there is no record of his reaction to this poetic panegyric on his philosophy. Four years earlier Wagner had sent the elderly recluse a copy of the *Ring* poem, which Schopenhauer read and annotated. His marginal comments are mainly adverse and he seems to have objected most to Wagner's cavalier treatment of the German language.

Apart from financial cares and concern for Minna's health, he had few other worries in Venice. When feeling fit he settled into a routine of work and relaxation: the morning spent in creative work; at two o'clock a gondola to the Piazza San Marco for lunch; then a walk, either alone or with Karl Ritter; in the evening a return by gondola for more work or a conversation with Karl. He later wrote that the cries of the gondolieri had impressed him deeply and may even have suggested the sad long-drawn wail of the shepherd's pipe at the beginning of *Tristan* Act Three. The Venice Diary reveals that Schopenhauer and Schiller provided his principal reading and that thoughts of Buddhism had led him to consider again the *Parsifal* subject, with its theme of compassion. He has come to see compassion for humanity's fellow-sufferers, and particularly for the suffering of dumb animals, as the strongest element in his moral being and as the fountain-head of his art. He feels that if all this suffering has any purpose, it must be to awaken pity in man, who will then perceive the error of existence and redeem the world. This will be the theme of his *Parsifal*, he says. Thoughts of that drama ran through his mind like a counterpoint to work on the latter part of *Tristan*. But at the end of May 1859 he tells Mathilde that the thought of composing music for *Parsifal* with all its suffering and agony, madness and despair, alternating with visions of inexpressible joy, of ecstasy and miraculous radiance, seems an overwhelming task. 'It is my *Tristan* of the third act inconceivably intensified.' The tale of *Parsifal* as told by the thirteenth-century Wolfram von Eschenbach he considers crude and helplessly confused; just as with

Gottfried von Strassburg's *Tristan*, he finds that the spiritual truth, the powerful core of the legend is clouded by the poet's ramifications and irrelevant asides. The broad, unwieldly complex of the *Parsifal* myth would have to be compressed into two or three powerful dramatic situations.

> And now – am I to undertake such a task? God forbid! This very day I bid farewell to the mad project. Let Geibel[1] write it and Liszt compose it! When my long-loved Brünnhilde leaps into the funeral pyre, I shall jump with her and hope for a blessed end! So be it. Amen!

At one point in the Diary he sees Mathilde as the suicidal Brünnhilde, and her ashes commingling with his own in the flames.

The early months of 1859 saw him approach the Saxon authorities once more with a plea for amnesty. A photograph of 'Father Geyer' lay before him on his desk in Venice, and he felt that if he and Minna were ever to set up home again together it would have to be in Dresden where she had her family and sympathetic friends. Above all, he was anxious for *Tristan* to be performed in Germany; Eduard Devrient at Karlsruhe was prepared for a production, but Wagner's presence could only be possible if the Saxon King made a move towards a pardon. He wrote a cordial letter to Lüttichau requesting his kindly intervention but received in reply 'a few business-like lines' that held out no hope of his return to Saxony.

The Austrian authorities, under pressure from the Saxon ambassador to Vienna, attempted to expel Wagner from Venice. Fortunately, his Swiss passport and the friendship of the sympathetic and cultured Venice Councillor of Police, forestalled any such move. But the new year brought the threat of war between Austria and Sardinia (backed by France). Venice no longer seemed a safe haven and in any case Wagner did not relish staying there during the hot summer tourist season. He was also missing the congenial Swiss countryside, the mountain air and those sturdy treks he so much enjoyed, for he had formed a deep love for his land of exile and was aware of the stimulus that the scenic background had given to his creations there. Later in the year he told Otto of his wish to continue the works 'I conceived in this tranquil and glorious Switzerland with my eyes resting on the towering, gold-crowned mountains. They are marvels and nowhere else could I have conceived them.' Accordingly, with Act Two of *Tristan* complete in full-score by mid March, he left Venice for Lucerne on the 23rd, the Erard being sent on in advance to the Hotel Schweizerhof. He said goodbye to Karl for the last time – they never met again. The Crimean War robbed the Ritters of the lands that provided their income, and Wagner's pension ceased that year.

In Lucerne the third act of *Tristan* was conceived. Wagner took a housekeeper, Vreneli Weitmann (later Frau Stocker) who pleased him so

---

[1] Emanuel Geibel (1815–84), poet.

17. Alexander Ritter (brother of Karl; married Wagner's niece Francisca) with his mother, Julie Ritter

Above 18. Minna

Right 19. Mathilde
Wesendonck

20. A page from the full score of *Das Rheingold*

Above left 24. Eduard Hanslick

Above 25. Caricature Wagner

Left 26. Tannhäuser asks to see his little brother, 'Les Troyen caricature of Berlioz Cham, Paris 1863

. Wagner in 1861

. Albert Niemann, 1877

29. Ludwig II of Bavaria

much that he later re-employed her in Munich and at Tribschen, and she assisted him with secretarial work. In April Wagner sent Mathilde this progress report on the work that was originally intended to be a practical and popular success:

Child! This *Tristan* is turning into something *frightful*!
That last act!!! –
I fear the opera will be forbidden – unless the whole thing is turned into a parody by bad production –: nothing but mediocre performances can save me! Completely good ones are bound to drive people crazy, – I can't imagine what else would happen! To such a state have things come!!! Alas! –

Apart from receiving a few, sporadic callers – the composer Felix Draeseke, Wilhelm Baumgartner, and Alexander Serov, the Russian composer and writer – Wagner accepted several invitations from Otto to the Wesendonck villa. These visits were designed to give the lie to rumours and gossip, but when Minna learned of them a new torrent of jealousy was unleashed. Wagner reminded her of her own entanglement with Herr Dietrich from Königsberg, twenty years before, and of how quickly he forgave her then. Minna merely countered this by dragging out references to the Laussot affair at Bordeaux.

Eking out an existence on the occasional theatre payment (Berlin gave *Lohengrin* in January and Dresden followed in August) he completed the composition sketch of Act Three on 19 July, in Lucerne, and by 7 August the entire work was ready in full score. Bülow, hard at work on the unenviable task of reducing the complex orchestration to pianistic terms, saw the opera as the summit of all music to date. With the conception of his child of sorrow, Wagner admitted to Carolyne's daughter, the Princess Marie, that an important chapter in his life had closed.

Eight

Misadventure in Paris

It seemed to me that the music was *mine*, and I recognized it as any man recognizes what he is destined to love.

Baudelaire on *Tannhäuser*

THE COMPLETION OF *Siegfried* and the performance of *Tristan* were Wagner's goals in the autumn of 1859. He was destined to achieve neither of these aims in the near future, but it was with them in mind that he chose to settle in Paris in September. On his first visit to the city he had arrived as a penniless refugee, unknown and without influence. Now, twenty years later, although still a refugee, his style of life was very different. He found a large house with a garden in the Rue Newton, and paid 12,000 francs as rent for three years in advance. Potentially it was a very elegant dwelling, but first Wagner had to spend a considerable sum on decoration and restoration: the decorator's bill ran to twelve pages and listed about 150 items. This expense was partly met as the result of a business transaction recently concluded with Otto. In reality Wagner lived on Wesendonck's charity, but neither man wished to regard it in that light. Otto preferred to 'do business' with Wagner by advancing sums for concerts, productions and the like. By the latest arrangement, Otto bought the publishing rights of *Rheingold* and *Walküre* for 12,000 francs. As Wagner proposed to live in a certain style and indulge in some fairly lavish entertaining, this sum was very quickly exhausted. By 19 October he was writing to Tichatschek in Dresden with an urgent request for 5000 francs:

> For heaven's sake prove to me that friendship's trust is not in vain. You would rid me of a terribly painful situation if you could help me. If the loan in its *entirety* could not be realized at once, half of it would suffice for an emergency provided that I could count on the remainder before the end of the year: but I wouldn't really be contented unless I had the whole sum right away. . . . Above all *my wife* must learn nothing about it; she would be terribly upset if she knew I were in such a predicament.

Wagner also corresponded with Dr Pusinelli in Dresden about the state of his wife's health. Minna was persuaded to join Wagner in Paris so that he

162

could ensure that she was properly cared for. On the way there by train, she opened a letter from Pusinelli to her husband. No secrets had been kept from the doctor about their marital relations and this letter was a particularly frank statement of the facts of her case and of the need for Wagner to handle her gently and avoid quarrels and excitement. When Wagner met her at the station on 17 November, she at once made it clear that she felt under no compulsion to live with him and that unless he treated her well she would go straight back to Dresden. Her defensive attitude and her opening of the letter infuriated Wagner, and the incident was a poor start to their final attempt at living together. Minna had brought with her the parrot and the dog, but Wagner insisted that Natalie remain in Germany: he was determined that she should have no opportunity to aggravate Minna's condition, and so the unwanted, unloved, unintelligent girl was left with Minna's relations. The only hope for her was that someone might marry her, despite her unattractiveness. Two servants were hired in order to relieve Minna of housework at the villa in the Rue Newton, where she had the first floor to herself. Even they found her intolerable, and shortly left.

Support and encouragement for Wagner's Paris ambitions came largely from unexpected quarters. When he called at the customs office to collect his belongings that had been conveyed from Lucerne, he was astonished when the official there introduced himself as one of his most ardent admirers. This was Edmond Roche, by vocation a poet and musician, and only by necessity employed as a customs officer. Another young enthusiast was Auguste de Gasperini, who immediately introduced Wagner to various men of influence. Both Gasperini and Léon Carvahlo, director of the Théâtre Lyrique, have left accounts of Wagner's visit to that institution, armed with the score of *Tannhäuser*. Carvahlo had provided two grand pianos for the audition, and was surprised to find that Wagner intended to play and sing the work entirely on his own. Wearing a blue jacket trimmed with red braid and a yellow cap embellished with a green fringe, he launched into the first part of *Tannhäuser*. After a while he withdrew, dripping with perspiration, and then appeared in fresh attire – yellow coat decorated with blue braid and red cap adorned with a yellow fringe – to attack the remainder of the work. 'He howled, he flung himself about, he hit all sorts of wrong notes, and on top of that he sang in German! And his eyes! The eyes of a madman! I did not dare to cross him – he frightened me,' recalled Carvahlo. Gasperini was astonished at the badness of Wagner's playing, through which Carvahlo sat impassively. 'When the last page was reached, M. Carvahlo stammered a few polite words, turned on his heels, and disappeared.'

Wagner had not been long in Paris when he learned that Karlsruhe had rejected *Tristan* on account of its difficulty. In turn, Dresden, Hanover and Strassburg all took fright at the score. There was some hope of a performance in Vienna, but for the moment Wagner concentrated his attention on Paris. He formed the ambitious idea of establishing a German theatre there, which would first mount the two earlier operas, *Tannhäuser* and *Lohengrin*, in model performances, before presenting *Tristan* but, in pursuing this scheme, he became involved in tedious, time-consuming business affairs and at the first whisper of Wagner's intentions the French press began a campaign designed to smear his name and discredit his artistic aims. In December Wagner was moved to publish a restrained and dignified protest, appealing for impartiality and the courtesy he expected as a guest in France. The recent deaths of Wilhelm Fischer, stage manager and chorus master at Dresden, and the composer Spohr, brought forth a moving obituary from Wagner which was published in the Dresden *Constitutioneller Zeitung*, and in the Leipzig *Neue Zeitschrift*. Another figure of his past, Schröder-Devrient, died in January 1860. Of less sorrow to Wagner was the news of the death of his old Dresden rival, Reissiger, in November 1859.

Much of Wagner's energy was spent in corresponding and negotiating with singers for his proposed model performances. Anyone not wholly in Meyerbeer's pocket was consulted and Belloni was brought in to help. Bülow, then in Paris, also came to Wagner's aid. A colossal amount of organization fell on Wagner's shoulders and any hope of continuing *Siegfried* was soon abandoned. Gasperini introduced him to a M. Lucy who seemed willing to finance a Wagnerian undertaking. Lucy remained sceptical of the plan for a season of German opera in Paris and instead a preliminary venture, consisting of three Wagner concerts, was agreed upon. Their hope was to give these concerts at the Opéra itself but, as a result of a long delay in negotiations, they had to resort to the Théâtre Italien (formerly the Théâtre de la Renaissance, also known as the Salle Ventadour). The director there, Calzado, a slippery character notorious as a gambler and cheat, only agreed to rent his theatre for a payment of 4000 francs per night. Artistically, the three concerts (on 25 January, 1 and 8 February 1860) fully justified all Wagner's hard work, and they attracted a great deal of attention and enthusiasm – the audience on the first night included Auber, Berlioz, Gounod and Meyerbeer. But the press, despite the fact that they had not been invited, wounded Wagner viciously. Only one independent voice sounded in his favour, that of Emile Perrin, painter, art critic and in later years, Director of the Opéra. Berlioz, unable to persuade the Opéra to take up *The Trojans*, had every reason to view Wagner's Paris ambitions with envy and annoyance, but his attendance at all three concerts (despite ill-health) and the honesty of his account of them in the *Journal des Débats* does him credit. He expressed genuine but reserved admiration for *The Flying Dutchman* overture and the extracts from *Lohengrin*, had considerably less enthusiasm for the *Tannhäuser* overture and found the prelude to *Tristan* incomprehensible:

It is a slow piece, beginning pianissimo, rising gradually to fortissimo and then subsiding to the quietness of the opening, with no other theme than a sort of chromatic moan, but full of dissonances, whose cruelty is further accentuated by long appoggiaturas which completely replace the true harmony-note. I have read and re-read this strange score; I have listened to it with the profoundest attention and an acute desire to discover the sense of it; well, I must confess that I still have not the least notion of what the composer intended!

This much at least was the frank critical reaction of a fellow musician who had no sympathy with nor understanding of Wagner's harmonic style. However, the remainder of the article descends into a sad piece of 'clever' journalism which illustrates that Berlioz had willingly swallowed all the popular notions of Wagner's theories, and in particular the long-current fallacy that he wrote his music to a 'system'. Wagner replied with a candid but not unfriendly open letter to Berlioz in the *Débats*, 22 February, designed to correct the notions of his 'theories' that Berlioz had repeated. It was not he, but a certain Herr Professor Bischoff of Cologne who coined the term 'music of the future'. This gentleman had misunderstood *The Art-Work of the Future* of 1849, a book that was not concerned with musical grammar but with the place of art in modern society. Wagner and Berlioz never came to blows over their differences in musical outlook: indeed, Wagner felt much sympathy for the world-weary French master, and blamed his coolness on the 'malignant' influence of his wife.

Of the older generation of French composers both Auber and Halévy welcomed Wagner with friendly interest. Among the new generation, Charles Gounod declared great admiration, and Wagner found in him an amiable and energetic champion of his cause, although *Mein Leben* confesses that 'no feeling of friendship had ever been able to induce me to hear his *Faust*'. The young Camille Saint-Saëns also joined the Wagnerian ranks as a staunch champion. But the most famous meeting was that with Rossini. The venerable Italian master had been made use of by an anti-Wagnerite journalist who circulated a malicious story claiming that Rossini had invited a friend to dinner and, upon learning that his guest admired Wagner, served him with fish sauce but no fish. Upon being asked the reason, Rossini declared that sauce without turbot was just the thing for a man who liked music without melody. Learning of this story, Rossini wrote to a Paris newspaper dissociating himself from any such unpleasant banter, and declaring that he would not resort to tasteless jokes at the expense of one who was trying to enlarge the scope of his art. All he knew of Wagner's work was the march from *Tannhäuser* which had pleased him very much. A friend of Rossini's arranged a meeting between the two men. They discussed many topics including Weber, Rossini's historic visit to Beethoven in 1822, the fickleness of the public, the cabals of the press, Wagner's ideas on the future of opera and the present state of Italian opera. They parted in mutual admiration and friendship, but never met again.

Other minor composers who joined the circle of the devoted were Louis Lacombe, Léon Kreutzer, the Belgian François Auguste Gevaert and the Hungarian Stephen Heller. In Frédéric Villot, custodian of the Louvre, Wagner found an intelligent supporter who had studied all his available scores. To Villot Wagner wrote the 'Open letter to a French friend' – '*Zukunftsmusik*' ('Music of the Future') – which appeared in the autumn of 1860 as preface to a French edition of prose translations of his operas. This expands the message of his *Débats* reply to Berlioz – that he did *not* write to a 'system'. In restating his artistic ideas, he hopes to trample underfoot all the misrepresentations of his writings from *The Art-Work of the Future* of 1849 onwards. But in restating his ideas Wagner confounds the issue by contradicting the views of *Opera and Drama*. That work, it will be recalled, dwelt on the primacy of poetry in the synthesis of music and words: music was but an intensified expression of the text. In *Zukunftsmusik*, ten years later, the shift in Wagner's thinking is apparent. Since the torrent of prose of the early months in Switzerland Wagner had discovered Schopenhauer who considered music 'by no means like the other arts but the copy of the will itself. . . . That is why the effect of music is so much more powerful and penetrating than that of the other arts, for they speak only of shadows but it speaks of the thing itself.' For Schopenhauer music does not 'depict one or other particular and definitive joy, or one or other sorrow or pain, or horror, or delight, or happiness, or peace of mind, but joy, sorrow, pain, horror, delight, happiness and peace of mind *themselves*, to a certain degree in the abstract: their essential nature, without accessories and therefore without their motives. Yet we understand them completely in this extracted quintessence'. Of the union of words and music he considered that 'if music is too closely united to the words, and tries to form itself according to the events, it is striving to speak a language which is not its own'. Melody, thought Schopenhauer, is totally independent: it exists quite freely from any text or stage action. The composition of *Tristan* also separated *Opera and Drama* from *Zukunftsmusik*. In that opera, it was the music, and not the text, that guided Wagner; during its creation he was conscious of pouring himself out in music. Whereas the *Ring* favours insistent alliteration in its text, the poem of *Tristan* returns to rhyming verse with an emphasis on vowel sounds. When the music was added, these words merge into the flow of sound, the orchestra often taking over completely, and the text conveying little meaning (especially in the huge love duet of Act Two). In *Zukunftsmusik* poetry is described as ascending to, or aspiring to the condition of music. All of Wagner's later writings on music contradict, to a greater or lesser extent, the stand taken in *Opera and Drama*. Yet both his friends and his enemies continued to regard that essay as the embodiment of Wagnerian law, and seemingly failed to observe that both in practice and in his later aesthetic pronouncements, he himself denied its teachings. Two facts contributed to the prevailing confusion and misrepresentation of his ideas: firstly

Wagner was constitutionally incapable of expressing his conceptions lucidly, and secondly, in adapting his vision of a synthesis of the arts to embrace Schopenhauer's philosophy, he continued to give the impression that he was ostensibly maintaining the original position of *Opera and Drama*.

Significantly, the boldest champions of Wagner's cause in Paris were not musicians. The artist Gustave Doré was among their number, and it is to be regretted that he never fulfilled his intention of providing illustrations to the *Ring*. Among men of letters, the novelist Champfleury (Jules Fleury-Husson) paid homage to Wagner in a pamphlet, and the poet Charles Baudelaire found in Wagner's 1860 concerts an art which was to be the most passionate love of the last years of his life. After the third concert he wrote to the composer expressing his gratitude, apologizing for the shameful behaviour of the French journalists and declaring that he was by no means alone in his enthusiasm. The postscript read, 'I am not adding my address because you might think I had something to ask of you.' However, Baudelaire and Wagner soon became personally acquainted and the poet was a regular visitor at his house.

The concerts of January and February were a financial disaster. Wagner's benefactor, M. Lucy had advanced several thousand francs towards the project, but deigned only to attend part of the second concert, during which he fell asleep. This enthusiasm did not allow him to risk further expenditure on Wagner's behalf. During February Wagner became conscious of an even greater calamity. Unknown to him, the street in which his house stood – the house which had cost him so much in rent, repairs and decorations – was to be demolished as part of a plan to reconstruct that area of the city. As work began which involved sinking the street level by ten or eleven feet, no one could approach his residence in safety. The landlord had previously been aware of this scheme and had deliberately cheated Wagner; now he refused to compensate his tenant but artfully invited Wagner to sue him, whereupon he in turn would sue the city authorities. Not only did Wagner lose two years' rent and all the money invested in improving the property, but he embarked on a costly legal action out of which he did not gain a single franc. In October 1860 he was compelled to move to another house in the considerably less pleasant Rue d'Aumale, near the Opéra, and thus became involved in further expense.

The year had begun on a more promising note. The publisher Franz Schott of Mainz paid Wagner 10,000 francs for the publishing rights of *Rheingold* and was given first option on the subsequent works of the *Ring* cycle. All of this money was consumed in the cost of the Paris concerts, although 6000 francs of it properly belonged to Otto Wesendonck. In the spring Wagner persuaded Otto to part with another 6000 francs for the rights of the unfinished *Siegfried* score. In July Wagner hit upon a way of balancing his debt to Otto with the suggestion that he regard the 6000 francs paid for *Rheingold* as an advance on the fourth section of the *Ring*, *Götterdämmerung*. Otto agreed to accept this ingenious and illusory settlement of his account. At the end of the year he received yet another loan from Otto, in lieu of royalties on *Tannhäuser*. In the last week of March Wagner repeated his Paris concerts in Brussels – a rash attempt to transform losses into profits which failed dismally. Three concerts were planned, but after the second, Wagner returned to Paris poorer than ever. It was Countess Marie Kalergis who made up the deficit by presenting Wagner with 10,000 francs. Her interest in Wagner dated from her visit to Dresden in 1845; they renewed their acquaintance during his stay in Paris of 1853, and from the time of this gift until her death in 1874 she ranked as one of his most prominent, though not uncritical, supporters. During his stay in Paris Wagner borrowed sums from several friends and from money-lenders including Julie Salis-Schwabe, a Jewish widow from Manchester, who provided 5000 francs. The French publisher Flaxland alsó came to his aid several times and bought the French and Belgian publishing rights of *The Flying Dutchman*, *Lohengrin* and *Tannhäuser* for 3000 francs. Wagner's arrangement with Flaxland led to a tangled maze of copyright problems, and legal wrangles with Wagner's former publishers, Breitkopf and Hermann Müller (who owned the Meser scores). Emil Erlanger, a Paris banker, showed practical evidence of his sympathy for Wagner by investing funds in the composer, apparently with an eye to being his business manager. This arrangement did not survive the disasters of Paris, but Wagner was ever grateful to the young Erlanger whose substantial loans greatly helped to support him.

Disillusionment with Paris and frustration at the business entanglements that were preventing creative work had by March 1860 reached the point where Wagner began to consider seriously the idea of returning to Saxony and offering himself for trial. There was now no hope of a *Tristan* production in Paris, nor even a means of approaching that goal, and no enthusiasm for the work had been shown by theatres elsewhere. In letters to the Wesendoncks Wagner spoke of his ardent wish to present *Tristan* to the public: then he 'can die in peace'. He was at this low ebb when, without warning, the Emperor Napoleon III commanded a performance of *Tannhäuser* at the Opéra and decreed that Wagner's wishes were to be carried out to the last detail. Various people seem to have influenced this decision, principally the remarkable and notorious Princess Pauline Metternich,* wife of the Austrian ambassador, Prince Richard von Metternich-Winneburg. She had long sought to play the role of patroness and saw in Wagner, whose *Tannhäuser* she had heard in Dresden, the ideal protégé. A shallow, frivolous, vulgar woman, she had endeared herself to Napoleon and the Empress Eugénie. Count Paul Hatzfeld, an attaché at the Prussian embassy, also appears to have caught the ear of the Empress and urged her to use her influence on Napoleon.

Wagner did not know what to think of this dramatic development. He wrote to Liszt from Brussels on 29 March: 'What will come of this projected *Tannhäuser*, God only knows; in my heart of hearts I have no faith in it . . .' But twelve days later he wrote to Mathilde describing the acceptance of *Tannhäuser* as of vital import for the cultural capacities of the unmusical French race. In the same letter he tells of his decision to rewrite the music of the Venusberg scene. The Dresden setting he now considers weak, ineffective and stiff. With the rich, transfigured scoring of *Tristan* behind him and with the choreographers, dancers and scenic designers of the Opéra at his disposal, he envisages a magnificently sensual and impressive recasting of the scene. It was obligatory that all performances at the Opéra be given in French, therefore Wagner, whose own knowledge of the language was rudimentary, was faced with the problem of finding a good translator. After several false starts with people who proved inadequate, Edmond Roche, Wagner's friend from the customs office, set about the task of fashioning decent French verses, assisted by a somewhat incompetent translator, Lindau. Their effort did not satisfy the Opéra management and the text was thoroughly revised by the keeper of the archives, Charles-Louis-Étienne Truinet, who also wrote the necessary new verses for the expanded first Venus scene. (These were later translated into rather uncomfortable German.) At his first interview with Wagner, and at every one of their many meetings thereafter, the director of the Opéra, Alphonse Royer, impressed upon him the absolute necessity of a ballet in the second act. The result of Wagner's refusal to comply with this custom will soon be revealed.

During the summer of 1860 Wagner displayed remarkable energy in a variety of directions. A common feature of his creative mood was that more than one idea would shape simultaneously in his mind. As he planned the Venusberg music his thought turned over the Parsifal idea. His correspondence with Mathilde flourished again, with boundless metaphysical reflections reminiscent of the Venice Diary. In August he drafted a drama, *Erec und Enide*, in which a doubting wife drives her husband to his death; then, overcome with sorrow she succeeds in reawakening him. Wagner's own doubting, invalid wife felt unhappy and out of place during the Wednesday evening social gatherings at their house. Malwida von Meysenbug arrived in Paris from London in the autumn of 1860. Her memoirs provide a valuable insight into the Wagner home life:

> Because of [Minna's] total inability to understand the nature of his genius and its effect on his relationship to the world, there now arose almost daily conflict and torment in their life together which, as they were childless, lacked any possible tenderness and reconciliation. Even so, Frau Wagner was a good wife, and in the eyes of the world it was she who was the better and long-suffering member of the pair. I judged the situation differently and felt boundless sympathy for Wagner, for whom love should have built a bridge across which he could have reached other men, instead of which it merely embittered the

already bitter cup of life. Actually I was on very good terms with Frau Wagner, who was friendly with me, confided in me and often came to weep on my shoulder. I did what I could then to make her understand her role in life better, but it was, of course, no use. She had not understood it in twenty-five years of marriage, and she never could, for it was simply not in her to do so.

One of Minna's complaints concerned Wagner's unconcealed fondness for Blandine Ollivier. She had few illusions about Wagner's intoxication with such intelligent and attractive younger women. Cosima she dismissed as 'a rather dissolute creature', and blamed her for the breakdown of Karl Ritter's marriage, in a letter to Emma Herwegh written on 24 March 1860.

Minna did share Wagner's hopes and fears for the coming *Tannhäuser*, however, for that work she considered far greater than his recent efforts. For real sympathy, though, Wagner desperately needed the company of faithful and devoted friends – but even they sometimes failed him. In May an informal performance of *Tristan* Act Two took place at the home of the great singer Pauline Viardot. Klindworth came from London at Wagner's expense and accompanied Viardot as Isolde and Brangäne and the composer as Tristan and Marke. The occasion was designed as a tribute to Wagner's friend and benefactress, Marie Kalergis. At the conclusion, the Countess said not a word, and Berlioz, the only other person present, merely congratulated Wagner on the ardour of his delivery. Afterwards Marie Kalergis gave it as her private opinion that the work would be impossible to stage: it was but an intriguing abstraction.

The French Emperor's commission of *Tannhäuser* conferred a new status upon Wagner. Unquestionably he was the most famous living German composer and yet he could not set foot upon German soil without fear of arrest. The position was no longer embarrassing to Wagner, but became increasingly so to the Saxon government. Among the famous exile's closest allies in Paris were some of the most influential diplomats. Apart from the Metternichs and Count Hatzfeld, the Prussian ambassador, Count Albrecht Alexander Pourtalès, was on friendly terms with him; and Princess Augusta of Prussia (consort of Wilhelm, and later Empress of Germany) had also declared a long-standing admiration for Wagner and personally intervened with the Saxon King. Fortunately Saxony's own ambassador in Paris, Baron von Seebach was another admirer and a relation of Marie Kalergis. The principal obstacle that confronted this impressive and united chorus in Wagner's support was the proud, easily-offended, rather narrow-minded character of King Johann of Saxony. He refused absolutely to grant Wagner either a pardon or an amnesty. It was only on account of the sheer pressure brought upon him that, with bitter reluctance, he agreed to allow Wagner to enter any German state *except* Saxony. Certain conditions were imposed: the concession would be revoked immediately if Wagner's behaviour was not satisfactory, and in order to enter any German state, he would first have to apply to the government concerned, which in turn would apply to the Saxon King, who would then grant permission.

In the last week of July Wagner sent a humble letter of thanks to His Majesty of Saxony, but confessed to Mathilde that the long-awaited news actually left him 'quite cold and indifferent'. In August he visited Germany for a few days, calling first at Frankfort to see his brother Albert. He considered calling on Schopenhauer but hesitated out of shyness, and decided to defer such a visit until a more favourable time. Thus he missed the chance of ever meeting the philosopher, who died on 21 September without being aware of how much his posthumous fame was due to Richard Wagner. Princess Augusta of Prussia was in residence at Baden-Baden, so Wagner called on her, ostensibly to express his gratitude for her intercession with Johann of Saxony. She received him very coldly with repeated assurances that she was completely powerless to help him further. It would seem that either his rough Saxon accent had upset her, or else she had been well informed about his character and was determined not to be made use of.

On his return to Paris he was at once preoccupied with the arduous preparations for *Tannhäuser*, the rehearsals commencing early in September. For the heroic tenor part Wagner chose Albert Niemann, for Tichatschek, the original Tannhäuser, was now rather old (although he sang Lohengrin for Wagner in 1867 and did not retire until 1872); and Ludwig Schnorr was engaged at Karlsruhe. Wagner would not deal with the Karlsruhe director, Eduard Devrient, whom he accused of personally wrecking the plan for *Tristan* there. Niemann seemed ideal in every respect – age, physique, vocal ability – and he knew the part well. He was engaged for nine months at the staggering fee of 54,000 francs. At their first meeting in Paris Wagner instantly became aware of the tenor's brusque personality when he appeared at his door with the words, 'Well, do you want me or don't you?' But for the first few weeks Wagner overlooked Niemann's haughtiness and vanity, realizing that in him he possessed a Heldentenor of rare ability who only needed to remedy various mannerisms and a certain vocal roughness. Marie Sax was chosen as Elisabeth, Fortuna Tedesco as Venus and Morelli as Wolfram. Wagner spared no effort in moulding their voices, shaping their phrasing and taking particular care over their stage gestures. In creating the Venusberg scene for Paris he became aware for the first time of the possibilities of ballet as an independent art form and as a potential factor in music-drama. He planned a wild Bacchanal, with cupids, nymphs, fauns, maenads, the three Graces, Sirens, Bacchantes, all kinds of strange beasts, tigers, panthers, rams, griffins, centaurs, water sprites, a Nordic Strömkarl, together with vast cloud-tableaux of Diana and Endymion, Europa and the bull, and Leda and the swan. Not all of this fantastic mythological menagerie was utilized, but Wagner had no cause to complain about the diligent preparations for the production in all its aspects.

Everything was done exactly as, and when, Wagner ordained it. He had absolute authority. He rejected the scenic designs three times before he was satisfied. The sets were those of Despléchin, who had designed the original Dresden production, with new designs for Act One Scene One and Act Two by other Paris artists.

Shortly after Wagner's removal to the Rue d'Aumale the campaign suffered a setback as the composer became seriously ill. The strain of the Opéra project combined with his acute financial plight resulted in a fever with hallucinations that absented him for six weeks. It was rumoured at the theatre that he was on his last legs. Minna and Gasperini were alarmed by his ravings: he begged to be taken to Naples were Garibaldi would cure him. When the fever subsided he was left partially blind for a time and with no energy to cope with the exertions of the rehearsals. The gravest aspect of this delay was that all impetus at the Opéra collapsed: doubts and disillusionment began to depress the company. Another obstacle to progress was the interruption to composition of the new episodes of Act One. On 16 December Wagner wrote to Otto, 'I have not yet finished the orchestration of the new scene between Tannhäuser and Venus; the first dance is still missing, and up to now, I have no idea how I shall carry it out.' When the score was ready, over a month later, there was very little time left for the choreographer Petipa to do justice to Wagner's ambitious and problematical scenario. The singers, and Tedesco in particular, were horrified to discover the length and difficulty of the new music. They had not anticipated such a large amount of it and were alarmed by its post-*Tristan* language, so very different from Wagner's Dresden style.

The matter of the Act Two ballet was continually raised. Wagner was told that the influential patrons of the Opéra cared for little else but the ballet and timed their arrival to coincide with its traditional place in the second act. Napoleon's Minister of the Household, Count Walewski, warned Wagner of the dangers if he refused to restructure the work accordingly. Petipa told him that none of the best dancers would take part in the Venusberg scene if it remained in Act One. But such an alteration to his work was unthinkable to Wagner. In vain did Royer warn him of the danger of incurring the hostility of the all-powerful Jockey Club. The rich young members of that organization could work more mischief than all Wagner's press enemies together. Royer suggested that a ballet-intermezzo be inserted somewhere in the second act. Wagner would not hear of such an absurdity, and refused to be tempted by promises of extra rehearsals, the finest scenery and lighting, or the best dancers in Europe. For Wagner, the Venusberg scene provided all that was required and more in the way of spectacle. He suggested beginning the work at eight o'clock to appease the Jockeys or providing a separate ballet after the opera. The dispute soon became a *cause célèbre* throughout Europe and in July 1860 Wagner made a declaration in the *Journal des Débats* that on no account would he incorporate a ballet in the central act of *Tann-häuser*.

Trouble with his leading tenor beset Wagner during the first weeks of 1861. Niemann had lost faith in the production and was upset at the idea of returning to Germany without having scored the personal triumph he sought. His vanity had led him to contact various journalists and from them he learned of the colossal prejudice against Wagner. His anxiety and conceit led him to suppose that he knew better than Wagner, and he ignored the composer's careful explanations and suggestions concerning the interpretation of the part. He was certain that failure lay ahead and as the performance approached his self-centred obstinacy increased.

The first full rehearsal with orchestra took place on 19 February. Altogether there were no less than 163 rehearsals for *Tannhäuser*, therefore there was little doubt that the singers knew their parts. The time had now come for Wagner to hand over the musical direction to the conductor of the Opéra, as the absurd rules of the institution did not allow a composer to conduct his own work. The conductor in question was Pierre Louis Philippe Dietsch who, twenty years before, had set Wagner's *Flying Dutchman* story as *Le Vaisseau Fantôme*. From the moment that Dietsch began working with the orchestra and singers, Wagner and his faithful assistant, Bülow, began to have serious worries; but at that first full rehearsal Wagner was more concerned with Niemann, whose stubborn approach to the title role was endangering the whole conception. In particular Wagner was annoyed by Niemann's method of saving his voice until the third act, in which he sang with heroic strength in order to create an effective, impressive ending. Patiently, Wagner explained that his approach to the third act should be quite different: the weary, tragic character of Tannhäuser at this point required a controlled, gentle, ghost-like tone. At this Niemann took offence. The next day Wagner wrote a very long letter to his peevish singer which carefully explains the artistic reasons behind the interpretation he desires. He begs Niemann to use his full strength in the second act and then he will come to feel the tenderness and delicacy of nuance that the last act requires. He does not spare the young tenor a rebuke in this plea for understanding and consideration. All the other singers have improved amazingly in the past six months, while Niemann seems to recoil and deteriorate. He has remained almost insultingly aloof, discourteous and deliberately insensitive to advice. Wagner ends by urging Niemann to take courage and prove worthy of the high opinion he has of him. Before he had signed the letter, a note arrived from the tenor. In blunt language Niemann demands that a passage from Act Three be cut. The previous day Wagner's refusal to cut it had 'caused me great embarrassment before a large audience *improperly* admitted by you, an embarrassment about which people are already talking everywhere and which will have a most harmful effect on my success'. If Wagner will not authorize the cut then he can look for another

Tannhäuser: 'Renouncing any personal success for myself, I shall be very happy indeed if I escape from this whole affair with my voice intact.' Wagner added a stern postscript to his own letter, declaring that Niemann has used language towards him which he can only understand by casting his mind back to the earliest years of his painful career. Nonetheless he hopes that this letter will not be too late to save the situation. He is prepared to make the requested cut and in return hopes for 'rather more regard on your part than is apparent from the tone of your letter of today'.

Greater heartbreak was to come. At the next rehearsal under Dietsch the carefully trained soloists, chorus and orchestra began to fall apart in chaos. Bülow expressed rage at his 'imbecile fumbling', wretched memory and total lack of musicianship. Wagner dubbed him the 'Schöps (simpleton) d'orchestre'. On 25 February Wagner told Royer that he would not permit Dietsch to ruin the months of hard work, and insisted on conducting the remainder of the rehearsals and the first three performances himself. On 7 March, having obtained no satisfaction, Wagner presented the same ultimatum to Count Walewski. On the following day he was told that in no circumstances could Dietsch be replaced. Wagner then took the only remaining course open to him and withdrew his score. Walewski replied that after such enormous expenditure and effort the performance could not be cancelled. As a last resort Wagner petitioned Napoleon himself, but received the same reply, although he was offered as many additional rehearsals as he might require. Clearly the prospect of another round of rehearsals would have a disastrous and demoralizing effect on the cast; indeed Wagner's attempted *coup d'état* with the Minister of the Household had already antagonized the orchestra. The press were virtually foaming at the mouth at Wagner's arrogance. There was no alternative but to let the disaster run its own course. The last rehearsal saw a steady massacre of Wagner's score, the tormented composer, seated on stage, thrashing his arms and legs about in a last attempt to correct the tempi of the incompetent Dietsch. At the final dress rehearsal on 10 March, to which Wagner invited about one hundred friends in an effort to quell the scandal-mongers, Niemann affected to suffer from vertigo during the first act: the remainder of *Tannhäuser* played without its hero.

The first performance, three days later, was attended by Napoleon, Eugénie and all the glittering court of the Second Empire. Despite their presence, Wagner's press enemies and the gentlemen of the Jockey Club were also there and spoiling for a fight. Wagner was unable to secure seats for all his friends, many of whom reproached him, pointing out that Meyerbeer's success lay in his insistence that the theatre be filled to the remotest corner with his own supporters. Bülow alone shared Wagner's distaste for claques, bribery and all the other underhand tricks of the theatre trade. To other supporters this lofty idealism was sheer folly.

Wagner was probably naive in that he did not foresee the sheer force of the opposition pitted against him. The antagonism was aimed not so much at Wagner's music, nor did it arise on account of the vexed question of the ballet, but it had its origin mainly in politics. The composer of *Tannhäuser* was regarded as a republican and, although he had ceased meddling in politics of any kind, he had associated with several men known for their republican sympathies, notably Emile Ollivier.[1] Wagner's reputation was still based largely on his activities and writings of over a decade earlier, and many people naively continued to think of him as an active republican. That suited Napoleon very well, for his adoption of Wagner would serve to enhance his reputation among democrats both in France and Germany. Among the members of the Jockey Club, however, were many Legitimists who were delighted to take the opportunity of turning this Imperial performance into a demonstration against Napoleon. Moreover, Princess Metternich was regarded with distrust as a detestable foreigner, using her influence at court to mend relations between France and Austria after the latter's defeat in the 1859 Italian Campaign. To humiliate her, to express contempt for Germany and Austria and to aim a blow at the Emperor himself were the motives of hatred that prompted the events of 13 March, made the Opéra their battlefield and caused one of the most celebrated theatrical scandals in history.

The overture and the scene between Venus and Tannhäuser were played to an encouraging and attentive silence. But at the transformation to the valley before the Wartburg, with the pastoral melody of the shepherd's pipe, a hue and cry commenced which was shouted down by the larger part of the audience. A little while later it began again: the Jockeys shouting abuse and blowing shrill hunting whistles as part of a carefully rehearsed plan of noisy protest. Those who wished to hear the music were equally vocal in their efforts to quell the demonstrators. The pro-Wagner party demonstrated their feelings with prolonged outbursts of applause lasting up to a quarter of an hour. Amazingly, the performance proceeded despite the furore which reached a crescendo of chaos in the third act. Little of it could have been effectively understood, but Wagner was gratified that the greater part of the public had shown tumultuous enthusiasm in an effort to drown the opposition. He thought it wise to withdraw his score but Bülow and other friends persuaded him to allow another performance. The second night was scheduled for the 15th but, as Herr Niemann was indisposed, it was postponed for a further three days. The Imperial couple were present again and the performance, with cuts imposed by Royer and unwillingly approved by Wagner, reached the middle of Act Two without interruption. Then the rumpus of

---

[1] Ollivier later became Minister of Justice in the Second Empire, and in January 1870, Prime Minister of France.

whistling, jeers and shouting erupted. Minna was insulted as the composer's wife; Bülow sobbed in her arms; the Wagners' servant, Therese, was sneered at until she screamed *Schweinhund* at her molestor; in Act Three an enraged Niemann flung his pilgrim's hat at the screaming mob. Again Wagner proposed withdrawing his score and again he was dissuaded. The third performance was arranged for a Sunday (24 March) – a non-subscribers' day – in the hope that the tickets would largely be obtained by sympathetic patrons. But by now, street sellers were offering 'Wagner whistles' and groups of police had to be positioned throughout the theatre corridors. They were there not to prevent outbursts of trouble, but to protect the aristocratic young hooligans of the Jockey Club from receiving richly deserved beatings from the other infuriated members of the audience. Wagner did not attend what proved to be the rowdiest evening of all. From start to finish there was almost continual uproar, the first act alone interrupted twice by fights lasting fifteen minutes each. During the evening various friends escaped from the tumult to report to Wagner at the Rue d'Aumale. At two in the morning Malwida arrived to find him calm and cheerful in the face of what must have been a profound and bitter disappointment. Eighteen months of work had been wasted on a brawl that provided him with the glorious sum of 750 francs, all of which he gave to Roche. Niemann, who returned to Hanover with 54,000 francs, had caused much of his suffering. Wagner wrote to Tichatschek, recalling his old love for the part, and bewailing Niemann and his tantrums – 'a miserable coward who runs around howling that he is ruining his voice with my *Tannhäuser*'. After some reluctance the authorities agreed to allow Wagner to withdraw the work. The Opéra made an inestimable loss. Berlioz gloated over Wagner's defeat and regarded himself as 'cruelly avenged'. And no full-length Wagner opera was heard in Paris for another twenty-five years, except for an airing of *Rienzi* in 1869.

The malevolent victory of the Jockey Club was not altogether without positive effects. Many younger men wrote to Wagner to express sympathy and indignation at his treatment. Baudelaire voiced his sentiments in a brochure of April 1861, *Richard Wagner et Tannhäuser à Paris*: 'What will they say of Paris in Germany?' he cried; 'A handful of rowdies have disgraced us en masse.' The nineteen-year-old Portuguese Jew, Catulle Mendès,* joined Wagner's French literary admirers in asking him to contribute to his newly founded and short-lived *Revue Fantastique* in 1861. Six years later Mendès married Théophile Gautier's daughter Judith, another ardent Wagnerian. Mendès, like Baudelaire, defended Wagner at length in books and articles, and his enthusiasm was shared by the writers Villiers de l'Isle Adam,* Edouard Schuré,* and the critic Léon Leroy. Wagner's oft-expressed hatred for France at the time of the Franco-Prussian War in 1870 impeded the progress there of his ideas and his music, but in the 1880s there was a new mania for Wagner, reflected above all in literature. Émile Zola, Paul Verlaine, Stéphane Mallarmé and, much later, Paul Valéry and Marcel Proust, all fell under his spell. In 1885 Edouard Dujardin, a composer turned novelist, founded the *Revue Wagnerienne* which had strong links with the Symbolist movement, and had many distinguished contributors including Mendès, J. K. Huysmans, Mallarmé, Villiers, Verlaine and Téodor de Wyzewa. Proust, Valéry, T. S. Eliot, James Joyce and W. B. Yeats owed much to the influence of the Symbolists and indirectly inherited from Wagner a literary equivalent of his 'endless melody' and leitmotif techniques. Two other literary giants who were among Wagner's heirs and boldest advocates ought to be noted here: Thomas Mann and Bernard Shaw. Among visual artists whose names have been linked with Wagner are Cézanne, Degas, Fantin-Latour, Gustave Moreau and Odilon Redon. Of the composers who joined Wagner's circle, Gounod summed up the reaction to *Tannhäuser* in his famous words, 'God give me a failure like that!' Until (and including) Debussy, the majority of French composers in the later nineteenth century could not escape Wagner's overwhelming influence. Particular mention should be made of Louis Bourgault-Ducoudray, Alfred Bruneau, Emmanuel Chabrier, Ernest Chausson, Henri Duparc, Camille Erlanger, Vincent d'Indy, Édouard Lalo, Giullaume Lekeu and Ernest Reyer.

The great period of French Wagnerism came after the composer was in his grave, but immediately after the *Tannhäuser* fiasco Wagner seems to have sensed the potential sympathy for him that arose as a direct result of the failure at the Opéra. There were many who sought to profit from his notoriety. The director of the Opéra-Comique even proposed to mount *Tannhäuser*. And for a considerable time Wagner contemplated the possibility of founding a theatre in Paris, exclusively devoted to his works. Soon it must have been clear to him that such hopes for Paris were as illusory as the *Rienzi* venture of twenty years before. Now, as then, his homeland beckoned again. It was in Germany alone that he could foresee any headway for his new works.

Nine

The Wanderer

The reasonable man adapts himself to the world; the unreasonable one persists in trying to adapt the world to himself. Therefore all progress depends on the unreasonable man.

Shaw, *Man and Superman*

THE QUEST FOR A *Tristan* production had lured Wagner to Paris, and for several years his travels and fortunes were guided and shaped by the elusive hope of securing a performance of that work. A glimmer of interest was rekindled at Karlsruhe when Wagner visited the Grand Duke of Baden there on 15 April 1861: he was given a friendly reception and soon a plan was laid to mount *Tristan*, under Wagner's direction, in September. The premiere would coincide with the Grand Duke's thirty-fifth birthday; Eduard Devrient was converted to the project; even *Rheingold* was proposed for the following summer. Above all, Wagner would settle at Karlsruhe permanently and complete the *Ring*. Not one of these happy prospects was destined to materialize. By sad mischance, Ludwig Schnorr and his wife Malvina, who were eventually to be the first Tristan and Isolde in Munich, had left Karlsruhe for Dresden one year before. Wagner knew Schnorr only by reputation and he had not heard Malvina for almost thirteen years. His reluctance to summon Schnorr to Karlsruhe was due to reports of his excessive corpulence: Wagner as yet had no idea that the tenor's abnormal bulk in no way detracted from his sensitive acting and exceptional vocal powers. He had received good reports of Aloys Ander* and Luise Meyer-Dustmann at the Vienna Opera, and resolved to go there and hear them for himself, and perhaps succeed in persuading them to undertake *Tristan* at Karlsruhe.

After returning to Paris for a few days to scrape some money together, he set out for the Austrian capital and arrived on 9 May, having called on the Grand Duke at Karlsruhe again on the way. Wagner was greeted like a hero in Vienna in the wake of the Paris scandal, and the management invited him to attend their productions of *Lohengrin* and *The Flying Dutchman* as guest of honour. They were justly proud of these items of their repertory and anxious to demonstrate the qualities of their singers to the composer. Wagner heard his *Lohengrin* for the first time in his life at a full rehearsal on 11 May. He wrote to Minna of the warmth and enthusiasm with which he was greeted and of the tears and emotion that overcame him on hearing his work at last. Everything about Vienna enchanted him: the orchestra was overpoweringly fine, the chorus and soloists outdid one another in vocal beauty, Ander was 'utterly perfect' and Dustmann 'capable of anything'. All this, together with the friendly sympathy of the Intendant, convinced him that there was little point in transferring singers to tiny Karlsruhe, when the ideal resources for *Tristan* were available here in Vienna. At the performance of *Lohengrin* on the 15th he received the most spectacular ovation of his career to date. At the end of the prelude he had to step forward from his box five times to acknowledge the overwhelming applause, and after every principal section in each act there were outbursts of similar enthusiasm. For *The Flying Dutchman*, three days later, he chose a less conspicuous seat but was recognized and brought on stage after the overture to take a bow. Throughout the remainder of the evening the opera was interrupted by wild demonstrations of approval.

Full of hope for future success in Vienna, Wagner returned to Paris at the end of May, partly to wind up his affairs there and partly to supervise Truinet's French translation of *The Flying Dutchman* for the publisher Flaxland. He found Minna sour and embittered. She blamed his stubbornness over the ballet issue, and his failure to bribe the critics, for the *Tannhäuser* débâcle. In Vienna he had appealed to a local choral society not to serenade him: she found fault in that. Tristan and Isolde she considered 'a much too enamoured and odious couple', and she knew that in her husband's plans, either for Karlsruhe or Vienna, she had little place. She felt old, ill and insignificant: she had no desire to stay in Paris and was faced with difficulties about returning to Dresden owing to her status as wife of the 'criminal' ex-Kapellmeister. On 22 June little Fips died. Wagner confessed in *Mein Leben*:

> The effect of this melancholy event upon Minna and myself was never expressed in words. In our childless life together the influence of domestic pets had been very important. The sudden death of this lively and lovable animal acted as the final rift in a union which had long become impossible.

Next day Wagner buried the dog in a friend's garden. Minna left Paris in the second week of July to take a cure at Bad Soden.

Having sub-let his apartment, placed his furniture in store, and settled his largest debts, Wagner spent his last three weeks in Paris as a guest of Count Pourtalès at the Prussian Embassy. His delightful stay there, enhanced by lively company and splendid views across the Seine and the Tuileries garden, resulted in an Album-leaf for piano in A flat major, dedicated to the Countess: *Ankunft bei den schwarzen Schwänen*, on 29 July. The title celebrates the black swans at the pool in the embassy garden, and the music is based on Elisabeth's Hall of Song aria in *Tannhäuser* Act Two.

Princess Metternich was similarly honoured with an *Albumblatt* for piano in C major on 18 June.

The state of Wagner's relations with Liszt is vividly reflected in their correspondence: after July 1861 no letters passed between them for eleven years. At the time of Wagner's move to Paris in the autumn of 1859, Bülow, in a moment of addle-headedness, sent Liszt a letter he had received from Wagner, dated 7 October. This not only contained Wagner's now famous grumble about an article that named Liszt as an influence on *Tristan*, but referred to Liszt's behaviour as cold and implied regret at the Princess's hold over him. Liszt informed Carolyne that Wagner 'seems to insinuate that you exercise a regrettable influence over me, and one contrary to my true nature'. Although they continued to correspond while Wagner was in Paris, the bright flame of their friendship had flickered very low. When he returned to Paris from Vienna he found Liszt in the city, basking in the brilliance of Parisian society to an extent that disgusted Wagner. He complained that he saw very little of his friend, but even so was able to abstract another loan from him. At the end of July Wagner left Paris and called first at Soden to see Minna, where it was agreed that she should return to Dresden while he went to Vienna. He guaranteed to provide her with an income of 3000 marks per year, and indeed he remained faithful to that commitment despite many later financial predicaments. From Soden he proceeded to Weimar, having promised to attend some performances of Liszt's orchestral music. In the absence of the Princess the two men drew closer together again in an atmosphere made congenial by a large gathering of distinguished and devoted friends, among them Brendel, Bülow, Cornelius, Leopold Damrosch, Felix Draesecke, Alwine Frommann, Blandine and Émile Ollivier, Tausig and Wendelin Weissheimer.* After a week of festivities, Wagner accompanied Blandine and Ollivier to Nuremberg where they spent a night and where Wagner's thoughts turned again to his old sketch for *Die Meistersinger*. The following evening they reached Munich and, in the company of Baron von Hornstein, spent some high-spirited hours sampling beer and making merry, largely at Hornstein's expense. An overnight journey took them to Bad Reichenhall where Cosima was taking a sour milk cure. After enjoying the society of the two sisters for a few days Wagner continued his journey to Vienna. *Mein Leben* recalls that as he said farewell, Cosima gave him 'a look of almost timid inquiry'.

In Vienna he was fortunate enough to meet by chance Dr Joseph Standhartner, physician to the Empress Elizabeth, with whom he had made friends on his previous visit to the city, and who offered him the use of his house for six weeks, as he and his family were about to leave for a holiday. The doctor's charming niece and housekeeper, Seraphine Mauro, added greatly to the enjoyment of Wagner's stay although this flirtation rather upset Cornelius, whose sweetheart she had previously been. Cornelius had lived in Vienna since 1859, his choice of residence being influenced by Wagner's association with the city; although he was unable to escape Wagner's powerful influence on his music – especially on *Der Cid*, the opera of his Vienna years – Cornelius, more than any of Wagner's intimate friends, was able to view the colossus with perspective and remarkable impartiality. In his many letters we find reasoned, critical and refreshingly unbiased accounts of Wagner's behaviour. Also close to Wagner at this time was Tausig, and another Liszt pupil, Alexander Winterberger (whom Wagner had known in Venice) joined his circle.

Despite the enthusiasm of the Isolde, Meyer-Dustmann, and of the orchestra, hopes for a production of *Tristan* early in October faded fast, even in Wagner's mind. The principal obstacle was the tenor Ander, who was continually suffering from hoarseness. Only later was it clear that his loss of voice was due to increasing insanity. His career struggled on for a year or two until the final breakdown; he died in an asylum on 11 December 1864. In the autumn of 1861, however, Wagner was prepared to go to any length to adapt the part for him, so anxious was he for a performance. Ander was terrified of the difficulties of the part, so Wagner suggested cuts, transpositions and all kinds of alterations to ease the strain. The press began to make capital out of Ander's affliction and stories of the 'unperformable' nature of Wagner's latest music abounded. Wagner was determined, so soon after the disaster in Paris, that he would not fail in Vienna. After struggling with Ander he tried another tenor, Morini (whose real name was Schrumpf), but found him inadequate. In desperation he attempted to secure Schnorr and even old Tichatschek from Dresden, but in vain.

Several of his friends thought it essential to attempt a reconciliation between Wagner and Hanslick. In May, during the rehearsal of *Lohengrin*, he had been introduced to the critic. Wagner recounts in *Mein Leben*:

> I greeted him shortly, like a perfectly unknown person; whereupon the tenor, Ander, presented him a second time with the remark that Dr Hanslick was an old acquaintance. I answered briefly that I remembered Dr Hanslick very well, and once more turned my attention to the stage.

Heinrich Laube, now director of the Burgtheater, invited both men to a dinner party. Wagner ignored Hanslick totally. In the autumn, at another evening party, Meyer-Dustmann introduced the two men yet again. Wagner tells us in *Mein Leben:*

> As I was in a good temper that evening I found it easy to treat Hanslick as a superficial acquaintance, until he drew me aside for an intimate talk, and with sobs and tears assured me that he could not bear to be misunderstood by me any longer.

If this report is to be believed, the critic confessed, with great emotion, that any misunderstandings of Wagner in his reviews were not due to malice but due to the limitations of his own knowledge. He now wished

Wagner to broaden his horizons. Wagner was at once soothing and sympathetic, and great relief and joy spread through Vienna that the two men were now friends. But within a few weeks the revised scenario of *Die Meistersinger* was ready – and the 'marker', that caricature of pedantic imbecility, was now christened 'Hanslich'.

When Standhartner and his family returned to Vienna at the end of September, Wagner moved into a hotel. Lacking the pleasures of Seraphine and now compelled to pay for his keep, he became disenchanted and saw little point in remaining in the town if *Tristan* was doomed to eternal postponement. His thoughts turned to finding a patron and a comfortable refuge to live and work. An appeal to the Grand Duke of Baden for a pension and accommodation in or near Karlsruhe was rejected on the grounds that Wagner would indulge in unwelcome interference with the theatre manager, Devrient. Next, he investigated the estate of Count Nako at Schwarzau and was quite put out when the family hurriedly made it very clear that there was hardly sufficient room for themselves.

With plenty of time on his hands, Wagner decided to work on the German translation of the Paris section of *Tannhäuser*. First, Cornelius volunteered to make a copy of the Venusberg scene as Wagner's original was now very tattered. The original score then disappeared for years, Cornelius having loaned it to Tausig, who took it upon himself to present it to Johannes Brahms. Weissheimer gained possession of the copy made by Cornelius and decided to keep it for himself. The Paris version of *Tannhäuser* had never been printed, so Wagner found himself totally without access to this large amount of music. In 1865 he traced the original to Brahms and demanded its return, pointing out that Tausig had had no authority to make a gift of it. In characteristically boorish fashion, Brahms refused to part with it. The affair dragged on for years, with Brahms ignoring appeal after appeal from Cornelius and Cosima. Eventually, in 1875, Wagner was forced to send Brahms a *de luxe* score of *Rheingold* in exchange for his own property.

On 8 October 1861, the *Oesterreichische Zeitung* published an article by Wagner on a new ballet, *Gräfin Egmont*, which was signed 'P.C.' When Peter Cornelius saw it he was annoyed, but Wagner appeased him with the promise that the fate of *Tristan* depended on the article, which praised the director of the Vienna Opera on his excellent production of the ballet, complimented him on the decision to perform *Tristan* and expressed the hope that another tenor would be found if Ander did not recover.

Cornelius was useful again in obtaining for Wagner the book that was to be his principal historical source for *Die Meistersinger*: Johann Christoph Wagenseil's *Chronicle of the Free City of Nuremberg*, of 1697, which contains an appendix, the *Book of the Mastersingers' most gracious Art*. Wagner's original sketch for a drama on this subject was made in July 1845 and *A Communication to my Friends* contained a lengthy summary of it. In

October 1861 he drafted a new scenario and told the publisher Schott at the end of the month that he could offer him within one year a popular operatic comedy, humorous and light in style, easy to produce, without the need for a Heldentenor or a great tragic soprano. The smallest German theatre would be able to cope with it and any reasonable bass would do for the jovial hero, Hans Sachs.

At a rehearsal with orchestra on 26 October of selected passages from *Tristan*, the players were keen to proceed with the work. Wagner too was delighted with Meyer-Dustmann as Isolde and Marie Destinn as Brangäne. But all his hopes for a suitable tenor and of receiving a fee for the work from the Vienna management had died. An invitation came to join the Wesendoncks who were on holiday in Venice, and Wagner did so on 7 November. In his autobiography he describes 'four dreary days' in Venice with his friends who were 'in very flourishing circumstances' but who did not seem inclined to listen to a recital of his financial woes. Clearly his motive in going to Venice was to assess his chances of another loan from Otto or of returning to the 'Asyl'. Rather than incur Minna's wrath, he did not mention Mathilde to her, but pretended his visit to Venice was with Dr Standhartner who was attending the Empress of Austria there. Otto insisted that Wagner join them in sight-seeing and no doubt the *Meistersinger* plan was discussed with Mathilde, who possessed the original sketch of 1845 which she promised to send to him. On the train journey back to Vienna he conceived the essence of the overture to *Die Meistersinger*, that remarkable and masterly exposition, celebration and combination of the principal melodies of the opera. Without waiting to receive the 1845 scenario from Mathilde Wagner rewrote his sketch afresh on reaching Vienna and appended a number of details concerning the customs and traditions of the Nuremberg Mastersingers, obtained from Wagenseil, with the help of Cornelius. On 19 November he sent the draft to Schott who was greatly interested. On the first day of December Wagner was with the publisher in Mainz; he read the scenario to him and Schott immediately offered him 10,000 francs. From Mainz he headed for Paris in the hope that the Metternichs would accommodate him at the Austrian Embassy, but neither they nor any of his other friends were able to oblige at that time.

It was therefore in a Paris hotel room that the poem of *Die Meistersinger* came to birth. The weeks leading up to its completion on 25 January were charged with that sheer joy in creation that had not possessed him since the completion of the *Tristan* score. Schott too must have been infected with enthusiasm when the eager composer descended on him to read the libretto early in February. Neither man could then foresee that the road towards completion of the score would be an exceedingly long one and that the first performance lay over six years away. The first problem facing Wagner was that of finding a suitable haven in which to compose. It is clear that at that time his arrogant and demanding attitude to his friends alienated many who might have aided him. His treatment of Cornelius is a particularly odious illustration of his selfish insensitivity. The industrious Peter was a man of very limited means and yet Wagner always expected, indeed insisted, that he drop everything and rush to his side at every beck and call. Cornelius did come to the reading at Mainz – all the long way from Vienna in the worst of winter weather, and on borrowed funds. Wagner had asked Cornelius to stay with him permanently so that they could 'belong to each other like a married couple'; he was astonished when, on the morning after the reading, Cornelius hastened straight back to Vienna.

Cornelius had no wish to pin his talents onto Wagner's sleeve; others were more alarmed at the likelihood of being bled of their fortunes. Baron von Hornstein was one, as we learn from *Mein Leben*:

> I thought I was conferring an honour upon him when I wrote to him at Munich asking permission to take up my abode for a time at his place in the Rhine district, and was therefore greatly perplexed when I received an answer expressing terror at my suggestion.

Wagner does not tell us that he had written cavalierly to Hornstein demanding an immediate advance of 10,000 francs, hardly a week after receiving that very amount from Schott. Hornstein had often been the butt of Wagner's rudeness and was determined not to sacrifice such a large sum to a man who would squander it in a matter of days. He informed him that he was not as rich as Wagner seemed to imagine and that there were far wealthier people among his admirers all over Europe to whom he would do better to apply. Perhaps at some future time Wagner could make an extended visit; in the meantime he wished him an early success with *Tristan*. Wagner retorted with an abusive letter of censure. It is his duty to show Hornstein the folly of his ways in rejecting his application; he resents Hornstein's effrontery in giving him any advice as to where to go for money; the refusal to grant him either accommodation or funds is insulting, and he has no interest in expressions of goodwill from people who are completely indifferent to his works. No doubt he felt much the same towards all the others who expressed alarm at his requests for hospitality: the Bülows, Liszt's friend Agnes Street, Cäcilie Avenarius, the Wesendoncks, the Grand Duke of Baden and all his Paris acquaintances politely but firmly refused him.

For a while he considered settling in Wiesbaden, but the eventual choice of residence was Biebrich-am-Rhein which had the advantage of being just across the river from Mainz and his publisher Schott, and was near to such musical centres as Frankfort, Karlsruhe and Darmstadt. He became the tenant of a first floor flat in a villa overlooking the Rhine and his furniture, including the Erard piano, was sent from Paris. On 14 February he wrote to Minna in Dresden telling her of his decision to settle there. In his letter he stressed his need for undisturbed peace and admitted his fear that, were she to join him, the old arguments, disturbances and needless jealousies would once more break out. He asks her to consider carefully whether to come to him and share his life in quiet congenial companionship, or whether to remain in Saxony and let Time heal the wounds of their marriage. Better that they should remain independent and apart rather than allow wretched misunderstandings and reproaches to cloud their lives again. But Minna did not hesitate or stop to think it over: determined to assert her rights as a wife, and without even answering his letter, she arrived at Biebrich one week later.

There ensued 'ten days of hell' as Wagner told Cornelius on 4 March. He welcomed her with tears in his eyes and felt real joy in the hope that she had come to him to share cheerfully in his creative life. The illusion was quickly destroyed. The very next morning, by mischance, he received a letter from Mathilde, followed a day or two later by a box of Christmas presents from her – tea, Eau de Cologne, an embroidered cushion and some pressed violets. They had been redirected from Vienna and delayed owing to Wagner's uncertain whereabouts. Minna at once let fly with accusations and insinuations about the 'love-affair' and regarded this untimely parcel as evidence of a new scandal. She nagged and whimpered and complained until he too lost all his forbearance and self-control and shouted at her furiously. A week of quarrelsome abuse, gloomy mistrust and smouldering resentment dragged by. It was the last and clearest illustration of their utter incompatibility. Even so, Minna returned to Dresden with the stubborn desire that he should follow her there. She was obsessed with the crazy delusion that, despite their irreconcilable differences, his true place was at her side. Tormented by jealousy she remained determined that it was her marital duty to shelter him from the clutches of other women. She was ill and frightened by the daunting prospect of loneliness and rejection, afraid of a future without him and insanely blind to the impossibility of living with him. Above all, she could not bear the thought that without her he could enjoy the fruits of his creations and that life might hold pleasures and rewards for him that she could never enjoy.

Without doubt, a great load of sorrow weighed upon Wagner. He felt immense grief at their separation, but the painful experience of her Biebrich visit finally taught him that his patience and his genuine wish to salvage something from the wreck of his marriage were of no avail. In his sorrow he was faced with three alternatives: petitioning the Saxon King for permission to live with her in Dresden; obtaining an amnesty with a view to visiting her occasionally in Saxony; or obtaining an outright divorce. To join her permanently in Dresden was clearly unthinkable and, on her account, he shrank from the idea of a divorce. The middle course seemed best, and on 25 March he sent Minna a letter addressed to King Johann pleading for amnesty on two counts: first, his need to have access to the Dresden theatre; second, the need for his sick wife to settle there permanently and for him to have access to her. The petition was accompanied by a letter from Pusinelli outlining the history of Minna's health in the last twenty years. Three days later he was pardoned and granted permission to enter Saxony. This decree, which once would have meant so very much to him, now held no joy whatever. It enabled Minna, however, to live in the town of her choice with the degree of respectability that meant so much to her, and it left open the possibility of a reunion. Had she been likely to contemplate divorce then he would certainly have agreed. On 14 June he wrote to Pusinelli asking him to confer with Luise Brockhaus as to the possibility of a complete break with Minna. The doctor consulted Wagner's sister and together they concluded that a divorce would be the best solution. The idea was put to Minna but she rejected it violently. The future of Wagner's marriage was confined to an exchange of letters: kindly and tactful on his part; on hers, reproachful and unforgiving. Now and then the old fond and friendly note sounds for a while, only to wither in a fresh outburst of injured wrath from the pathetic invalid in Dresden.

To Minna, to Malwida and to the world at large, Wagner described Biebrich as a peaceful retreat where he intended to avoid people as much as possible. After all, *Meistersinger* was promised to Schott for September 1861. In fact, from the evidence of his own pen and the accounts of his friends, it would seem that Biebrich witnessed an endless round of social gatherings and intimate soirées, with Wagner basking in the sunshine of friendly adulation and contentedly spending every franc that he could borrow. At the end of March he approached Countess Pourtalès for a loan: she had expressed delight with the *Meistersinger* libretto and at once complied with a gift of 1200 thalers. Work at the score was slow and fitful. The overture was scored by the third week of April, and in May he composed the prelude to Act Three and the 'Wach auf!' chorus. He was considerably distracted by the charms of two young women, Friederike Meyer and Mathilde Maier, both of whom served to compensate for his lonely and loveless state. Friederike was the sister of Luise Meyer-Dustmann, the proposed Viennese Isolde, but had severed all connection with her family and was now living as the mistress of the Frankfort theatre director, who kept her in fine style. Mathilde, on the other hand, was the essence of domesticity and took time off from running her mother's household in Mainz in order to cater for Wagner. Also living in Mainz was Wendelin Weissheimer, currently assistant conductor at the theatre there, who was a regular visitor to Biebrich. According to *Mein Leben*, Weissheimer was anxious that Wagner influence his father in favour of the young man's choice of a musical career. Wagner's encouragement of Weissheimer's modest talents, and even of his compositions, was not unconnected with the fact that Papa Weissheimer was a wealthy farmer. Wagner went so far as to hear a performance of Offenbach's *Orpheus* under his friend:

I was horrified that my sympathy for this young man should make me descend so low as to be present at such an abomination, and for a long time I could not refrain from letting Weissheimer see the annoyance I felt.

Another former acquaintance, the composer Joachim Raff, lived in nearby Wiesbaden. Wagner found himself attracted to the gambling tables of that town, and Weissheimer was astonished at his ability to predict the winning numbers in roulette when others were playing. Fortunately Wagner resisted the temptation of staking anything himself, although he proudly recounts in his autobiography his supernatural feat of winning back a small sum lost on another occasion by Cosima.

The most important guests at Biebrich that summer were Ludwig Schnorr and his wife Malvina. Wagner heard Schnorr for the first time in a performance of *Lohengrin* at Karlsruhe on 26 May. At the singer's first entry Wagner was enraptured with his voice and all his doubts about Schnorr's obesity marring his performance were instantly dispelled. The couple stayed for two weeks by the Rhine and their visit to Wagner coincided with that of Bülow and Cosima. With Bülow at the piano, Wagner guided Schnorr and Malvina through *Tristan*, helping them to overcome the vocal difficulties and physical strain of the work by a deeper understanding of the drama and a clear enunciation of the words. Despite the fact that he was exhausted through overwork, nervous and irritable, Bülow made a copy of the first half of Act One of *Die Meistersinger* which was already sketched. In the presence of Wagner's greatness his own modest talents seemed as nothing. 'With Wagner as a neighbour,' he told Pohl, 'everything else shrivels into insignificance, becomes so puerile, so null and void.' One evening when in particularly exuberant mood Wagner outlined to his friends his plans for works beyond *Die Meistersinger* and the *Ring*, and gave them details of his ideas about *Parsifal* and even *Die Sieger*, as Weissheimer recalled in his memoirs:

> He went on to talk about an Indian subject that fascinated him; but he said that he thought it would hardly come to anything, for he always had the premonition that *Parsifal* would be his last work. He had obviously talked himself into quite a state of emotion. Tears were to be seen on Frau Bülow's face – there was a pause. I slipped out onto the balcony and Hans von Bülow quietly followed me, and whispered the prophetic words: 'However faint the hope, and however slight the prospect of his realizing his plans – you will see, he will attain his goal and achieve even *Parsifal* too.'

Of the many callers that summer – Luise Meyer-Dustmann, Alwine Frommann, Ferdinand David and August Wilhelmj (one day to lead the orchestra at the first Bayreuth Festival) – none surprised Wagner more than August Röckel, recently released from prison. He walked unannounced into the hotel where Wagner was dining with the Bülows, the Schnorrs and other friends, and seemed astoundingly unchanged in appearance despite his thirteen-year incarceration. In addition to all the visitors a painter arrived to execute a portrait of Wagner that had been commissioned by Mathilde Wesendonck. As Wagner found the sittings very tiresome, Cosima sat and read to him. When the time came for the Bülows' departure, Wagner accompanied them as far as Frankfort:

> This time we could take leave of one another cheerfully, although the increasing and often excessive ill-humour of Hans had drawn many an involuntary sigh from me. On the other hand, Cosima seemed to have lost the shyness she had shown towards me in Reichenhall a year before, and a very friendly manner had taken its place. When I was singing Wotan's Farewell to my friends I noticed the same expression on her face as I had seen, to my astonishment, in Zurich on a similar occasion, only the ecstasy of it was now exaltedly transfigured. Everything was veiled in silence and mystery, but the belief that she belonged to me grew to such certainty in my mind that in moments of extraordinary excitement my behaviour became recklessly exuberant. As I was accompanying Cosima to the hotel across a public square, I suddenly suggested that she should sit in an empty wheelbarrow which stood in the street, so that I might wheel her into the hotel. She complied instantly. I was so astonished that I lost all my courage and was unable to carry out my mad scheme. (*Mein Leben*)

One or two things upset Wagner a little during the summer. Rent had to be paid for the nest at Biebrich and his funds were now very low. He continually kept an eye open for free accommodation on some aristocrat's estate and considered for a time a little castle in the grounds of the Duke of Nassau, a medieval tower at Bingen, a property at Rheingau belonging to Count Schönborn and the Metternich's castle of Johannisberg. He was very much put out by the failure of Cornelius and Tausig to respond to an invitation to Biebrich. About eighteen years later, when dictating the appropriate part of his autobiography, the grudge against them was not forgotten.

> Cornelius having accepted immediately, I was the more surprised to get a letter from Geneva, whither Tausig (who suddenly appeared to have funds at his disposal) had carried him off on a summer excursion – which was no doubt more important and pleasanter. Without the least mention of any regret at not being able to meet me that summer, they simply informed me that 'a glorious cigar had just been smoked to my health'. When I met them again in Vienna, I was unable to refrain from pointing out to them the insulting nature of their behaviour; but they seemed unable to comprehend what I could object to in their preferring a beautiful tour of French Switzerland to a visit to me at Biebrich. They obviously considered me a tyrant.

Schott helped finances a little by buying the *Wesendonck Lieder* for 1000 francs, but Wagner grew more and more irritated by his refusal to advance any more for *Die Meistersinger*. Progress with that score halted entirely late in July when Wagner was bitten on the thumb of his right hand by his landlord's bulldog, Leo. For almost two months the resultant swelling made writing impossible. Schott, unmoved by this misfortune, kept his purse shut. He had a good idea of the astonishing speed with which Wagner spent large sums of money. After the summer visit to Biebrich, Bülow wrote to Weissheimer:

> It is incredible how much money he can spend in a fortnight. . . . It puzzles me how he always knows how to get hold of the necessary when it is absolutely essential to him – perhaps he is an even greater genius in matters of finance than he is as a poet and composer.

At the end of August the financial wizard was so hard up that he journeyed to Kissingen to face Schott, who was taking a cure. To Wagner's fury he found the publisher's wife, Frau Betty Schott, posted outside the door of his sickroom like a guardian angel, obstinately refusing him entry. Begging letters failed to soften Schott's heart, so on 20 October he tried a more vigorous attack, accusing Schott himself of responsibility for the delay of *Meistersinger*. The publisher's parsimony and failure to think of Wagner's needs and comforts is ruining the project. He can no longer sleep because of anxiety:

> You are mistaken, my dear Herr Schott, you are greatly mistaken as to the manner in which a man of my type is to be handled. Much can be extorted under pressure of hunger but not works of the higher kind.

Schott's stiff rejoinder to this was simply to point out that not he, but only some enormously rich banker or a prince with millions to spend could provide for Wagner's needs and comforts.

For the first time in his life, Wagner conducted *Lohengrin* in an uncut performance at the Frankfort theatre on 12 September, at the invitation of the manager, Friederike Meyer's lover. He welcomed the chance of once more directing his work in this way, but the prospect of touring as a conductor in order to make ends meet, daunted him. Yet there was no other way out of his financial predicament. Weissheimer had arranged a concert in Leipzig on 1 November, largely to promote himself as conductor and composer. To add lustre to the programme Wagner was invited to conduct the *Tannhäuser* overture and the first performance of the *Meistersinger* overture. Bülow was engaged to play Liszt's Second Piano Concerto and the event was transformed for Wagner by the presence of Cosima, dressed in mourning for her sister Blandine who had died on 11 September. Apart from a few friends and relatives, the hall was empty for the concert – the Leipzigers stayed away *en masse*, and Weissheimer's father had to pay off a large deficit. To help pay Wagner's travelling expenses, Bülow sold a ring that had been presented to him by the Grand Duke of Baden. Wagner's new overture succeeded in winning great approval from both the tiny audience and the orchestra, and was encored.

With no hope of a fee for the concert he found himself penniless at a most inopportune moment: not only was Minna's quarterly allowance due, but the advance rent for another year at Biebrich had to be paid. Fortune smiled, however, in the shape of an unlooked-for gift of 1500 marks from the Grand Duke of Weimar. He was now able to take Minna's money to Dresden in person, and to return to the town he had last seen in the smoke and bloodshed of 1849. Wagner's sister, Klara Wolfram, stayed with Minna during his visit in order to prevent the awkwardness and embarrassment that arose when husband and wife were alone. Minna had done everything to make him comfortable in her new flat: a study and drawing room were provided for his use. Fortunately the four-day visit was largely spent in the company of friends – Pusinelli, Heine, Friedrich Brockhaus and the Schnorrs – and no controversial subjects were aired; nor were there any outbursts of recrimination or opening of old wounds. She accompanied him to the station on the day of his departure, and the moment of parting was cheerless and desolate. Her anguished forebodings proved justified: Richard and Minna never met again.

On reaching Biebrich he managed, with some difficulty, to secure his rooms there for another six months. With some surprise he had learned from Vienna that Ander was fully restored and rehearsals for *Tristan* were to be resumed. Before setting out for Austria he called at Mainz to find Friederike Meyer, now separated from her Frankfort manager; she volunteered to accompany Wagner, and they arrived in Vienna together on 15 November. As soon as Luise Meyer-Dustmann learned that Wagner had brought with him her notorious sister, a new threat to the performance emerged. Meyer-Dustmann had until then been one of Wagner's staunchest supporters in the *Tristan* project. Now that the composer was openly consorting with Friederike, whom she and her family despised and disowned as a kept woman, her commitment to the role of Isolde began to diminish rapidly. It had been Friederike's hope to join the Burgtheater but she failed to secure an engagement. Recent illness and the strains attending her private life had taken their toll on her looks: she was haggard, extremely thin and almost completely bald, but would not wear a wig. Wagner suggested she leave for Venice to recover her health and, to his relief, she agreed. For many months Wagner regretted the loss of his paramour, who would gladly have returned to him, but for the threat of a serious scandal. It was well known in Vienna that Wagner had enjoyed sharing Friederike's money, all provided by her protector in Frankfort. Ultimately, after a disastrous attempt to start her own theatre in Coburg, she returned to the arms of her original lover and played no further part in Wagner's life.

Once rid of his *fille de joie*, Wagner's problems were not at an end. Meyer-Dustmann seemed set to wreck the performance and Ander's fear of the part of Tristan increased daily. It seems that the resurrection of the scheme was due in part to the management's belief that Hanslick now favoured Wagner. When Standhartner arranged a reading of the *Meistersinger* libretto at his home on 23 November, it seemed natural to invite the critic. The character of the marker (later called Beckmesser) was then known as 'Hanslich' and Wagner must have relished the effect that his huge joke would have upon his guest. *Mein Leben* records the scene piously:

> We noticed that as the reading proceeded the dangerous critic became ever paler and more ill at ease, and everyone remarked on the fact that he could not be persuaded to remain after the reading, but took his leave at once in an unmistakably vexed manner. My friends all agreed that Hanslick looked on the whole libretto as a lampoon aimed at himself, and felt our invitation to the reading to be an insult. And undoubtedly the critic's attitude towards me underwent a very remarkable change from that evening. He became uncompromisingly hostile, with results that were obvious to us at once.

As the *Tristan* plan foundered and eventually sank into oblivion owing to Ander's complete loss of voice, Meyer-Dustmann's feigning an illness and the anxiety of the management at such a protracted failure, Wagner turned to concert-giving. It was of paramount importance that his music from *Rheingold* onwards be heard, even in concert version, in order to counteract the damaging but widespread rumour that his works since *Lohengrin* were simply unperformable. In November 1862 Marie Kalergis secured an invitation for a concert tour of Russia. At the same time Wagner planned some concerts for Vienna. Copyists were soon busy preparing selections from *Rheingold*, *Walküre* and parts of *Meistersinger* and *Siegfried* – Cornelius, Tausig, Weissheimer and Brahms all shared in the work. Two concerts at the Theater an der Wien, on 26 December and 1 January 1863, proved immensely popular but financially disastrous. The Empress of Austria was present at the second, and at a third on 8 January which Wagner gave in a futile attempt to cover his losses. True to form, he gave a magnificent dinner for his friends and performers, in spite of the deficit. In compensation, he was rewarded by the obvious artistic success, by a gift of 1000 gulden from the Empress, and with a profit of another 1000 gulden when he gave a Wagner concert in Prague on 8 February. In Prague Wagner met a friend of his youth, Marie Löwe-Lehmann, who had retired as a singer and now played the harp, and her pretty teenage daughter, Lilli Lehmann.* Fifty years later Lilli wrote of her terror at seeing Wagner for the first time – dressed in a yellow damask dressing gown, pink tie and black velvet cloak with rose satin lining.

The Russian visit was a triumph. Three concerts in St Petersburg (the first on 3 March), consisting of Beethoven symphonies and extracts from his own operas, were repeated in Moscow to great acclaim. He returned to St Petersburg for two benefit concerts – one for himself, which was poorly attended, and one in aid of those imprisoned for debt, which was completely sold out. Among the many members of the Russian aristocracy who befriended him, the Grand Duchess Helene showed especial interest by sitting through four readings of the *Ring* poems and presenting him with 1000 roubles. He returned to Vienna with a very considerable profit. Astonishingly this tidy sum of roubles, quite sufficient to have bought him two modestly comfortable years in which to complete *Meistersinger*, was squandered in a matter of weeks.

He decided to give up his quarters at Biebrich and have his furniture removed to Penzing, a suburb of Vienna, where he acquired the upper part of a large house at a rent of 2400 marks per year. The décor and furnishings were on the most lavish scale. From an account he sent to Mathilde Maier we learn that the dining room was dark brown with little rosebuds, the work room glossy lilac with garnet-coloured velvet drapery bordered with gold, the study matt brown-grey with lilac flowers and dark brown velvet drapery, the tea-room glossy green with violet drapery bordered with gold, the bedroom glossy lilac with green velvet drapery and gold borders, and so on throughout each of a dozen rooms: an orgy of colour, festooned with satin curtains, portières, soft deep carpets, and sofas, armchairs and cushions to match. The light hangings cast a dim and delicate radiance; the maid was fitted with pink knee-breeches and had to be exquisitely perfumed. A seamstress, Bertha Goldwag, carried out his wishes to the last detail and provided him with twenty-four dressing gowns, a quantity of silk suits, all lined with fur and in a variety of colours, with slippers and neckties to blend. In addition to the pretty maid he employed two servants, Franz and Anna Mrazek. An extensive garden came with the property and a wine cellar which he stocked with a fine and ample supply. In such comfort he celebrated his fiftieth birthday: he was serenaded with a torchlight procession by local choral societies, and wined and dined in splendour with Tausig, Cornelius, Standhartner and the Prague musician Heinrich Porges, who all marvelled at his lordly way of life.

Only the occasional unhappy letter of reproach from poor Minna reminded him of the harsh outside world. He wrote to Natalie with the suggestion that even their correspondence should cease. To his Dresden relations he described his life as nothing but work and loneliness. But to Mathilde Maier he painted a very different picture; that of his luxurious home in which he longed for her to join him in love and devotion. When she declined to accept he turned instead to the feminine charms of the two daughters of a local pork butcher. To complete his domestic happiness he adopted an elderly dog named Pohl.

He had turned his thoughts again to the *Meistersinger* score, but before long the spectre of poverty hovered before him. He had exhausted all the income from his Russian tour and in order to maintain his life-style in Penzing more fund-raising concerts were essential. In July he gave two concerts in Pest where the Hungarians received him enthusiastically, and he netted 1000 gulden. For part of the summer he was engaged on a substantial article on *The Vienna Court Opera House* which contained sensible suggestions for improving the standards of German opera, but which, like all his other efforts towards theatrical reform, was ignored.

Two unprofitable concerts in Prague, early in November, inaugurated another concert tour. At Karlsruhe he was greeted by a number of friends, notably Marie Kalergis, who, by a recent marriage, was now Frau Muchanoff. She introduced him to the Russian writer Ivan Turgenev who professed to admire the Wagnerian orchestral extracts, but could not stand the singing. The Grand Duke and Duchess of Baden were present, together with Queen Augusta of Prussia. With his share of the Karlsruhe profits Wagner bought a fur coat. It cost 220 marks, and when he pointed out that his takings were only 200 marks the extra twenty were knocked off the price. From Karlsruhe Wagner visited the Wesendoncks in Zurich and asked for a loan. He met with no response, and fared little better at his next port of call, Mainz, with the publisher Schott. He had planned to visit Minna in Dresden but chose instead to head for Berlin and the hospitality of the Bülows. While Hans was rehearsing, Wagner and Cosima went for a drive. *Mein Leben* describes this profound and decisive moment in their lives:

> This time our jesting died away in silence. We gazed speechless into each other's eyes; an intense longing for an avowal of the truth overpowered us and led to a confession, which needed no words, of the boundless unhappiness that weighed upon us. With tears and sobs we sealed our confession to belong to each other alone.

By selling a gold snuff-box presented to him one week before by the Grand Duke of Baden, Wagner realized 270 marks, and set out for Löwenburg where he was to conduct the private orchestra of the Prince of Hohenzollern-Hechigen. The prince was an enthusiastic patron of new music and entertained Wagner with the same warm hospitality which Berlioz had enjoyed on his visit to the Silesian estate six months before. He presented Wagner with a generous fee of 4200 marks and apologized that economic circumstances prevented it being larger. More delightful still was the presence at Löwenburg of Henriette von Bissing, a wealthy widow and sister of his close friend of the Swiss years, Eliza Wille. She lent a sympathetic ear to his complaints about the cruelties of life – how an artist like himself seemed unwanted by the world – and promised to provide for his needs so that the hardships of concert touring would no longer be necessary. He in turn hinted at a proposal of marriage.

In cheerful mood Wagner returned to Vienna on 9 December. Although he had little to show for his tour – Minna's allowance and the settlement of debts exhausted the prince's gift – he looked forward to a bright future. On Christmas Eve he threw a lavish party for his friends, giving each of them what his autobiography calls 'an appropriate trifle' from his Christmas tree. From a letter of Cornelius's we know that he alone received a heavy overcoat, an elegant dressing gown, a scarf, a waistcoat, a cigar case and tinder box, silk handkerchiefs, gold shirt studs, pen wipers embossed with gold mottoes, cravats, a cigar-holder engraved with his initials, a leather purse containing a silver thaler, a sash and other 'trifles'!

On 27 December he collaborated with Tausig for a concert in Vienna, but was forced to ask Tausig to endorse a note for him – an action that was to have serious repercussions for the young pianist. As the year 1864 opened Wagner began to be frightened by the consequences of his wild extravagance. He had pinned his hopes on another profitable Russian tour, but owing to the delay of a letter arranging this, the whole venture collapsed. He began to borrow frantically. Henriette von Bissing was his other hope, but she, having heard the worst reports of his profligacy, suddenly withdrew her offer of help. Ruin seemed inevitable: not only was his property at Penzing endangered but there was every likelihood of a court action leading to debtor's jail. He wrote to Eliza Wille asking her to persuade the Wesendoncks to allow him to escape to the 'Asyl', but again Otto declined to help. He then begged the Grand Duchess Helene of Russia to pay at least Minna's pension. She apparently complied. One of Wagner's last social evenings in Vienna was spent in the unlikely company of Brahms. At that time the two men seemed to get on pleasantly enough, although their ideas were remote indeed. After Brahms played his 'Handel Variations' Wagner remarked that 'one can see what can still be done with the old forms in the hands of one who knows how to deal with them'.

But all the social pleasantries of Vienna were over for Wagner. His staggeringly extravagant behaviour of the past year was perhaps the desperate gesture of a middle-aged man anxious to show the world that he counted for much more than it was willing to credit. It was a gesture doomed to failure, for no one, no prince, no banker, was willing to indulge his luxuries. Wagner escaped from Vienna on 23 March and aimed for Switzerland via Munich. The Bavarian capital was in mourning for King Maximilian II and Wagner noticed a portrait of the new young king, Ludwig II, in a shop window. Eliza Wille harboured Wagner at Mariafeld for the month of April. He cannot have been an easy guest: a severe cold aggravated his condition of despair; just as in 1849, he had burned his boats and was, as then, a wanted man. None of his works since that date had reached the stage and there was little hope that they ever would, or that he would ever find the means to complete *Meistersinger*, let alone the *Ring*. 'Only a miracle can save me now,' he wrote to Cornelius.

> My situation is extremely perilous. It is most delicately balanced: a single jolt – and all is over, and nothing more can ever come out of me, nothing, nothing! A *light* must show itself; a *man* must arise who will give me energetic assistance now . . .

Ten

Rescue

In the year of the first performance of my *Tannhäuser* (the work with which I first entered my new and thorny path), in the month in which I felt impelled to such excessive productivity that I sketched *Lohengrin* and *Meistersinger* at the same time, a mother bore my guardian angel . . .

> Wagner to Elize Wille
> 26 May 1864

LUDWIG FRIEDRICH WILHELM OF BAVARIA was born on 25 August 1845, a few weeks before the first *Tannhäuser* performance. In the following year, his grandfather, King Ludwig I, commenced a scandalous affair with the pseudo-Spanish dancer and adventuress Lola Montez,* who counted Liszt among her previous conquests. The sentimental old King, who was a zealous patron of the arts and who created nineteenth-century Munich, not only ennobled Lola as the Countess Landsfeld, but fell so completely under her spell as to allow his temptress virtually to dictate affairs of state. A constitutional crisis ensued, and amid scenes of uproar remarkable even for that tempestuous year 1848, Lola was driven from the city and Ludwig abdicated in favour of his son Maximilian. The baby Ludwig was now Crown Prince. An abnormally sensitive child, he soon showed a keen interest in the arts, and the universal childhood pastime of building with toy bricks held an unusual attraction for the future creator of Neuschwanstein, Linderhof and Herrenchiemsee. Holidays were spent at the castle of Hohenschwangau, restored by his father, where the walls were painted with scenes from the legends of Tannhäuser, Lohengrin and the Grail. Ludwig immersed himself in German mythology and in particular with the tales of the Swan Knights and their contests. The symbol of the swan pervaded Hohenschwangau and captivated the boy who would seal his letters with the sign of a cross and a swan.

In February 1858 his governess attended the Munich premiere of Wagner's *Lohengrin* and infected her twelve-year-old pupil with an enthusiastic account of it. That Christmas he received from his tutor a copy of *Opera and Drama*, and before long he read and memorized the libretti of *Tannhäuser*, *Lohengrin* and, later, Wagner's other dramas. In February 1861 he heard *Lohengrin* for the first time and was so overwhelmed that he cajoled his father into ordering another performance in the following June in which Schnorr sang the title role. In December 1862 he heard his first *Tannhäuser*. A year later the poem of *Der Ring des Nibelungen* was published, and like all Wagner's available works it was acquired by the eager young prince. This 1863 edition was prefaced by an essay in which Wagner outlined his plan for a Stage Festival in a specially built auditorium in the shape of an amphitheatre, with the orchestra invisible to the audience, in order to create the perfect illusion and an excellent acoustical balance of singers and instrumentalists. His *Ring* tetralogy cannot be conceived in the debased, conventional repertory theatres, but only in the conditions of such a festival, which would be able to utilize the finest singers from all over Germany. Only a German prince could find the means to make this plan a reality:

> By this act he would found an institution which would assuredly earn him an immeasurable influence on German artistic taste, on the development of the German artistic genius, on the formation of a true, not an illusory, national spirit, and which would bestow eternal renown on his name.
>
> Is such a prince to be found?

In February 1864 Albert Niemann sang *Lohengrin* and *Tannhäuser* in Munich and was summoned by Ludwig to the palace, and presented with gifts and tokens of royal esteem.

On 10 March King Maximilian died and Ludwig II, not yet nineteen, was proclaimed King. One of his first thoughts was to summon Richard Wagner to his court. A rumour reached him that Wagner had been seen in Munich, and one day his Cabinet Secretary, Franz Seraph von Pfistermeister,* found the King searching the town's Strangers' List. He told Pfistermeister that he was looking for Wagner. As Wagner was a very common name, his Secretary asked which Wagner the King had in mind. The young monarch replied that for him there was only one Wagner – Richard Wagner, the composer – and he instructed Pfistermeister to search for him and bring him to Munich at once. On 14 April Pfistermeister began his quest which led him first to the house in Penzing. There he found Franz and Anna Mrazek who told him that their master had left three weeks before, and they could not say where he had gone. All Wagner's furniture had been sold, but he noted one hundred bottles of champagne in the cellar which had not been taken by the creditors. Presumably it was thought that these belonged to someone else, and not to a bankrupt like Wagner. Pfistermeister telegraphed Ludwig with news of Wagner's disappearance. The King replied on the 17th:

> The contents of your telegram horrify me! My resolution is quickly taken: go after R. Wagner as swiftly as possible, if you can do so without attracting attention. I hope this will be possible; it is of the utmost importance to me that this long-cherished wish of mine shall soon be gratified.

The Cabinet Secretary, in his new, unaccustomed role as detective, learned that Wagner had fled to Switzerland. He returned to Munich and, after a delay owing to court mourning for Princess Augusta, resumed his search on 30 April. Information from Wagner's friends led him to Mariafeld where he discovered that the elusive composer had only just left. His stay there had ended when François Wille returned from a trip to Constantinople and made it clear that Wagner could not be harboured indefinitely at his estate. Now hot on the trail, Pfistermeister proceeded to Stuttgart.

On the evening of 2 May, Wagner was at the home of the Stuttgart Kapellmeister, Karl Eckert,* when a card was handed to him with the inscription 'Secretary to the King of Bavaria'. Convinced that this was the ruse of some creditor, and alarmed that his whereabouts were no longer secret, Wagner gave word that he was not there. On returning to his hotel he found that the suspicious stranger had been making inquiries of the landlord, and had asked to see Wagner on urgent business. His doom appeared to be sealed, so, with great reluctance he made an appointment for the next morning at ten, and spent a night disturbed with worry.

At the subsequent interview Pfistermeister confirmed his credentials with a letter from King Ludwig and gifts of a ring and a royal portrait. He begged Wagner to accompany him to Munich at once. Before leaving Stuttgart an amazed and delighted Wagner lunched with Karl Eckert and Weissheimer. During the meal a telegram was handed to Eckert which announced the death of Meyerbeer in the early hours of the previous day. Two such decisive tidings of Fate within a few hours greatly affected Wagner. He wrote in rapture to his new-found prince and saviour:

> Beloved, gracious King!
> I send you these tears of the most heavenly emotion, to tell you that now the marvels of poetry have entered as a divine reality into my poor, loveless life. That life, all the poetry and all the music contained in it, belongs henceforth to you, my gracious young King: dispose of it as your own!
> In utmost ecstasy, faithful and true,
> Your subject,
> Richard Wagner   *Stuttgart, 3 May 1864*

That evening he travelled with Pfistermeister by train to Munich. The first audience was arranged for the following afternoon.

It has been speculated that Ludwig's ministers may have actively encouraged his adoption of Wagner in the hope that the dreamy lad, lost in ecstatic worship of his friend, would be diverted from interfering with their political schemes. They may have been encouraged in this hope by what they knew of his boyhood characteristics, for he was unquestionably a romantic, highly sensitive and shy. His very youth led not only the politicians, but older members of his family such as ex-King Ludwig and the Grand Duke of Hesse, to hope that he might be easily manoeuvred and manipulated. They were very quickly divested of these ambitions for, from the moment he ascended the throne, Ludwig displayed an authority of command, a sureness of judgment and a determination to rule firmly that astonished all. One of the first misconceptions about Ludwig that must be corrected is that he was a weak ruler. As sovereign, his sense of duty and his ability to take political decisions were above question. Bismarck, a well-qualified judge of statesmanship by any standards, had a high regard for Ludwig's political judgment.

Another error is the notion that he allowed his devotion to Wagner to influence the practical responsibilities of his office. He was in fact no more Wagner's puppet than that of the politicians. On matters concerning artistic ideals, he and Wagner were of one accord, but at no time did Wagner's political views sway him, except perhaps when Wagner exhorted him to have courage or, in friendly wise, urged him not to lose faith in himself. There is no doubt that he drew immense consolation throughout his reign from Wagner's art, and that he regarded his ability to help Wagner as one of the highest joys of his life. At times he would gladly have abdicated and thrown away the cares of kingship for his love of art. But he never did so. He found instead that Wagner's operas gave him renewed strength to turn again to affairs of state. To his shy, lonely, sensitive personality, many of his activities and obligations as King were abhorrent, and he felt a strong urge to withdraw into himself. This tendency towards isolation was most strongly accentuated in later years when, as his repugnance for politics, paper-work and public gatherings grew, his eccentricities became more marked.

The Ludwig that Wagner met in May 1864 was not the so-called 'mad king' of later years: the builder of fairy tale castles or the recluse who took nocturnal sleigh rides in the Alps. Nor was it Wagner who turned him into such a figure. He was, at the time of their first encounter, a strongly individual young man with a staunch conviction of the ideals and duties of kingship. He already had a vision of his divine mission as a leader of the German people. He was heir to the great traditions of his ancient family line, and shared with his predecessors an instinctive feeling for the essence of kingship and the character of the monarchy which they had preserved and fostered. In befriending what he saw to be the greatest figure in contemporary art he displayed the hereditary trait that led his father and grandfather to patronize painters, sculptors, architects, poets and scientists. In Wagner, in Wagner's composite art, he found confirmation of his inner beliefs. To claim that Wagner manipulated or perverted or weakened the King's character is nonsense: he was but a mirror of one aspect of Ludwig's complex soul. Wagner and all he stood for formed part of Ludwig's already nurtured vision of Germany – her heritage, her folk-soul and his own place as one of her princes – so to claim that Wagner was a 'bad influence' on the King is to miss the point. Before they even met, Wagner was an outer manifestation of Ludwig's deepest held spiritual hopes and aspirations. Of course Wagner the man subsequently pervaded Ludwig's private life; and to imagine Ludwig without Wagner is as impossible as the earth without the sun. In the story of Wagner's life, Ludwig's importance lies in his great act of patronage: he gave Wagner the means (almost 1,000,000 marks in fact) to complete his life's work, his later music-dramas and the establishment of Bayreuth. It can be left to the biographer of Ludwig to explain the reasons for his attraction to Wagner from his tenderest boyhood. But there can be no doubt that in his kingship and in his patronage of Wagner, Ludwig pursued two independent courses and, in doing so, displayed enormous courage and strength of mind in the face of criticism, malicious gossip and the overwhelming temptation to throw his crown aside.

The King's homosexual character must be mentioned here before continuing the narrative, as it has frequently, perhaps inevitably, been linked with his friendship for Wagner. In a note made in 1873 Wagner wrote that 'There is one thing about the Greeks we will never be able to understand, a thing that separates them utterly from us: their love – pederasty.' At no time did Wagner indulge in or show any leanings towards a homosexual relationship. Among his closest friends, though, there were several homosexuals, notably Ernst Kietz, Karl Ritter and, later, Paul Joukowsky. As an experienced man of the world, connected from earliest youth with artistic and theatrical circles and never burdened with bourgeois morality or the confines of any religious dogma, Wagner displayed a tolerance towards the subject that was not characteristic of his era. It did not trouble him greatly to know what pleasures or what modes of behaviour the sexual temperament of his friends led them to pursue. His own reputation until the time of the call to Munich was as something of a womanizer. Heinrich Esser wrote to Schott in March 1863:

> If he starts a new love affair in every town he happens to visit, that's his business, and nothing to do with me. Perhaps his tender heart is incapable of resisting the eccentric, enthusiastic ladies who throw themselves at him, and with all my heart I wish him joy in the soft embraces of so many gentle arms.

After he was established as the favourite of the Bavarian King, speculation crept abroad that he might have experienced a sexual reorientation. This was never more than malicious gossip, but the causes behind it deserve examination. Firstly, as Wagner grew older his passion for dressing up in silks and furs and his fondness for exotic perfumes increased and came as a gift to gleeful satirists and cartoonists. Far from being mere effeminate affectations, these indulgences were part of his psychological need for luxury and comfort when composing. His mode of dress was never orthodox: radiant colours, sumptuous fabrics and delicate scents stimulated the strongly erotic element in him, created the illusion of voluptuous well-being and induced a rich and sensual aura of nestled comfort which he apparently found necessary to encourage creativity. The smooth texture of silk suited his abnormally sensitive skin and the perfumes, necessarily strong on account of his habitual snuff-taking, bestowed a benign and rosy freshness. To the irreverent these indulgences were evidence of an unwholesome, foppish and degenerate personality and it was easy to deride and jeer at such an unconcealed exhibition of apparent moral decay. In 1877 an unscrupulous Viennese journalist obtained and published Wagner's letters to his Putzmacherin (milliner), Bertha Goldwag, after an unsuccessful attempt to blackmail Wagner into buying them back. Brahms was instrumental in encouraging this base act of public mockery: by some low means he came to possess the Putzmacherin letters and gloated over such a valuable trophy with which to make merry at Wagner's expense.

The style of Wagner's correspondence with Ludwig, at a first glance, might give a misleading impression of their exact relationship. Today, the flowery, high-flown terms of endearment, the protestations of undying love and exuberant confessions of mutual affection seem to be unbearably affected and sentimental. From the first to the last of their hundreds of letters, both men consciously adopted a romantic, lofty, almost otherworldly tone of address which mirrored the exalted nature of the great task to which they were pledged. As Newman has pointed out, the modern reader of these letters in English translation must bear in mind the conventions of the period, the language and the peculiar circumstances of the artist and the young King. Apparent expressions of ardent love did not imply the connotations of physical attachment that we are tempted to read into them. Ludwig was not in love with Wagner in the physical sense. He worshipped Wagner the artist and revered as a hero the creator of *Lohengrin* and *Tannhäuser*, but had no illusions about the less attractive features of Wagner the man. It is in this sense that Wagner's account of his first audience with the King should be understood. He wrote to Eliza Wille on 4 May:

> He loves me with the intensity and fire of first love: he knows everything about me and all my works, and understands me like my own soul. He wants me to stay near him always, to work, to rest, to have my works performed; he wants to give me everything I shall need for that purpose; I must finish the 'Nibelungen' and he will have it performed as I want.

When he described this first meeting to Mathilde Maier as 'a love scene both seemed unwilling to end', he was still intoxicated with the joy of his extraordinary change of fortune. The rescue has all the charm and unreality of a fairy tale: Ludwig was regarded, not only by Wagner but by his subjects generally, as the personification of the romantic ideal of kingship. He was tall, strong and handsome; indeed a veritable Prince Charming. The older man cannot have foreseen the young King's future of pathetic and unhappy relationships with a succession of equerries, soldiers and actors, but he probably realized that the youth had an unusual sensitivity, an abnormally feminine emotional nature that would require delicate and careful handling.

Rescue

It was not until the breakdown of his engagement to Duchess Sophie in Bayern, in 1867, that serious speculation began as to the King's real nature. At that time Wagner, who understood his friend thoroughly, counselled him with tact, wisdom and affectionate concern. As the years passed by and circumstances kept Wagner apart from him, the King followed his true inclinations and indulged in a series of passionate relationships with members of his all-male retinue. If his posthumously published diaries are to be believed, they confirm that these 'falls' were frequent, and that he was constantly racked by guilt, regret and anguished self-reproach. He was by nature deeply religious, and by breeding unable to come to terms with his own temperament. Whatever joy he found in his various attachments was quickly replaced by a pathetic frenzy of anguished regret. He continually struggled against the sensual part of his nature and, in despair, he would look to Wagner's works for strength and fortitude. Like Tannhäuser, he was torn between penitence and the sensuous pleasures of love lust. At an early point in their relationship Wagner realized Ludwig's dependence upon his art: it was not Wagner himself, but the ideal world manifested in his works that Ludwig saw as the way to salvation. The tragedy of the King's life was not caused by Wagner, but was the result of the conflict between the ideal world of Ludwig's imagination and the real world in which he had to live and rule. Had circumstances unfolded differently, had some wise hand prevented the separation of the two men, had their mutual artistic plans been allowed to develop as projected in their eager, dream-like early meetings, then Ludwig's fate might have been very different. His lonely path, his growing isolation and his tragic death in the cold dark waters of Lake Starnberg were ultimately the result of the total failure of the court camarilla, the politicians, the journalists and the gossips, to understand either man correctly. Not Wagner's ambitions, nor Ludwig's eccentricity, but the campaigns and conspiracies of lesser men sealed the King's doom.

While admitting that Wagner and Ludwig did not have an overtly homosexual relationship of the ordinary kind, certain writers have concluded that Ludwig's attraction to Wagner's work was on account of its alleged homosexual content.[1] Having seized upon the fact that Wagner's nickname for Ludwig was 'Parzival', they conclude that his last opera was written specifically to pander to his patron's sexual predilections. This is an inversion of the truth, for if anything, it was from, not for, sex that Ludwig turned to Wagner. To pursue such a line of thought is merely to keep alive the discredited notion that Wagner was a cunning, calculating tormentor of the young King's mind. From all that follows of the Wagner story, with which the fate of his adoring benefactor is so closely inter-

---

[1] For example, R. Gutman (see Bibliography) finds an 'aura of homosexuality vibrating throughout' *Tristan*, and also concludes that 'the opulent art of *Parsifal* grew from hatred, from growing impotence, and an ever more disturbing sexual ambiguity'.

wrought, the reader is free to judge whether Ludwig's devotion was the result of mystical idealism or moral perversion.

The King described Wagner's reaction to his promise to provide the means for the completion and performance of the *Ring*, in a letter to his cousin Sophie:

> He bowed low over my hand and seemed moved by what was so natural; he remained a long time in that position, without saying a word. I had the impression that our roles were reversed. I stooped down to him and drew him to my heart with the feeling that I was taking an oath to be true to him until the end of time.

On the day after the first audience he wrote to Wagner:

> Rest assured that I will do everything in my power to make up to you for what you have suffered in the past. The petty cares of everyday life I will banish from you for ever; I will enable you to enjoy the peace you have longed for, so that you will be able to spread the mighty wings of your genius undisturbed in the pure air of your rapturous art! Though you did not know it, you were the *sole source of my joys* from my earliest boyhood, my friend who spoke to my heart as *no other* could, my best teacher and mentor.

What particularly delighted Wagner was that Ludwig had no official post or duties in mind; he did not intend to appoint him his Kapellmeister, but was to leave him free to create as his own master.

The King's first gift was of 4000 florins with which to settle his most outstanding debts. Wagner left for Vienna where he vented his fury on his friends for having sold all his possessions to his creditors. It was a characteristically ugly failing of his not to see that his friends had acted as wisely as they could in difficult circumstances which were really no concern of theirs. Instead, he raged and stormed at the loss of his furniture, including the Erard piano. Rather than buy another, he persuaded Bechstein, through Bülow, to part with one of his. His first concern was not to honour all his debts, but to keep the knowledge of Ludwig's patronage secret for as long as possible. His Vienna friends were told not to spread a word of it. Despite the gift of 4000 florins and the promise of a salary of 4000 florins per annum he told Minna that his allowance was a mere 1200 florins and that for the moment Dr Pusinelli would have to help him out with her quarterly allowance. He also kept quiet about a gift of 20,000 florins from the King on 10 June.

He returned from Vienna with his dog and his servants, the Mrazeks, and settled in the Villa Pellet near the King's summer residence, Schloss Berg on Lake Starnberg, on 14 May. Each day the royal carriage called for him and he would spend hours of rapture discussing art with Ludwig. They evolved a plan of action for the coming years: in 1865 *Tristan* and *Meistersinger* would be produced; in 1867–8 the *Ring*; in 1869–70 *Die Sieger*; and in 1871–2, *Parsifal*; 1873 would see 'my happy death', wrote Wagner. In October 1864, an official contract was drawn up whereby Wagner would complete the *Ring* within three years. He was to be paid 30,000 florins, in instalments, and the manuscripts and performing rights would be the property of the King. Ludwig would also have the right to decide when, where and how the works would be produced. Wagner had no worries over this last condition: after all, he and the King were of one mind in agreeing that a new, ideal theatre had to be created. The sum of 15,000 florins was paid to him at once and, in the same month of October, the King gave him 40,000 florins as a personal gift. Not including gifts of property, furniture, removal expenses and other sundries Wagner received 75,000 florins all told in the first six months of his friendship with the King. Yet to Minna he described the rumours of his high income as 'malicious' and 'crazily exaggerated'. In October he admitted to her that his annual income would be 4000 florins, but he did not mention the other gifts he had received. Even 4000 florins was a very large salary in Bavaria at that time; 75,000 florins was a simply staggering sum.

Everything augured well: Pfistermeister as yet displayed no ill-will; the press, the politicians and the older members of the royal family all seemed pleased that the new King had found a cause that brought him such joy. There are ominous words, however, in Wagner's earliest letters from Starnberg. To Eliza Wille he confidently claimed:

> Gradually everyone will come to love me, and even now the young King's immediate entourage are glad to discover and know that I am *what* I am, for everyone sees that my enormous influence on the mind of this prince can only do good and can do no one any harm.

Yet to Weissheimer he admitted:

> You can imagine the prodigious envy I have to face: my influence on the young King is so great that all who do not know me are very uneasy. The large salary that the King has settled on me will therefore be designedly given as less than it actually is.

Such boastful claims concerning the extent of his influence on the King's mind, and the public outcry when the extent of Wagner's salary became known, were to contribute to his undoing.

As soon as he was settled in the Villa Pellet, Wagner began to invite, or rather summon, his friends. The call went out to Eliza Wille and her family, to Heinrich Porges, to Cornelius, to Klindworth, to the Bülows, and to Mathilde Maier. He was lonely in his ivory tower and unable to understand why his friends did not run to his side at once. That Cornelius should refuse on the grounds that he wished to finish his opera *Der Cid*, irked him considerably, as is clear from a letter of 31 May:

> I have told you again and again that I have carefully made all arrangements here for your reception. We two, and others as well, could live together here side by side, quite independent of each other, each free to follow his work or his whim, and yet with the ever-present possibility of enjoying each other's society at any

moment. Your piano, which would not disturb me, stands ready; there is a box full of cigars in your room, etc. This, my dear Peter, *is ardour*! It demands a response or – the wind will blow from another quarter! You have sent me not one line in answer to all mine, and yet you get H. Porges to tell me that you are sorry you cannot come, that you intend to revise your *Cid* during the next three months, and must therefore remain in Vienna. Now, which is better, dear Peter, – that we should discuss this curious behaviour – or say nothing? I am almost inclined to think it is better to say nothing, for obviously there is something hidden here that will not be made clearer by discussion but, on the contrary is likely to be distorted and blurred.

After pointing out that this is not the first time that Peter has disturbed him by declining his favours, he continues:

Your present behaviour is (in view of the warmth of my feelings) nothing short of wounding – and so I feel it already. Therefore, my dear Peter, do not take it amiss if I tell you of the irrevocable conclusion to which my conflicting feelings have brought me. Either you accept my invitation immediately and settle down with me for the rest of your life in a sort of domestic treaty – or you scornfully reject my proposal, and so expressly renounce the wish to unite your lot with mine. In the latter case I, for my part, renounce you wholly and finally, and in future will cease to consider you in any way in planning my life.

But Peter was not to be moved. He knew that in Wagner's company he could not create anything, but would be compelled to be an intellectual lap dog. On 11 June Wagner made a three-day visit to Vienna to pay off his most clamorous creditors with some of the 20,000 florins he had received from the King the day before. He took the opportunity to pour out the phials of his wrath upon poor Porges – Cornelius taking care to avoid him in such a dangerously irascible mood. It is sad to observe that his new-found fortune had made him even more tyrannical.

A few days after Wagner's return to Starnberg, Ludwig left Schloss Berg for several weeks. In his desolation Wagner wrote to Mathilde Maier on 22 June, imploring her to join him on any conditions. He must have a woman to look after his household. Three days later he wrote again enclosing a letter for Mathilde's mother which begged her to send her daughter to him: she is the only woman who can redeem his life. Then, suddenly, on 29 June, another letter followed, asking her not to come after all: he could never allow her to enter into a relationship that might be emotionally disastrous, and might bring unendurable grief upon him. The reason for this unexpected and casual dismissal of Mathilde was the arrival at Starnberg that very day of Frau Cosima von Bülow, with a servant and her two daughters, Daniela and Blandine.

Cosima had arrived without her husband who was unable to join Wagner until 7 July. Fifty years later, at a court hearing to determine the paternity of her daughter, Isolde (born 12 April 1865), Cosima testified that from 12 June to 12 October 1864 she had lived in intimate relations with no one but Wagner. There is no doubt Isolde was Wagner's child. What is unclear is whether Bülow was aware or unaware, or simply unable to face up to the reality of Wagner's parentage. At the 1914 hearing the servant Anna Mrazek testified that during Bülow's stay at the Villa Pellet, Cosima shared his bedroom. It is possible that Bülow actually convinced himself that the child was his own, and certainly he never admitted otherwise to the world, but when Cosima became pregnant he must have known the truth of the matter, if her 1914 testimony is true. In a letter to Raff of August 1866 Bülow admitted that 'from February 1865 I was in no doubt whatever as to the rottenness of things'. He was a very sick man when he arrived at Starnberg where both the emotional atmosphere and the unseasonable chilly weather worsened his condition. On Ludwig's return to Berg, Bülow was summoned to play to him and was granted the honour of dining alone with the King. In addition he joined in music making at the Villa Pellet with Klindworth who had just arrived from London. Wagner and Ludwig were anxious to secure Bülow's services as conductor in Munich; Wagner himself did not relish the task and was unwilling to entrust his works to Kapellmeister Lachner or his assistants. The post of Court Pianist was created for him at a salary of 2000 florins.

Bülow was in a sorry state of health and broken nerves when given this news. Paralysed temporarily in both legs and one arm he left Starnberg for a Munich hotel on 19 August, in order to recuperate. At the same time, Cosima left for Karlsruhe where Liszt was attending a music festival. She discussed the King's offer to Hans with her father, and his dangerous illness; she may also have given her father some hint of her relationship with Wagner. On 28 August Liszt and his daughter arrived in Munich to see the sick man, and the following day Cosima went to Starnberg to fetch Wagner. He came to the capital and persuaded Liszt to stay overnight at the Villa Pellet. His old friend complied, no doubt curious to see at first hand Wagner's new station in life. On this short visit the two men resumed their mutual interest in each other's work – the completed sections of *Meistersinger* and Liszt's *Christus* were eagerly scanned. Next day, 31 August, Liszt returned to Munich and Wagner joined him there on 2 September, perhaps in order to see Cosima once more before she returned to Berlin with Hans and the children.

Wagner's pen was busy throughout the summer of 1864. Ludwig had requested a summary of how Wagner's views on politics and religion had changed since his writings of 1849–51. His answer came in the form of a long essay, *On State and Religion*, which Wagner presented to him on 16 July. It is not known how much sense Ludwig extracted from this example of his protégé's graceless and wandering prose, but he no doubt noted Wagner's assertion that he had 'never descended to the arena of Politics proper': a disclaimer intended no doubt for the eyes of the court. The bulk of the essay is a metaphysical improvisation on the theme of the supreme ideal of kingship. Briefly: the King has an almost superhuman mission as the personification of all that is highest in the state, and as the active embodiment of true religion. He needs, and will be given, strength, comfort and dreams of divine revelation by (Wagnerian) art, which manifests the (Schopenhauerian) illusion and nothingness of the world. These extraordinary words of wisdom intended for his nineteen-year-old master are couched in a tangled mass of verbiage, spiced with absurdly primitive analogies and metaphors, at once obscure, disordered and repetitive. The style pervades all Wagner's later discourses on politics. It is as if he were writing his thoughts at random, thinking aloud on the page. He is quite incapable of putting over a simple idea without becoming involved and discursive, while complex subjects he deals with cavalierly in absurd generalizations.

The exuberance and the poverty of his prose were equalled in his next offering to Ludwig, *Huldigungsmarsch* (March of Homage), written for the King's birthday on 25 August, but not performed until October. A poem followed in September, *An meinem König*, to which Ludwig responded with some equally effusive verses of his own, entitled *An meinem Freund*. Cosima was the recipient of another poem *An Dich*!, on 1 October, in which she is hailed as a bright star risen in the dark night of his life. Of more significance was a theme inspired by her visit to Starnberg. Wagner jotted it down with a chamber work in mind; later it formed the opening theme of what is now called the *Siegfried Idyll*, and it appears also in the third act of *Siegfried* when Wagner symbolically linked his love for Cosima with that of Siegfried and Brünnhilde. Work on the full orchestral score of *Siegfried* began at Starnberg.

Early in October Wagner settled in Munich, in a house at first rented by the King, but bought for Wagner in the following May. This extensive and elegant property in the most fashionable part of town had a large garden containing a cottage. From the veranda two peacocks could be observed strutting in the shade of a great ash tree. In November Wagner's stipend was raised to 5000 florins per annum. Bertha Goldwag was summoned from Vienna, and on two visits to the house she decorated every corner, wall, recess, window, frame, cornice, border and ceiling with an array of white, gold, lilac, yellow, red, brown, green and blue silks and satins. As Wagner had lost his Penzing wardrobe she recreated it for him with multi-coloured shirts, suits and dressing gowns to match the fabrics and furnishings. He chose Bertha in an effort to avoid gossip among the Munich retailers and she travelled incognito, informing curious customs officials that her lavish wares of lace, satin and silk were intended for a Countess in Berlin. The luxury in which this wild spender and incorrigible borrower was living did not remain a secret for long. Former creditors, court officials who called at the house and inquisitive journalists soon spread the word of his extravagance. Envy was inevitable; resentment grew at such a drain upon the purse of King and country, and memories of Lola Montez revived. Wagner was soon nicknamed the new Ludwig's 'Lolotte' or 'Lolus'.

Another more serious cause for complaint was the invasion of Wagner's friends into Munich's artistic life. Established members of the town's musical community began to feel threatened. Wagner's aim was to remodel Munich's musical life entirely. The Bülows arrived in November, Cornelius followed shortly and later Heinrich Porges and the Leipzig singing teacher Friedrich Schmitt (whom Wagner had first known at Magdeburg) joined the ranks. The citizens of Munich were also to be transformed: Wagner declared that their minds must be elevated by theatrical performances of only the highest and most significant works of art: Shakespeare, Calderón, Goethe, Schiller, Mozart, Beethoven, Gluck and Weber.

And, needless to say, Wagner. On 4 and 8 December he conducted two performances of *The Flying Dutchman*, both attended by the King. A concert of Wagner extracts followed on the 11th, the regular Munich patrons displaying their enthusiasm for the new régime by mostly staying at home. Musically *The Flying Dutchman* succeeded well, but its inadequacies of presentation reinforced Ludwig's determination that a theatre specifically suited to Wagner performances must be built. On 26 November he had told the composer of his resolution to erect 'a large masonry theatre'. Wagner wrote to his old friend Semper, commissioning him for the task. On 29 December the architect was received by Ludwig and given a definite commission for a monumental festival theatre to be situated on the Gasteig hill. It was to be conceived according to Wagner's specifications; the most essential features being the amphitheatre form of the auditorium, a complete separation of the 'ideal world' on the stage from the 'reality' of the audience, and the necessity for the orchestra pit to be lowered and therefore unseen. Optical and acoustical considerations were of paramount importance; from every seat in the theatre the desired illusion must be perfect. The eye would not be distracted by conductor and players but would be led across a neutral space to the dream-like world of the stage.

Semper was not given any kind of written contract by the King, but Wagner assured him he need not doubt the King's word. This worried Semper, as did the fact that the press were ordered to deny any rumours that the theatre plan existed. Ludwig and Wagner were anxious to keep the project secret until definite moves had been made. In a wise attempt to form a strategy that would prove acceptable to Ludwig's advisers, Wagner suggested the building of a temporary theatre within the Glaspalast, a huge building of the Crystal Palace type, used mainly for exhibitions. The King was set upon a monumental stone structure, however, and as his enthusiasm and impatience grew, Pfistermeister's doubts about the project hardened into outright opposition. The court, the cabinet and, when they gathered details, the press and the public all had objections to the idea. The expense would be enormous and even the King's Civil List was not inexhaustible. Few could see what necessity there was for the King's favourite to have a theatre entirely his own, particularly as the works intended for performance there were largely incomplete or yet to be written. In addition, there was every possibility that the young King's enthusiasm for this wildly ambitious composer would one day fade and a vast sum would have been needlessly wasted. Controversy raged in the press and the King's ministers determined that the plan would die a slow death if they took care to delay and vacillate over it for as long as possible. Poor Semper was the innocent victim of these intrigues, and as events unfolded in Munich during 1865, Wagner could do very little to save the situation.

Linked to the theatre scheme was Wagner's plan for a music school in Munich, principally to train singers for Wagnerian roles, and the arrival of Friedrich Schmitt was the first step towards this goal. The new year began with real hope; both King and artist had every expectation that their aims would be realized. On 13 January Cornelius was presented to the King for the first time. Ludwig and Wagner indulged their optimism by drawing up a revised schedule for the performance of all his works, written and unwritten, and by planning an edition in several volumes of his complete prose writings.

February 1865 saw the first concerted effort to drive Wagner out of Munich. The suddenness and savagery of the attack took him by surprise. A series of misunderstandings fed the press with ammunition, and in the court, Wagner's enemies did their best to poison the King's mind against his friend. At the end of the previous year Baron von der Pfordten became Minister-President and Foreign Minister of Bavaria. He was Wagner's implacable foe, having detested the man and his works since the revolutionary Dresden days, and having done all in his power to prevent the old King Max promoting Wagner's operas in Munich. Wagner still regarded Pfistermeister as an amiable ally, but before long the secretary was in league with Pfordten; and Pfi and Pfo, as Ludwig and Wagner called them, became the evil twins intent upon destroying the Wagnerian cause in Munich. In the events of February 1865, Pfistermeister was already indulging in duplicity. Lesser figures at court including Huber, the King's adviser on current events, the cabinet treasurer Hofmann, and Leinfelder, his reader and private secretary, were eager to do what they could to counteract Wagner's influence on their royal master. The first cause for gossip had no real foundation. The newspapers made much of the fact that Ludwig had not attended performances of *The Flying Dutchman* on 5 February and *Tannhäuser* on the 12th. This, they implied, illustrated that Wagner was out of favour with the King. In fact, Ludwig had come to an agreement with Wagner that he would not attend repertory performances of his operas until the projected model performance of *Tristan* with Schnorr.

Of greater seriousness was a scandal that arose over a portrait of himself that Wagner presented to the King on 30 January. That this affair became public knowledge was clear evidence to Wagner that he had an enemy, or enemies, within the court, who fed the press with malicious reports. Ludwig had long desired to commission an oil portrait of Wagner, so the composer decided to surprise his friend with just such an item. Friedrich Pecht, his old acquaintance from early Paris and Dresden times, was now resident in Munich, and he carried out the work. The King was delighted with the result and wrote to thank Wagner warmly. Some days later Pfistermeister consulted Wagner as to payment for the portrait and it was agreed that the matter should be settled directly with Pecht. On 5 February, Wagner requested an audience with Ludwig, which was granted for the following day, but on arrival at the Residenz he was astounded by the news that he would not be admitted as the King was profoundly displeased with him. Two things apparently contributed to this unprecedented repulse. Pfistermeister seems to have misled the King over the payment for Pecht's portrait, and given him to understand that Wagner was demanding 1000 florins for it. Also, when in conversation with Pfistermeister prior to the arranged audience, Wagner had inadvertently referred to the King as 'mein Junge' ('my boy'), and when this intolerable breach of etiquette was duly reported to Ludwig, the sensitive young ruler reacted angrily by refusing to admit Wagner to his presence.

Speculation and gossip about Wagner's disgrace and rumours of his supposed arrogance over the Pecht affair abounded in the town. On 12 February Ludwig published an official denial that Wagner was 'in disgrace', pointing out that it was purely pressure of work and legislative duties that had prevented the King receiving the composer in recent weeks. This did not satisfy the journalists, and, acting on information supplied by spies at court or in the cabinet, they continued to assure their readers that Wagner had forfeited the King's favour and was leaving Munich. Published denials by Wagner, appeals to Pfistermeister to prevent the press attacks, the resumption of a friendly correspondence with Ludwig, and an audience with him on the 17th, did not stem the tide of malicious innuendo. On the 19th the most devastating attack on Wagner was published in the *Allgemeine Zeitung*. In a lengthy anonymous article, the poet Redwitz claimed on the highest authority that Wagner had left Pecht's portrait in the King's room with a bill for 1000 florins. The resultant disfavour brought upon the former revolutionary Wagner, will be joyously welcomed by all except the composer's partisan associates. This man's 'demands in matters of everyday life and comfort seem to be of so exquisitely sybaritic a nature that not even an oriental *grand seigneur* would object to the prospect of living permanently in his house . . . and eating at his table.' Wagner is moreover ostentatious, ungrateful, arrogant, and insatiable in his demands. The article rejoices that the King has decided to confine his enthusiasm for Wagner to music alone and not extend it to the composer's personality, and concludes that if Wagner and his friends should ever again 'thrust themselves between us Bavarians and our beloved King' they will be 'really and truly overthrown and can turn their backs forever on our good Munich and Bavaria itself'.

In his reply in the columns of the same newspaper three days later, Wagner vigorously objected to the personal nature of the attack on him. He claimed that his income from the King was not excessive when compared with payments for works of art by former Bavarian rulers. All that he earns is by way of fair compensation for loss of alternative income during the completion of the *Ring*. He categorically denies the allegations concerning the Pecht story. Above all, how he spends his income and how he chooses to decorate his own home is entirely a private matter with which no one else should have any concern. It is not he who has harmed the monarchy, but the press in publishing such articles. This clever reply adroitly avoids the heart of the matter: whether it is right for someone to run up huge debts through lavish living and then expect them to be paid by the privy purse. And, although the lampoons, cartoons, rumour-mongering and town-talk did not cease, Wagner survived this first attempt to oust him from the side of his prince.

The real ill-effect of the February fracas was the sudden appearance of creditors from remotest times and places, who, having read of Wagner's privileged position, redoubled their insistent claims upon him. Others sought to use his much talked of influence over the King for personal and political ends. Within months of his rescue by Ludwig he was approached by all sorts of people seeking his intervention with the King, among them a man condemned to death and the orphans of a female poisoner. But the royal favourite refused to become involved in political affairs of any kind. At the time of the February troubles he had to tread especially warily. Bavaria was, next to Prussia, the largest German state, and was bitterly opposed to Bismarck and his aims for German unification. A fervent nationalism was in the air, and with it a distrust of foreigners (such as Wagner) and a hatred of Prussians (such as Bülow). It was therefore all-important that Wagner should not be seen to abuse his position. Prince Max von Thurn und Taxis was set upon creating a little kingdom for his eldest son in the Westphalian Rhineland together with half of Belgium. Seeking the support of the Bavarian King he sent two agents to Wagner in February, with the offer of a generous share in a large financial enterprise and future artistic support if he would help to remove Pfister-meister from office. In turn, Pfistermeister, realizing his position was precarious, began to side with Wagner and countered the Prince Taxis offer with assurances that he would receive the music school, the Semper theatre, endless credit and so forth, if the composer would stand by him. Wagner affected to be dense when approached with these bribes and made it clear to Pfistermeister and the foreign agents that he had no interest in politics, either domestic or foreign, but only in artistic enter-prises. Another ambition of the reactionary politicians was to steer Lud-wig towards a despotic, absolutist concept of monarchy. It was put to Wagner that his own aims could only benefit from such a move and that he was in an ideal position to influence the King, but Wagner refused to prove accommodating, which immediately led the conspiring ministers to assume that he had democratic ambitions of his own. If this pawn would not play their game, then he would have to be removed from the board.

Ironically, his struggle to avoid political involvement thrust Wagner to the centre of the game of power. Horrified by what he saw and heard of the machinations and aspirations of those surrounding the King, he resolved to protect his friend from the evils that threatened him. He was encouraged in this mission by a curious visit from an elderly fortune-teller, Frau Dangl, who told him on 22 February that two previous Bavarian monarchs had gone astray by not following her advice. She had read in the stars that Wagner was called to protect the young King from the conspiracies of those who would destroy him as they destroyed his father and grandfather. Next day, Wagner wrote to Mathilde Maier of 'an almost supernatural experience' which had revealed to him his lofty destiny: the fate of King, indeed of all Germany itself lay in his hands! 'Why this cup to *my* lips?' he cried. Clearly the old sibyl had turned his head.

Meanwhile, work proceeded on the full orchestral score of *Siegfried* Act Two, although much of his time was spent drawing up 'A Report to His Majesty King Ludwig II of Bavaria on a German Music School to be founded in Munich'. This lengthy manifesto, on which he collaborated with Bülow, appeared in the early spring. Its principal contention is that, unlike France and Italy, Germany has no national style of theatrical performance. The new school will devote itself to the cultivation of a vocal style suited to the great German musical tradition; a new standard of teaching resulting in a new breed of singers is envisaged. Contemporary musical journalism is criticized as lacking any constructive or ethical basis. What is required is a new music journal to deal with problems of style and performance and to bridge the gap between artists and public. To the music teachers of Munich, this report, far from seeming a noble endeavour to raise artistic standards to a level of excellence hitherto unknown, was nothing less than an attempt to supplant them and install in their place an institute geared solely to the furthering of Wagner's ends and the creation of singers for the *Ring*. Journalists, too, saw their inde-pendence threatened. The local teaching community regarded Wagner's sensible plans as a sentence of death upon themselves, a sweeping away of all that impeded the only important goal – Wagnerian opera.

To the politicians, these ideas were of small account. What concerned them far more was the vast, costly, unwieldy plan for an all-Wagner festival theatre. Recent events had shown that it would not be easy to rid Ludwig of his passion for Wagner, and as long as the King set his heart upon his theatre, they could do little to hinder the scheme except to pursue a policy of procrastination. Not until 8 April did Semper receive any official word about the matter, when Pfistermeister requested plans for both the monumental stone theatre and the temporary Glaspalast theatre. No decision had been made as to which of these projects would be carried out, nor was the unfortunate architect given any help, technical information, specifications of proposed sites, facts about dimensions and drainage, or the complex difficulties involved in erecting a provisional structure within the Glaspalast. Despite this deliberate lack of co-operation, Semper worked hard at his designs, and with painstaking care conceived plans for both schemes that overcame the immense problems involved. His devotion to the undertaking was rewarded by further delays and little or no advice from Munich.

Owing to the presence of the hostile Queen Mother, Wagner saw little of Ludwig in the aftermath of the February storm. The King expressed regret at this but reaffirmed his undying love for Wagner. In order to be really sure where he stood, Wagner wrote to the King asking whether he ought to go or to stay: one word from his 'glorious Friend' would decide his fate. He must have known what reaction Ludwig would show to the slightest hint of losing his friend. The King replied:

Dear Friend!
Stay, oh stay! Everything will be as glorious as before. I am very busy. Till death,

Your Ludwig.

Wagner answered in three ecstatic words, 'Ich lebe noch!' – 'I live again!'

Thus satisfied, Wagner turned to the major preoccupation of the spring and early summer, the first production of *Tristan und Isolde*. Ludwig had arranged with the King of Saxony for Ludwig and Malvina Schnorr to be released from the Dresden Opera for three months. Wagner was given personal command over the 'model' production but he felt unequal to the physical task of conducting. He had no intention of allowing the Court Kapellmeister, Lachner, to direct the performance, so Ludwig created Bülow 'Court Kapellmeister for Special Services'. An hour or two before the first orchestral rehearsal on 12 April, Cosima gave birth to Wagner's first child, a daughter christened Isolde Ludowika Josepha. It was Wagner's hope to give *Tristan* in the tiny, intimate Cuvilliés theatre in the Residenz. At the early rehearsals he was delighted by the fact that the singers' facial expressions could be clearly seen and that every word they sang was heard perfectly in the exquisite little auditorium. But Ludwig's fears that the work was on too large a scale for the Cuvilliés proved correct: with the full orchestra the sound was overpoweringly great and Wagner reluctantly moved to the large court theatre. Bülow, who knew the score intimately, having already made the piano arrangement, worked immensely hard and inspired superb playing from the orchestra, but he was difficult to work with, and as the sessions proceeded he became more nervous and irritable, actually collapsing in a faint on one occasion. On 2 May he asked for the orchestra pit to be enlarged. When he was informed that this would mean removing thirty seats from the stalls, he shouted, 'What does it matter if we have thirty *Schweinehunde* more or less in the place?' The press made enormous capital out of this insult to the Munich citizenry by the already unpopular Prussian. One paper carried a huge headline for over a week declaring 'Hans von Bülow is still here!' The cry went up to throw him out of the city like Lola Montez. He received threatening and abusive letters; word spread that there was a plot to assassinate him. The whole production seemed jeopardized by one indiscreet remark, but Bülow apologized publicly and disaster was narrowly averted.

As the great day approached, Ludwig could hardly contain his ecstatic emotions. On 10 May he wrote to his friend:

> My loved one, I shall never forsake you! Oh *Tristan*, *Tristan* will come to me! The dreams of my boyhood and youth will be realized! You should have nothing to do with the common things of the world; I will bear you high above earthly cares!. . . My love for you and for your art grows ever greater, and this flame of love shall bring happiness and salvation.

Admirers from all over Europe began to gather in Munich including Anton Bruckner, Damrosch, Draesecke, Eckert, Gasperini, Adolf Jensen, Johann Kalliwoda, Klindworth, Eduard Lassen, Pohl, Porges, Raff, Röckel, and Schuré. But many of those closest to Wagner wounded him by staying away: Liszt, Cornelius, the Willes and the Wesendoncks. Pusinelli was invited, but was asked not to tell Minna. The doctor wrote back with the news that he could not come: Minna was dying.

The King and six hundred guests attended the dress rehearsal on 11 May. Ludwig marked the occasion appropriately by pardoning all those in prison for their part in the revolutions of 1849. Better news concerning Minna came early on the day of the projected first performance. Then followed a rapturous letter from Ludwig. The remainder of that morning of 15 May, however, was one of the most heartbreaking of Wagner's life. First, the bailiffs arrived to seize his furniture, on account of an upaid debt of five years before: a sum received in Paris from Julie Schwabe. Cosima was sent at once to the treasury and returned with 2400 florins, and the matter was settled.

Schnorr then arrived, in tears, with the calamitous news that Malvina was hoarse: there could be no performance of *Tristan* that evening. When the news of the postponement was made public late in the afternoon, sensational reports swept the town: Malvina's voice had been ruined by Wagner's impossible music; Bülow was too afraid to appear in public; the orchestra had gone on strike, and so forth. Predictably the press gloated over Wagner's tragedy: the *Schweinehunde* were cruelly revenged. The *Volksbote* sneered that Wagner's opera now was truly the music of the future. Parodies of the opera filled the Munich comic papers. It was over three weeks before Malvina returned to Munich from her convalescence and by the first actual performance on 10 June, most of Wagner's friends had left Munich. That evening Ludwig sat alone: elsewhere in the house were ex-King Ludwig I, Duke Max and Prince Luitpold. At the end of each act there was some hissing but it was drowned out in the general applause. To prevent a demonstration against Bülow the general public were not admitted until the prelude had commenced. To all but a few, this long-awaited première must have been strange and puzzling. No one, however, doubted the heroic accomplishment of Ludwig and Malvina Schnorr. The tenor's performance was beyond Wagner's powers of praise. The great goal had been accomplished: the unperformable had been performed. On reaching the residence, Ludwig wrote to Wagner:

> Unique One! Holy One!
> How glorious! – *Perfect*. Overwhelmed with rapture!. . . . To drown . . . to sink down – unconscious – supreme bliss. *Divine* work!
> Eternally true – till death and beyond!

Three more performances followed and after the last Ludwig was so overcome that on the train home to Berg he pulled the communication cord and wandered into a forest to cool his excitement before continuing the journey. Wagner too was profoundly moved by the excellence of the orchestra and leading singers, but sadly aware that very few had even the faintest understanding of his work.

On 21 July, three weeks after the final performance, Wagner received a telegram from Dresden announcing the death of Schnorr. Puzzled, and knowing that the twenty-nine-year-old tenor had many relatives, he wired back, 'Which Schnorr?' The unbelievable answer came – Ludwig Schnorr. Wagner recalled with horror Schnorr's complaint on the evening of the third performance about an icy draught that worried him as he lay on the stage hot and breathless from his huge monologues in Act Three. The young singer had said darkly that chills had serious consequences for him. He had left Munich with Malvina on 13 July and Wagner had noted a certain excitability in his manner. He had confessed to the composer his dread of returning to Dresden and a diet of Verdi and Meyerbeer, and was filled with despondency at the thought of the uphill struggle that lay before Wagner and himself. As Wagner relaxed by calling on Ludwig at Berg and, on the 17th, commencing the dictation of *Mein Leben* to Cosima, Schnorr's final illness developed rapidly. On the 16th, having sung in fine form at a Dresden rehearsal on the day before, he was attacked by agonizing rheumatism. Within two days his condition deteriorated and, in the soaring summer heat, fever gripped him and he became delirious. Before the final apoplexy of the brain his frenzied thoughts were only of Wagner. He sang lines from *Götterdämmerung* to his own wild music and cried, 'My Richard loved me! I die happy: *He* loved me!' He called for Wagner to come quickly: 'Richard, do you not hear me?' And lastly, 'O Siegfried, Siegfried, Farewell! Console my Richard!'

On 22 July Wagner and Bülow hastened to Dresden, but arrived too late for the funeral. In the brilliant July sun, the town was thronged with 20,000 singers gathered for a festival. The irony struck Wagner: *the* singer had but just departed. After consoling Malvina and hearing the tale of Schnorr's last hours they returned; Wagner sick in mind and body. For weeks he was obsessed and tormented with the fate of his Tristan. He later wrote, 'In him I lost the great granite block needed to raise my building and I found myself having to seek his replacement in a pile of bricks.' In the first agony of loss he saw Schnorr as a martyr for his cause. In the Brown Book for 25 August he wrote:

> My Tristan! My Beloved! I drove you to the abyss! I was accustomed to standing there: my head does not reel . . . I lay hold of him to stop him, to draw him back, and I push him over, just as we kill the somnambulist when we cry out to him in our alarm. Thus I pushed him over. And myself? My head does not reel. I look down: it even delights me. But – the friend? I lose him! *Mein Tristan! Mein Trauter!*

To the King he wrote, again quoting the dying Kurwenal's words, '*Mein Tristan! Mein Trauter!* For me he lived, for me he died!'

Eleven

Art and Politics

The megalomaniac differs from the narcissist by the fact that he wishes to be powerful rather than charming, and seeks to be feared rather than loved. To this type belong many lunatics and most of the great men of history.

Bertrand Russell, *The Conquest of Happiness*

AMONG THE HUNDREDS of letters from Wagner to Ludwig there is perhaps none more remarkable and revealing than that of 8 August 1865. The composer was resting after the excitements of the *Tristan* production and brooding over the fate of Schnorr. With the death of the singer, he told the King, the old Richard Wagner died, leaving behind a new Richard Wagner who can achieve 'everything – more than the *Nibelungen*, every-thing – if it be made possible'. His annual allowance of 5000 florins had only days before been raised by 1200 florins to help him maintain a carriage. The reborn artist needed more than a coach and pair to reach his goals, however, and he attached to his letter a modest demand for 200,000 florins: 40,000 to be paid at once, the remainder to be invested and the interest paid to him in quarterly instalments of 2000 florins. In addition, his Munich residence should be provided free of rent for the rest of his life, during which he will, of course, never bother the treasury again. Only Wagner would have seen nothing remarkable in sending such airy suggestions along with a letter that claimed he was no longer capable of desiring anything for himself. The request made, he retired with servant, dog and Holtzmann's translation of the *Ramayana*, to the royal hunting lodge of Hochkopf, where for almost two weeks he mused on future uncertainties, present unhappiness and past misfortunes.

The intimate jottings in the Brown Book testify to Wagner's real state of mind while at Hochkopf and on his return to Munich from that spartan and uncongenially furnished retreat on 21 August. In that journal, far more than in his letters (always written, it seems, with half an eye on future publication), his horror at the loss of Schnorr and his unhappiness at Cosima's absence (she was away in Pest with Bülow and Liszt until 13 September) are expressed with uninhibited candour. That Frau von Bülow spent most of her time at Wagner's side, and less and less with her husband, was now common knowledge in Munich. Not for the first time

216

Wagner saw a husband as the obstacle preventing the full realization of his ardour and happiness, but in this instance the unwanted member of the triangle was devoted heart and soul to Wagner's cause: Bülow once declared his willingness to be Wagner's boot-black. An entry in the Brown Book for 20 August cries to Cosima, 'Stay with me and do not leave me again! Tell poor Hans frankly that without you I cannot go on. O heaven, if only you could calmly take your place as my wife before the world!'

Scoring of *Siegfried* Act Two occupied him at Hochkopf and on his return to the capital; the full orchestral score of that act was complete by December. In addition to two poems for Ludwig, the Brown Book for 27–30 August contains a detailed prose sketch for *Parsifal*. A fair copy was sent to the King who wrote on 5 September:

> My Only One! My godlike Friend!
> At last I have a moment to myself, at last I am free to thank my beloved friend from the bottom of my soul for the sketch of 'Parcival'; I am filled with the fire of enthusiasm; each day that passes my love glows more ardently for the only one I love in this world, the one who is my sublime joy, my comfort, my trust, my all! O Parcival, when will you be born? I worship this highest love, this immersion, this surrender of self in the anguished suffering of a fellow man! The story grips me strongly! Truly this art is holy, is the purest and noblest religion. –

Such effusions did not in themselves alarm Ludwig's ministers. What worried them was the more radical nature of some of the King's Wagnerian ambitions. In July, the Munich Conservatoire of Music had been closed – the first step towards establishing a school on the lines laid down by Wagner. Pfistermeister, in gratitude to Wagner for his non-interference in the Taxis plot, had made a show of enthusiasm for the *Tristan* production, but in private he cursed the whole enterprise. By the summer Wagner had sensed that Pfistermeister was not wholly for his cause and he tried to persuade Ludwig to appoint a new official to take over Pfistermeister's duties in artistic matters. Nothing was done about this, nor about Wagner's plan for improving the pay of 'rank-and-file' musicians in Munich: the reaction of the press was greatly feared, for already there were indignant protests at the closure of the conservatoire, wild speculations about future Wagnerian projects and dismay at the composer's private life-style. On top of his outrageous demand for 200,000 florins and free accommodation for life, the ministers were forced to consider the Semper theatre project.

The architect visited Munich in September to examine the proposed sites and give the King details of his plans, but Ludwig did not receive Semper on the pretext of ill-health. Wagner did nothing to help the scheme for fear of jeopardizing his own financial hopes, neither warning Semper off nor interceding with the King, as it suited him to delay the theatre project. The *Ring* was far from complete and ready cash was of much more immediate importance than laying foundations for monuments. Ludwig too remained vague as to which plan he wanted – stone theatre, or temporary structure. Thus the game of double-dealing at Semper's expense continued; the architect returned to Zurich in ignorance of the real state of affairs and applied himself to a rigorous preparation of estimates, working models, plans and elevations.

On his birthday the King received from Wagner the manuscript score of *Rheingold*, and from Cosima an embroidered cushion. Ludwig was impatient for Wagner's autobiography and in the meantime Cosima supplied him with neatly copied extracts from Wagner's diaries. On 14 September Wagner began a 'Journal' for Ludwig, outlining his views on German affairs. In 1878 parts of this 'Journal' were published under the title *What is German*? When Cornelius learned that Wagner was supplying the King with political commentary of this kind, he wrote to his fiancée: 'A shudder ran through me: I saw the beginning of the end.' The King was delighted with the 'Journal' and promptly had a copy made for Pfordten and his other ministers. For Pfi and Pfo, this was welcome evidence of the kind they had been seeking: for, through the welter of incoherent and longsome prose, it was clearly seen that Wagner was feeding the King with political notions of a particularly dangerous kind.

Wagner's main contention is that the German spirit is the finest thing on earth. Sadly, this true, virtuous and glorious German spirit has been sullied and corrupted, mainly by Jews and Frenchmen. Modern Prussia represents most of the evil in Germany, for Berlin is populated by French immigrants, 'while the Jews came in from underneath in large numbers to take charge of "business" and to dish out alcohol instead of things of the spirit to the Folk, in order to dissipate their phlegm'. Because the German people have not been watchful, it is the Jews who now run the press, the theatres, and the key institutions of the nation. The salvation of Germany is dependent on a prince who has the true sense of his historic duty to his subjects. All other German princes have failed to lead, indeed have betrayed, the German people. In Ludwig there has been born an enlightened ruler capable of true leadership in the spirit of the Germany of old and better times. Bismarck, with his Prussian aims for the unification of Germany is 'with appalling frivolity playing with the destiny of the noblest and greatest nation on earth'. The destiny of Germany is to concern itself only with its own lofty development, for 'the German feels no thirst for conquest, and the lust to dominate foreign peoples is unGerman'.[1] A people's army (*Volkswehr*), on the model of Switzerland,

[1] 'When I talk of peace I am doing nothing but giving expression to the profoundest and most sincere wish of the German people' were Hitler's words in 1935 as he rearmed Germany and increased compulsory conscription. Five years after the 'Journal' Wagner was screaming for war with France and gloating over Prussian victories. All anti-Prussian remarks were deleted when the 'Journal' was reprinted as *What is German*?

would provide Germany with an armed force of millions, which would be entirely defensive, and would become 'a beneficial branch of body culture'. The Jew would benefit from membership of such a German Folk army: he would 'either vanish or be transformed into a true German'.

On 10 October Cosima learned from Pfistermeister that Wagner was to be gifted his house in the Briennerstrasse, but that the King had no intention of providing him with 40,000 florins merely to pay off his debts. Although he was to receive 8000 florins per year as interest on the 160,000 florins, Wagner was enraged at the refusal of the 40,000 and he and Pfistermeister had a furious argument. The cabinet secretary told Ludwig that he would no longer tolerate being a 'speaking-tube' between the King and the composer. He was relieved of these duties and in future his subordinate, Johann Lutz, dealt with Wagner. Lutz proved no friend of Wagner's, and kept Pfi and Pfo well informed about his communications with the King. On 18 October, court and cabinet were astonished to learn that Ludwig had changed his mind and offered the 40,000 florins to Wagner. Wagner had no desire to collect the money in person so Cosima was sent to the treasury. According to her own account she was told by an official that they had insufficient notes for the sum, which would have to be paid to her in silver coins. If this was an attempt to make things awkward and embarrassing, Cosima remained unruffled. She calmly ordered two cabs and, with the help of her eldest daughter and the children's governess, loaded them with the heavy sacks. Half of the money was spent at once discharging debts and, on 20 October, Wagner left for Vienna to gather more wares from Bertha Goldwag. In addition to consulting his doctor (Standhartner) and his dentist in Vienna, Wagner sought out Julius Fröbel,* journalist and former revolutionary, whom he hoped to lure to Munich as editor of a proposed Wagnerian musico-political paper.

At Hohenschwangau in mid November, Wagner was the King's guest for one week of mutual happiness. Neither of them guessed that within a month Wagner would be banished from Bavaria. In the mornings, while the King worked, messages and verses were passed between them. From midday they were constantly together. Military bandsmen from Munich were posted on the castle ramparts and the landscape echoed to themes from *Lohengrin*. On 21 November, after Wagner's departure, Ludwig ordered a fireworks display and the arrival of the Swan-Knight was enacted on the Alpsee: Ludwig's favourite, young Prince Paul von Thurn und Taxis, dressed as Lohengrin, was drawn across the lake in a flood-lit boat by a large artificial swan. Before leaving Hohenschwangau, Wagner had impressed upon the King the necessity for several appointments: he wished to see artistic matters dealt with by a newly created official, instead of by the cabinet secretariat; he wanted Bülow appointed director of the new music school, and Fröbel brought to Munich as editor of a new journal. The watchful Lutz took care to remain within earshot when these suggestions were made.

An article prompted, if not actually written, by Wagner appeared in the Nuremberg *Anzeiger* on 13 November. It consisted of a pointed attack on the cabinet secretariat, Pfistermeister, Lutz and the treasurer, von Hofmann. On the 26th a reply appeared in the *Volksbote* which suggested that Wagner 'may not have been wholly unaware' of the contents of the recent attack, and indeed the removal of the cabinet secretary would be to the advantage of those who wished to exploit the royal treasury. This same Wagner, continued the article, had received 190,000 florins of Bavarian money in less than a year, and recently had insisted on another 40,000! This monstrous sum had been paid to him despite objections from Cabinet Secretary Pfistermeister.

As soon as Wagner read this article he sent it to the King with a covering letter expressing exasperation at Pfistermeister and the court officials. He advised Ludwig to dismiss Pfordten and replace him as Minister-President with Max von Neumayr. Wagner did not know Neumayr well, but felt that he had been removed unjustly from office by Pfi and Pfo. To reinstate him as head of the cabinet would be a victory over Pfistermeister. The King replied on the 27th with a wise letter, pointing out that he too had little time for the stupidities of insignificant little 'Mime' (as he and Wagner called Pfi) but adamantly refusing to summon Neumayr to form a new Cabinet. Wagner should ignore the silly chatter of the press and turn his thoughts to his work. Wagner wrote back at once with a more venomous attack on Pfistermeister, whom he saw as an archtraitor, an unscrupulous, disloyal blackguard. The King *must* summon Neumayr – let him ride out from Hohenschwangau like a hero and bring Neumayr to Munich to set all to rights! At the same time Wagner wrote an anonymous article in response to the calumnies expressed in the *Volksbote*. This appeared in the Munich *Neueste Nachrichten* on 29 December. It was a furious, thoughtless and uncontrolled rejoinder, in which Cosima took a hand; but the style and sentiments left no one in doubt as to the authorship. The article makes cavalier use of the name of the King, and calls for 'the removal of two or three people who do not enjoy the least respect among the people of Bavaria'.

Pfordten promptly warned the King that His Majesty's friendship for Richard Wagner was in danger of causing a serious constitutional crisis. Ludwig replied that Wagner's role was entirely artistic and not political. On 1 December, Pfordten wrote again in sterner terms, advising Ludwig that Wagner's article, the unspeakable effrontery of his references to the King's friendship, his demands for the removal of the highest officials, his extraordinary income and his meddling in non-artistic matters, can no longer be tolerated. The King 'stands at a fateful crossroads and has to choose between the love and honour of his faithful people and the "friendship" of Richard Wagner'. That man is resented and despised by

Bavarians of every class and calling. Pfordten concludes with a timely note of caution: 'When the very existence of states and thrones is under serious threat from many quarters . . . there is a far greater need for action in the real world than for dreaming in the ideal world.' The crisis caused by Wagner's article forced the King to leave Hohenschwangau for Munich. He arrived on 6 December after the newspapers and satirical magazines had enjoyed an unprecedented week of rich scandal and innuendo. After studying petitions and police reports, and discussing the matter with his family, he reluctantly gave the awaited command: Wagner must leave Bavaria.

Wagner and Cosima were at dinner when Lutz brought news of the King's decision. While she almost fainted with shock, he exploded with rage, screaming insults and oaths about Pfistermeister and his abominable intrigues, until Lutz ordered him to control himself with a curt reminder that he was present in his official capacity. Next day Ludwig wrote to his friend expressing grief at the decision, about which he had no choice, and assuring him that he remained faithful, and hopeful that the parting would not be a long one. Wagner presumed the King had lost his head, and could not forgive him for giving way. The press was loud in its praise of the King's decision and hoped that Wagner would be an exile forever. The gloomy departure of the fallen favourite on 10 December, with his faithful servant and his sick old hound, was described by Cornelius:

> We went to the station at 5 o'clock in the morning, and had to wait quite a long time for Wagner. At last the carriage arrived. Wagner looked like a ghost; pale, distraught, his long lank hair looking quite ashen. We accompanied him to the train, Franz and Pohl were travelling with him. Wagner had a last, urgent conversation with Cosima, and Heinrich [Porges] particularly made out the words, 'Keep silent'. Cosima was completely broken down. As his train disappeared beyond the pillars, it was like the fading of a dream.

Wagner was dazed and bitter; Ludwig was heartbroken; Cosima lived in fear of a threatened assassination. For a long time the King lived in the hope that Wagner would return to Munich – a hope that faded slowly as his loneliness and isolation grew. Wagner's future visits to the city were brief and infrequent. Had he returned on a permanent basis then a political crisis would have been inevitable: the Seven Weeks' War of 1866 and the Franco-Prussian War of 1870 were periods when no such crisis could be contemplated. In addition the relationship between Wagner and Cosima was to prevent his settling in Munich and bringing a new scandal upon the royal household. Ludwig realized that he could never be with Wagner unless he abdicated, and that was the last thing his friend wished him to do. He was a prisoner on his throne.

To be a fugitive was not a new experience for Wagner, and the one great consolation of the flight from Munich was that he began this latest exile as a rich man, with his income still guaranteed. Reaching Switzerland, he spent a week at Vevey, and then three days at Geneva where he found a spacious country house in the vicinity of the town, called 'The Artichokes', with magnificent views towards Mont Blanc, thirty miles distant. He rented this villa for three months as from 23 December, and promptly had its rooms festooned with silks and satins. Composition of *Die Meistersinger* Act One was resumed on 12 January but, finding the house uncomfortably cold and damp, he left for the south of France ten days later, in search of a warmer home in which to complete his task. On the night of the 25th he retired in the comfort of the Grand Hotel at Marseilles.

In Dresden, at two o'clock next morning, Minna stirred from her bed choking and gasping for air. She opened a window, turned, half fell across her bed, and died. Her servant found her some hours later with foam around her mouth. Pusinelli wired Munich; Cosima forwarded the message to 'The Artichokes' and it was relayed to Wagner at Marseilles. He responded unemotionally, simply sending a telegram to Pusinelli asking the doctor to arrange the burial. Minna's last act on Wagner's behalf was to send, at Bülow's suggestion, a denial of newspaper reports that her husband had left her to starve while he basked in luxury. Her letter appeared in the *Volksbote* on 16 January:

> ### Honour to the Truth
> As a result of an erroneous report in the *Münchner Weltbote* I hereby truthfully declare that so far I have received sufficient support from my absent husband, Richard Wagner, to live a decent life, free from care.
> > Frau Minna Wagner
> > *geb*. Planer

Instead of rushing to Dresden, as he did at the time of Schnorr's death, Wagner returned to 'The Artichokes', complaining of an inflamed finger. A strange incident followed, an attempt perhaps to expiate his guilt about Minna. He found that the dog Pohl had died and had been roughly buried in his garden. He had the animal unearthed and reburied in a proper grave under some trees. At the ceremony he almost fainted with emotion, tied a collar round Pohl's neck and put a coverlet over his body. A monument of Jura stone was commissioned to mark the spot.

On 28 January Wagner sketched a drama in the Brown Book, on the death of the hero of the *Chanson de Roland*. A revised copy was sent to the King that same day. The symbolism was clear enough: the false counsellor Ganelon (Pfistermeister) persuades Charlemagne (Ludwig) that Roland (Wagner), whose horn is heard, is not in distress, but that the sound is an echo of the hunt. Roland suffers and dies, but not before attempting to destroy his magical sword. In dashing it against a mountain, the rocks are splintered but not the sword. Finally he throws the blade into a deep lake. When Charlemagne learns of Ganelon's deceit, the traitor and his kind are horribly punished: four thousand enemies are destroyed, three hundred cities are burned.

Die Meistersinger now occupied his thoughts; Act One was complete in orchestral sketch by 21 February. Nuremberg, the setting for that drama, now suggested itself as the ideal place for the realization of his plans. He told Bülow that the ancient town would be the ideal seat for German art, for the music school and for his operas. 'I wish that the King would grant me a pavilion of the Bayreuth Schloss as a country seat – Nuremberg nearby, all Germany surrounding me.' To Ludwig he described Munich as a vile place, corrupted by Jesuits and Jews. If only the King could move his court to Nuremberg! But however romantic the young King's ideas, the one thing he could hardly command was that his court should fly to the town which happened to be the backdrop for Wagner's latest opera. As Wagner's letters castigating Munich arrived, the King stared at his new and rather pathetic toy – a beautiful model of the proposed provisional Munich Festival Theatre. On Wagner's departure from Bavaria, Ludwig had assured Semper that recent events would not hinder the theatre plan. In the early months of 1866 the disgraceful saga dragged on, Pfistermeister and others steadily poisoning the King's mind with doubts and objections, and at the same time sending Semper hollow assurances that the project would one day materialize. No one told the architect that Wagner had no further interest in Munich, and the composer himself shamefully avoided his former friend while in Switzerland.

Cosima and her daughter Daniela joined Wagner at 'The Artichokes' in the second week of March. Dictation of *Mein Leben* continued and on 23 March the full score of the first act of *Meistersinger* was finished. Four days later they made an excursion to Berne until 30 March when, on the return journey, they discovered a house near Lucerne, set in magnificent grounds and commanding breathtaking views of surrounding peaks and across Lake Lucerne. This was Tribschen and, at a first glance, Wagner and Cosima knew it would be the ideal haven. She returned to Munich next day, while he wrote to Ludwig with news of their discovery. The King had set his heart upon Wagner living in Bavaria, therefore his prompt and handsome offer of 5000 francs to secure tenure of Tribschen was a truly noble and open-hearted act of devotion. Later in the year the Briennerstrasse house was sold and the sum realized put towards the rent of Tribschen. Wagner occupied his new home on 15 April and Cosima joined him there early in May, while Bülow remained in Munich until 6 June, before which date Cosima had conceived Wagner's second child. Liszt regarded his daughter's behaviour as an abomination; he foresaw not only the scandal that would ensue, but that such an open liaison would alienate the King and end Bülow's Munich career. For the moment Ludwig knew of Cosima only as Wagner's secretary and amanuensis. He corresponded with her as with a fellow worshipper of the Master.

In Tribschen he earned that title, 'der Meister', for there he completed *Meistersinger* and *Siegfried*, and composed *Götterdämmerung* and the *Siegfried Idyll*. Never one to hide his light under a bushel, Wagner saw his art as intimately bound up with the greatness of Germany. He wrote to Constantin Frantz* that one thing was clear, 'my art-ideal stands or falls with Germany's well-being'. During work on *Meistersinger*, Wagner's consciousness of his mission to regenerate Germany through the theatre took an almost fanatical turn. At the same time he began to dress almost like a character from his own opera, donning the famous Dürer hat, and encouraging visitors to address him as the Master. His brown hair, slightly receding behind that massive forehead, was now shot through with flecks of grey; his eyes had lost none of their piercing brightness. Those eyes were 'as blue as the lake of Lucerne', wrote Judith Gautier,* 'beaming eyes, where blended the most beautiful shades of sapphire'. And August Lesimple, an admirer from Cologne, remarked that 'whoever has looked once into those eyes will never again forget the deep and mysterious expression which shone there. There was something marvellous about his eyes.' His expressive eyes, his powers as an actor which could bewitch his listeners, and his remarkable mode of dress, gave him a magnetism unexpected in a man so small of stature – he was 5 feet 5½ inches tall. Mrs Burrell thought in looking at pictures of Wagner 'that he had a narrow escape of Deformity; he was not in the least deformed, yet the immense Head was poised on the Shoulders at an angle peculiar to Hunchbacks; it caused him to fall an easy prey to Caricaturists'. At Tribschen his general health improved considerably and he would astonish visitors with his acrobatic feats such as climbing the trees in his garden or the façade of his house. His eyesight was to cause him some concern, but the fact that Cosima relieved him of most of his correspondence and wrote most of his prose to his dictation, probably averted serious ocular damage. As a result it was she who spent her old age in near-blindness. In Cosima Wagner found his ideal help-mate; one who willingly sacrificed all to protect, encourage and inspire the genius she loved, who placed his interests above those of herself, her reputation, her husband, her family, even her health. Of all the men and women who fell under his spell, she alone tolerated, understood and forgave his every weakness. Early in 1867 she told Ludwig, 'We are now working at the biography every evening as busily as ants. "Why, you write as if the Holy Ghost were dictating to you!" he said to me recently. "Well", I replied, "there is something very like a Holy Ghost concerned in it." '

Cosima had only been at Tribschen for a day or two when, on 15 May 1866, a telegram and a letter arrived from the King which announced his wish to abdicate in order to be with Wagner forever: at all events he must be with the composer for his birthday in one week's time. Both of them wrote to Ludwig with reasoned advice and timely words of caution. Were the King to renounce his throne then Wagner's income from the privy

30. Wagner at the age of fifty-two; photograph by Hanfstaengl

31. Cosima Wagner

32. Wagner attacking the ear
of the universe; caricature by
André Gill

At the Treasury Door, Mur
(" Punsch." Munich, 186

34. Wagner at Tribschen, 1868

35. Friedrich Nietzsche

36. Cosima and Richard, 1872

Opposite below 38. The Margraves' Opera House, Bayreuth

At Rehearsal.   By Gustave Gaul.
(Vienna, 1875*.)*

Above 39. The Festival Theatre, Bayreuth

Below 40. Wahnfried

41. Wagner as Siegfried: a cartoon from 'Schalk von Leipzig', 5 January 1879. Paul Lindau, an anti-Wagnerian critic crouches by the dragon; Frau von Schleinitz (or perhaps Amalie Materna) is the wood-bird; Liszt and Cosima appear at the sides of Wahnfried, and the notice on the door reads 'Jews forbidden to enter'

Top 42. The interior of the Festival Theatre, Bayreuth. The original set for the Grail scene in *Parsifal* can be seen on stage

Above left 43. Wagner on the stage of the Festival Theatre during rehearsals, August 1875

Above right 44. A subscription certificate for the 1876 Festival, signed by Wagner purse would cease; were Ludwig to join him in Switzerland then Cosima's position would be made very awkward. Wagner's advice was that the King should be patient, devote himself energetically to his duties to the nation, and allow Wagner to create his works in undisturbed tranquillity. In all their minds was the extremely delicate political situation. At that moment Austria and Prussia were set on a collision course; Bavaria would be forced to take sides in the inevitable war. On 10 May Ludwig had reluctantly agreed to the mobilization of the army. At a moment when his very kingdom was in peril, his first desire was to be with Wagner on the composer's birthday, which also happened to be the day of the state opening of parliament. If Wagner would not, or could not, come to Bavaria, then the King resolved to go to Tribschen for the occasion. His plan was concealed from his anxious ministers and subjects. On 20 May he sent his aide-de-camp Prince Paul Taxis to Tribschen. At dawn on the morning of the 22nd he telegraphed birthday greetings to Wagner from Berg to which Prince Paul arranged that Wagner send a reply. After receiving secretary Lutz in his customary early morning audience, he set out for his usual ride. Having thus duped his courtiers into accepting that day to be one of customary routine, he made his escape, with a groom, to the station at Biessenhofen, took an express train to Lindau, crossed the Bodensee to Rorschach and reached Tribschen at midday. The groom announced the arrival of 'Walther von Stoltzing'. For two days Ludwig delighted in the joy of being with Wagner and, on the return journey, he expressed his happiness in three ecstatic telegrams.

Very different was the reaction of his family, his ministers and his people. Widespread indignation greeted the news that, at a time of national crisis, Ludwig's priority had been a pleasure trip. Because of it the opening of parliament had been postponed until the 27th. There was no cheering when the King drove to the *Landtag* and his speech from the throne was received in icy silence. But the great weight of public opprobrium fell on Wagner, Cosima and Hans. Open references to 'the carrier-pigeon Madame Dr Hans de Bülow' and the nature of her relations with her 'friend' at Tribschen filled the Munich newspapers. Wagner, his mistress and the detested Prussian, Bülow, were blamed for leading the King astray. Hans fled to Switzerland, but not before he had printed a tactless and ill-considered letter defending his honour and challenging the editor of the *Volksbote* to a duel. In Wagner's eyes it was essential that the truth behind the press campaign of vilification, the real nature of his relations with Bülow's wife, be concealed from the King. Together with the Bülows, he conspired to trick Ludwig into signing a letter deploring the recent abuse of Hans, commending his artistic achievements in Munich, urging him to remain at his post, attesting to the 'noble and high-souled character' of his wife, and ordering the strictest punishment of the evil perpetrators of these criminal calumnies. Cosima also wrote to the King begging him to sign the letter and show that there was not a word of truth in the shameful allegations:

> My royal lord, I have three children, to whom it is my duty that I should preserve their father's honourable name unstained; for the sake of these children, that they may never cast aspersions on my love for our Friend [i.e., Wagner], I beg you, my most exalted friend, write the letter!

To foist this piece of deceit upon the young monarch was the basest act of Cosima's life. Nor did Wagner ever stoop to anything as low and mean in his whole career. His guilt was made more shameful by the sending of a telegram to Prince Paul Taxis, which hinted that Ludwig would lose Wagner for ever if he did not sign. The King did sign the letter and Bülow published it on 19 June. It convinced few people, many suspected that Wagner had written it, and the press did not withdraw their 'slanders'. More important matters now occupied the newspaper columns, for on 16 June the Seven Weeks' War began, with Bavaria taking Austria's side against Prussia. Having lied to the King and persuaded him to sign the letter affirming Cosima's innocence, those at Tribschen had in effect placed themselves in a more perilous position than before. For there was the ever-present possibility that at any time Ludwig would realize the truth and the deception.

Ludwig had no heart for the war. On the very day of its declaration he was enjoying a fireworks display on the Roseninsel with his beloved Prince Paul and his groom. When Pfordten called upon him he was at first refused entry but forced his way to the King's presence, only to find him with his favourite, dressed up as Barbarossa and Lohengrin in a grotto lit by an artificial moon. It was on Wagner's wise prompting that Ludwig stirred himself to visit his regiments in the field on 26 June. The war went swiftly and Bavaria, like all the other allies of Austria, was overwhelmingly beaten by the Prussian forces. Not so much the bitterness of defeat, but a deeper, spiritual torment prompted an anguished letter from the King to Cosima on 21 July:

> Dearest friend, I beg you to prepare the beloved one for my decision to lay aside my crown. He must have mercy on me; he must not demand that I should endure these torments of hell any longer. My true and God-given mission is this: to live at his side as a faithful, loving friend, never to leave him. Tell him . . . that our plans can be carried out by this means, that I shall die if I must live without him. I shall be able to do more then than I can now as King; then we will have the power to work and live for coming generations. My brother is now of age, and I will hand over the government to him . . .

Cosima replied with calm and soothing words, calculated to give the King hope and strength. Wagner's own reply which followed, is equally diplomatic, and an exhortation to take courage. He skilfully reiterates the vision they have each shared of Ludwig's great destiny as King and urges him to have patience: as he grows older then his hopes and dreams can all be fulfilled. Let the King look forward to the day that Nuremberg, not Munich, will be the centre of German art and Bayreuth the royal residence. Even if Prussia crushes all Germany, 'let *us* prepare quietly and tranquilly the noble hearth at which the German fire can one day rekindle itself'. A telegram brought Ludwig's response: 'Marvellously strengthened. I feel as brave as a hero. I shall hold on.'

Before the end of the war, Wagner's views on Prussia changed and, as the new Germany emerged, his admiration grew for its architect, Bismarck. When Bismarck's peace terms allowed Bavaria to retain her independence, and when Wagner realized the new political importance of Prussia, his former hatred for the powers in Berlin was transformed into enthusiastic praise. Another cause for celebration that resulted from the war was the dismissal of Pfi and Pfo, Mime and Alberich. All his life Pfi claimed his surrender of his post was due to Wagner's interference in Bavarian politics. Pfo cried before his downfall, 'I consider Richard Wagner the most evil man under the sun, a man who would ruin the young King in body and soul.' Of Pfordten's fall, Ludwig remarked that 'the contemptible dragon is now trampled in the dust'. Bülow rejoiced at the enforced departure of Pfistermeister, 'this most abominable beast'. Late in 1866, Pfi was succeeded by Max von Neumayr and Pfo by Prince Hohenlohe-Schillingsfürst.*

All through the turmoil of that year, steady progress was made with *Die Meistersinger*. The orchestral sketch of Act Two was completed on 23 September and the composition sketch of the last act was begun on 2 October. In September Bülow left the awkward ménage at Tribschen and settled in Basel. Wagner now told Ludwig that Cosima was staying at Tribschen where she would be best cared for during her confinement; he had more funds than Bülow to allow her to live in comfort. She in turn dutifully wrote to the King of her plans to visit her husband and provided him with reports of domestic arrangements at Tribschen and the progress of *Mein Leben*. In October a new young disciple came to live at the house: Hans Richter,* a horn player from the Vienna Opera. He quickly endeared himself to the Master and Cosima, who found him refreshingly good-natured and remarkably willing to help with every chore, from amusing the children to copying out the *Meistersinger* score. Richter's diary provides us with an inventory of the Wagner household: there is 'Wagner, Baroness Bülow and the children, Lulu, Boni, Loldi;[1] the housekeeper Vreneli; her niece, Marie; the children's governess; Agnes the nurse; Marie the cook; Steffen, the valet; the boots, Jost; and myself. In addition, two peacocks, two cats, one horse; friends Russ and Koss (dogs),[2] plus a lot of mice.' Soon Richter was recognized by Wagner as the

---

[1] Lulu, or Lusch, was Daniela; Blandine and Isolde were nicknamed Boni and Loldi. The subsequent children were Eva (Evchen) and Siegfried (Fidi).
[2] Russ was Wagner's gigantic Newfoundland; Koss was Cosima's terrier, so named in order to prevent friends applying the abbreviation to herself.

ideal conductor with whom to entrust the *Ring*, a work for which Bülow had little enthusiasm. In any case Bülow would now be something of an embarrassment, and in the young horn player Fate had seemingly provided his successor. As a first step, Wagner resolved to find him a post at the Munich Opera.

On 10 November Malvina Schnorr arrived at Tribschen. In ordinary circumstances she would have been a most welcome guest. As Isolde, she had exceeded Wagner's highest expectations; he had described her performance as incomparably perfect and had likened her to his youthful model, Schröder-Devrient. It was natural that Malvina should feel strong emotional links with Wagner. For the last five years of their married life, she and her husband had lived and breathed *Tristan*, and Ludwig Schnorr had died in a paroxysm of Wagnerian ecstasy. Malvina felt that his untimely end was a direct result of his efforts over *Tristan*, and that she should therefore have a place in Wagner's future life and works. In 1868 Wagner published an essay in praise of Schnorr. Neither in that article, nor in any other printed work does he mention, let alone praise, Malvina. The explanation is to be found in the strange and fateful events of November 1866.

Soon after her sudden and grievous loss, Malvina turned to spiritualism and claimed to have communicated with the spirit of Schnorr through the mediumship of her pupil Isidore von Reutter, whom she brought to Tribschen. Cosima was handed a report of Schnorr's spirit messages which she sent up to Wagner's room. The gist of the communication was that Malvina and Isidore were to play a vital part in Wagner's artistic plans. The spirit had told Isidore that Wagner must arrange a meeting between her and King Ludwig, whom she was destined to marry and guide along the right path. It added that Wagner should in future make less demands on the human voice and write more songs so that his music would be more popular! 'Malvina is correct – out of love for Richard I became a sacrifice to art.' Having perused this extraordinary document, Wagner came downstairs and greeted the women politely. Isidore, he later told Röckel, 'had the figure of a military policeman', and Malvina appeared alarmingly determined upon her mission to rescue Wagnerian art before it went astray. Next morning, Wagner sent her a letter refusing to have anything further to do with her until she dismissed the charlatan Isidore. But not only did Malvina descend upon Tribschen for lunch that day, she also intercepted Wagner on his afternoon walk, regaling him with reports of her husband's tormented last hours and how he now desired her to redeem Wagner's art. Before leaving for Munich on 12 November, she wrote to inform Wagner of her conviction that he would follow them to Bavaria and enact Isidore's prophecy.

Wagner had often speculated on the possibility of communication with the dead. The idea was not unacceptable to him; he frequently saw in ordinary events a portentous significance, and he credited Cosima with psychic powers. With Isidore's ludicrous revelations it was another matter entirely. Normally he would have dismissed outright the ramblings of this feeble-brained, hysterical impostor, but it shortly became evident that Malvina did not intend to let the matter rest. Having realized that Cosima did not believe in Isidore's powers, and having ascertained the nature of her intimacy with Wagner (Cosima was then seven months pregnant), she threatened to expose her as an unclean spirit of darkness, a demon who flouted the will of heaven and placed ignominious fetters upon Wagner's noble spirit. Clearly there was great danger if these women were to gain the ear of the King. The only way to prevent this was to discredit Malvina as a lunatic. Cosima wrote urgently to the King on 14 November with the news that she and Wagner had been alarmed by Malvina's behaviour and it would seem that her mind had been unhinged by Schnorr's death. Eight days later, Wagner wrote to Ludwig warning him that Malvina had lost her reason and, on account of her insane hatred of Cosima, precautionary measures including police protection might be necessary. Meanwhile, letters from Schnorr's widow arrived at Tribschen denouncing Cosima as an infernal spirit on whose head God's vengeance would fall. On 6 December Ludwig wrote to Tribschen with the hope that all was now peaceful there. The King then began to receive letters from Malvina which openly discussed the scandal of Wagner's relations with Bülow's wife. These he duly forwarded to Tribschen. In a bombardment of letters, Wagner begged the King to silence Malvina by threatening to banish her from Bavaria or forfeiting the state pension she had received since Schnorr's death. He enclosed the account of Isidore's vision in which the King was referred to as a 'weak character'. He suggested that Malvina and Isidore are in league with the King's political enemies and that their calumnies and malicious attacks are aimed at discrediting the monarchy. He stressed that the crazy delusions of these women were causing untold suffering to Bülow and that Cosima, 'who in complete innocence showed nothing but kindness to this worthless woman', is now ill, strained and sleepless on account of the affair.

Ludwig did not doubt Wagner's word. He ordered Malvina out of the country or she would lose her allowance. In reply to this, Malvina simply provided him with explicit details of how Wagner and Cosima had duped the King into signing the Bülow letter in June. There were many people ready to testify to the truth of this if only the King would make private inquiries. Ludwig reported this to Wagner and sent for Franz Mrazek in order to gain confirmation. The faithful former servant revealed nothing however. In the end the King did not expel Malvina from Bavaria or confiscate her pension, but merely asked her to leave Munich for a while. Thus her claims seemed vindicated to some extent, and she was free to repeat the truth about Tribschen to all and sundry. Wagner was furious and continued to demand that she should be punished. It may have been that the very insistence and agitation of Wagner's protests of innocence led the King to consider the possibility that he really had something to hide. But Ludwig could not bring himself to accept Wagner's adultery, and became angrily impatient with the entire business. As late as 9 December 1867 he wrote to court secretary Lorenz von Düfflipp:*

> Recently I received a letter from Richard Wagner, in which he asks me to punish Frau Schnorr – in what fashion you will see from the passage from the letter which I enclose herewith. Return it to me quickly; I await your suggestion with regard to this matter. The eternal wrangles and complaints on the part of Wagner, Porges, Fröbel and the rest of them have become thoroughly repugnant to me. I have shown these people so much indulgence and patience, conferred so many benefits on them, that they ought to have every cause to be satisfied and grateful; the thread of my patience is at last beginning to break.

Düfflipp told him frankly that Wagner was lying and that the King had been tricked all along. Ludwig replied:

> If it should be that this sorry rumour is true – which I was never able to bring myself to believe – if it really is a case of adultery after all – then, alas!

Düfflipp was a skilful politician who was able to manipulate Wagnerian affairs without antagonizing the composer as Pfistermeister was wont to do. It was Düfflipp who engineered the final, slow death-scene of the Semper theatre tragedy. In January 1867 Ludwig received Semper's model of the monumental theatre. Like Wagner, the King was greatly impressed with its beauty, and he summoned the architect to Munich to explain its details. Both Ludwig and Düfflipp assured Semper that the building was to go ahead as soon as the necessary land was acquired, and sent him back to Zurich with requests for detailed estimates of costs. After a month Düfflipp informed him that the site for the theatre was unobtainable and it was now proposed to erect it in the Hofgarten. This effectively turned Semper's complete plan upside down, and may well have been intended to discourage him altogether. Incredibly, the affair was prolonged for a further two years. Throughout 1867 Semper waited in vain for any written instructions from Munich or any payment. In November, his son investigated the delay and was told that once a number of political and economic problems were solved, the scheme would be set in motion. His father was invited to settle in Munich as Chief State Architect, and the papers confirming this would be posted to Zurich without delay. No papers ever reached Zurich: Düfflipp pretended to Cosima that they must have gone astray in the post. Cosima's intervention with Düfflipp was Semper's last attempt at gaining satisfaction. All that resulted was a fresh recital of meaningless promises and false hopes. Throughout 1868 Semper's lawyer was engaged in lengthy negotiations with the Bavarian treasury in an attempt to compensate the architect for three years' wasted effort. It was January 1869 before his client received any payment. The shameful humiliation of a great architect, the indignities to which Semper had been exposed, and the futile interruption to his career, were small matters to the victorious politicians. Their successful delaying tactics ensured that the King grew weary of the project; if Wagner would never return to Munich then Ludwig no longer cared about his festival theatre. The King was never aware how badly Semper had been treated, and seems to have thought the architect's behaviour stubborn and unreasonable. That is forgivable if the King was not in possession of the full facts. What is really unpleasant is Wagner's subsequent criticism of Semper's 'mistrustful' attitude. Semper's name must be added to that enormous list of former friends who were ruthlessly kicked aside by Wagner as soon as their usefulness was over.

At the beginning of 1867, the King foresaw none of this. Indeed with Pfistermeister and Pfordten removed, there seemed every chance that Wagner might return to Munich, and the music school, the theatre, the 'model' performances, the Wagnerian journal, and all their other early dreams would now materialize. Wagner preferred, however, to remain at Tribschen and complete *Die Meistersinger*; the prospect of conducting rehearsals or superintending the school did not attract him. Instead he planned to install Bülow as his emissary in Munich. That plan also had its drawbacks: where was Cosima to go? And Bülow had no desire to return to the town where he was hated as a Prussian spy. Were the King to call him, it would have to be under special conditions.

The composition sketch of *Meistersinger* neared completion late in January. Wagner intended to end the opera with the Prize Song and the joyful chorus of the townsfolk, thereby omitting the big speech of Hans Sachs about German art. Cosima protested vehemently at this and spent the whole of 27 January persuading him to change his mind. Ultimately he relented and composed Sachs's address between two and three o'clock in the morning of 28 January. Bülow arrived at Tribschen for a few days on 17 February, the day on which Cosima gave birth to Wagner's second child, named Eva Maria in fitting celebration of the opera's heroine. Wagner was overjoyed. Good news had come from Munich too: announcing his engagement to Sophie, daughter of Duke Max in Bayern and sister of the Empress Elizabeth of Austria, Ludwig worded his telegram on 22 January: 'Walther informs the dear Sachs that he has found his faithful Eva, Siegfried his Brünnhilde.' Following the gossip about the King's lack of interest in women, this news was greeted everywhere with warm approval.

Sophie dutifully adopted Ludwig's love for Wagner, and a secret meeting between them was arranged during Wagner's visit to Munich from 9–18 March. Afterwards she wrote regularly to him. Wagner expressed the hope that the wedding would take place soon. While in the capital he had two audiences with Ludwig, taking the opportunity to explain his need to remain at Tribschen for reasons of health and work, and to arrange with the King favourable terms for Bülow's return to Munich. It was agreed that Hans would be created a regular Kapellmeister, director of the music school, and as a bonus, awarded the Order of the Knight's Cross of St Michael, first class. Wagner also met the new minister-president, Prince Hohenlohe. This clever and experienced tactician gave Wagner the impression that he was wholeheartedly sympathetic, and the composer in turn modestly admitted that Hohenlohe owed his position to Wagner's influence with the King. The minister listened patiently to a recital of Wagner's political principles and prejudices, and having ascertained that he had no intentions of returning to Munich, bade him a cordial farewell and dismissed him from his mind. Wagner's brief return to Munich occasioned a cartoon in *Punsch*, showing the composer knocking at the door of the royal treasury above the caption, 'Just a passing visit'. The jest cost the paper 12,000 florins when Wagner sued for damages.

Hans accepted his royal commission to return to Bavaria, and on 18 April settled in Munich with Cosima, in a large apartment with two rooms reserved for Wagner's use. For Cosima and Wagner this separation was the cause of great anguish, but Bülow's position would have been impossible if he had not brought his wife to the capital. His first duties were to staff the music school (Cornelius, Joseph Rheinberger and Franz Wüllner were among those engaged), and to prepare for the model performances of *Lohengrin* and *Tannhäuser* at the court opera.

Wagner was busily engaged upon the full orchestral score of *Meistersinger* Act Two, but found time to send the occasional word of political advice to Ludwig. He still regarded himself as the 'saviour' of Bavaria, and anxiously suggested changes in the cabinet and the importance of a strong alliance with Prussia. Ludwig tactfully ignored all this, maintaining a polite silence on all matters unconnected with art. If Wagner had not learned the folly of interfering in politics, then the King was well aware of the dangers, and ardently wished the composer would confine himself to his real task. To satisfy a pressing invitation from Ludwig, Wagner agreed to stay at Starnberg for his birthday on 22 May. A villa had been prepared by Cosima, and various gifts were laid out for him including an ingenious combination of piano and desk, presented by the King who had specially commissioned it from Bechstein. Wagner was irritated by the fact that personal contact with the King was confined to two meetings, which hardly justified the interruption to his score. Clearly Ludwig was keen to avoid any more gratuitous political advice from his friend. The Master was in a dark mood when he found himself called from Starnberg to supervise the final rehearsals of *Lohengrin* in Munich, which had not been going well. He had selected the redoubtable Tichatschek for the title role, but at the final rehearsal on 11 June, the King expressed disgust at the choice of the ageing singer, with his flabby powdered face, his uncertain gait, his leering expressions and his marked tremolo. This was not Ludwig's ideal of the youthful romantic Knight of the Grail. To cap it all, Tichatschek wore his own favourite costume, not the one requested by the King, and the Ortrud was also poorly cast. Ludwig returned to

Berg with the peremptory command that both singers must be replaced before the first performance in five days' time. At this, Wagner too became furiously angry and at once stormed back to Tribschen, where he completed the scoring of *Meistersinger* Act Two on 22 June. Poor Bülow was left to cope with the unenviable task of preparing the premiere with the two new principals, Heinrich Vogl and Therese Thoma. After the performance, which was successful, Cosima informed the King how much the absent Wagner suffered. As expected, Ludwig melted and expressed his regret at the incident. Wagner took advantage of this and replied at length on 25 June, pointing out that the King would do better to leave Wagner to decide on theatrical matters, taking the opportunity to inform the King of his displeasure at being virtually ignored at Starnberg, and demanding that the Intendant of the opera, Wilhelm Schmitt, be replaced by a Wagnerite. To this tirade Ludwig responded with suitably conciliatory and penitent words, without actually agreeing to act on Wagner's suggestions. For years Ludwig had looked forward eagerly to the model performance of his beloved *Lohengrin*: the shadows which darkened the event, not least Wagner's sulks and tantrums, must have been hard to bear.

July brought compensatory rewards. The music school was established by royal decree, and the King made a highly successful visit to Paris, encouraged by Wagner. He had been reluctant to go to the French capital, considering it to be a stronghold of 'materialism, base sensuality and godless frivolity'. But Wagner, in a noble admonition, urged him not to miss this opportunity of broadening his knowledge of the world, of seeing the city which was the centre of civilization and where he himself had learned so much about stage-craft. For Bülow's model performance of *Tannhäuser*, at Munich on 1 August, Wagner was conspicuous by his absence. The King could not attend himself owing to court mourning for the King of Greece,[1] but Wagner's aloof attitude disturbed him. Cosima joined Wagner at Tribschen from 11 August until 6 September; she brought news of the disorder and indiscipline at the Munich theatre, and of the dubious attitude of Intendant Schmitt. Liszt arrived in Munich for further performances of *Lohengrin* and *Tannhäuser* late in September. Having no doubt discussed the Wagner affair with Hans and Cosima, he journeyed to Tribschen to see the composer for the first time in three years. Wagner dreaded his visit, but it passed off very agreeably. Liszt was amazed by *Die Meistersinger* and Wagner's warmth of feeling towards his old friend is shown by his efforts to secure Liszt an appointment as director of Catholic church music in Munich, although nothing came of this plan.

On 11 October the King's engagement to Sophie was publicly broken off. For many weeks Wagner had felt anxiety about the continued

---

[1] A private performance was given for Ludwig on 3 August.

postponement of the wedding date, and from Ludwig's letters it was clear that the more he thought about the marriage, the more wretched, tormented and unhappy he became. The annulment of the engagement, despite the inevitable public scandal, lifted a great weight from both the King's and Wagner's shoulders. Ludwig wrote to Cosima:

> What would have become of all our plans if this unhappy marriage had been concluded; if I had been driven to despair by inward suffering, grief and mourning; where should I have found the inspiration to give me enthusiasm for our ideals? My very soul would have been crushed, my golden dreams would have evaporated like idle fancies. No school of art would have been established, no festival theatre would have arisen. *Die Meistersinger* would not have existed for me, the *Ring* and *Parsifal* would not have brought me their blessing. Only a shadow of myself would have dragged out a gloomy existence, devoid of peace and joy, and a tenfold death would have brought me a longed-for happiness. Now all, all will come to pass. I have awakened from an agonizing, torturing dream, and feel again unbending strength, which will be true to its noble mission.

Throughout this difficult period Wagner's letters to the King were understanding and sympathetic, and on 25 October, the day after *Meistersinger* was completed in full score, he wrote to him with advice of the soundest kind: Ludwig should not give way to the temptation to live in isolation, he should be seen more by his people and devote all his energies to affairs of state.

It would have been well had Wagner applied corresponding advice to himself, and had been seen to confine his activities to artistic matters. But before work on *Meistersinger* was ended, he commenced a series of articles, *German Art and German Politics* in the Munich *Süddeutsche Presse*. This was a newly established daily paper, supported by the Bavarian treasury, and intended to reflect the views which Hohenlohe, the King and the Wagner party wished to project as those of the new Bavaria, holding the balance of power between Austria, Prussia and France, in the Europe that emerged from the Seven Weeks' War. The editor, at Wagner's suggestion, was Julius Fröbel, who was to prove sufficiently independent of Wagner's fanatical ideas to incur the eventual wrath of Tribschen. The first of the fifteen instalments of *German Art and German Politics* delighted the King. Although published anonymously, no one could mistake the painful and prolix prose style of Richard Wagner. The glorious German spirit is once more celebrated in a plethora of superlatives; the universal mission of the reborn German Folk-spirit is to 'extend its blessings' beyond its own frontiers. A German prince can achieve this task of redeeming Germany by spreading German goodness and German greatness to less happy lands. Bavaria and her worthy monarchs are duly praised. German music will give birth to a dramatic art of such expressiveness that it will surpass that of ancient Greece. The articles began with a quotation from the pan-German Constantin Frantz, which urged Germany to free itself from the tyranny of French materialism. France, claims Wagner, is 'spiritually bankrupt'. Now that the might of Prussia had been revealed, the flame of French civilization can in a moment be extinguished for ever.

Such extremism of national sentiment was nothing new, and Wagner was not alone in relishing Germany's growing might and the prospect of France's downfall. The ideas expressed in these articles are but one link in the chain between the prophet of National Socialism, Friedrich Ludwig Jahn (1778–1852) and the author of *Mein Kampf*. But the *Süddeutsche Presse* was regarded as the official organ reflecting Bavarian policy, and such hysterical pan-Germanism and open attacks on France at a time of delicate international relations, could not be tolerated. The King realized that the articles were 'suicidal' and, on 19 December, ordered the breaking-up of the type of the fourteenth instalment. Fröbel was perfectly happy to abandon the embarrassing series before the last two articles appeared, and announced the cessation that day. Wagner and Cosima were indignant at this disgraceful public insult. Ludwig was tired of Wagner's folly; he was angry and impatient at the composer's reawakening of the Malvina Schnorr affair, his imprudent articles, and the political meddling of Wagner and Cosima for their own ends. *German Art and German Politics* was published in book form in 1868. It did little to further Wagner's cause in France. When Bizet read Wagner's opinion that it was Germany's destiny to destroy France, he wrote, 'This pasteboard republican would amuse me greatly if he did not make me sick. I would like to rub his nose in his article.' Faced with the diatribes that flowed from Wagner's pen, posterity has tended to Mahler's view that 'one almost has to forget Wagner's writings in order to give his genius due admiration'. It is a tribute to both men, Bizet the Frenchman, Mahler the Jew, that Wagner's baser pronouncements did not blind them to his artistic greatness. Bizet (who was in Rome at the time of the Paris *Tannhäuser* and did not become familiar with Wagner's scores until 1869) wrote movingly to Madame Halévy after she had expressed disgust at Wagner's published opinions of her late husband in 1871:

> Wagner is no friend of mine and I hold him in but mediocre esteem, but I cannot forget the immense enjoyment I owe to his revolutionary genius. The fascination of his music is indescribable. It is all voluptuousness, tenderness, love. . . . The whole of nineteenth-century German thought is incarnate in this man.

Whenever Ludwig expressed dislike of Wagner the man, he was quickly reconciled by his reverence for Wagner the artist. At Christmas 1867 he received Wagner in audience, and the score of *Die Meistersinger* was presented to him. Wagner was delighted with developments at the court theatre: Lachner and Schmitt were leaving; the apparently amiable Baron von Perfall* was to become Intendant; and Hans Richter gained a post as operatic coach. All seemed set fair for a *Meistersinger* production.

The King's attitude over Fröbel irked him though: he had hoped Ludwig would order the publication of the two abandoned articles, and suitably punish the miserable editor if he dared refuse. Ludwig would not comply and did not receive Wagner again, although the composer remained in Munich until February. A gap of three-and-a-half months in their correspondence indicates that all was not well. Before returning to Tribschen, Wagner sent an important letter to Düfflipp, on 5 February; important because it clearly indicates that he was not averse to the idea of presenting the *Ring*, in instalments, in Munich:

> . . . it might not be impossible, should His Majesty wish it, for the separate parts of the cycle to be experimentally performed, following each other year by year.

As will be seen, when this plan came to be enacted, Wagner's behaviour caused an almost fatal breach with the King.

On 9 March 1868, a distracted Ludwig broke the unbearable silence with his friend in a letter confessing the agony this recent estrangement had caused him. Once more Wagner seized the advantage of the penitent royal mood. His reply of the 12th was calculated to wring the heart of the lonely young King. As expected, this woeful lament of Wagnerian self-pity drew a sorrowful letter of repentance from Ludwig, four days later. Wagner returned to Munich for a month in mid March; although the King did not receive him, their letters eagerly discussed the forthcoming *Meistersinger* production, Wagner's plan to complete *Siegfried* by the end of the year, and the issuing of his complete prose and poetical works in ten volumes. It must have amused those who did not share in these lofty dreams, that the illustrious Master had not been twenty-four hours in Munich before he was threatened with arrest on account of a twenty-one-year-old debt to a Frau Klepperbein of Dresden. Hurriedly, Wagner arranged for the treasury to settle this tiresome demand for 2200 florins.

Almost a year was to pass before composition of *Siegfried* was resumed. Wagner's fifty-fifth birthday was spent with the King on the Roseninsel. The *Meistersinger* rehearsals next claimed his attention; he worked hard with the singers, who were greatly impressed with his gifts as producer, and valued his helpful advice. His personal charm was less evident to those who knew him better. Bülow's dedication and enthusiasm were above reproach, but the strain of his private life, the occasional outburst of trouble from the orchestra (led by the antagonistic horn player Franz Strauss, Richard Strauss's father), and the sheer size and complexity of the score, led to displays of exasperation with Wagner. The composer behaved towards his closest friends with more than his usual arrogance and tactlessness: he quarrelled with Cornelius; Weissheimer found him 'changed for the worse' and 'hardly recognized him this year'; Draesecke remarked that 'it isn't exactly pleasant to have anything to do with him at present'; Porges was taken aback by Wagner's offensive attitude to Weissheimer. The latter had rather indiscreetly insisted upon showing Wagner his latest opera, *Theodor Körner*. With *Die Meistersinger* on his mind, Wagner understandably refused to look at the work. It was the end of another friendship.

The premiere took place on 21 June. It was the summit of Wagner's triumphs to date. The work was perfectly in tune with the current awakening of German national consciousness, the magnificent (and historically authentic) costumes delighted all, and the singing was of a high standard of excellence. Franz Betz* sang Sachs; Gustav Hölzel, Beckmesser; Franz Nachbaur, Walther; Mathilde Mallinger, Eva; Schlosser,[1] David; and Sophie Dietz, Magdelene. Ludwig had insisted upon Wagner sharing the royal box, something no commoner had ever done before. 'Horace by the side of Augustus,' remarked Bülow. When the composer acknowledged the overwhelming applause from his place in the royal box, he created a sensation. A leading dissident voice was that of Heinrich Laube, Wagner's boyhood champion, writing in Hanslick's journal the *Neue Freie Presse*. His malicious review was prompted by the mistaken belief that Wagner had conspired to prevent him gaining the Intendantship of the Munich theatre. Hanslick himself found the work 'unbeautiful and unmusical'; apart from a few 'engaging details' he would have been 'tempted to seek refuge in slumber'. Here is a sample of the great critic's acrimony:[2]

> The overture is hardly calculated to win the listener. All the leading themes of the opera are dumped consecutively into a chromatic flood, finally tossed about in a kind of tonal typhoon . . . and must excite in the uninitiated the impression that the Nuremberg Mastersingers were predominantly concerned with cyanide. The only thing which prevents me from declaring it to be the world's most unpleasant overture is the even more horrible Prelude to *Tristan und Isolde*. The latter reminds me of the old Italian painting of that martyr whose intestines were slowly unwound from his body on to a reel. The Prelude to *Die Meistersinger*, at best, goes about it quickly, with spirit and a club.

Such opinions mattered little against the massive chorus in favour of the work; demands for it poured in from all over Europe.

A far more serious criticism reached Wagner's ears upon his return to Tribschen after the first performance. As *Meistersinger* continued to fill the Munich theatre, the King informed Cosima that the old Malvina Schnorr allegations were once more current in the town. In letters of 16 and 19 July, Wagner told Ludwig of his disgust at these scandals issuing from the lowest depths of human depravity which had tormented and besmirched the Bülow marriage. It might lead to Cosima having to leave Munich forever. Ludwig replied with the hope that Cosima would do no

---

[1] Referred to variously as Max, Karl or Anton Schlosser (1835–1916).
[2] In fairness, Hanslick later regarded his first review of the work as hasty and overharsh. He later formed a higher opinion of it.

such foolish thing: that would merely fan the flames of the evil rumours. On 22 July, however, Cosima fled from Munich to Tribschen. No clearer confirmation of her adultery could be conceived. Eight years were to pass before Wagner saw the King again.

August brought forth a sketch for a comic drama on the subject of Luther. The hero symbolized Wagner the redeemer of Germany; Cosima was Luther's bride. In the previous May, when parted from her, the tragic nature of their love had given birth to a musical theme, subtitled 'Romeo and Juliet'. Later Wagner intended to use this melody in various projected instrumental works (including a *Trauersymphonie*, 1871, and a proposed tragic sequel to the *Siegfried Idyll*, 1873); it found its ultimate place in the music for Titurel's funeral procession in *Parsifal*.

From 14 September until 6 October, Wagner and Cosima holidayed in Italy, visiting Stresa, the Borromean Islands, Genoa, Milan, Lake Como (Cosima's birthplace) and Lugano. From Italy Cosima wrote to Bülow announcing her intention to devote her life to Wagner alone. She returned to Munich on 16 October in the hope that her husband would agree to a divorce. Wagner meanwhile wrote to the King to prepare him for such an event. In carefully veiled phrases he depicts Cosima as 'belonging to a different world-order from this', and hints that as a result of a decisive crisis and much suffering, Bülow will shortly find himself alone. These resolutions are things that do not concern the 'shallow world'. Clearly he was hoping for a sign of forgiveness from Ludwig that would enable him to unburden himself with a full confession of the real state of affairs. But the King conveyed his displeasure in eloquent silence: every one of Wagner's letters was left unanswered. Bülow proved no more amenable to Cosima's demands for a divorce. The first obstacle to this was Cosima's Catholicism and Bülow's reluctance to offend the staunch religious feelings of her father. In addition, Bülow was now very content with his position in Munich; a divorce, with the attendant scandal, the inevitable displeasure of the King and the possibility of serious damage to Wagner's cause, would put an end to his career. On 1 November Wagner returned to Munich. He found that Cosima had left Hans and was staying with the Mrazeks. Bülow refused to consider a divorce; the King refused to receive Wagner.

For some mysterious reason Wagner left to visit his relatives, Ottilie and Hermann Brockhaus, in Leipzig. The cause of this secret journey remains obscure, but its result was a most fateful encounter. On 8 November, a young student of classical philology, Friedrich Nietzsche,* joined the evening company at the Brockhaus home. Already a convert to Wagner, through enthusiastic study of the *Tristan* vocal score, Nietzsche was overwhelmed at meeting his hero. Wagner was in his best form that evening; for the young man's benefit he read an amusing episode from *Mein Leben* describing his own Leipzig student days, and delighted Nietzsche by expressing his debt to Schopenhauer. Before the evening was over Wagner extended a cordial invitation to Nietzsche: they must continue their discussion of music and philosophy at Tribschen.

Wagner returned home on 11 November. Five days later Cosima joined him, having left Bülow for ever. From that time until his death, Cosima never left Wagner's side. She was constantly there to worship, to encourage, to protect him from any unwelcome influence. In later years he would wander about the rooms of his house like a soul in torment if she happened to be out for a few hours. To Tribschen Cosima brought Wagner's daughters Isolde and Eva. Daniela and Blandine joined the household in the following April, Bülow having by then abandoned the pretence that his wife was visiting relations in France. The wreck of Bülow's life, and her part in the public deception of the King, weighed heavily in Cosima's mind. She never forgot the high price that was paid when she accepted the higher call of destiny. On the first day of 1869 she began her diary which records, until the day before Wagner's death, not only every detail of every hour of their life together, but the great stain of sorrow and guilt that could never be cleansed from her soul. In these pages she addressed her children, born and unborn, with a plea for understanding and forgiveness. At that time Wagner's pension could have been withdrawn. At any moment the King's displeasure could divest him of everything. The thought of living together with the children in a garret in Paris seemed a real possibility. With her decision to follow the only One unto death, and with his acceptance of her, they knew that they had sealed their fate irrevocably, for good or ill.

A less complicated union had been effected during the *Meistersinger* year. In 1868, Natalie at last found a husband, Herr Bilz of Dresden. The allowance Wagner had made to her since Minna's death now ceased. His principal anxiety was to repossess from Natalie all letters from himself to Minna. She sent him 269 of these and pretended the others were lost or destroyed. Despite Wagner's threat of legal action if any letters were withheld, Natalie retained a large selection of them, carefully choosing those which revealed him in the worst light. Wagner would never have credited her with such subtlety. When Bilz died, he again provided her with a pension. After Wagner's death Cosima continued to support Natalie in the poorhouse where Mrs Burrell discovered her, with her precious hoard of documents.

In addition to *Mein Leben* Wagner found time for other literary work. The *Recollections of Ludwig Schnorr von Carolsfeld* of May 1868 was followed at the end of the year by *Recollections of Rossini*, the Italian master having died on 13 November. The major effort of this period was a lengthy appendix to *Judaism in Music* which was published in book form in March 1869. The reissue of this work was very unwise and was greeted with dismay by most of his friends. The new edition was dedicated to Marie Muchanoff who had innocently inquired why the press was so hostile to Wagner. The answer, declared Wagner, was because it lay in the hands of the Jews. The new postscript to the original essay named Hanslick as the typical Jewish, anti-German critic. 'Hanslick's gracefully hidden Jewish origin' was a reference to the critic's ancestry on his mother's side: Jewish merchant forbears whom Hanslick took care to conceal. No less unpleasant was an anonymous article (subsequently issued as a pamphlet under the pseudonym Wilhelm Drach) of early 1869, pouring scorn upon the reputation of Eduard Devrient. *Herr Eduard Devrient and his Style* masquerades as a review of his former friend's memoir of Mendelssohn, but consists of a cheap, small-minded and rather pointless attack on Devrient's use of language and his admiration for the Jewish composer. The stab-in-the-back technique was familiar to Wagner, but it is particularly distasteful to note that he considered betraying no less a friend than the King himself. It was Cosima who warned him of the folly of making an approach to Bismarck for patronage. Thankfully, Ludwig was unaware how lightly his beloved friend would have turned to the coffers of Prussia had the wind been favourable in that direction. Cosima was right: Ludwig would never have tolerated such an act of treachery.

The first letter from the King in five months is dated 10 February. In the old tones of exuberant friendship, Ludwig turns to Wagner again for strength and solace; he is eagerly awaiting the productions of *Tristan* and *Rheingold* later in the year. Wagner replied with news about Tribschen but concealed the fact of Cosima's presence from the King. On 1 March he took up composition of *Siegfried* after twelve years, and told Ludwig how marvellously he had recaptured the mood of the work. By the middle of the month, plans were under way for the production of the first drama of the *Ring* cycle at Munich. Perfall sent the theatre machinist, Friedrich Carl (Fritz) Brandt to Tribschen, in order to discuss the complexities of the stage movements in *Rheingold*. On Brandt's visit Wagner gave the first clear indication that he opposed the Munich production of the *Ring* in instalments. He told Brandt curtly that the King would be better off with a concert performance, and that Munich was incapable of mounting the work effectively. These were only excuses: his real objection to Munich was that, owing to the unresolved Cosima affair, he dared not go there in person. Wagner hoped that if he refused to collaborate then the King would abandon the production.

On 15 May Nietzsche, now a youthful professor of classical philology at the nearby University of Basel, called at Tribschen while on an excursion. As he neared the house he heard a sequence of chords being repeated over and over at the piano. Later he identified the passage as *Siegfried* Act Three, at Brünnhilde's words, 'Verwundet hat mich, der mich erweckt' – 'I am wounded by he who awakened me'. Words of ominous significance. Wagner was delighted to see the intelligent young man he had met in Leipzig, and invited him to return in two days' time. It was the first of countless happy visits. Wagner's birthday a few days later marked the beginning of a series of innocent household pantomimes that came to celebrate every such anniversary in the Wagner family, and were reminiscent of the charades and children's dramas that Geyer had loved so much. On this occasion Wagner was wakened by Hans Richter playing Siegfried's horn call; Cosima's four daughters, dressed up as the Messengers of Peace from *Rienzi*, recited ancient Greek poems in praise of spring; and the Maurin-Chevillard string quartet arrived from Paris to serenade him with late Beethoven. Nietzsche was a house guest at Tribschen during a weekend in early June. At dawn on Sunday 6th, a cosmic event occurred in the Wagner calendar: Cosima presented the Master with a son. Her diary piously recalls Wagner's reaction to the news, brought to him by Vreneli the housekeeper:

> Then he was surprised by an incredibly splendid glow as of fire, which blazed upon the orange wallpaper beside the bedroom door with a glow of colour such as he had never seen before, and was reflected on the blue casket with my portrait on it, so that the picture . . . was transfigured with an unearthly beauty. The sun had just risen above the Rigi and cast its first rays into the room. The most glorious of sunny days was shining. Richard melted into tears; and now the chime of the bells floated across the lake from Lucerne, ringing for the early service on Sunday morning.

To celebrate the birth of the child, christened Helferich Siegfried Richard, Wagner inserted the Starnberg theme (later the opening theme of the *Siegfried Idyll*) into the final duet for Brünnhilde and Siegfried. From the words 'Ewig war ich' onwards the style of the third act of *Siegfried* is in marked contrast to all that has gone before. The text seems oddly wedded to the newly sprung themes; but musically and theatrically, no better ending to the work could be imagined. To the mood inspired by that splendorous sunrise, the world owes one of the greatest of operatic finales. The composition sketch was completed on 14 June; the orchestral sketch of the act begun on the 25th.

With the birth of her son, Cosima wrote to Bülow (who had learned of the event from the newspapers) and begged him to consent to a divorce, thereby ending an intolerable strain upon them both. Bülow had already resigned his post at Munich, but was waiting to conduct his last work of the season, indeed the one that had first brought him there: *Tristan*. In his reply, he commented on the fatal nature of that work, which had drained his very life away. Although he still refused to contemplate a divorce, his letter is noble and generous. In the breakdown of their marriage he acknowledges all the faults to be on his side; he has given her poor return for her devotion and he has poisoned her life. But now that he is without her he has lost all the support of his own life:

> Your mind, your heart, your friendship, your patience, your indulgence, your sympathy, your encouragement, your advice, and, above all, your presence, your glance, your words, all these have formed and determined the basis of my

life. The loss of this supreme good, whose value I recognize for the first time now that it is lost, and which crushes me both morally and as an artist, makes me realize that I am a bankrupt.

She has abandoned him for one who is pre-eminently superior in every respect: this he accepts. The one consolation in his future agony will be the knowledge that Cosima is happy.

July brought an unexpected and delightful visit from three French admirers: the beautiful, intelligent and lively Judith Gautier, her husband Catulle Mendès and the writer Villiers de l'Isle Adam. They stayed for two weeks at a hotel in Lucerne, but visited Wagner each day at Tribschen. The youthful high spirits of this trio infected Wagner. In her book, *Richard Wagner at Home*, Judith recalled many stories of his wild exuberance. Cosima was still rather weak following her confinement, but Wagner was determined she should join in the fun. One day he began pushing her higher and higher on the children's swing:

Cosima grew white; her hold relaxed and she was about to fall. 'Do you not see that she is fainting?' I cried, throwing myself toward Wagner. He grew pale in his turn, and the danger was quickly averted. But, as the poor woman continued to be dizzy and trembling, the Master concluded it would be wise to create a diversion. He ran rapidly toward the house, and by the aid of the shutters, the mouldings and projections of the stones, he climbed nimbly up the side, and reaching the balcony of the floor above, leaped over it. He had obtained the desired effect, but in replacing one evil by another. Trembling with anxiety, Cosima turned to me, saying under her breath: 'Above all things, do not notice him; do not look surprised, or you can never tell where he will end.'

The happy invasion came to an end. One side effect of Judith's stay was an unwelcome invasion of swarms of curious tourists at Tribschen, for she had published an article on her visit to Wagner, which was reprinted in a Lucerne journal. The famous house was keenly surveyed by holidaymakers on Lake Lucerne; some tried to gain entry to the grounds. Others railed against the immorality of the occupants, and the neighbouring parish of Horw demanded their expulsion from the district.

Wagner continued to behave shabbily over the Munich *Rheingold*. The court theatre had been closed since 28 June for the reconstruction of the stage, installation of complex machinery and lowering of the orchestra pit. With Bülow gone, Wagner ensured that Hans Richter became his new musical ambassador in the capital. As a young man of barely twenty-six, Richter did not command the same respect from the management that Bülow had enjoyed, but Wagner was determined to increase Richter's powers, for his own ends. In July they formed a plan to blackmail the management. Richter agreed to threaten Perfall with his resignation at a crucial point in the rehearsals, unless Wagner's instructions were carried out to the letter. With such a difficult premiere it would be easy to find fault somewhere and use it to gain a tactical advantage. When the designer, Christian Jank, who had delighted Wagner with his lighting and scenery for *Meistersinger*, called at Tribschen, the composer found fault with his ideas. Despite the problems of communication with Tribschen, and the deliberately unhelpful response from there, Perfall and the Munich management went to extraordinary lengths to please Wagner. They secured the best singers, and the finest technicians and players of the first rank were brought from abroad to augment the orchestra. Wagner's hypocrisy led him to encourage Judith Gautier and her friends, together with another visitor, Serov from Russia, to attend the performance; at the same time he hatched his plot with Richter to make life as difficult as possible for Intendant Perfall.

Orchestral rehearsals in the theatre began on 11 August. Two days later Wagner began urging Richter to hand his resignation to the King on the grounds that Perfall was obstructing Wagner's wishes. He hoped that by playing this card, Ludwig would be forced to dismiss Perfall and Richter would gain absolute power in the theatre. For the moment, rehearsals proceeded according to schedule and, on the 18th, Wotan, Loge and Alberich joined the endless procession to and fro, from Bavaria to Switzerland, to consult Wagner. In the face of such compliance with his wishes, his pettifogging complaints had a very hollow ring. At the conference with the three male singers, Wagner attempted to win them over to his plan of sabotage. With Franz Betz, the proposed Wotan, he succeeded. The first performance, arranged for 25 August (the King's birthday), had to be postponed owing to technical shortcomings. The town was full of expectant celebrities, including Liszt, Joachim, Turgenev, Manuel Garcia, Pauline Viardot, Pohl, Hermann Levi,* Saint-Saëns, Klindworth, and the critics Chorley from London and Hanslick from Vienna. The final rehearsal on the 27th, attended by the King and about five hundred others, went through without interruption, and various failings of the stage machinery were compensated for by the musical excellence. Next day Richter wired Wagner suggesting the performance be postponed owing to the scenic problems. Having been fed with the worst reports from Betz, Wagner telegraphed Ludwig the same day demanding a postponement until the difficulties had been resolved, and followed this on the 29th with a letter to the King denouncing the management for failing to obey royal orders, and enclosing Betz's account of the chaos at the theatre. Ludwig did not reply.

On the 28th Richter had played his trump card, sending a letter of resignation (drafted by Wagner) to the King. Next day he was summoned to a meeting of the Intendant at which Düfflipp represented the King. Perfall told the young man of his contract and his obligations to the theatre. Richter replied haughtily that he chose to take orders from no one but Wagner. He was promptly suspended. The management knew that the scenic problems could be overcome; all that was needed now was a willing conductor. Ludwig entirely endorsed this view and wrote to Düfflipp:

> The way Wagner and the theatre rabble are behaving is truly criminal and quite shameless; it amounts to open defiance of my orders and I cannot endure it. Richter may on no account conduct again and must be dismissed at once; that is final. The theatre personnel are to obey my orders and not Wagner's whims . . . for if Wagner's loathsome intrigues were to succeed, the whole mob would grow more impudent and shameless, and would finally become uncontrollable; the evil must therefore be uprooted. – Richter must go, and Betz and the others must be brought to heel. I have never experienced such effrontery in my life.

Düfflipp informed Wagner of the intention to go ahead and hoped that the composer would now respect the King's wish and not prevent the performance. Wagner realized the extent of the King's anger, and wrote to him in pleading tones. Richter must conduct! Surely the King will not insist upon a *Rheingold* that is against the composer's will? Again, Ludwig made no reply. Learning that Wagner had resolved to come to Munich, the King left Berg and moved to the remote Hochkopf. His last instruction to Düfflipp was in the clearest possible language: 'If W. dares to offer any more opposition his allowance is to be taken from him and not another work of his is to be produced on the Munich stage.'

When he arrived in Munich early on 1 September, Wagner was confident that his personal intervention would ensure the reinstatement of Richter. He could not now withdraw his demand for Richter without losing face. Despite threats, insistent telegrams to the King and demands for rehearsals, the theatre door remained closed to him. Both Düfflipp (or Tartufflip as he was now called in the Wagner camp) and Perfall firmly conveyed to him the King's wishes. Completely defeated and humiliated, Wagner returned to Tribschen on the 2nd. Yet another letter to Ludwig, begging the King to countermand the production, was sent and left unanswered. Wagner's clumsy and selfish behaviour also sparked off a fiery response from the press: he and Cosima were attacked mercilessly with a virulence unknown since his expulsion from Munich in 1865. The court theatre approached various conductors to replace Richter – Bülow, Lassen, Herbeck, Levi and Saint-Saëns all declined for one reason or another – and the eventual choice was Franz Wüllner, teacher at the music school. Wagner wrote to this gentleman in the following pretty tones:

> Hands off my score! That's my advice to you, Sir, or to hell with you! Go and beat time for singing clubs, or if you really must have opera scores, get hold of the ones your friend Perfall has written! And you can tell that fine gentleman that if he doesn't frankly admit to the King that he is incapable of mounting my work, I will light such a blaze around him that not all the gutter scribblers who are financed out of the *Rheingold* pickings will be able to blow out. You gentle-

men are going to have to take a lot of lessons from a man like me, before you realize that you have no understanding of anything.

The premiere of *Rheingold*, under Wüllner, took place at last on 22 September. Betz had resigned, so August Kindermann sang Wotan; Heinrich Vogl* was Loge; Karl Fischer, Alberich; and Schlosser sang Mime. Loge's 'narration' (Scene 2) was applauded by the audience who thought they had found a melody among the otherwise endless 'recitative'. Despite Wagner's frenzied agitation, the stage machinery worked perfectly and was in many ways more successful than the subsequent Bayreuth production. Wagner reacted with a nasty little poem, *Rheingold*, which stated that stupid dwarfs could play with the Ring if they liked, but their reward would be the curse of the gold.

One month went by, and Ludwig's anger cooled. On 22 October he re-established friendly correspondence with Wagner, expressing his grief at the recent quarrel, and defending his behaviour as the result of his intense longing to see Wagner's works performed. But despite all his contrition, he gave no indication that he was prepared to abandon plans for *Die Walküre* in Munich in the following year. Wagner had meanwhile begun the full orchestral score of *Siegfried* Act Three on 25 August, but resolved not to hurry this work, or it too would be pushed into premature production at Munich. The task occupied him until February 1871, and even then, as will be seen, he pretended to the King that *Siegfried* was not yet ready. Composition of *Götterdämmerung* began on 2 October 1869. One of his most important essays, *On Conducting*, was serialized in the Leipzig *Neue Zeitschrift* between October and January, and afterwards issued as a pamphlet.

The task of printing the first parts of *Mein Leben* was now underway. Wagner chose an Italian printer, Bonfantini, who worked in Basel. The preparation of this edition of eighteen copies was shrouded in the greatest secrecy, Bonfantini being chosen for the task as he understood no German. Wagner corresponded with him in French, continually reiterating the need for discretion in the undertaking. (It was this air of mystery that prompted Bonfantini to print one unauthorized copy for himself, which was eventually acquired by Mrs Burrell.) For a while Nietzsche was entrusted with the negotiations with Bonfantini, and he read the early proofs. Indeed, their professor in Basel began to prove useful in countless ways, among them shopping in the town for Cosima. He discharged this task with the utmost diligence, ensuring that the goods were of the highest quality, and in particular selecting the children's toys for Christmas with loving care. Nietzsche was a guest at Tribschen for Christmas, when Cosima read to him Wagner's *Parsifal* sketch. As a present, Wagner received from her a newly published edition of Geyer's play *Der Bethlehemitische Kindermord*. He also received a number of Geyer's letters from his sister Cäcilie, which may have convinced him that Geyer was his real father. At the same time he asked Nietzsche to order the motif of a vulture as the decorative emblem for *Mein Leben*: the German for vulture is Geier or Geyer. In a footnote to *The Wagner Case* of 1888, Nietzsche announced to the world that Geyer was Wagner's father. In all probability he based this statement on what he had learned during confidential talks with Wagner.

Early in 1870 Nietzsche sent Wagner the manuscripts of two of his lectures *The Greek Music Drama* and *Socrates and Tragedy*. The composer recognized the boldness of Nietzsche's scholarship, and his first thought was that Nietzsche's talent should be directed towards Wagnerian ends. Here was a passionate admirer who was likely to be of great influence in the academic world. Nietzsche may well have found Wagner and Cosima rather patronizing, but for the moment he looked upon the Master as the best possible influence on his mode of thought, the confirmation and enrichment of his ideas on life and art. He was prepared to overlook Wagner's personal weaknesses, the immoral liaison with Frau von Bülow, Cosima's condescending and ignorant comments on philology or the Classics, even the Master's own pompous criticism of subjects he scarcely understood. Wagner, in later life a fanatical vegetarian, was horrified by Nietzsche's adoption of such a diet, and grew angry when his advice on the necessity of meat was ignored. But, like Cosima, the young professor forgave Wagner his outbursts of vehemence, his frequently coarse manners, and his well-meant but misguided advice. All that mattered to Nietzsche was that he was in the closest proximity to this trans-figured world, this concept of a higher order, a profounder truth, that dwelt in Wagner's mind. He was happy to follow the man who seemed the perfect embodiment of the Greek ideal and the spiritual architect of modern Germany. Wagner began to grow upset when there was a gap of any length between Nietzsche's welcome visits. He formed such a high opinion of his new friend that he considered appointing him Siegfried's legal guardian, since he feared he himself would not live to see his son reach manhood. Despite her frequent irritation because Nietzsche was not sufficiently Wagnerian in his writings, Cosima always gave a warm welcome to the devoted professor. Not surprisingly he was soon very much in love with her.

Some years before, when considering Nuremberg as the ideal platform for presenting *Die Meistersinger*, Wagner had thought of staying in Bayreuth. He had recalled in *Mein Leben* his passing the little town when it was lit by a glorious sunset, long ago in 1835. On the evening of 5 March 1870, Cosima and Wagner looked up the town in the pages of Brockhaus's *Konversationslexicon*. There Wagner read of Bayreuth's rise to fame in the eighteenth century, when the Margrave Friedrich built, among other things, an opera house with – *the largest stage in Germany*. At once Wagner thought of Bayreuth as the home for his long-desired festival, where the *Ring* could be presented in ideal conditions. The town had the advantage of being within Bavaria, but was so near to its northern border that it commanded a fairly central position in Germany as a whole. He began to collect what information he could concerning Bayreuth, and soon discovered its further merits. There was no regular theatre season there, nor was it a popular summer resort, nor near to any spas or tourist centres. In other words, there would be nothing to detract from his own festival in such a place, and it was likely that the town authorities would welcome a venture that would bring new life and commerce. For the moment, Wagner breathed not a word of his Bayreuth idea to Ludwig. The King, in his own letters, avoided another topic: the forthcoming premiere of the second drama of the *Ring* cycle, *Die Walküre*.

Wagner had laid down his conditions concerning a Munich *Walküre* performance in a letter to the King on 12 January. He must be given full command of the production; the court theatre should be entirely his for six weeks; he may choose his own conductor, singers and assistants; he will not be responsible to the Intendant but take his instructions direct from the Court Secretariat; Perfall should be given leave for the duration of the rehearsals and production, which itself should not take place until 1871. Ludwig was not prepared to grant one of these demands, and he ignored Wagner's letter. Düfflipp made an approach to Bülow but, writing from Italy, Hans refused the invitation to conduct *Walküre*. It was therefore to Franz Wüllner that the honour again fell of conducting a Wagner premiere. The composer was frustrated and annoyed: his various attempts from April till June to persuade the King to abandon the idea, or to make the performance a private 'rehearsal' with no admittance to the public, had been disregarded. There were still signs of royal regard, however. For Wagner's birthday the King sent an equerry to Switzerland with the gift of a horse, named 'Grane'. On the great day, 22 May, Wagner was greeted by the girls of the house, adorned with garlands of roses, and a regimental band, forty-five men strong, and secretly rehearsed by Cosima, serenaded him with his *Huldigungsmarsch*.

Die Walküre was first performed on 26 June. Heinrich Vogl and his wife Therese sang Siegmund and Sieglinde; Kindermann, Wotan; Sophie Stehle, Brünnhilde; Anna Kaufmann, Fricka. Wagner of course remained away, and hoped his friends would do the same. The audience that night included Liszt, Brahms, Joachim, Saint-Saëns, Duparc, and Judith and Catulle Mendès. The opera was presented again three days later, and in July there were three performances of *Rheingold* and *Walküre* in sequence. Both press and public were most favourably impressed. The mood of the country was warlike, and the audience warmed to Wagner's warrior maidens. There was wild cheering and applause at Brünnhilde's battle cry, and at Wotan's words 'denn wo kühn Kräfte sich regen, da rat' ich offen zum Krieg': 'for wherever bold powers stir, there I openly encourage war.'

War between France and Prussia (backed by Bavaria) broke out on 19

July. Wagner could hardly contain his joy and patriotic fervour. Ironically, there was a French invasion of Tribschen just as the Master was screaming for Gallic blood. The Mendès couple, Villiers, Saint-Saëns and Duparc were entertained with extracts from the *Ring* and exhibitions of crude German chauvinism: 'War is sublime!' declared Wagner. As the weeks went by his intoxication knew no bounds. He wanted to write to Bismarck and beg him to bombard Paris, as the burning of that city would be the symbol that at last the world was to be set free from the oppression of all evil. Their friend Nietzsche took part in the war as a medical orderly, and fell victim to dysentery and diphtheria. Meanwhile Wagner and Cosima studied his essay *The Dionysian Outlook*. On 20 August Wagner sent the King the orchestral sketch of *Götterdämmerung* Act One, which together with a poem, *Gesprochen ist das Königswort*, congratulating Ludwig on the mobilization of the army, had been completed early in July. On 18 July Cosima obtained her divorce, Hans having at last consented. She and Wagner were married on the King's birthday, 25 August, at the Protestant church in Cologne. Liszt read of the event in the newspapers, and showed his feelings by instructing his bank to continue sending her allowance to 'Baroness von Bülow'. He was spiritually far removed from his daughter at this time: the fall of France grieved him as much as it seemed to delight her.

The now legitimate Siegfried was christened on 4 September. On the first day of that month the French suffered a crushing defeat at Sedan, and the Second Empire was over. On hearing the news Wagner declared, 'This is a christening present for Fidi. . . . God in heaven, what a destiny! I am fatal to the Napoleons. When I was six months old there was the battle of Leipzig, and now Fidi has made mincemeat of the whole of France!' In this outburst of nonsense and delusion, Wagner may have hinted at a truth. His intense hatred of France may well have stemmed from his earliest boyhood, when the first stories he ever heard were of the atrocities of the detested Napoleonic troops.

The centenary essay, *Beethoven*, was written during the Franco-Prussian War. It evolved from a sketch of seven short paragraphs in the Brown Book headed 'Beethoven u.d. deutsche Nation', where it is clear that, without naming him, Wagner conceived his essay as a reply to Hanslick, specifically the critic's seminal study *Vom Musikalisch-Schönen* (Beauty in Music) of 1854. This brochure was Hanslick's most important contribution to musical aesthetics, in which he defended the 'integrity' of musical structure against the prevailing contemporary view that music was the expression of poetic content or emotion. What cannot be said in purely instrumental terms is beyond the realm of music proper; the boundaries of music cannot therefore be extended by union with poetry, programmatic explanations or descriptive titles. Music is limited to the sphere of sound, to pure tones and rhythms; it cannot depict or explain people, objects or philosophical systems. Its beauty lies in its inherent formal structure. These views were anathema to Wagner, and he criticized their author for devising an aesthetic theory that denies music's essential relationship to the Sublime. Hanslick had been appointed professor of the history and aesthetics of music at the University of Vienna in 1861. The Brown Book sketch ends by asking what was to be thought of a nation who raised to high academic distinction someone 'who babbles such wretched stuff'. *Beethoven* is Wagner's most important treatise on musical philosophy, and it leans heavily on Schopenhauer, seeing music as a presentation of the inner essence of all phenomena. The real category of music is not beauty, but the Sublime. Harmony is beyond physical time and space. The true world of sound is like a dream world of which our waking consciousness perceives only an allegory. Beethoven's music strove not towards mere beauty, but transcended our earthly concepts and touched upon sublime serenity and joy. In his *Parerga und Paralipomena*, Schopenhauer discussed visions, dreams and clairvoyance. Wagner extends Schopenhauer's theory of dreams to the world of sound. There is a sound-world parallel to the familiar sight-world of dreams. The inspired act of composition is a clairvoyant experience; the composer receives his inspiration in an ecstatic dream-like state. To the aware listener his music has the power to shut out all outward phenomena, to draw him into his undisturbed inner world.

The philosophic nature of this essay is absent from his other literary efforts of the following months. During the horrors of the Siege of Paris, Wagner gloated over the terrible privations and hardships of the French in a merry 'farce', *Eine Kapitulation*, which he held to be in the style of Aristophanes. This foul and ugly specimen of mockery, with its clumsy attempts at plodding Teutonic humour, is one of the saddest illustrations of the level of crudity to which a great mind could sink. Through Hans Richter he attempted to print it in a Berlin journal; it was wisely rejected, whereupon Wagner tried to persuade Richter to set it to music as a parody of Offenbach. The sorriest incident in the story was the publication of *Eine Kapitulation* in 1873, when there was no longer the excuse of war hysteria in its defence. This public display of his coarse and boorish hatred of France caused an angry reaction against Wagner's music in that country, which lasted until his death. It was not the only product of his reaction to the German victory. In January 1871 he sent Bismarck a poem, *To the German Army before Paris* in which he insults France, extols militarism and hails the new German Reich. A *Kaisermarsch* followed, with a choral finale which Wagner hoped might become the national anthem of the Empire. The music matches the banality of the text. Wagner's admiration for the German army only lasted for a few years. His nationalism was in exact ratio to his hopes that Bismarck and the Empire would be of use to him.

Thomas Mann remarked that 'German spirit was everything to Wagner, German state nothing'. When Hitler took Wagner's dramas to signify the glorification of power and world domination, he succeeded in reversing their meaning. Mann correctly interpreted Wagner's *Ring* as a warning: his portrayal of power and the will to dominate shows that the result is total corruption and destruction, indeed the complete annihilation of a race. In this sense alone was his art prophetic of National Socialism. The much criticized nationalism of *Die Meistersinger* Mann fairly compared with that found in the English Histories of Shakespeare. Wagner was not a nationalist composer; he in no sense reflected folk art. His nationalism was opportunism. In the early 1870s he tried hard to woo the powers in Berlin, and spoke grandly of the *Ring* coinciding with the victories of the Reich. When Bismarck and the Kaiser showed that they had no intention of patronizing him, his regard for all things German quickly vanished and he came to detest Prussian militarism. His subsequent opinion of the Iron Chancellor was very low: 'a man who could reap but could not sow'. As his son Siegfried grew older Wagner was sickened by the thought that he might be conscripted into the German army. Very different were his feelings in 1871 when his patriotism knew no limits. During the early Bayreuth years, his favourite reading was the German General Staff's account of the war with France. The *Kaisermarsch* was but an offshoot of a grander plan for a *Trauersymphonie*, a symphony of mourning for the fallen, intended to be performed during a victory parade in Berlin. This was never realized. Instead, Wagner the nationalist is remembered by such things as his sorry *Kapitulation* which depicts Hugo and Offenbach as sewer rats. It is hard to believe that the same mind conceived the *Ring*.

On quite a different level was his gift to Cosima upon her birthday on Christmas Day 1871. Hans Richter rehearsed a group of musicians in Zurich and Lucerne in a work filled by Wagner with themes intimately connected with Cosima. This *Tribschen Idyll*, later published as the *Siegfried Idyll*, contained a trumpet part of thirteen bars which Richter played himself, having reportedly rowed out to the middle of the lake to practise out of earshot of Tribschen. On the morning of the 25th Cosima learned the reason for Richter's sudden and mysterious devotion to the trumpet. Her diary reads:

> As I awoke, my ear caught a sound, which swelled fuller and fuller; no longer could I imagine myself to be dreaming, music was sounding, and such music! When it died away, Richard came into my room with the five children and offered me the score of the symphonic birthday poem – I was in tears, but so was the rest of the household. Richard had arranged his orchestra on the staircase, and thus was our Tribschen consecrated for ever.

She also received from Nietzsche a manuscript, the *Genesis of the Tragic Idea*, from which his *Birth of Tragedy* was to develop. She was pleased: 'I am particularly glad that Richard's ideas can be expanded in this field.'

On 1 March 1871 Wagner wrote to the King claiming that the full score of *Siegfried* was not yet ready (which was a barefaced lie) and that he wished to withhold the work until *Götterdämmerung* was complete. He has an idea for a festival somewhere in Bavaria where there is a theatre, and the entire *Ring* can be presented ideally. He does not mention Bayreuth by name, but it was to view that town that he and Cosima left Tribschen in mid April.

Twelve

The Master of Bayreuth

Es gilt wohl nur ein redliches Bemühen!
Und wenn wir erst in abgemessnen Stunden
Mit Geist und Fleiss uns an die Kunst gebunden,
Mag frei Natur im Herzen wieder glühen.

Goethe

THE FINAL TWELVE YEARS of Wagner's life were predominantly concerned with the establishment of his festival theatre at Bayreuth. In addition to the completion of the *Ring*, his energy was devoted to the organization of the 1876 festival, the fight to save the enterprise from financial ruin, the composition of *Parsifal* and the achievement of the second and last festival of his lifetime, in 1882. His capacity for work was boundless, but the accomplishments of these years took a heavy toll: chest and heart pains, that had worried him as early as 1866, recurred with alarming frequency. At Tribschen Cosima told him that he would be doing his finest work at ninety. Had it not been for the uphill effort that every step towards the Bayreuth goal entailed, then her prophecy might have proved correct. The creation of Bayreuth was as important a part of Wagner's legacy as any of his dramas; the burdens and struggles it entailed meant that he died, in Newman's words, 'a sacrifice to his idealism'.

The first problem was with the King. By the terms of Wagner's 1864 contract with the Bavarian state, the *Ring* was Ludwig's property, and he had the right to perform its parts as and when he liked. He was already anxious to hear *Siegfried*, even to perform the two acts he knew to be complete. Düfflipp made this clear to Wagner when they met in Augsburg on 15 April 1871. The composer was set against the idea, and continued to pretend that the final act was still unfinished, knowing that no one could dispute this. Ludwig had the legal power to prevent Wagner performing any part of the *Ring*; therefore to win him over to the Bayreuth idea was a task requiring delicacy and diplomacy. These were not qualities which Wagner possessed in abundance. One tactless move and all his hopes could be ended. At their Augsburg meeting, Wagner told Düfflipp of his plan for Bayreuth. The court secretary at once informed

252

the King, who wrote to Düfflipp on 19 April: 'I dislike Wagner's plan very much: it will be perfectly impossible to produce the entire Nibelungen cycle in Bayreuth next year.' Wagner and Cosima had meanwhile arrived in the little Franconian town. An inspection of the Margrave's opera house quickly revealed its unsuitability. This rococo gem of 1747 enchanted the connoisseur of theatres, but its formal tiers of boxes and tiny seating capacity in relation to stage size, ruled it out for his purposes. The town itself greatly pleased him and he was given an enthusiastic reception by the civic authorities. Not only was a location chosen for the proposed festival theatre, but, near to it, he found a site upon which to build his home. With Cosima he proceeded to Berlin, calling *en route* at Leipzig, where he heard a rehearsal of his *Kaisermarsch*, and at Dresden, where they spent two days with Pusinelli.

Outwardly, the Prussian visit was the result of his election to the Berlin Royal Academy of Arts, where, on 28 April, Wagner read his installation thesis, *On the Destiny of Opera*. Like *Beethoven*, this was the product of a lifetime of reflection on music and the theatre, and it further develops Schopenhauer's ideas. Interestingly (and as in *Beethoven*), music and mime are regarded as the essential features of the complete art-work, the poet's task being only to shape the framework. Yet only three years before, *Opera and Drama*, with its emphasis on poetry's supremacy over music, had been reissued with a new preface, and the introduction to the published version of *On the Destiny of Opera* rather perplexingly refers the reader to his earlier Zurich essay.

Wagner had other aims in Berlin besides making a speech and receiving an academic tribute: the Bayreuth idea would need massive financial and practical support. While crowds gathered outside his hotel to catch a glimpse of him, while he attended the inevitable dinners, accolades and serenades that were a feature of his visits to most towns in these years, while the Emperor, Empress and all the Imperial court were present at concerts in his honour, he set about finding support for his project in Berlin. Marie, Countess von Schleinitz* was to prove a pillar of support in the Prussian capital, and Tausig, who now resided there, joined her in helping to plan fund-raising. Wagner met the proposed architect of the Bayreuth theatre, Wilhelm Neumann, and on 3 May had an interview with Bismarck. The Imperial Chancellor listened respectfully to Wagner's plan but made no promise to help, perhaps out of a desire not to offend the King of Bavaria.

Ludwig quickly came to the support of his friend's ambitions. He knew that Wagner would never come back to Munich, although the Cosima problem was now resolved. The Semper theatre project was dead, and the composer's opinion of the court theatre was in no doubt following the *Rheingold* and *Walküre* episodes. Above all, Ludwig knew that the personal, spiritual bond between Wagner and himself, forged so lovingly in the early months of their friendship, had been broken asunder for ever. In

Bayreuth, Wagner had found the final and highest ideal of his career, and the King knew that Wagner's idealism could never be thwarted or compromised. It was Bayreuth or nothing. He studied Wagner's papers, *On the Destiny of Opera* and *On the Production of the Stage-Festival-Play 'The Nibelung's Ring': a Communication and Summons to the Friends of my Art*. On 12 May Wagner publicly announced his intention to mount the *Ring* in a specially constructed theatre at Bayreuth in 1873. Money would be raised by means of Patronatscheine (patrons' certificates) which, at 300 thalers each, gave a comfortable donation towards the building costs of the theatre, and guaranteed the purchaser a seat for the *Ring* cycle. Baron Loën, Intendant of the Weimar theatre, became chairman of the Patronat Committee. Wagner's original estimate of the cost of building the theatre was 300,000 thalers. Emil Heckel,* a music publisher in Mannheim, suggested the formation of Wagner-Vereine (Wagner societies) throughout Germany which could arrange fund-raising events and purchase Patronatscheine to share out among members who could not afford individual certificates at 300 thalers. Wagner approved this scheme and Heckel became president of a network of Wagner-Vereine.

Wagner was back at Tribschen on 16 May, having called at Leipzig, Frankfort, Darmstadt and Heidelberg to summon support for Bayreuth. A letter from the King followed on the 26th, declaring that 'the gods have inspired your plan for performing the Nibelungen work in Bayreuth'. Ludwig's principal doubt is whether the theatre can be ready in one year. The birthday celebrations on 22 May followed the now-familiar pattern: on this occasion Wagner rose to be greeted by a tableau – Cosima as Sieglinde with tiny Siegfried in her arms, Daniela as Senta, Blandine as Elizabeth, and Isolde and Eva as their operatic namesakes.

The early death of Tausig on 17 July, news of which reached them on the day the terrier Koss died, was a grievous blow to the early plans. For a short while his enthusiasm had given great impetus to the appeal. Throughout the summer and autumn Wagner composed the second act of *Götterdämmerung*. The composition sketch was begun on 24 June; the orchestral sketch completed between 5 July and 19 November. The loss of Tausig was not the only worry of that year. Response to the Patronatscheine scheme was slow; initial interest in Berlin waned when people realized Wagner was set upon building his theatre in faraway Bayreuth. Other towns (not only in Germany but as far away as London and Chicago) offered sites, and were prepared to lend financial assistance if Wagner changed his decision as to where to place his theatre. But he never wavered from the choice of Bayreuth, where the sympathy of the town council and the friendship of a local banker, Friedrich Feustel, proved invaluable. On 7 November the town formally approved Wagner's scheme, granted him a free site for building, and pledged its wholehearted support. Early in December Ludwig agreed to buy the land for Wagner to build his home in Bayreuth, and on the 14th of that month the composer inspected the new theatre site, the first one having proved impractical.

In order that the Wagner-Vereine should attract sufficient interest, Heckel advised Wagner that he would be required to visit these clubs and conduct concerts. As the Patronatscheine continued to find few supporters, he therefore became involved in the most exhausting aspect of the Bayreuth preparations: strenuous concert tours which strained his health, and hampered progress with *Götterdämmerung*. The first of these concerts occurred in Mannheim on 20 December. Cosima naturally attended, and Nietzsche came from Basel. Wagner returned to Tribschen for Christmas and wrote to the King on the 27th, expressing, as well he might, his great debt of thanks to Ludwig for all his loyal help. Knowing Ludwig's fear that Bayreuth would become a showpiece of Prussian patronage, Wagner is careful to make it clear that he has not turned to any other German prince for aid. He does not mention that he would have leapt at any such offer, particularly if the Prussian Hohenzollerns, whom Ludwig detested, had shown willingness to open the Imperial coffers to him. Turning to the festival itself, Wagner proposes that the King will be given a private performance of the *Ring* cycle in the guise of a 'final rehearsal'. Ludwig's reply of 3 January is in his noblest vein, with not a word of reproach concerning Wagner's past behaviour:

> In spite of all the storms that often seem to divide us, of all the cloud-racks that gather between us, our stars will yet find each other . . . when we at last reach the holy goal we had set ourselves from the beginning, the life-giving, all-illuminating central sun of the eternal godhead for which we suffered and fought undaunted, we shall account for our deeds, the meaning and object of which were to spread that light over the earth, to purify and perfect mankind with its sacred flames, making it the partner in everlasting bliss.

Literary work continued alongside composition and the Bayreuth appeals, throughout 1871 and 1872. The death of Auber, on 12 May 1871, prompted his *Recollections of Auber*; the commencement at last of a long-desired publication brought forth a *Preface to the Collected Edition* of his prose and poetical works. Boïto, in his capacity as translator, was the recipient of a *Letter to an Italian friend on the Production of 'Lohengrin' at Bologna*. In 1872 there followed *To the Burgomaster of Bologna, Actors and Singers* (which includes his last tribute to Schröder-Devrient), *On the Name Music-Drama, Letter to an Actor*, and an *Open Letter to Friedrich Nietzsche*.

Nietzsche's first book, *The Birth of Tragedy out of the Spirit of Music* arrived at Tribschen early in 1872. The original conception of this work had little to do with Wagner, but was primarily involved with ancient Greek culture and its relevance to modern Germany. Nietzsche's visit to Tribschen of April 1871 altered his approach to the book, and throughout the summer and autumn he worked at its final section, linking his ideas on Greek tragedy with Wagner's art. Nietzsche defines two elements of early Greek culture, the form-creating force which was Apollonian, and the emotional element, characterized pre-eminently by music, which was Dionysian. The two elements were antithetical, the Dionysian element tamed by the Apollonian, Apollo harnessing Dionysus. The revival of music through Wagner's genius would infuse new life into tragic myth. In modern Germany there will be a rebirth of the Hellenic world. Naturally Wagner and Cosima warmly approved of this book. Hans von Bülow was so taken with it that he travelled around with a supply of copies to give away. Nietzsche's university colleagues reacted differently to his poetic metaphysics, his spurious marriage of classical philology with a modern musical cult figure, and not one student enrolled for his classes in the autumn of 1872. In the open letter mentioned above, Wagner defended his friend against his critics in self-important, amateurish language, which served only to damage Nietzsche's academic reputation even more.

Composition of the final act of *Götterdämmerung* began on 4 January 1872. Owing to a new problem over the site for the festival theatre, he journeyed to Bayreuth later in the month. The third and final site was then chosen and, with 12,000 florins from the King, he bought the plot of land for his house. Returning to Tribschen, he commenced the orchestral sketch of *Götterdämmerung* Act Three, and sent to Bayreuth meticulous details regarding his house – its size, situation, layout of the garden, types of shrubbery, position of the drive, all minutely described like an elaborate set of stage directions. During March, Düfflipp conveyed to Wagner the King's displeasure at the withholding of the *Siegfried* score. The order to perform this work in Munich had been given one full year before; Perfall had already had designs made, and piano rehearsals were under way, using the published vocal score, but without the full score nothing more could be done. Düfflipp wrote that 'The extremely disagreeable sentiment evoked by your refusal of the orchestral score of *Siegfried* still persists and this disharmony can only be removed by the fulfilment of His Majesty's wish.' Furthermore, in answer to Wagner's question as to whether to invite the King to the ceremony of laying the foundation stone of the Bayreuth theatre, 'such an invitation is not desired'. On 10 April Wagner completed the composition sketch of *Götterdämmerung* and twelve days later he left Tribschen for ever.

On the eve of his departure, a new disciple had joined the Wagner household: Joseph Rubinstein,* who was to remain at the composer's side ever after, as a faithful amanuensis, assistant pianist and musical jack-of-all-trades. Rubinstein had introduced himself to Wagner with a remarkable letter which reached Tribschen in February. It began, 'I am a Jew. This tells you everything.' There followed an account of the hardships and dangers for Jews like himself in contemporary Germany. He was approaching Wagner not for pity, but to offer his services in the completion and production of the *Ring*. Gloomy and withdrawn by nature, he often proved an embarrassment and a burden to the family and their friends, but his devoted work and untiring willingness fully compensated for this. In his original letter to Wagner he confessed to having attempted suicide. When Wagner invited him to join his household, he gave the young man a reason for living. In the year after Wagner's death, Rubinstein took his own life.

The Fantaisie Hotel at Donndorf, a short distance from Bayreuth, was Wagner's residence from 24 April (until September), Cosima joining him there on the last day of the month. On 6 May he was in Vienna for a Wagner-Verein concert. This set the pattern for all such events: a concert of Wagner extracts and a Beethoven symphony, speeches and a banquet, surrounded by an exhausting bustle of publicity and excitement. He was back at the Fantaisie on 14 May, ready to organize the most important event of the year – the laying of the foundation stone. The eleven-year silence in the Wagner-Liszt correspondence was broken on 18 May with the following letter from Wagner:

My great and dear Friend!

Cosima maintains that you would not come, even if I were to invite you! Well, we should have to endure that as we have had to endure so much else! But I cannot forbear to invite you. And what do I say to you when I speak the word 'Come'? You came into my life as the greatest man whom I was ever privileged to address as an intimate friend. Gradually you drifted apart from me, perhaps because you never felt so close to me, as I to you. Instead of your personal presence, there came to me the reborn, inmost essence of your spirit, and this fulfilled my longing to have you close to me. Thus you live in full perfection before me and within me, and we are united as if beyond the grave. You were the first to ennoble me with your love; to a second higher life I am now wedded in *her*, and can do what I could never have achieved alone. Thus you could become all to me, while I could remain so little to you. How immeasurably, then, have I the advantage of you!

And so when I say to you, 'Come!' I say 'Come to yourself!' For here you will find yourself. Blessings and love to you, whatever you decide!

Your old friend,
Richard.

Liszt did not come, but he sent this reply, which was delivered on the day of the ceremony by Baroness Olga von Meyendorff:

Dear, noble Friend,

I am too deeply moved by your letter to be able to thank you in words; but from the depths of my heart I hope that every shadow, every circumstance that holds me fettered far away will disappear, and that we shall soon meet again. Then you will see clearly how inseparable my soul remains from *both of you*, and how intimately I live again in your 'second' higher life, in which you will accomplish what you could never have accomplished alone. In this is heaven's pardon for me: God's blessing on you both, and all my love. (*Postscript*) It goes against the grain with me to send these lines through the post. They will be handed to you on the 22 May by a lady who has been for several years acquainted with my thoughts and feelings.

Wagner took Liszt's refusal to come in bad part, and was pointedly rude to Baroness Meyendorff, whom Cosima regarded as a 'spy'.

In later years, the prevailingly wet weather was the one feature of Bayreuth that Wagner came to detest. On the morning of the ceremony it behaved characteristically and poured down upon the group of staunch supporters who climbed up the muddy hill to the theatre site. Among them were Cornelius, Porges, Nietzsche, Marie Muchanoff, Malwida von Meysenbug, Countess Schleinitz and Countess Dönhoff. The stone was set in place to the strains of the *Huldigungsmarsch*, and a metal casket was also lowered into the ground. This contained a telegram of good wishes from the King, and a verse of Wagner's:

> Hier schliess' ich ein Geheimnis ein,
> Da ruh' es viele hundert Jahr':
> So lange es verwahrt der Stein,
> Macht es der Welt sich offenbar.

(Here I enclose a secret, may it rest there for many centuries: so long as the stone preserves it, it will declare itself to the world.)

Three times Wagner struck the stone with a hammer and cried, 'Be blessed, my stone! Stand long and hold firm!' He turned away and it was observed that he was deathly pale and there were tears in his eyes. Other hammer blows followed and then, owing to the weather, the company repaired to the Margrave's opera house to hear Wagner's speech. He referred to the unique nature of the event, and described what his friends would find when they next met in Bayreuth:

> You will see an outer shell made of the very simplest material which will remind you at best of those wooden structures which are knocked together in German towns for choral gatherings and the like, and pulled down again as soon as the festival is over. But as soon as you step inside this building it will become clear to you which part of it has been built to last. . . . The subsequent mysterious entry of the music will next prepare you for the unveiling and distinct portrayal of scenic pictures that appear to manifest themselves out of an ideal world of dreams.

Otto Brückwald was the final choice of architect and together with Karl Brandt* he was to adapt Semper's Munich theatre plan to Bayreuth conditions. The features of the Riga theatre that had interested Wagner thirty-five years before – the sunken orchestra pit hidden from the audience by an acoustic cover, the amphitheatre layout of the seating – would here be brought to perfection. In his Paris story, *A Happy Evening* of 1841, the desire for the orchestra to disappear is clearly expressed:

> We were agreed that when a beautiful instrumental piece is being performed, nothing is more prosaic and off-putting than the spectacle of the wind players'

horribly swollen cheeks and distorted physiognomy, than the unaesthetic scrabbling of the double basses and cellos, than the boring up-and-down movements of the violinists' bows. Therefore we had chosen a place from which we could hear the orchestra's every nuance without being distracted by the sight of the players.

'. . . oh, my invisible, sunken, – transfigured orchestra in the theatre of the future!' Wagner had cried to Ludwig in May 1865. Now at last it was to come into being, not only for acoustical reasons but so that the eye would be carried unhindered to that magical stage, the gulf between audience and actors making the scenes appear at once unreal and yet larger than life.

The climax of events on 22 May was a memorable performance of Beethoven's Ninth, under Wagner, in the old opera house, with singers and orchestra brought from all over Germany. The soloists were Marie Lehmann (Lilli's sister), Johanna Jachmann-Wagner (the composer's niece), Niemann (now having been reconciled with Wagner ten years after the Paris catastrophe) and Betz. The celebrations were no doubt extended well into the night in the hostelries of Bayreuth. But next morning Wagner rose with the all-too-real task before him of solving the innumerable practical problems of the scheme, raising money, writing endless letters, planning concert tours, and, not least, orchestrating *Götterdämmerung*. It was apparent that there could not be a festival in 1873, but Wagner hoped that all would be ready for the following year. On 22 July 1872, he completed the orchestral sketch of *Götterdämmerung* Act Three and, in August, Niemann stayed with him in order to study the role of Siegmund.

Having ascertained that they would be welcome, Cosima and Wagner set out on 2 September for a three-day visit to Liszt, who was staying at Weimar. Cosima, anxious to discuss her decision to become a Protestant with her father, was saddened by his seeming depression, world-weariness and 'spiritual lassitude'. He was a little more cheerful on visiting Bayreuth (15–20 October, staying at the Wagners' new house, a rented property in the Dammallee) and devoted admiring hours to studying Wagner's work, also playing through *Christus* to his son-in-law. Unfortunately the return visit was marred by displays of jealous ill-temper on Wagner's part. Poor Cosima was regularly subjected to her husband's legendary coarse language whenever she was tactless enough to show a little too much affection towards her father. She told her diary on 30 October, the eve of her reception into the Protestant church, 'I must indeed have been guilty of some neglect . . . but it seems to me that it is not right of him to fly out at me so violently time after time.'

The year was not without public controversy. In June, Wagner did himself little good by becoming involved in a nasty sequence of corres-pondence in the Augsburg *Allgemeine Zeitung*, which was gleefully spread about by the press all over Germany. He began by denying a report that the performance of Weissheimer's opera, *Theodor Körner*, in Munich, was due to his influence there. This was true enough, but Wagner's irritable, indeed insulting letter, followed by a dignified protest from Weissheimer, led to a distasteful and unnecessary public wrangle. In the autumn a certain Dr Puschmann published a book to demonstrate that Wagner was insane. He concluded to his own personal scientific satisfaction that Wagner was suffering from megalomania (belief that he was a philosopher, politician, musician, dramatist, economist, a redeeming Saviour, a Messiah), persecution mania, irrationality, moral perversity and mental alienation. Nietzsche rose to Wagner's defence with a letter to a musical journal in January 1873. Ironically Wagner was seriously offended with Nietzsche just at that time owing to the fact that the philosopher had dared to refuse an invitation to spend New Year at Bayreuth.

From a letter of Liszt to Princess Carolyne in November we learn that, in addition to his own generous contribution to the Patronatscheine scheme, the subscribers included Baroness Meyendorff, Duchess Helene of Russia, the Sultan of Turkey (who sent 3000 thalers) and the Khedive of Egypt (who donated £500 sterling). Otherwise the response was poor, and in particular the royal houses of Germany and Bismarck's government had displayed an almost hostile lack of interest. To provide a much-needed stimulus to the enterprise, Wagner and Cosima embarked upon a hectic tour in search of likely singers, on 10 November. They also saw and encouraged the various Wagner-Vereine. For Cosima it was a chance to see the haunts of Wagner's peripatetic youth. In Würzburg (where they saw *Don Giovanni*) memories of *Die Feen* days were revived. On to Frankfort which, says Cosima, was 'most abominable' not only on account of a performance of Meyerbeer's *Le Prophète*, but because the town was filled with Jews. At Darmstadt they were entertained by Karl Brandt; on reaching Mannheim they saw *The Flying Dutchman* and Cosima noted that 'we are a little wearied by these entertainments'. In Stuttgart they were horrified by *Les Huguenots;* Strassburg proved congenial owing to a meeting with Nietzsche who 'looked very well and was vigorous and cheerful'. Wagner and Nietzsche discussed their mutual problems: the recent attack on Wagner's sanity, and Nietzsche's academic isolation following *The Birth of Tragedy*. On to Karlsruhe for *Tannhäuser* and Grand Ducal hospitality, followed by Mainz, Wiesbaden and then to Cologne by boat down the Rhine. Wagner reflected on Liszt's *Lorelei* song as they passed the famous rock. From Cologne they proceeded north to Hanover for an awful *Oberon*. In Magdeburg Wagner showed his wife his old house and the theatre which had not been altered since then. He recalled the similar tour in quest of singers that he had made from there long ago, the disastrous Schröder-Devrient concert, the sky-blue swallow tail coat with monstrous cuffs he had worn as Kapellmeister. In Dessau they experienced the finest production of their tour, a performance of Gluck's *Orfeo*. Wagner decided that the ballet master, Richard Fricke,* would be an excellent choice for the Bayreuth production. Now homeward bound, their last stop was at Leipzig where they encountered Heinrich Brockhaus. His sin of forfeiting Wagner's library at the time of the Dresden revolt was forgiven him. Cosima noted that his wrongs had been cruelly punished: he was now totally blind. They reached Bayreuth in good time for the Christmas celebrations, having had a fairly fruitless journey. Wagner was disgusted at the universally poor standards of singing, acting, conducting and production. The experience reinforced his belief in the urgent necessity for a regeneration of German theatrical art.

Early in the new year, 1873, they set out upon another exhausting and equally fruitless tour, consisting of concerts, fund-raising events, banquets, visits to the opera, speeches to the Wagner-Vereine, and earnest conversations with crowned heads and politicians. In Dresden he saw Tichatschek, Pusinelli and the Wesendoncks, who had settled there after the Siege of Paris, which had provoked serious anti-German feeling in Zurich. In Hamburg, Berlin and Schwerin Wagner was wined, dined, serenaded and showered with laurel wreaths, but he returned to Bayreuth on 6 February without having achieved any material gains from this sacrifice of time and energy. Wagner railed against the tight-fistedness of his fellow countrymen. There was an unwillingness to part with money owing to the post-war financial depression but the real cause of the problem was simply apathy. The Wagner-Vereine were well-intentioned but unco-ordinated in their efforts. By April only 200 of the hoped-for 1300 Patronatscheine had been bought. Unfounded rumours damaged the cause, such as the gossip that Wagner was using the certificate subscriptions to build himself a lavish mansion.

Through pamphlets and articles Wagner ensured his voice was widely heard. During the year there appeared *A Glance at the German Operatic Stage of Today* (a penetrating and understandably caustic glance); *The Rendering of Beethoven's Ninth Symphony*; *Prologue to a Reading of 'Götterdämmerung' before a select audience at Berlin* (the select audience in January included Adolph Menzel, Field Marshal Count Moltke, Lothar Bucher, Hermann von Helmholtz, Prince George of Russia, the Crown Prince of Württenberg and other potential aristocratic subscribers); and in August he issued a *Final Report* on Bayreuth, with descriptions of the theatre, explanations of how the concept had evolved and a summary of progress so far. Nietzsche spent some days at Bayreuth in April and found Wagner in anxious mood. On 3 May the full score of *Götterdämmerung* was begun.

Cosima's secret preparations for his sixtieth birthday celebrations were of a very special nature. To conceal her plans she even had special copies of the local paper printed for her husband, omitting any news of them. The first sound that greeted his ears that morning was the *Wach auf* chorus from *Meistersinger* sung from the garden by a local choir. At the old opera house in the evening, festivities began with an overture which Wagner could not identify. Was it Beethoven? Or Bellini, perhaps? Cosima waited in amusement until he gradually recalled his own Overture in C major of 1831. There followed a performance of Geyer's *Der Bethlehemitische Kindermord* and during the interval the orchestra played the folksong Wagner had strummed on the piano on the eve of Geyer's death. After performances of his *Albumblatt* of 1861 and the Wesendonck song *Traüme*, the evening ended with his cantata of 1835, *Beim Antritt des neuen Jahres* with a new text provided by Cornelius. One week later Wagner and Cosima visited Weimar for the first performance of Liszt's *Christus* oratorio. He did not attend out of mere politeness but because the work had intrigued him when Liszt played it through in the previous autumn. Cosima's diary records that 'Richard passed through every phase of transport to downright revolt, arriving finally at the profoundest, most affectionate fairmindedness.'

One year had passed since the laying of the foundation stone and the number of subscribers was still dangerously small. A rather desperate plea to Bismarck in June brought no response. The Festspielhaus was completed in the rough on 2 August, and there was now every danger that things would come to a standstill. That month Wagner turned to Ludwig, with the news that the German people had failed him, preferring to invest their money in 'Jewish or Jesuitical undertakings'. He pleads for a loan in order to complete the theatre and commission the stage machinery. Such a sum would merely be a guarantee of funds and would be repaid when sufficient Patronatscheine had been bought. Düfflipp replied that the King could not spare any money at present owing to his own building schemes at Neuschwanstein and Linderhof; in any case Wagner had made it clear that the 25,000 thalers already contributed by the King was all that would be requested. Next, Wagner turned to Schott and succeeded in obtaining 10,000 francs from the publisher as an advance on *Götterdämmerung*. On 31 October a large group of patrons and Vereine members assembled in Bayreuth to inspect the theatre. Once again it poured with rain. A new appeal was drawn up by a Dresden member (one by Nietzsche having been rejected by the meeting as too vehement) and nearly four thousand German book and music shops received copies. It met with absolutely no response. Another request was made to eighty-one German theatres to give a charity performance in aid of the Bayreuth funds. Three theatres replied with a refusal; the other seventy-eight ignored the appeal completely. Although no offer of help came from Ludwig, he awarded Wagner the Maximilian Order for Art and Science in December, but the composer was irritated at the officious way in which he was summoned to the President's office to receive the decoration. When he later learned that Brahms had been honoured in the same way he was livid, and wanted to send his medal back. Cosima dissuaded him.

The Master of Bayreuth

After Christmas, which was marked by a chorus for the children to sing to Cosima (*Kinder-Katechismus zu Kosel's Geburstag*), the horizon brightened. On 25 January 1874, Ludwig informed Wagner that if the theatre was otherwise doomed, he would lend financial aid, despite his own heavy commitments. A long letter from Wagner followed, eagerly grasping at the hope now held out to him. On 26 February the Bayreuth theatre committee signed an agreement with the court secretariat whereby the King would lend 100,000 thalers which would be repaid by means of income from Patronatscheine and fund-raising events. The story of Ludwig's help from 1874 to 1876, and his willingness bit by bit, in the face of his own near-bankruptcy, to relax the conditions laid down in this contract, is too complex to be unravelled here in full. Wagner had been characteristically over-optimistic in estimating the income from subscribers, and the speed with which things could be achieved. By the autumn of 1874 it was clear that the festival would be delayed until the summer of 1876. It was not until June 1876 that Ludwig's final concession with regard to repayment (effectively granting Wagner free access to Patronatscheine money) enabled the festival to become a reality. Ludwig saved Bayreuth through his understanding of, and sympathy with Wagner's enormous burden. It should be stressed that throughout these years, despite the seriousness of their mutual financial worries, relations between composer and King were of the friendliest.

February 1874 brought not only the King's loan but the generous sum of 10,000 florins from Schott, as an advance for 'future works'. Wagner had told him that after *Götterdämmerung* he planned to write six large orchestral works. This was one of Franz Schott's last kindnesses to Wagner, for he died in May. Many friends and relations did not live to see the fulfilment of Wagner's great dream: in that year alone came the deaths of Franz Mrazek, Luise Brockhaus, Peter Cornelius, Heinrich Wolfram, Albert Wagner, Marie Muchanoff, and (in March 1875) Klara Wolfram.

Wagner occupied his newly-built Bayreuth home on 18 April 1874. This magnificent villa was given the very Wagnerian name Wahnfried ('peace from illusion'), intended to symbolize his having at last found refuge from the illusions of the outer world. Engraved across the portal were the words

Hier, wo mein Wähnen Frieden fand –
WAHNFRIED
Sei dieses Haus von mir bennant.

(Here, where my illusion found peace – 'Peace from Illusion' let this house be named by me.)

which greatly amused the townsfolk of Bayreuth. Indeed, in reading reports of the pious and pompous way of life at Wahnfried, the self-dramatizing of their lives which the Master and Frau Cosima cultivated, the lofty and noble tones in which Glasenapp and du Moulin-Eckart (their biographers) solemnly describe their most trivial doings as though they were events of world-shaking import, it is difficult to suppress a smile. Needless to say, the villa was furnished and decorated throughout in the most sumptuous fashion. A magnificent large drawing room, lined with books, opened out upon the garden which had a gateway (by special permission of the King) leading to the grounds of the Neues Schloss. A bronze bust of Ludwig, set on a granite column, stood in front of the house. A sgraffito panel decorated the façade, with Germanic Myth represented by the figure of Schnorr, Wotan's ravens flying down to him; on one side stood the figure of Schröder-Devrient as the spirit of Tragedy; on the other, Cosima as the spirit of Music holding Siegfried (a portrait of his son) by the hand. Inside the house were all the treasures Wagner had amassed: gifts from the King, Lenbach paintings, fine sculpture, marble busts, rare items of furniture. Susanna Weinert, a governess at Wahnfried whose diary is in the Burrell Collection, reported that there was 'a solemn quiet in the house; even the noise of footsteps is stifled by soft carpets'. Cosima demanded strict formality of behaviour. The servants (of whom there were a great many) had to address the tiny son of the house as 'Herr Siegfried', while the children always rose when their parents entered a room and one by one kissed Cosima's hand. She intended them to regard Wagner 'like a god'. A barber, with the singularly appropriate name of Bernhard Schnappauf, manicured the Master. A Swiss maid supplied him with endless silk dressing gowns, and he would wander the house in preposterous Meistersingerisch costumes. Cosima too adored fancy dress. But the humour was always to be on a lofty plane: Judith Gautier observed Cosima's annoyance when Wagner joked familiarly. She wished him 'to be more reserved, more Olympian'.

In the majesty of this Valhalla Wagner felt he would be happy to live to 'an absurd age'. However, when the moment of death came, he was prepared for it. Believing that Cosima would die with him 'in a kind of euthanasia', he provided a sofa in his room from which their souls would one day float together into the Beyond. Their grave was all ready at the foot of the garden. While Wagner worked in his study, which had a portrait of Geyer on the wall that he considered to have a strange resemblance to his son Siegfried, the rest of the household was busy moving around on tiptoe. Wahnfried's doors were rarely closed to visitors and Cosima can have found few quiet moments between stage-managing servants, children, callers of all sorts from the most distinguished to the idly curious, not to mention the menagerie of Newfoundland dogs, terriers and other pets that were privileged to roam around undisturbed.

From a letter to the King we have a description of a typical day at Wahnfried.[1] From ten o'clock, after breakfast with Cosima, Wagner

---

[1] The house was badly damaged by a bomb during the Second World War. It was restored and reopened as a Wagner museum in July 1976.

attended to work or business in the drawing room until one. At lunch, the children joined them, and coffee was taken in the garden (if the notorious Bayreuth weather permitted). Wagner then read the only newspaper he permitted in the house, the Bayreuth *Tagblatt*, and discussed life, philosophy or art with Cosima. In the late afternoon it was time for a walk or a drive, usually to the Eremitage or the Fantaisie, or occasionally to the Festspielhaus. At seven they took a light meal with the children, after which they would read for the remainder of the evening unless visitors arrived to talk or make music. Cosima, Hans von Wolzogen,* Glasenapp and du Moulin-Eckart have preserved the Master's conversations during evenings at Wahnfried. On musical matters he spoke with assurance and perception. Among his very favourite items for evening soirées were the preludes and fugues of Bach. Rubinstein would play, while Wagner lectured on them, made up stories about them for the children, and occasionally danced to them. He was never happier than on those evenings when a devoted circle of disciples gathered to listen to his every word on politics, religion, art, science, economics or whatever branch of universal wisdom he chose to touch upon. To these disciples his opinion on any aspect of knowledge was received as a sacred truth. To the less reverent reader of today his utterances appear as no more than the hazy, hazardous, and laughably high-flown reflections of a loquacious dilettante.

Once settled in Wahnfried, Wagner began casting the *Ring* – by no means a small or easy task. For only a few of the major parts was he certain about the right singers. Betz as Wotan, Niemann as Siegmund, and Karl Hill* as Alberich were among the early choices. During the summer Emil Scaria* stayed in Bayreuth studying the part of Hagen. For Loge, Georg Unger* was selected but later he was allotted the role of Siegfried. For the moment Wagner was at a loss to find the ideal Siegfried. Niemann wanted the part, seeing in it an appropriate 'star' role for himself, but Wagner refused to consider Niemann, now well into his forties, for his youthful hero. In July, Amalie Materna* was selected to sing Brünnhilde. The summer work of 1874 was largely devoted to auditioning singers, most of whom were rejected as unsuitable. To aid him in this task, Wagner gathered together a group of young men who became known as the 'Nibelungen Chancellory'. Apart from Richter and Rubinstein, Felix Mottl, Anton Seidl* and Hermann Zumpe* assisted in accompanying and coaching artists, conducting rehearsals, copying and proofreading parts and so on. Max and Gotthold Brückner of Coburg made the sets which were designed by Joseph Hoffmann of Vienna. Carl Emil Doepler of Berlin designed the costumes (an aspect of the production that was to disappoint Cosima, and upon which Wagner had given very little guidance); Karl Brandt designed the stage machinery; and Richard Fricke studied the scores to plan choreographic movement of such scenes as the Rhinemaidens'.

In co-ordinating all this complex activity, while still engaged upon the huge task of orchestrating *Götterdämmerung*, Wagner had no time to concern himself with anyone who was not involved heart and soul with his work. In February 1874 the second of Nietzsche's *Thoughts out of Season* had been received coldly by Wagner and Cosima, as nowhere did it touch upon their own great work. Cosima even suggested Nietzsche should improve his German! Their professor caused further annoyance by refusing an invitation to Wahnfried early in the summer, and when he did arrive at Bayreuth in August, there was a series of awkward scenes. Nietzsche and Wagner were both under considerable strain at the time. By nature they were both self-centred, violent in their opinions, intolerant and proud. Inevitably they would one day come to blows, simply on account of their all-too-similar weaknesses, for each of them came to see himself as the saviour of civilization, and neither of them could suffer any contradiction. Exactly when Nietzsche began to realize that their natures were incompatible is not clear. The old idea that he experienced a sudden and decisive revulsion during the 1876 festival is quite untenable. Nor was it *Parsifal* that caused the schism, for Nietzsche had known the gist of that work since Christmas 1869. It would seem that during the visit to Wahnfried of August 1874, he decided to put his friendship with Wagner to the test, by indulging in a series of petty and perverse actions, designed to irritate his host. Firstly he upset Wagner by denouncing the German language and feigning a desire to express himself henceforth in Latin. He then repeatedly produced a vocal score of Brahms's *Triumphlied*, a feeble celebration of the German victory over France. Every time Wagner saw this red-bound score, he reacted (in his own words) like a bull confronted with a red rag. Cosima shared the Master's rage and disgust at seeing this sample of 'Handel, Mendelssohn and Schumann swaddled in leather' deposited on their piano in all its crimson glory. It was Nietzsche's last visit to Wahnfried for almost two years. He was repeatedly invited back, but partly due to the embarrassment of the *Triumphlied* incident, partly owing to ill-health, and partly, one suspects, out of a growing consciousness that he and Wagner could not survive together in the same world, he stayed away. But his championship of the Bayreuth scheme was for the moment undiminished. The third of his *Thoughts out of Season*, 'Schopenhauer as Educator', was greatly indebted to Wagner, and the fourth was entitled 'Richard Wagner in Bayreuth'. Early sketches for the Wagner essay show that Nietzsche's doubts about his friend's art and personality were already coherently formed. On the appearance of the published version, however (neatly coinciding with the first festival when every visitor was seen to be reading a copy), none of these doubts was expressed. On the contrary, the essay was a glowing tribute to Wagner, an enthusiastic appreciation of what his art and his friendship had meant to Nietzsche for so many years.

With the completion of the full score of *Götterdämmerung* on 21

November 1874, the *Ring* was finished. The final double bar-line was added to the mighty conception which had first been sketched twenty-six summers before. The great event was marred by a very unfortunate incident. That morning Cosima handed Wagner a letter from Liszt which dealt with family news and a proposed Wagner-Liszt concert in Pest. Before lunch she found him reading the letter. Knowing of his delicate state of nerves, and that he disliked anyone discussing or viewing incomplete work, she timidly avoided looking at his score, and confined her remarks to the way in which to answer Liszt's kindly letter. At this he took bitter offence, complaining that all she could find to talk about was her father and his letters. Such was her sympathy for him at such a moment! In his wrath he continued to rail at her for the rest of the day. The tormented woman confessed to her diary that evening:

> During the midday meal I concealed my suffering, but when Richard repeated his harsh complaints later, I could not help bursting into tears, and I am still weeping as I write this. And so I have been robbed of this supreme joy, but not by the stirring of any bad motives within me. The fact that I have dedicated my life to this work in suffering has not won me the right to celebrate its completion in joy. And so I celebrate it with pain; I consecrate this exalted, wonderful work with my tears, and thank the eternal God who has laid upon me the burden of being the first to expiate this completion by my suffering. To whom can I tell my pain, to whom lament it? With Richard I can only keep silence. I will confine it to these pages, that they may teach my Siegfried to cherish no anger, no hatred, but boundless pity for that most pitiful of creatures, man. And so I rejoice in my pain and fold my hands in gratitude! It was nothing evil that brought it upon me, and the only support left to me is to accept it with my whole heart, without railing against my fate, without reproaching anybody. May all my sufferings be ineffably swallowed up in this one! The children saw me weeping and wept with me, but they were soon comforted. Richard went to bed with a last bitter remark . . .

For almost two weeks she was too upset to make any entries in her diary. When she took it up again on 3 December, she recounted that later in the evening of that fateful November day, 'Richard came and took me in his arms and said that we loved each other too passionately; that was the cause of our sufferings. And then on the 22nd we really celebrated the completion of the work.' Even so, Cosima arrived at a party that evening with her eyes red with tears.

The one great consolation in her suffering was the thought that she had played no small part in enabling him to complete the *Ring*. In fact she had decisively influenced the ending of *Götterdämmerung*. In 1872 she persuaded him not to set the final lines of the last scene, which had caused him so much trouble and revision. Ludwig had particularly admired the discarded verses[1] and voiced his disappointment at Wagner's decision.

---

[1] These can be found in Volume VI of Wagner's *Gesammelte Schriften*.

To satisfy the King's desire for a musical setting of the lines in which Brünnhilde extols love as the supreme element rather than power or riches, Wagner sent him a composition sketch in which they were set for voice and piano, in August 1876. In other ways the *Ring* owed much to Cosima; notably the final love scene of *Siegfried* in which she is enshrined in musical symbolism. But in a sense her greatest contribution to the work was still to come: her selfless devotion, her watchful, protecting love, and her untiring adoption of every duty and chore that would smooth his path during the preparations for its first performance.

Thirteen

The First Festival

My blunder was this: I travelled to Bayreuth with an ideal in my breast, and was thus doomed to experience the bitterest disappointment. The preponderance of ugliness, grotesqueness and strong pepper thoroughly repelled me.

Nietzsche, Aphorism (1878)

THE SIX-MONTH PERIOD from December 1874 until May of the following year was a restless, care-laden and difficult time for Wagner, who travelled ceaselessly, conducting, consulting his colleagues and collaborators, attending one opera after another in search of singers, and making encouraging visits to the scattered Vereine. In December he called at Coburg, to consult Brandt and the brothers Brückner, and at Leipzig, where he heard Eugen Gara in Spohr's *Jessonda*, and selected this baritone for the part of Gunther in the *Ring*. Christmas was spent at Bayreuth. For Cosima he orchestrated the *Kinder-Katechismus* introducing the 'Redemption' motif (from the final scene of *Götterdämmerung*) in an epilogue. In addition to pondering over the *Parsifal* subject, he sent a lively and humorous review of *Jessonda* (*On an operatic performance in Leipzig*) to the *Musikalisches Wochenblatt*, and on 1 January Cosima told Betty Schott that Wagner was writing an *Albumblatt* for her. This E flat major piano piece was sent to the publisher's widow a month later, as a gesture of thanks for her part in returning to Wagner his unpublished 1830 transcription of Beethoven's Ninth.

In addition to his appointed task as conductor of the first festival, Hans Richter was expected to help Wagner by taking the rehearsals for orchestral concerts in Vienna and Pest. To the great annoyance of Wahnfried, he chose to marry and, having used up his permitted leave from his post at the Pest theatre for his honeymoon, he was unable to supervise the Vienna rehearsals for Wagner's concert. Cosima was especially displeased at this lack of consideration. In her diary there are hardly any words of praise for Richter from this time onward. To her own satisfaction his faults were explained by his racial origin: he was a native of Hungary. Just as a Jew was to be entrusted with conducting the Christian *Parsifal*, a 'non-German' was handed the baton for the thoroughly Teutonic *Ring*. As long as the right people were being useful to the cause in the right way, racial faults took second place. The moment they stepped out of line, weakness of race was found to be the cause. It is piquant to observe the Franco-Jewish-Hungarian Cosima as arbiter of what was German. To explain Nietzsche's later betrayal of the Wagner cause she pointed to his supposed Slav origins. Similarly Wagner, equally erroneously, accused Brahms of being a Jew.

To rehearse his own concert, then, Wagner left Bayreuth for Vienna on 20 February. Cosima left the children in the care of Nietzsche's sister, Elizabeth. The concert on 1 March, attended by the now familiar fuss of toasts and tributes, contained extracts from the *Ring*, including the closing scene of *Götterdämmerung*, with Materna as soloist. In Pest, Liszt and Wagner joined forces. The legendary pianist played Beethoven's Fifth Concerto, and a new work of Liszt's, *The Bells of Strassburg*, was performed. 'A curious work; very effectively written, but so alien to us,' was Frau Cosima's verdict. Of Richter's performance of *The Flying Dutchman* she was more scathing. He fell further in her estimation by agreeing to conduct a performance sung in Hungarian and Italian, heavily cut, and in which he had introduced extra effects such as clashing cymbals! On 12 March they were back in Vienna for a repeat of the previous concert there. After a few weeks at home Wagner commenced another tour on 9 April visiting theatres at Hanover (where he found his Gutrune, Mathilde Weckerlin), Leipzig and Brunswick; and conducting two Wagner concerts in Berlin. After a day or two at Bayreuth, saddened by the death of his dog, Russ, he proceeded to Vienna for a third Vereine concert. The financial result of all this effort was still not sufficient to stave off bankruptcy.

Wagner now had his complement of singers for the *Ring*, but many of those selected needed a great deal of patient coaching to rid them of bad habits acquired in the repertory theatres. By mid June, Wagner had decided to give the work's most arduous tenor role, Siegfried, to Georg Unger, having considered two others before him, Franz Glantz and Hermann Schrötter. Julius Hey,* a teacher of singing from the Munich music school, was in Bayreuth throughout the summer. His particular charge was the transformation of Unger, whose pronounced Saxon accent had to be corrected, his vocal mannerisms broken, and his technique thoroughly overhauled. At the outset, Unger's voice was colourless and strained, his diction poor, his confidence lacking and his general manner rather vague and self-defeating. But Wagner saw in him a reserve of energy and sufficient intelligence, together with a vigorous and powerful physique, that held the promise of an ideal Siegfried. It would be a strenuous task, not only to give his voice the free resilience and necessary clarity of intonation, to shape his phrasing, build his confidence, instil in him a natural awareness of the visual aspect of performance, but also to remodel his entire personality: to transform him into the character-mood of Siegfried – healthy, bright, positive and with natural, unforced strength of temperament. To this end, and at Wagner's expense, Unger obtained leave from his theatre for an entire year to study with Hey in Bayreuth and Munich. Gradually Wagner's confidence in him reaped results, and by the following summer his voice and personality had changed beyond recognition.

General piano rehearsals began at Wahnfried in July 1875. Members of the Nibelungen Chancellory assisted and in addition to the huge cast, the house was filled with visitors including Liszt, Countess Schleinitz, G. A. Kietz, Hermann Levi, Hülsen from Berlin, and various friends of Nietzsche, although the professor himself could not attend owing to illness. On 24 July the theatre was ready for the first trial of the scenery for the opening sections of *Rheingold* and *Walküre*. The effect was magical: from every part of the fan-shaped auditorium the stage could be seen and, more important still, the acoustics were perfect. The original Semper plan for a double proscenium, creating Wagner's desired effect of illusion, worked wonderfully. No orchestra, no prompter's box distracted from the magic. The conductor, invisible to the audience, commanded an excellent view of both the stage and his submerged players. On 2 August the orchestra played in the theatre for the first time. The leader was the distinguished August Wilhelmj who presided over 114 of the finest players from all over Germany (including sixty-four strings, and of course six harps), attracted to Bayreuth from artistic, not mercenary, motives: none of them received a fee, only expenses for travel and maintenance. When Wagner entered the theatre he was greeted by Wotan's opening lines, 'Vollendet das ewige Werk' from *Rheingold*, sung by Betz. Ten days of rehearsals with orchestra followed: Richter conducted, and Wagner sat on stage directing energetically from a small desk lit by a petroleum lamp. Kietz feared he would knock this over in his excitement, and persuaded Brandt to fix the table securely to the stage.

Wagner's main aim was to cultivate a German vocal technique that would be a worthy national equivalent of the bel canto style of Italy. Linked to this, he strove to achieve with his singers a union of vocal precision, careful understanding of the text and perfection of dramatic expression that would create a single, vivid, all-pervasive performance. He astonished his young cast with his prodigious energy, his animated illustration of every gesture, his almost violent participation in each activity, his ability to do everyone's work in addition to his own. He was greatly impressed with Betz as Wotan, Hill as Alberich, Vogl as Loge, Schlosser as Mime, and Scaria as Hagen. Of the ladies he was equally pleased with Materna as Brünnhilde, Therese Vogl as Sieglinde, Grün-Sadler as Fricka, Jaïde as Erda, and the three Rhinemaidens: Lilli and Marie Lehmann and Minna Lammert. His most serious worry was Unger as Siegfried, and he even considered the possibility of giving that part to Niemann, but three factors led him to hesitate. First was Niemann's stout, middle-aged appearance. Second, it was artistically undesirable to have Siegmund and Siegfried played by the same singer. Lastly, Niemann's temperament had not matured since the Paris days; his selfish, surly, arrogant, rebellious nature began to affect the entire cast when he arrived in Bayreuth late in July. He wanted to be more important than anyone else; he did not share in the communal festive spirit of the enterprise; he resented the necessity for so many rehearsals in out-of-the-way Bayreuth; he was irked at being given what he considered to be a subordinate part (Siegmund); and he frequently lost his temper, on one occasion pulling poor Rubinstein from his place at the piano and shaking him angrily. At that Wagner remained calm, and quietly suggested they continue the rehearsal. Afterwards Rubinstein left, while Wagner invited the remainder of the company out to the garden for refreshments. Niemann sulked and refused to eat anything, until Louise Jaïde offered him a piece of ham. He then helped himself to something more from her plate, thanked her and left. Cosima had observed all this with displeasure and somewhat tactlessly took Frau Jaïde indoors and scolded her for encouraging the tenor's boorish behaviour. Jaïde was mortified by this reprimand; when Niemann heard of it he left Bayreuth with the injured contralto, telling Cosima he would never return. Betz, always game for a fight, threatened to follow his Berlin colleague. The incident was petty and unnecessary, but illustrated how easily one man could jeopardize the whole festival and cast a shadow over the entire company. Some weeks passed before Niemann informed Wagner, through Betz, that he would graciously condescend to take part in the festival after all.

Cosima's part in that unfortunate episode was characteristic of her ability to rub the artists the wrong way. None of them liked her haughty and self-important manner, her refusal to join in the fun or to adapt in friendly spirit to the variety of artistic temperaments that such an enterprise brought together. It was inevitable that after the strain of a day's exhausting rehearsal, a group of young, light-hearted theatricals would let their hair down and indulge in some harmless pranks. Hagen had two pet monkeys which created amusing havoc when let loose; Gunther and Fasolt frolicked in front of their hotel wearing sheets and performing wild tribal dances; Felix Mottl went shopping in drag; boots and shoes would be playfully mixed up; and the répetiteurs once caused a scandal by smoking some hashish. While the pious Cosima looked upon this without humour, Wagner, the experienced old man of the theatre, happily encouraged such displays of nonsense. Despite the cold frowns from his wife, he once stood on his head to show how much he had enjoyed their high-spirited games in the Wahnfried garden. A garden party for the 140 singers and players marked the end of the rehearsals for that year, but by then the press had printed rumours of the discord between frosty Frau Cosima and certain of the singers. Hans Richter had taken part in the gossip and for some weeks his further involvement in the festival was, like Niemann's, in doubt. But all in all, the preliminary rehearsal period had been successful: 12,000 marks, provided from Wagner's concert takings, had covered the expenses of singers and orchestra, the theatre had fulfilled all his hopes, and the stage equipment was now in place. Installation of gas lighting had begun; the furnishing of the auditorium, the completion of scenery and the making of costumes were the priorities of the coming months. In September Ludwig allowed Wagner free access to Patronatscheine money, until the six-hundredth certificate had been sold, and therefore financial difficulties were momentarily eased. That month Wagner took a welcome week's holiday at the Bohemian spa of Teplitz. During the autumn the Kaiser was approached for a gift of 30,000 thalers and would apparently have acceded to this request but for the opposition of his ministers.

In November and December Wagner was in Vienna, supervising productions of *Tannhäuser* and *Lohengrin*. As can be imagined, he had no enthusiasm for this task, which put an extra strain on his health, but the Vienna management had threatened not to release Materna and Scaria for Bayreuth unless Wagner collaborated on their terms. Artistically the visit was highly successful, but Wagner was constantly depressed by the thought that Vienna had no real sympathy with his true theatrical aims. Two young men were immensely impressed with Wagner on this visit to Austria however. Angelo Neumann,* a tenor with the ambition of becoming a theatrical director, received tremendous inspiration from watching Wagner in rehearsal, as he recounted in his memoirs:

These rehearsals convinced me that Richard Wagner was not only the greatest dramatist of all time, but also the greatest of managers, and a marvellous character actor as well. Now at the end of these long thirty years I can still distinctly recall certain incidents of his wonderful mimetic powers. I never hear a performance of *Tannhäuser* or *Lohengrin* without his image rising before me in certain scenes. How wonderfully he took the part of Tannhäuser finding himself at the crossways in the forest after his release from the enchantments of Venusberg. Riveted to the spot, he stood like a graven image, with arms upraised; then gradually, at the entrance of the pilgrims, came to life with a tremendous shuddering start, and finally, overcome with emotion, sank to the ground as the chorus proceeded; to break out at the end in his great cry – 'Ach, schwer drückt mich der Sünden Last!' What stately dignity and what knightly fire he put into this role as Tannhäuser listens to the song of Wolfram. Then in the great final scene of the first act how he dominated, moved, and inspired his company – assigning places, prescribing gestures, and arranging expressions, till the tableau was perfect and the whole cortège, Landgrave, knights, chorus, horses, and dogs took their places with utmost artistic precision. These were moments to make an indelible impression on my mind.

After being overwhelmed by a performance of *Tannhäuser*, another young enthusiast, Hugo Wolf,* took to hanging around the Imperial Hotel simply to catch a glimpse of the revered Master who was staying there with his family. On one occasion he greeted Wagner as he was leaving his hotel and held open the door for him. Then he ran as fast as he could to the opera house and arrived there before Wagner's cab. The astonished composer found himself being greeted at the end of his journey by the same young man he had noticed at the hotel. Later, with the help of the hotel manager and a chambermaid he gained access to Wagner's rooms. When the Master arrived, as Wolf told his parents, 'I saluted Cosima very respectfully, but she did not consider it worth the trouble to bestow on me a single glance; indeed she is known to the whole world as an exceedingly haughty and conceited lady.' Wagner too was about to ignore Wolf, but the chambermaid drew his attention to the young artist who had been patiently waiting for him. For a short while they were alone. Wolf was anxious to have Wagner's opinion on his talents as a composer. Wagner explained he was too busy to give proper attention to the boy's compositions, but urged him to work hard. Wolf told him he took the classics as his models and Wagner said with a smile, 'Yes, that's right, one cannot be original all at once. I myself was not either.'

While in Vienna Wagner heard several works, always with an ear for singers of Bayreuth quality, including *Carmen*, the Verdi *Requiem*, Goldmark's *Queen of Sheba*, Gounod's *Romeo and Juliet* and Meyerbeer's *L'Africaine*, which so revolted him that he left after the first act. Of Bizet's opera *Carmen* Cosima used the adjective 'repellent' but admitted it displayed talent. Glasenapp tells us that the Master 'had to endure even Bizet's *Carmen*'. But Wagner's own reaction to the French masterpiece was, 'Here at last, thank God, is somebody with ideas, for once in a while.' Strangely, he especially admired the relatively conventional duet of Don José and Micaëla in Act One. At a chamber music concert he heard Brahms take part in a performance of his C minor Piano Quartet. He renewed his acquaintance with Bruckner, who had visited Bayreuth a year before and had dedicated his Third Symphony to Wagner, but Wagner did not hear one of his works either at this or at any other time. Johann Strauss was another devoted friend among the many admirers in Vienna, whose enthusiasm eclipsed the antagonism of such journalists as Hanslick and his henchman Ludwig Speidel.

At Christmas Wagner was able to send Ludwig the first three printed instalments of *Mein Leben*. Dictation and publication of the fourth and last part was delayed until after the *Ring* festival. (The final part was published at Bayreuth in 1881.) At the turn of the year he responded to an invitation from a New York committee to write a work commemorating the centenary of American independence. The *Centennial March* ('Festival March for the celebration of the centenary of American Independence'), completed in February 1876, is not one of his greatest inspirations. His own view was that the best thing about it was the welcome 5000 dollars he received for the commission. Oddly, when he was at work on this march, he hit upon a theme that was to be used in the Flower Maidens' chorus in *Parsifal*.

Wagner's travels were not over. Nor were his financial troubles. Early in March he returned to Vienna to show his gratitude to the opera chorus there by conducting a performance of *Lohengrin* for their benefit. He was serenaded on his departure, but in his own mind he resolved never to return to the town of Hanslick again. Nor did he do so: for the future the world would have to travel to his own ideal theatre at Bayreuth. Before devoting himself to the final preparations and rehearsals there, he had to fulfil a promise to Berlin, to supervise the premiere of *Tristan* in that town. Hülsen, although never a wholehearted admirer of that work or of the *Ring* (excepting *Die Walküre* which attained a popularity in its own right and which many theatres sought in vain to produce individually), now treated Wagner with great cordiality. He made full amends for his earlier opposition to Wagner, by insisting that not only should the composer receive royalties on all performances of *Tannhäuser* at Berlin since 1844, but that the profits from *Tristan* should be donated to the Bayreuth fund. This was a most welcome contribution, for by February 1876 only 490 out of the hoped-for 1300 Patronatscheine had been subscribed for.

In addition to the financial worry, there were problems with the cast. The singers had mostly agreed to appear at Bayreuth for little or no fee, being content with expenses. Emil Scaria now demanded payment of 7500 marks for appearing at Bayreuth in August, plus 250 marks for each day of rehearsals during July. This Wagner could not contemplate, so he was faced with finding another singer for the part of Hagen, and also another first Norn, for that lady had withdrawn along with Scaria. Within a week or two of the first rehearsals another blow fell: Vogl wrote to tell Wagner that his wife was expecting a child and would be unable to take the part of Sieglinde in the festival. With commendable good spirit, Wagner replied that he would be happy to stand as godfather to the child which he hoped would turn out to be a true Volsung. For Frau Vogl's part he now selected Josefine Scheffzky of Munich. This soprano had for a while the distinction of being one of those theatrical ladies chosen to entertain King Ludwig in his lavish, fantasy paradise, the Winter Garden, on the roof of the Residenz. On account of her large size she was always hidden in the shrubbery when called upon to sing. Her period of favour did not last long. It was the practice for such performers to make costly gifts to the King in return for the royal presents they had themselves received. This was purely a charade, for they then submitted a bill to the royal treasury. Fräulein Scheffzky sent Ludwig a Persian rug, and sent the treasury a bill for five times the amount she had paid for it. Her reward was the humiliation of exposure before the entire court and company, followed by prompt dismissal. It may also have been the same Josefine who attempted to attract the King's attention by 'accidentally' falling into the lake in the Winter Garden, hoping that Ludwig would jump in and rescue her. But, as Wilfred Blunt tells us, 'she misjudged her man;

Ludwig merely rang the bell for a servant and gave orders for her to be fished out, dried, and removed from the royal presence'. Wagner appears to have been little more impressed by her. She was chosen for Sieglinde (and the third Norn) purely out of necessity; for strength of voice rather than vocal or physical beauty.

From late April, singers, musical assistants and technicians began to gather in Bayreuth. On 30 May three gymnasts tried out the Rhinemaidens' swimming machines. At Munich in 1869 this scene had caused difficulties. There, the girls were to be wheeled up and down and round and round on trolleys. After one Rhinemaiden had become sea-sick at her first attempt, the other two flatly refused to mount their trolleys. Ballet dancers were brought in to fill their places, while the singers performed from the wings. When Lilli Lehmann saw the infernal contraption designed for the Bayreuth production she was horrified. Fricke, who had designed the machines, eventually persuaded Lilli's sister Marie to be strapped into one of them, and soon she forgot the perils and began to enjoy the sensation of swimming. At this Lilli and Minna Lammert joined in and soon all three were singing and gyrating in the waters of the Rhine as if in their natural element.

Other crises were resolved less harmoniously. Brandt began to behave in rather a conceited fashion, threatening to resign over all sorts of issues from dissatisfaction with the hard-working Fricke, to an inaccuracy in his name as printed on the programme. Apart from Grane the horse, who was throughout a model of best behaviour, almost everyone reacted to the strain and tension by indulging in the occasional loss of temper. A grossly over-taxed but resourceful Wagner had to exert himself to keep his forces in order, from time to time being conciliatory, flattering, encouraging; now and again ruthless and occasionally contradictory in his instructions, but in general patient and expedient in weathering a countless series of little storms. The timetable of events was divided into three rehearsal cycles, a general rehearsal attended by the King, and three performance cycles:

First Rehearsal Cycle:	sectional rehearsals with piano and orchestra.
3 June–12 July	
Second Rehearsal Cycle:	with orchestra, scenery and props.
14–15 July	*Rheingold*
17–19 ,,	*Walküre*, one act per day as with
20–22 ,,	*Siegfried*
24–26 ,,	*Götterdämmerung*
Third Rehearsal Cycle:	in costume, without breaks unless necessary.
29, 31 July	
2, 4 August	
General Rehearsal	
6–9 August	

The First Festival

First Performance Cycle: 13, 14, August 16, 17 ,,	with acts starting at approximately 4 p.m., 6 p.m. and 8 p.m. Refreshments served in long intervals. Audience summoned back to theatre by fanfares from Terrace.

Second Performance Cycle
20–23 August

Third Performance Cycle
27–30 August

As late as 15 July Wagner had to import a new singer for an important part. Scaria's replacement, Kögl of Hamburg, had proved inadequate as Hagen, so Siehr of Wiesbaden stepped in to learn the part at short notice. The final list of singers was as follows:

Wotan (and the Wanderer): Franz Betz
Donner, and Gunther: Eugen Gara
Froh, and Siegfried: Georg Unger
Loge: Heinrich Vogl
Alberich: Karl Hill
Mime: Schlosser
Fasolt: Albert Eilers
Fafner: Franz von Reichenberg
Fricka, and 1st Norn: Friedericke Grün-Sadler
Freia, and Gerhilde: Marie Haupt
Erda, and Waltraute: Louise Jaïde
Woglinde, and Helmwige: Lilli Lehmann (also Woodbird)
Wellgunde, and Ortlinde: Marie Lehmann
Flosshilde, and Rossweisse: Minna Lammert
Siegmund: Albert Niemann
Hunding: Joseph Niering
Sieglinde, and 3rd Norn: Josefine Scheffzky
Brünnhilde: Amalie Materna
Schwertleite, and 2nd Norn: Johanna Jachmann-Wagner
Siegrune: Antonia Ammann
Grimgerde: Hedwig Reicher-Kindermann
Hagen: Gustav Siehr
Gutrune: Mathilde Weckerlin

As rehearsals proceeded, certain sections of the press inaugurated a campaign aimed at ruining the festival. There was widespread publicity concerning an anonymous Catholic pamphlet which prophesied that the Festspielhaus would be destroyed by fire, and described in ghoulish detail the ghastly fate awaiting the audience enjoying the 'sinful sounds' of Wagner. Newspapers in Vienna and Munich grossly exaggerated the report of one or two cases of typhus in the Bayreuth army barracks. Fear of an epidemic virtually halted inquiries for Patronatscheine, and discouraged some who had already bought them. When Scaria dropped out of the cast, the journalists claimed that the whole production was doomed

277

to disaster. Malicious reports appeared claiming that only two cycles would be given and, as a result, there were few applications for the final cycle. A few critics set out to damn the performance in their previews and reviews of the first cycle, and thereby discourage people from attending the others.

Another major threat to the festival was the dangerously delayed arrival of the dragon and various other pantomime props which were constructed in England. The London firm which made the £500 dragon sent it to Bayreuth in sections. The tail arrived first, during the third week of July, and some days later the middle portion came. It was a fabulous beast with a caterpillar motion and covered with bristles a foot long. But sadly, its head was still missing for the performance of *Siegfried* before the King on 2 August. By the first public performance, a fortnight later, the dragon had a head, but no neck. This part of the monster never arrived; it was rumoured that it was sent in error not to Bayreuth, but to Beirut in the Lebanon! London also supplied the snake for Alberich's transformation scene, described by Fricke as 'a masterpiece of fancy and machinery: it opens its mouth wide, rolls its eyes horribly, and the body is covered with bright scales'. In addition there was sent, also at the very last moment, a bear, a car with a yoke of rams for Fricka, a magpie and an ouzel for *Siegfried,* and sacrificial beasts and a pair of ravens for *Götterdämmerung.*

When he was not too exhausted by his labours, Wagner spent his free hours and 'rest days' entertaining at Wahnfried. At these gatherings, ranging from small dinner parties to receptions on a grand scale, visitors would remark with astonishment upon his whimsical good humour and exuberance, his remarkable equilibrium and ability not to lose his nerve despite all the arduous cares of the undertaking. A galaxy of celebrities descended upon Bayreuth in 1876, including Princess Bariatinsky from Russia, Ludwig Bösendorfer, the Emperor Dom Pedro of Brazil, Anton Bruckner, Leopold Damrosch, Count and Countess Danckelmann, Edward Dannreuther* from London, Dessoff, Countess Dönhoff, the Eckerts, the Emperor of Germany and other assorted royal figures, Heckel, Klindworth, Lassen, Lenbach, Levi, Liszt, Mathilde Maier, Judith and Catulle Mendès, Baroness Meyendorff, Malwida von Meysenbug, Angelo Neumann, Elizabeth and Friedrich Nietzsche, Saint-Saëns, Count and Countess Schleinitz, the Schurés, Professor Stern of Berlin, Wilhelm Taubert, Tchaikowsky and Wolzogen. Every day and every evening Wagner had to attend to the social niceties such a gathering necessitated, and although he did not reveal it, the strain of such entertaining began to tell upon his health. Bülow had been invited to the festival (and was even offered the musical directorship at one point) but he did not come. Recently returned from a successful American tour, he was in an exceedingly bad physical and mental state. The last place he wanted to be was Bayreuth.

The guest of honour was the one man who had made the festival possible: King Ludwig of Bavaria, whom Wagner had not met for eight years. Ludwig desired no publicity or ceremonial of any description and wished to avoid meeting any other German royalty. Although the town was decorated for his visit and the royal waiting room at the station sumptuously prepared and furnished, he arranged for his train to arrive at one in the morning at a station outside Bayreuth. There Wagner met him and they drove together to the Erimitage and talked well into the night. The King would not visit Wahnfried on account of the crowds which regularly gathered outside. When he drove to the theatre he avoided the town by taking a circuitous route through the countryside, and when he did ride through the streets (after the rehearsal of *Rheingold*) it was in a closed carriage. The Kaiser attended the first two operas of the cycle. He was in a jovial mood, warmly congratulating Wagner on his 'national' achievement. Wagner later remarked to Ludwig, 'It was well meant, but I saw only the irony of it. What has the "nation" to do with my work and its realization?' It irked him that he had to sacrifice half a rehearsal to meet the Kaiser at the station. This was *his* vision come to reality, *his* moment of triumph, *his* own historic achievement: *he* had created a festival, built a monument to his own art, accomplished an ideal undreamed of by any other composer in history. In the face of that, Emperors and princes paled into insignificance. At his own wish, Ludwig returned to Bayreuth for the third and final cycle. Again he insisted that there should be no public tributes to him, a partition should be erected to separate his box from any neighbouring princes, and police should guard it during the intervals.

On the final evening, 30 August, after a tumultuous ovation, Wagner made a restrained and serious speech. He could not tell whether or not there would be another festival. He paid tribute to the two men who had made the Bayreuth venture possible. First, the King, whom he praised not only as benefactor and protector, but as a co-creator of his work. Later, at the concluding banquet, he approached a venerable figure, with long white locks and Roman cassock, and declared:

This is the man to whom the highest honour is due. At a time when I was quite unknown it was he who reposed the fullest confidence in me. Without him, you would probably never have heard a single note from my pen. What I have and what I am I owe to him alone, to my dear, unwavering and wonderful friend Franz Liszt.

There were also many defects and disappointments concerning the first festival. Brandt's stage machinery had failed to match Wagner's expectations. A considerable number of faults with the technical apparatus were never solved. At the first *Rheingold* the scenery jammed between the opening Rhine set and the transformation to Valhalla. Fricke considered the final scene of *Götterdämmerung* dreadfully botched. Neumann found the wall of magic fire feeble in comparison with the Munich production of six years before. Cosima intensely disliked the costumes, which reminded her of Red Indian chiefs, and was depressed by the final tableaux. Wagner despaired of Brandt's failures and criticized Richter for not being sure of a single tempo. 'Affliction! Collapse!' wrote Cosima in her diary, 'Richard very sad, he says he would like to die.' The King was bitterly disappointed with the Brückner brothers' sets. Less respectful visitors giggled at the elements of pantomime including the comical dragon and Fricka's mechanical chariot. Feustel and the theatre committee viewed with alarm the rows of empty seats at the second and third cycles. Of the performers, Wilhelmj and the orchestra, Materna, Siehr, Lilli Lehmann, Hill and Jaïde won Wagner's highest praise. He was tired beyond measure with the prima donna tricks of Betz and Niemann and wished to have no more to do with them. Unger was the greatest disappointment. He was unable to produce an effective mezzo-forte, and Wagner had been forced to ask him to sing the part of Siegfried at full voice throughout. But he still had faith in the young man whom he considered ideal in physique, and whose personality and demeanour had improved so dramatically in less than a year. He arranged for Unger to receive a subsidy of 12,000 marks to enable him to study further with Hey in Munich, the main aim being to cultivate a greater variety of tone-quality.

Bayreuth itself had created problems. When things went wrong, if a musical instrument was damaged, or a piece of mechanism required replacement, the little town did not have the facilities to help. Visitors found the amenities deplorably wanting, especially in the matter of food. Tchaikowsky noted that 'the service is very bad. We had booked a room in advance, our room is very nice, but on the first day I had the greatest difficulty in getting luncheon, and I owed my breakfast yesterday to a stroke of luck.' There was resentment at the fact that local merchants had not been slow to raise their prices for the period of the festival. And already the souvenir industry was in full swing, offering Wagner mementos, 'Rheingold' wines, Wagner cravats, Nibelung caps and other items of bric-à-brac.

Hanslick's account of the 1876 festival is well worth reading to gain an insight into the conditions and the atmosphere of that remarkable event, described by one who was emphatically not sympathetic to the Wagner camp. His opinions about the music are of slight interest; his observations on the Festspielhaus itself, the scenic effects, the poor amenities of the town, the questionable necessity for Wagner's own theatre in such a place, and his objection to the morality of the *Ring* (and *Walküre* Act One in particular) are, however, valuable testimonies, presented fairly and honestly, and refreshing on account of their very independence. Hanslick admired Wagner's energy, his theatrical genius and his tenacity in fulfilling his long-cherished dream of the ideal theatre. His principal objections are to Wagner's ecstatic celebration of incest, the dramatic reliance on magical potions, the degrading and morally repulsive treatment of 'de-

ceit, prevarication, violence and animal sensuality'. It was not only Hanslick who found the *Ring* morally repulsive; that was the prevailing view of
both that work and *Tristan* for many decades. Nor was Hanslick alone in
remarking upon the wealthy, affluent and exclusive patrons seen at
Bayreuth: they seemed oddly unrepresentative of a work inspired by and
written for 'the German Folk'.

With two visitors to the festival Wagner became involved in relations
that were to bear significant fruit during the last years of his life. Judith
Gautier, who was to play the part of a Wesendonck-like Muse during the
creation of *Parsifal*, received Wagner in her hotel room one day. He fell
upon her breast and sobbed like a child, for once releasing all the emotion
that had been pent up inside him as a result of the weeks and months of
ceaseless work and worry. Angelo Neumann, now joint-manager of the
Leipzig theatre, approached Wagner with the offer of mounting the *Ring*
there. For the moment Wagner expressed no interest: it was his hope that
the work would be given again at Bayreuth in 1877.

That hope faded before the year was out. During the third cycle Feustel
had told Wagner that there would be a deficit. To mount another festival
with improved stage machinery, better payment for the artists, cheaper
tickets to attract larger audiences – all these optimistic prospects vanished
when the magnitude of the loss was realized. The failure of the German
public to support his venture, the poor response to the Patronatscheine
scheme, resulted in a disastrous deficit of 142,000 marks. Wagner was
weary and despondent. In all probability there would never be another
festival; the theatre and even Wahnfried would have to be sold either to
the Bavarian state or to the highest bidder; the future prospect was of an
endless and exhausting round of fund-raising concerts to clear the crippling debt. For all the difference his achievement was likely to make to the
general condition of German theatrical art, the last five years of building
Bayreuth might as well have never taken place. Low in spirit, Wagner,
with Cosima and the children, left for Italy on 14 September.

They made a leisurely journey south, through Munich and Verona,
spending a week in Venice (20–27 September), two days in Bologna,
where Wagner was given a civic welcome and made an honorary burgess
of the town, and stayed for another week in Naples (29 September – 5
October). From there they proceeded to Sorrento, on the south shore of
the Bay of Naples, where they remained until 7 November at the Hotel
Victoria, a short distance from the Villa Rubinacci, which was the home of
their friend Malwida von Meysenbug. Malwida's guest for the winter was
Nietzsche, and he and Wagner spent a good deal of time together in
Sorrento. It was their final meeting. To understand the historic parting of
these two great minds, the era of Nietzsche *contra* Wagner, we must
retrace our steps a little, and view the first Bayreuth festival through
Nietzsche's eyes.

It was Schopenhauer who drew the two men together, and it was their respective interpretations of Schopenhauer as time went by, that gradually pulled them apart. Nietzsche was thrilled to learn that Wagner had once read *The World as Will and Idea* five times in the space of nine months. In the early years of their friendship, Wagner was reissuing his prose works. Nietzsche read these and eagerly digested them. His own *Birth of Tragedy* closely follows the argument of *The Art-Work of the Future*. He came to see the Tribschen triangle in the light of his own reflections on Greek tragedy: Wagner was Dionysus, Bülow was Theseus, Cosima was Ariadne. For a while, Brahms was the candidate for Apollo in this allegorical modern German rebirth. Having admired Handel for some years, Nietzsche found in Brahms's *Triumphlied* 'a rebirth of the spirit of the Handelian chorus'. Here was the spirit of Apollo, just as Wagner represented the spirit of Dionysus.

Wagner's reaction to this passing infatuation of his friend was recounted in Chapter 12. At that time Brahms had not established himself as a symphonist (the premiere of his First Symphony was not until November 1876) and Wagner had little reason to consider his talents as anything more than old-fashioned and mediocre. In addition, he had not much liked Brahms as a personality during his stay in Vienna, he knew of him as a signatory to the notorious Manifesto of 1860 which attacked Liszt and the 'New German School' of composers, and he had experienced something of Brahms's bad manners in his efforts to have his Paris Venusberg score returned to him. The *Triumphlied* itself was an unworthy product of Brahms; it was reminiscent of oratorio form which Wagner loathed as an unnatural abortion, and it perhaps aroused his jealousy, for it had achieved a popularity in the wake of the Franco-German war not shared by his own *Kaisermarsch*. Oddly, both Wagner and Brahms vied with each other in patriotic fervour during and after the war, and both included accounts of the campaign among their favourite reading. Nietzsche did not share these nationalist emotions. His enthusiasm for Brahms soon waned, and in later years he openly disparaged his music. Ironically, he then began to express the same blind prejudice against Brahms that Wagner indulged in, condemning him as a hollow imitator of borrowed forms, whose music reflected the mediocrity of his dull, average, middle-class German admirers.

It was not, therefore, over Brahms that Nietzsche and Wagner came adrift. Music had in fact very little to do with the sundering of their friendship. The explanation is to be sought inside Nietzsche's mind. It was he, not Wagner, who underwent a radical change in thinking, indeed experienced a fundamental change in his philosophical outlook around the time of the first Bayreuth festival. He questioned whether Wagner's art really did unite the Dionysian and Apollonian elements in the manner of ancient tragedy, as he had claimed in *The Birth of Tragedy*. He began to reconsider Schopenhauer and reject much of his pessimism, upon which Wagner had built his own aesthetic. Before he met the composer

Nietzsche had been a frenzied admirer of Wagner through studying the vocal score of *Tristan*. The music, not the theatrical aspect, not even the sensuous orchestral sound, converted him. In reading Wagner's prose, he had taken it for granted that the ideal setting envisaged for the *Ring* would completely destroy the old concept of the theatre. For, all his life, not only in his later writings, Nietzsche displayed a strong antipathy towards anything theatrical, a revulsion against the 'naturalism' of acting and singing. He was by temperament anti-theatrical, whereas Wagner was through and through a man of the stage, one who adored the world of acting, who dramatized his own private life, and delighted in the little household mummeries that celebrated birthdays and anniversaries in his childhood home and in his old age at Wahnfried.

Nietzsche made nearly thirty visits to Tribschen before Wagner left for Bayreuth. During the years of preparation for the festival they met very rarely, and not at all between August 1874 and July 1876. Late in 1874 Nietzsche sketched his ideas about Wagner in a series of preliminary notes for the fourth of his *Thoughts out of Season*. When published, that essay, 'Richard Wagner in Bayreuth', did not express the doubts about Wagner's art revealed in the early sketches, but he had already realized that Wagner's art was not what he had originally seen it to be. In embryo, the gist of Nietzsche's late writings on Wagner is present in this sketch, in the same strange mixture of admiration and disgust. He reflected on the sectarian nature of Wagner's cult, the misgivings aroused in him by Wagner's most ardent champions, and Wagner's presumption in believing he could steer Germany to a greater destiny through the theatre. That Nietzsche could think these thoughts and then omit them entirely from his published essay is the clearest indication of the ambivalence, the confusion in his mind.

We have seen that Wagner's own view of the first festival was that it fell far short of his ideal. The reasons for this were manifold, but, given time and sufficient finance, he believed that the faults and shortcomings of 1876 would be overcome. Nietzsche's vision of what the festival would be like was of a very different order from Wagner's. He had believed that Bayreuth would resemble 'the morning sacrament on the day of combat'. In 'Richard Wagner in Bayreuth' he wrote:

> Without a doubt in Bayreuth even the spectator will be worth seeing . . . . All who take part in the festival will seem like men out of season: they have their home elsewhere than the present age, and find elsewhere both their explanation and their justification. . . . As for us, the disciples of this revived art, we shall have the time and the will for thoughtfulness, profound and holy thoughtfulness.

This essay was written in 1875, with some final sections added in June 1876. Serious illness had prevented Nietzsche attending the 1875 rehearsals, but his thoughts were constantly with Wagner. In the summer of

1876, his health was no better – he complained of stomach upsets, repeated vomiting, blinding headaches that lasted for days, immense exhaustion, and the inability of his eyes to bear the light. Despite this sorry condition he was determined not to miss the *Ring*. His essay arrived at Wahnfried in the second week of July. Cosima sat up half the night to read it and sent a telegram to the professor on the 11th, thanking him for 'the only refreshment and uplift' she had lately received besides the *Ring* rehearsals. Wagner followed this with a letter the next day: 'Friend! Your book is prodigious! However did you learn to know me so well? Come soon, and get accustomed to the impression by means of the rehearsals.'

Realizing that he could gain admittance to the rehearsals and did not have to wait until August to experience the *Ring*, Nietzsche set out for Bayreuth, arriving there on 23 July. In about ten days he was able to see the three-day rehearsal of *Götterdämmerung* from the second rehearsal cycle, plus *Rheingold*, *Walküre* and possibly *Siegfried* in the third rehearsal cycle. His poor vision, migraines and general weakness did not enhance the experience. Worse still, the crowds of patrons that were gathering in Bayreuth horrified him. The lively receptions at Wahnfried he found sheer torture. He longed for solitude and left Bayreuth for Klingenbrunn, where he made some sketches for *Human, All too Human*, the first of his books to reveal an antipathy to Wagner, although the composer is not named. He then returned to Bayreuth and joined his sister for the first performance cycle. Instead of finding a group of uplifted disciples indulging in 'holy thoughtfulness', he saw a crowd of rich, fat, well-dressed holidaymakers, thoroughly enjoying themselves, and thinking mostly of food and beer when not listening to Wagner. 'Where was I?' cried Nietzsche in his *Ecce Homo*, 'I recognized nothing; I scarcely recognized Wagner. In vain I called up my reminiscences. Tribschen – a remote island of blessed spirits: not a shadow of a resemblance!'

Bayreuth was not discussed by Wagner or Nietzsche as they walked the beach at Sorrento. For the present, Wagner could not ignore the spectre of financial ruin which was conjured up in every communication from the Bayreuth theatre committee, but he preferred not to discuss it. One topic of conversation irritated Nietzsche: Paul Rée, a radical Jew, close friend and companion of the philosopher, whom Wagner suspected of influencing him against Bayreuth. On one of the last days at Sorrento, as they strolled along the coast, Wagner spoke of *Parsifal* and his own religious experiences. Nietzsche remained silent: he presumed Wagner was merely acting, the old atheist shamming Christian piety in the hope that a drama concerned with Christian redemption would succeed at the box office where the one concerned with pagan Gods and heroes had failed. In this Nietzsche misjudged his friend. Wagner had not suddenly become a Christian. *Parsifal* was not the result of a Pauline conversion. He had considered the subject as suitable for dramatic treatment since his first readings of Wolfram von Eschenbach in the Dresden years, over thirty years before. Now it filled his mind constantly, and naturally its associations with Christian belief turned his thoughts more and more to that religion. But he never saw religion itself as holding the way to the renewal and rebirth of civilization. Only art could do that. Art would effectively become religion: hence the unwieldy term for Parsifal – a *Bühnenweihfestspiel* or Stage-Consecration-Festival-Play. To Nietzsche this was all madness, weakness and delusion. He deplored Christianity and was revolted at Wagner's apparent acceptance of it. The great artist seemed to be abdicating in favour of bourgeois morality. As Nietzsche began to consider that the destiny of Europe lay in his own hands, that it was he who was to be the prophet of the future, he came to view Wagner's work as 'the death agony of the last great art'. Wagner was revealed to him as a tyrant, an artist of excess, unbeautiful, un-German, unmelodious, suffocating, heavy, undulating, rolling, obscure, unhealthy. At Bayreuth he had seen no new ideal, but all the theatrical trappings of the grandest grand opera. In 1878 he wrote, 'I feel as if I had recovered from an illness; with a feeling of unutterable joy I think of Mozart's *Requiem*. I can once more enjoy simple fare.' Wagner was no longer a god in Nietzsche's universe: he was 'human, all too human'.

Without entering the realm of what is properly Nietzsche biography, it is necessary to depart for a moment from the chronological account of Wagner's life in order to examine the consequence of their quarrel. At Sorrento and during the months that followed, Nietzsche was philosophical and self-contained. For the moment Wagner did not grasp that they had come to the parting of the ways, and no doubt attributed the professor's sombre mood to his recent illness and depression.

In October of the following year, it was Wagner who provoked the first open acrimony by informing Nietzsche's doctor that he considered the young man's sufferings were due to excessive masturbation, and recommended a water cure. Nietzsche was understandably enraged. After Christmas 1877, Wagner sent him the *Parsifal* libretto, humorously inscribed, 'To his dear friend Friedrich Nietzsche, from Richard Wagner, High Ecclesiastical Councillor.' Nietzsche's first reaction was

more Liszt than Wagner, spirit of the Counter-Reformation; for me, since I am much too accustomed to Hellenism and the human universal, everything is too Christian, temporally limited; nothing but fantastic psychology; no flesh and too much blood (the Communion in particular gets too full-blooded); and then I don't care for hysterical females; many things that are bearable to the inner eye will be unendurable in performance; just imagine our actors praying, quivering, and with throats stretching in ecstasy. Likewise the interior of the Grail Castle *cannot* work on stage, any more than the wounded swan. All these lovely inventions belong in an epic and, as I have said, to the inner eye. The language reads like a translation from a foreign tongue. But the situations and their sequence – is not this sublime poetry? Is not this the ultimate challenge to music?

These remarks (characteristically bitter-sweet, his old admiration welling up in spite of himself) were not conveyed to Wagner, whose next communication from Nietzsche was a copy of *Human, All too Human*, sent in May 1878. Before receiving it, Wagner was in no doubt that 'certain startling changes' had taken place in his friend, as he told Professor Overbeck of Basel, 'and those of us who have had the opportunity to observe him for years in his psychical convulsions would almost be justified in saying that a long-threatened but not unexpected catastrophe has come upon him.' Wagner may or may not have suspected that Nietzsche had syphilis, but he was convinced that this book indicated mental derangement. There could be no other explanation for his betrayal of Bayreuth. In the third of his essays, *Public and Popularity* (August 1878), Wagner aimed a few darts at the author of *Human, All too Human*. Just as Nietzsche had not named Wagner in his book, the composer does not name the philosopher, but sneers at those who feel obliged to indulge 'in the act of criticizing all things human and inhuman'. 'Every German professor is bound at one time to have written a book that makes him famous,' writes Wagner (alluding to *The Birth of Tragedy),* and he makes a pointed reference to 'philosophers and philologists' who practise self-gyrations, 'now flying from accepted opinions, now flying back to them in some confusion'.

Cosima was less subtle, and wrote to Nietzsche's sister Elizabeth denouncing her brother's treachery. She saw the evil influence of the Jewish Dr Rée in Nietzsche's book. The verdict of Wahnfried that Nietzsche's apostasy was the result of insanity was convenient, but it is not credible. The years 1878–88 were to witness the appearance of his greatest philolosophical writings – books that have little bearing on the Wagner story, although they contain countless allusions to the composer. Throughout that decade Nietzsche searched for the ideal music to replace Wagner's. He turned to works of simplicity, considering the scores of his closest friend and admirer, the now forgotten Peter Gast,* to be those of 'a new Mozart', the true Dionysian art of the future, guaranteed to eclipse Wagner within ten years. His quest for other immortals (Brahms and late Beethoven were rejected) led him to bestow extravagant praise on the operas of August Bungert, Edmond Audran, Goldmark, Lalo and Offenbach. Above all, Bizet's *Carmen*, which he saw times without number, was for him the perfect 'stimulus to life'. All the while he expressed regret at the loss of Wagner's friendship. He wrote to Gast in August 1880:

> Nothing can compensate me for the fact that during these last years I have lost the sympathy of Wagner. How often I dream of him, and always of the intimacy of our one-time meetings! Never did an ill word pass between us – nor in my dreams – but many a merry and heartening one; and with no one else perhaps, have I laughed so much as with him. Now that is all over; and what does it matter that in many things I am right as against him? As if that could blot out the memory of this lost sympathy!

While the Master of Bayreuth preached to his devoted disciples, no one read Nietzsche's books. Undoubtedly he felt jealousy in addition to his almost unendurable pangs of regret. In the early Bayreuth years, Nietzsche had been envious of Wagner's energy, the drama of his life, his ability to win friends and supporters. Five days after Wagner's death he wrote to Peter Gast:

> It was hard being an opponent for six years of the man whom one venerated the most, and I am not coarse enough for this. In the end it was an ageing Wagner against whom I had to defend myself; as for the real Wagner, I want to a great extent to be his *heir* (as I have often told Malwida). Last summer I felt that he had taken from me all the people who it made sense to influence, and that he had started drawing them into the confused and wild hostility of his old age.

In 1887, four years after Wagner's death, he told Gast of his emotional reaction to the *Parsifal* prelude. He doubts whether Wagner has written anything better, and praises the perception, sublimity of feeling, clarity, and consummate workmanship of the music. 'Has any painter ever depicted so sorrowful a look of love as Wagner does in the final accents of his prelude?' And to his sister he confessed:

> I cannot think of it without feeling violently shaken, so elevated was I by it, so deeply moved. It was as if someone were speaking to me again, after many years, about the problems that disturb me . . .

In the following year, Nietzsche wrote the books which elaborated in the plainest terms his challenge to Wagner: *The Wagner Case* and *Nietzsche-contra-Wagner*. These two short books were separated by the writing of three others, *Götzen-Dämmerung* ('The Twilight of the Idols'; the title being an obvious parody on that of Wagner's fourth *Ring* drama), *Der Antichrist* and *Ecce Homo*. In certain passages of these works (particularly the Wagner volumes and *Ecce Homo*) an exaggerated megalomania, violence of language and uncontrolled use of insults betray the impending collapse of his sanity. In October 1888, when Bülow failed to react favourably to Gast's overture *Der Löwe von Venedig*, Nietzsche cried, 'He will be sorry for it. For it was *I* who had written him a rude and entirely justifiable letter so as to finish with him once for all. I gave him to understand that "the first mind of the epoch had expressed a wish in the matter": I allow myself to speak like that now.' *The Wagner Case* was published under Nietzsche's supervision in the autumn of 1888, but it is doubtful whether he would have published the more virulent *Nietzsche-contra-Wagner*, at any rate in the form in which it did appear, long after his breakdown.

Nietzsche's challenge to Wagner was a moral rather than a musical one. Despite the vehemence of his attacks on the man and his ethics, there is always an element of respect for the music. W. H. Auden noted that 'Savage as he is, Nietzsche never allows the reader to forget for one instant that Wagner is an extraordinary genius and that, for all which may be wrong with it, his music is of the highest importance.' Thomas Mann described these late writings as 'like a panegyric with the wrong label, like another kind of glorification. It was love in hate, it was self-flagellation.' Nietzsche's concise, aphoristic style (his ability, as he put it, 'to say in ten sentences what everyone else says in a book – what everyone else *does not* say in a book') is impossible to condense further. The works themselves must be read. That said, the essence of Nietzsche's argument in *The Wagner Case* can, with temerity, be put as follows:

The artist, and particularly the musician, can redeem corrupt society. Music is the means whereby man can revalue his values; transform, at least temporarily, this base world into a better place to live. Wagner's great fault was to abuse his gifts, by resorting to romantic fantasy and Christian ideology, and by turning his back on life. He had exalted the will in *Tristan*, and then annihilated it in *Parsifal*. He meted out illusion and false values. He belonged to the damp north and the fog; grey, gruesome and cold. Bizet on the other hand was southern and tawny, life-enhancing, of sunburnt sensitiveness, 'light feet, wit, fire . . . stellar dancing . . . the vibrating light of the south, the calm sea – perfection . . .' Bizet understood love. Wagner misunderstood it. Wagner demanded unquestioning belief – it was a crime against the holiest to be scientific or sceptical. 'Oh, the rattle-snake joy of the old Master precisely because he always saw "the little children" coming unto him!' 'Ah, this old Minotaur! What has he not already cost us? Every year processions of the finest young men and maidens are led into his labyrinth that he may swallow them up, every year Europe cries out "Away to Crete! Away to Crete!" . . .' Wagner and the Wagnerites adopted the notoriously obscure German of Hegel and Schelling in which lucidity is clouded and logic refuted. The blind obedience they demanded was characteristic of the age of the *Reich*, the classical age of war. Their belief in the pre-eminence of the theatre is absurd. 'Bayreuth is grand opera – and not even good opera.' Wagner was not a man but a disease which made music sick. His disease is symptomatic of a decaying civilization.

Nietzsche-contra-Wagner is an intensified counterpart to all this, with particular reference to the 'poisonous' morality of *Parsifal* and the dangerous cultism of Bayreuth. He describes the turning point in his life:

> Already in the summer of 1876, when the first festival at Bayreuth was at its height, I took leave of Wagner in my soul. I cannot endure anything double faced. Since Wagner had returned to Germany, he had condescended, step by step, to everything that I despise – even to anti-Semitism. As a matter of fact, it was then high time to bid him farewell: but the proof of this came only too soon. Richard Wagner, ostensibly the most triumphant creature alive; as a matter of fact, though, a cranky and desperate *décadent*, suddenly fell helpless and broken on his knees before the Christian cross . . .

On 3 January 1889, nine days after completing that book, Nietzsche saw a

Letzte Bitte an meine lieben Genossen.

! Deutlichkeit!

Die grossen Noten kommen von selbst; die kleinen Noten und ihr Text sind die Hauptsache. —

Nicht dem Publikum etwas sagen, sondern immer den Anderen; in Selbstgesprächen nach unten oder nach oben blickend, nie gerad' aus. —

Letzter Wunsch:

Bleibt mir gut, Ihr Lieben!

Bayreuth, 13 August 1876.   Richard Wagner

5. Wagner's final instructions and good wishes to the cast of the *Ring*, Bayreuth 1876

6. Amalie Materna as Brünnhilde

Above 47. *Die Walküre* Act One; Bayreuth, 1896

Below 48. *Siegfried* Act Two; Covent Garden, 1892

Above 49.
Götterdämmerung Act
Two; Covent Garden,
1892

Right 50. Ludwig and
Malvina Schnorr as
Tristan and Isolde;
Munich 1865

Top 51. *Tristan und Isolde* Act Three; design by
Adolphe Appia, La Scala Milan 1923

Above left 52. Wagner acknowledges an
enthusiastic crowd; from 'Puck', Leipzig 1876

ove 59. The Palazzo
endramin Calergi,
enice, where Wagner
ed

ght 60. Wagner's
ave in the garden of
e villa Wahnfried.
is picture was taken
mediately after the
neral and the grave
d not yet been
osed

61. Richard Wagner: painting by Lenbach

coachman flog a horse in the streets of Turin. He rushed towards the animal and collapsed with his arms around it. He was carried home and, after recovering consciousness, wrote and posted a number of letters which mirrored the sudden outbreak of his madness. One was to August Strindberg, appointing a day for a meeting of monarchs in Rome. 'I will order the young Kaiser to be shot' and signed 'Nietzsche Caesar'. Another, to Peter Gast, was signed 'The Crucified'. Another, to the King of Italy, arranged a meeting with the Pope for the following week. But the most pathetic letter of all was sent to the widow at Wahnfried. When Cosima opened it she read simply, 'Ariadne, I love you. Dionysus.'

He was taken to an asylum at Jena, where he spoke little, and only about music. Occasionally he burst into boisterous song. He found peace by improvising at the piano, with gradually decreasing skill. He was released in the care of his mother in May, and remained with her at Naumburg until 1896 when he was moved to Weimar, the city of Goethe and Schiller, as part of his sister Elizabeth's plan to start a Nietzsche cult. He died in August 1900 after eleven full years of mental darkness. His insanity came as no surprise to Cosima, who considered it to have been evident since the time of the first Bayreuth festival. Nietzsche's sister remained on excellent terms with Wahnfried, a model disciple of all Wagner's darker teachings. In 1885 she had married Dr Bernhard Förster, a fanatical anti-Semite; and in the following year she left Europe with him and settled in Paraguay where they founded Nueva Germania, to put into action Wagner's teachings about racial purity and vegetarianism. The venture collapsed in 1889 when Förster, having swindled his followers, committed suicide. On her return to Germany, Elizabeth took the collecting and publishing of Nietzsche's works out of Gast's hands and set about creating a false picture of her brother as a pan-German, militarist, racist and anti-Semite. She singed, tore and dropped ink-spots on his letters to achieve her ends, and altered the accounts of her relationship with Nietzsche so as to place herself in a better light.

Thus Nietzsche's real warning – against Wagner's baser Germanism, his anti-Semitism, the intellectual and moral danger of an unbalanced devotion to the darker aspects of his art and writings – was effectively confounded. Not until Karl Schlechta's edition of Nietzsche's works (Munich, 1954–8) was the extent of Elizabeth's manipulation fully revealed. Before then, the Nazi ideologists had used Nietzsche for their own ends. Even so, with Nietzsche they had to edit, censor, pervert and quote out of context. With Wagner's prose works they had no need of blue pencil or scissors. The next chapter, which returns to the main narrative with the *Parsifal* period, must also relate the sad truth that Wagner's mind was more than ever obsessed with anti-Semitism, racial purity and other themes that foreshadow Hitler's doctrines even in such refined details as anti-vivisection and vegetarianism. *The Wagner Case*, in referring to the effect of Wagner's obscure notions upon German youth, observed that 'Wagner did *not* conquer these boys with music, but with the "idea": – it is the enigmatic vagueness of his art, its game of hide-and-seek amid a hundred symbols, its polychromy in ideals, which leads and lures the lads.'

Fourteen

Art and Religion

'Believe me, my friend, our art is a religion. It has been made possible for art to rescue what is most holy to us from all dogmatism and rigid formalism.'

Cosima Wagner to Hermann Levi

As NIETZSCHE'S STAR began to fade out of the Wagnerian constellation, a new one arose. Joseph Arthur, Count de Gobineau* had attended the 1876 festival and Wagner met him again in Rome in November. Here the family stayed for almost a month, having left Napoli owing to bad weather. As a novelist and writer of short stories, poems, plays and literary criticism, Gobineau was to be acclaimed long after his death by Cocteau, Gide and Proust. Today there is an annual Étude Gobiennes (founded 1966), devoted to the literary aspect of his work. A French aristocrat and widely travelled diplomat, he also left a number of travel books and writings on the Orient, but his greatest claim to fame rests on his *Essay on the Inequality of the Human Races*. This book, in the words of Michael Biddiss,[1] 'elaborated a racial philosophy of history and society that surpasses in scope and sinister grandeur even the pages of *Mein Kampf*', and in it Wagner thought he had found scientific evidence of his own racial prejudice. The *Essay* had been written in 1853–5, and since then had lain virtually neglected. Entirely thanks to Wagner, this compendium of inconsistent, pseudo-scientific, racist ideology was given a rebirth. There were many marked differences between Wagner and the exquisitely refined anti-democratic French aristocrat. Gobineau's racial theories were highly complex and it is extremely doubtful if Wagner understood much of the *Essay*. Gobineau was not an orthodox anti-Semite and in fact his treatment of the Jews displays some traces of admiration. Even the Negro race is seen as a necessary agent in artistic creation. His main thesis is that the Aryan race (which he does not equate with the German) is superior to the black and yellow races. However, the Aryan race is doomed: it has been irrevocably contaminated by the mixing of its blood with that of inferior races. This pessimistic outlook was not shared by Wagner, who remained an optimist, and maintained a faith in

[1] See Bibliography.

291

Christianity which Gobineau had rejected. For Wagner, racial regeneration was possible. Gobineau presumably found the Saxon Wagner uncongenial at times, and realized that he had not fully grasped his views; nevertheless, it must have been flattering to meet such an ardent admirer.

Also in Rome was a Liszt pupil, Giovanni Sgambati,* in whose chamber music Wagner found 'truly great and original talent'. This rare example of the older Wagner praising a young composer has occasioned sneering remarks from some commentators. Sgambati may be virtually forgotten today, but his chamber and symphonic music, songs and *Requiem* were landmarks in the Italian music of his time. He was a precursor of the modern Italian musical movement and, without reading too much into Wagner's championship, the older German was not blind to the pioneering elements in his work, foreseeing a new awakening of Italian culture, departing from the one-sided operatic past, and providing a refreshing antidote to the dullness of much modern German chamber music. It was to take greater figures than Sgambati to achieve this, but that is no reason to disparage Wagner's selfless recommendation of the young man, his help in arranging publication, funds and a wider hearing for his music.

From Rome he sent letters to his valued but troublesome colleagues Betz and Niemann, praising their artistry and expressing a hope that the strains of the recent festival, which led to their outbursts of dissatisfaction and ill-temper, can be forgotten and forgiven. For him the Italian holiday has brought no peace of mind:

> All my worries follow me, the eternal anxiety about the deficit. Even if I put the material cares of my enterprise out of mind, *you* will understand me if, after all the extraordinary heart-stirring zeal which these performances called into being, I regard all our efforts as little more than waste of strength, aimless and useless.

As he journeyed north, the burden of care weighed ever more heavy. From Florence he wrote to Heckel:

> You actually ask me about the Festival medal, which I naturally countermanded at once when I was told of the constantly mounting deficit. What people expect of me! – Well, I can tell you now quite definitely that I shall spend the whole of the coming summer in restoring my health, if possible. On account of my increasing abdominal troubles, I think I shall go for a prolonged water-cure in Marienbad and elsewhere. Should I find my health restored, we will see what are the prospects for the year after next. If the deficit has not been covered in the meantime – and that without further efforts on my own part – I am considering handing over the whole theatre to some manager or other, perhaps to the Munich court theatre, and I personally shall never trouble myself about it again. This, dear friend, is where my powers give out. What I have accomplished so far was in the nature of a question to the German public, 'Do you want this?' Now I take it that people do not want it, and that ends it for me.

For the moment, troubled days and sleepless nights did not end. Passing through Munich, Düfflipp was consulted and informed of the extent of the loss. Cosima handed over to the fund a legacy of 40,000 francs received following the death of her mother in March 1876. Düfflipp visited Bayreuth on 22 January 1877 to discuss the financial crisis with Wagner and the theatre committee. No solution could be found: the King's finances were so precarious that there was no hope of help from Munich.

Wagner wrote a revised prose sketch for *Parsifal* between 25 January and 23 February. Act One of the poem was complete by 29 March, Act Two by 13 April, and Act Three by 19 April. During this retreat into creativity, a possible solution to his financial crisis was suggested from an unexpected quarter. A London firm of concert agents, Hodge and Essex, invited Wagner to conduct twenty concerts of his music at the Albert Hall. With its seating capacity of 10,000, there was an alluring prospect of £500 profit per evening. Even the agents' revised offer of six concerts and a fee of £1,500 was enough to tempt Wagner, despite the warnings of friends such as Liszt who knew how hazardous such ventures could be. Wagner and Cosima arrived in London on 1 May and stayed for five weeks with Eduard Dannreuther in Orme Square, Bayswater. The composer conducted the first half of each concert, but his health was poor and he appears to have failed to do himself justice. Seidl and Franz Fischer* assisted at rehearsal, and Hans Richter conducted the other items in the programmes, intended to illustrate Wagner's output from *Rienzi* to the *Ring*. The orchestra was enormous (48 violins, 15 violas, 20 cellos, 22 double-basses, 28 woodwind, 8 horns, 5 trumpets, 5 trombones, 5 tubas, 7 harps, 6 percussionists) and therefore very expensive. The singers (including Unger and Hill who both suffered hoarseness) commanded very high fees. About a third of the seats at the Albert Hall were owned by subscribers and remained empty throughout the series. Wagner's fee was reduced to £700 (despite two extra concerts), and the damage to his health was incalculable.

The artistic effect of this, his last tour as conductor, cannot be measured in the simple terms of profit and loss. The more discerning members of the London public began to realize what Wagner's conducting was all about. In his essay *On Conducting* of 1869, he spoke of his lifelong dissatisfaction with conductors, and those of the Mendelssohn tradition in particular, who misunderstood the tempo of such works as the Beethoven symphonies, tending to take them at a uniformly brisk pace. Not enough distinction was made between the spirit of, for example, a Mozart and a Beethoven slow movement. The inherent drama of a movement, together with the inner life of a musical phrase, the elements of melody, harmony, dynamics and accents, should dictate the tempo, if the conductor is not to become a mere human metronome. At Bayreuth even Richter's four-in-a-bar beat was too rigid and inflexible for Wagner. As a young man he must have been horrified at Mendelssohn's practice of conducting only the opening bars of a symphonic movement and then sitting back to listen to the remainder, taking up the baton again merely to stress the occasional dynamic contrast. In 1886 Hanslick expressed astonishment at Sullivan's conducting of a Mozart symphony in London, 'from the comfortable recesses of a commodious armchair, his left arm lazily extended on the arm-rest, his right giving the beat in a mechanical way, his eyes fastened to the score . . . as if he were reading at sight. The heavenly piece plodded along, for better or worse, listlessly, insensibly.' In the same report from London, Hanslick recorded how much Richter had improved the art of conducting in England since the Wagner concerts of 1877. Wagner's early experiences of great conducting were the examples of Habeneck and Berlioz. Historically viewed, though, it is Wagner who was the father of the modern art of conducting. His belief that only a thorough insight into the score, an understanding not only of the practicalities of the music, but of its inner spiritual life could lead to a meaningful interpretation; his mastery of rubato; the intensity he brought to dynamic shading; his insistence on technical perfection – these ideals and achievements provided a shining example for an entire new generation of conductors. Hans von Bülow was the first to inherit and evangelize the Wagnerian approach to conducting; followed in later years by Hans Richter, Felix Mottl, Hermann Levi, Anton Seidl and, indirectly through Karl Muck, Arthur Nikisch and Richard Strauss into our own century. Siegfried Wagner (who conducted at Bayreuth from 1896 until 1928) spoke in his memoirs of the 'plastic simplicity and great clarity' of his father's conducting: he

> used his eyes above all else, and repeatedly referred to them as the most important means of communicating the conductor's wishes. Consequently his outward passion was more restrained; it revealed itself at the end when people noticed his very heavy perspiration. The sight was always an aesthetic one for the audience, without any of the exaggerated gesticulation which is so popular nowadays and creates the impression that the ultimate object of the music is the conductor, and the work being performed is incidental. It was his eyes that electrified.

Socially, the London visit was a marked success. The Prince of Wales and the Duke of Edinburgh attended several concerts, and on 17 May Wagner was received at Windsor by Queen Victoria and the Duke of Albany. In addition, he met Robert Browning, George Eliot and George Henry Lewes, renewed his acquaintance with Sainton and Lüders, and had his portrait painted by Herkomer. Cosima spent her days exploring the art treasures of the London galleries and met Burne-Jones and William Morris. On 4 June they left London and rested for four weeks at Bad Ems. The sense of wasted effort for such poor financial return filled Wagner with melancholy. He thought of selling Wahnfried and emigrating to America with his family. There was now no shortage of requests to perform his work; he was more famous than ever before. But this did not affect his disillusionment, for it seemed no one cared a jot about his dearest creation – Bayreuth. To Ludwig he sent news of the gloomy situation, begging an audience with the King, to induce him to save the Bayreuth idea. He enclosed the libretto of *Parsifal*, signing it 'Erlösung dem Erlöser! R.W.' Ludwig sent ecstatic thanks, but did not refer to the financial crisis.

From Bad Ems the family went to Heidelberg, where they were delayed as Siegfried contracted a serious throat infection; then on to Mannheim and Lucerne, where they made a sentimental visit to Tribschen, and on 20 July to Munich, where Wagner met Düfflipp and laid before him the grim details of the Bayreuth deficit: about 100,000 marks were still owed to various contractors in addition to 216,152 marks owed to the Bavarian treasury. Düfflipp recorded Wagner's reaction upon learning that the King had no instructions regarding the theatre. He 'looked astonished and aghast: he fell back in his chair, drew his hand across his brow and said in a tone of profoundest emotion, "Ah! Now I know where I am! So I have nothing more to hope for! And yet the King's last letters were so cordial and kind that I thought the old days had come back again!"' There was no possibility of another Bayreuth festival unless the debt could be cleared, and if it was not cleared soon there was the danger of serious legal action against Wagner by his creditors. One solution would be to mount the *Ring* in Munich in 1878 and use the proceeds to liquidate the Bayreuth scheme. That would, however, sorely damage both Wagner's cause and the town of Bayreuth which had sacrificed so much on his behalf. Düfflipp succeeded in reconciling Wagner with his old enemy Perfall, who considered how the Munich theatre could best help Bayreuth out of its difficulties.

Wagner was beset by a problem to which there was no easy solution. Collectively, the Kaiser, the various German governments, and theatre managements throughout the country could have saved the day by responding to Wagner's appeals, but they gave no sign of interest. Another possibility was for other theatres to mount the *Ring*; both Vienna and Neumann at Leipzig were keen to do this. The obstacles were negotiating worthwhile financial arrangements and overcoming the problem that the *Ring* was the property of the Bavarian King, who could prevent its performance elsewhere than the Munich court theatre. To add to the deadlock, the hiring-out of the *Ring* to other theatres would remove from Bayreuth its unique attractiveness. A performance of the work at Leipzig was very nearly agreed to, early in 1877; but suitable terms could not be arrived at, and Neumann's partner, August Förster, got cold feet.

In desperation, Wagner was forced to sell various trifles to the firm of Schott, including the Album Sonata for Mathilde Wesendonck of 1853. It was with immense sorrow that he parted with the *Siegfried Idyll*. This tender, domestic tone poem was never intended for publication: parting with it was like selling his closest, most confidential secrets to a greedy world.

Early in the thirteenth century, the poet Wolfram created his epic of *Parzival* at Eschenbach. Six-and-a-half centuries later, but only about twenty miles away, Wagner began the music of his *Parsifal* in Bayreuth, during August 1877. The work was a welcome escape from material cares. By 26 September, the prelude was sketched (although slight adaptations were made to it in 1881). The last notable amorous relationship of Wagner's life spurred on its early creation. As with *Tristan* in Venice, when Mathilde Wesendonck filled Wagner's thoughts, so Judith Gautier became his absent muse during the first months of writing *Parsifal*. And as with Mathilde, Judith faded from his mind as soon as the composition was well advanced. Like the Venice Diary, his twenty-one letters to Judith of the autumn and winter of 1877 are rapturous in tone, and the passion is mystical, metaphysical rather than physical. He remembers the ecstasy of her sweet embraces and her warm kisses, but his 'love' is, as it was with Mathilde, a *longing*, a yearning for unattainable delights. Cosima observed her husband's infatuation and tolerated it without comment. Unlike Minna, his second wife understood the necessity for his intoxication with youth, beauty and charm. She saw it as a passing ideal rather than a threat to their marriage, and indeed, with his letter of 10 February 1878, the flow of tender exchanges ceased abruptly. Judith had served her purpose. She had also, in the meantime, supplied him with exotic scents, powders, cold creams, bath salts, and expensive fabrics from Paris. Many of his letters contain extraordinarily detailed instructions as to the fragrance of the perfumes or the exact shade and texture of the pink and yellow satins he desired. The Putzmacherin letters had recently been published, so to avoid further gossip about the unusual creative aids needed by the Master, Judith addressed her packages to his Bayreuth barber, Schnappauf. Swathed in silk, the composer received these gifts, sampled the delicate bouquets with childish excitement, and would playfully label the bottles 'Extract R.W.' or 'Eau de Richard' and place them on Cosima's dressing table.

In a letter to the Wagner–Vereine, dated 1 January 1877, he had expressed a hope that at future festivals there would always be free seats available for those who could not afford Patronatscheine, and in particular for young people who would benefit from the artistic experience. In September at a meeting of Vereine delegates he put forward another hope. Last year's performances did not measure up to his ideal. The goal of Bayreuth was to create a style and an art that could not be cultivated in the wretched conditions of contemporary repertory theatres. He now proposed the founding of a 'school' at Bayreuth to train singers, instrumentalists and conductors in the correct performance of the great works of the German repertoire. This new idea was worked out with exceptional care, and it embraced a wide syllabus of studies in music and interpretation, with a timetable planned for the next six years. Such a 'school' would provide a nucleus of musicians who would be equipped for future festivals, and from their number would emerge teachers and exemplars for coming generations. This noble scheme was ignored: the advantages of such a fellowship of musico-dramatic artists were not sufficiently apparent to those who could have financed such an undertaking.

Instead, another way of preaching the Wagner gospel was found. In February 1878 there appeared the first issue of the *Bayreuther Blätter*: a newspaper intended to inform the friends of his art on all subjects related to it. Hans von Wolzogen, whose private income enabled him to devote his life to the cause of Wahnfried, was the editor. In his introductory article, Wagner expressed disgust and horror at the power and prejudice of the German press. No doubt the newspapers would condemn his publication as 'a nook-and-corner tract'. If so, let them remember that' in Germany it is always the "nook" and not the large capital' that has produced the greatest flowering of culture. Having already produced nine volumes of his own thoughts, Wagner now proposes to let others fill the columns of the *Bayreuther Blätter*. This will enable him to devote himself in peace to *Parsifal*, which he announces for performance in 1880.

On 31 January the first act was complete in orchestral sketch. We learn from Cosima's diary that Wagner told her, 'he feels so well that he wants to compose *Die Sieger* immediately after *Parsifal*, so as to prolong this condition'. His excellent humour was enhanced by the saving of Bayreuth, for in the early months of the year, the solution to the deficit was found. Credit must go to the able Bayreuth administrators, Feustel and Muncker, who saw that the only way to satisfy the creditors' demands was from royalties on Wagner performances at the Munich Court Theatre. On 16 January, unknown to Wagner, Cosima sent a letter of Feustel's, expressing this view, together with a plea of her own, to Ludwig. On the 25th, Perfall recommended to the King that Wagner should receive his share of the handsome profits Munich was making from his works. He suggested that the composer receive ten per cent of the gross receipts of all performances until the Bayreuth debt was paid off. Ludwig von Bürkel, who had recently succeeded Düfflipp as Court Secretary, supported Perfall's proposal. Ludwig consented, and at his instance the agreement which rescued Bayreuth was signed on 31 March. The prospect of financial ruin was now removed from Wagner's path, and he could contemplate *Parsifal* with renewed confidence. The saving of Bayreuth by Munich is somewhat ironic, as Wagner's *raison d'être* for founding Bayreuth was the supposed hostility and deficiency of Munich. Stranger still that Perfall, the object of Wagner's most violent abuse ten years before, should play such an important part in the rescue. The Munich Intendant suddenly becomes 'highly gifted' in Wagner's letters.

Royalties from performances of the *Ring* operas all over Germany also brightened the financial outlook. Wagner was more or less blackmailed into permitting single performances of *Walküre*. To obtain the release of Richter for his London concerts he allowed Vienna to present the work in 1877, and a similar bargain with Schwerin, who employed Hill, led to a performance of *Walküre* there in January 1878. By February 1879 Vienna had added the other operas and was performing the complete cycle. By November 1878, Munich too had added *Siegfried* and *Götterdämmerung* and was able to present the whole *Ring*. Neumann produced the *Ring* splendidly at Leipzig during that year. He hoped to take it to Berlin, but met with the opposition of Hülsen and the resident singers (including Niemann, Betz and Lilli Lehmann) who objected to imported artists taking the parts they had created at Bayreuth. Separate performances of parts of the cycle were given at Brunswick, Cologne, Hamburg, Mannheim and Weimar, during 1878–9, with *Die Walküre* proving especially popular.

It would have been well if Wagner had kept to his suggestion, and allowed the columns of the *Bayreuther Blätter* to be filled with the words of others, for his own articles betray his intellectual decline, his growing fanaticism and absorption with crackpot but nonetheless sinister theories about race and German society. Apart from *A Glance at the Stage Festivals of 1876*, which contains his reasoned, retrospective assessment of the festival, his contributions to the paper in 1878, despite their confused and rambling prose, reveal a mind darkened by hate and self-delusion. The 1865 'Journal' for Ludwig he reprinted as *What is German?* In March appeared *Modern*, a vicious anti-Semitic diatribe which blames the Jews for all that is bad in contemporary society. In addition to writing worthless music, they have usurped the press, ruined the German language, created false cultural values, and they infiltrate politics, science, art and philosophy in the subtle guise of exquisite and borrowed surnames. *Public and Popularity* appeared in three parts between April and July. In the third of these we are informed that the identification of the Christian God with Jehovah, 'the tribal god of Israel', is 'one of the most terrible confusions in all world-history'. Modern theology has cast in its lot with Judaism. (He presumably felt that it was now the task of the new Wagnerian Art–Religion to prove that Jesus could not have been a Jew.) The human race is reverting to barbarism: taking two thousand years as 'the period covered by the great historical cultures in their evolution from barbarism back to barbarism', civilization will come to an end somewhere about the middle of the next millenium. A similar dreary view of world history, past and future, permeates *The Public in Time and Space* of October. At one or two points in this essay his lofty delusions hit upon a semblance of reality and logical thinking when he discusses Mozart and Liszt.

None of the apparent senility of these articles is found in the music of *Parsifal*. It is certainly the music of an old man, but while his verbal style grew more dense and tortuous, his musical style became more refined and clear. The subtlety of nuance, the harmonic sensitivity, the finely balanced orchestral colours and textures, reveal no weariness, no decline in inventive power or lack of abundance in ideas. The second act was completed in orchestral sketch on 11 October. For the double festival of Christmas and Cosima's birthday, he orchestrated the *Parsifal* prelude, rehearsed it in secret with the Duke of Meiningen's orchestra and performed it on the morning of 25 December in the Wahnfried hall. The third act was ready in orchestral sketch by 26 April 1879. Wagner's own birthday one month later was celebrated in the usual quaint fashion. One curious and striking remark he made to the King when describing this occasion is to be noted for the light it casts on the vexed question of Wagner's parentage. Ten-year-old Siegfried, says Cosima in her diary, was standing in front of her portrait, 'pretending to be painting it, dressed like Father Geyer and with his hair arranged in the same way as his'. Wagner told Ludwig that 'he was supposed to represent my father Ludwig Geyer, significantly reborn'.

Earlier in May Wagner had sent Ludwig a poem celebrating the fifteenth anniversary of his call to Munich. In the previous October, Cosima's diary gives us a rare glimpse of her true feelings towards Wagner's relations with his patron. He had shown her his latest letter to the King:

> A most strange and indescribable feeling came over me when I read at the end of it that Richard's soul belonged for ever to the King. It was like a serpent's tooth at my heart, and I really do not know what I should prefer. I should not like what he has written to be a mere phrase, yet I should not like it to be true, and even if it were in my power to do so, I would not have it unwritten; for all he does is well done. Yet I suffer and pine in the effort to conceal my suffering. All hail, sorrow, I am ready to greet thee as a guest! I can once more approach him with serene composure, and how it purifies me to think that I may deem myself worthy to be at his side!

The essay *Shall we hope?* (*Blätter*, May 1879) finds Wagner riding his familiar hobby horses: the Jews, the Jesuits, the press, the Reichstag, the French are all attacked, a few insults being thrown at Brahms, Nietzsche and Disraeli for good measure. Germany is sinking into barbarism: the only real hope left is the superiority of German blood, and of course *Parsifal*. The *North American Review* published an autobiographical sketch, *The Work and Mission of my Life* (drafted in fact by Wolzogen) which again stressed the greatness of 'German spirit' and 'German blood', this time seen as the civilizing element in North America. America will be dependent on German greatness in the future. With relief one turns the pages of the *Bayreuther Blätter* to find Wagner touching again upon the only two subjects that he was capable of discussing fairly rationally, if not quite lucidly – music and drama. Later in the year appeared *On Poetry and Composition*, *On Operatic Poetry and Composition in Particular*, and *On the*

Application of Music to the Drama. Apart from a short *Word of Introduction to Hans von Wolzogen's 'Decay and Rescue of the German Tongue'*, the only other prose offering to be mentioned is his *Open letter to Herr Ernst von Weber, author of 'The Torture-chambers of Science'*. Weber was a former African explorer and diamond miner, now founder-president of the Dresden Society for the Protection of Animals and a leading anti-vivisectionist. On the surface Wagner's sentiments in this letter are admirable: many would share his revulsion at the exploitation and torture of helpless animals, and his contention that human dignity only begins to assert itself when man becomes distinguished from the beast by his pity for it. But Wagner confounds and confuses his case, muddles his thinking and strays away from anti-vivisection to his anti-Semitic obsession. Man's mistreatment of animals is traced to the Jewish Pentateuch, where beasts are seen as created solely for the use of man. Nietzsche's disavowal of the Schopenhauerian concept of pity is challenged by Wagner, who regards pity as 'the only true foundation of morality'. The open letter ends, unaccountably, with a parting shot at Brahms's *German Requiem*.

Almost every day, Cosima began her diary with a report on Wagner's health. The entries for 1879 reveal a steady decline, not helped by the Bayreuth climate, which was persistently wet and cold. Wagner slept less and less well; the weather depressed him and prevented him taking sufficient exercise; his erysipelas returned, together with rheumatism, chronic catarrh and crippling chest and heart pains. Progress with *Parsifal* was seriously affected: he ruled out the bar-lines for the full orchestral score on 7 August, and began the immense labour of the final instrumentation on the 23rd. The proposed 1880 production was publicly postponed, with the offer of a refund on subscriptions already taken.

Rather than suffer another Bayreuth winter, the family left for Italy at the end of December. The visits to Italy from 1876 onwards greatly influenced the boy Siegfried: his young eye drank in the architectural features of the land, and it was soon apparent that he had considerable promise as a visual artist. Recently Heinrich von Stein* had joined the Wahnfried household as Siegfried's tutor. Although only twenty-two, his fine intellect and wide culture were apparent to Wagner, who hoped for a while that he had discovered another Nietzsche. Interestingly, Nietzsche too admired Stein, and hoped that after Wagner's death he would join him as a friend and disciple. When Stein died, aged only thirty, Nietzsche wrote: 'I really loved him; I felt as though he were reserved for me for a later age. . . . He was by far the finest species of man among the Wagnerians.' Wagner described Stein to Ludwig as 'slim and blond, like one of Schiller's young men'.

The family occupied the Villa Angri at Posilipo, near Naples, from 4 January 1880. In his new year greeting to the Vereine, Wagner had bewailed the fate of Germany which was now in the hands of the Jews, and hoped that the spirit of German music would soon redeem the prevailing misery. Bad weather followed Wagner south – the Italian winter was unusually severe – and facial erysipelas confined him to his room for two weeks on his arrival. Throughout the ten-month stay in Italy the elements were unkind to Wagner, although he enjoyed the scenery in the neighbourhood of Naples, and persisted with cold-sea-bathing.

Another personable young man joined his circle at the Villa Angri and remained ever after at Wagner's side. Paul Joukowsky had attended the 1876 festival and was staying by chance at Posilipo. A modestly talented painter, he came from a very cultured background and counted Turgenev and Henry James among his friends. He seems to have charmed everyone with his agreeable manner, and Wagner quickly decided that he was the ideal choice of scenic designer for *Parsifal*. In turn, the young Russian was overwhelmed by Wagner, abandoned all thought of his own career and vowed henceforth to serve only the cause of Bayreuth. When Henry James called at Villa Angri he was horrified at the change that had taken place in his friend who was lost in rapt admiration of the Master. James found Wagner, Cosima and their entourage repulsive, and was alarmed that Joukowsky could so readily accept every statement of the composer as unquestionable and universal truth. He abandoned his friend to Wagner, and so ended one of the closest attachments of his life.

In addition to the two other acolytes, Rubinstein and Stein, visitors to Posilipo included Engelbert Humperdinck*, Malwida, Liszt and Sgambati. All the while, Wagner was preoccupied not with *Parsifal*, but with a lengthy article which filled the entire issue of the October *Bayreuther Blätter*. This was *Religion and Art*, a preposterous assault upon subjects of which he had no understanding and yet expounded with the unabashed assurance of a dilettante street-corner orator; linguistics, geography, ethnology, Mariolatry, medieval and renaissance art, temperance, socialism and trades unionism. That such inflated claptrap could be regarded by many as the highest wisdom, that Wagner could draw men of no small intelligence into the orbit of his own absurd self-delusions, is truly mysterious.

Art, says Wagner, must save the spirit of religion by revealing the truth of mythic symbols. Art is incapable of this high task as long as it is bound to false dogma. Religion has stifled art and become artificial. The human race has degenerated because it has failed to grasp the great truth of the Schopenhauerian reversal of the will to live – the kernal of all true religion. The Christian God has been erroneously identified with the Jewish tribal god: the god of punishment and war, not the redeeming all-loving Saviour of the poor. The Church has been ruled by the Jewish Old Testament, not the Christian New Testament. Strife-bound civilization, and events like the Puritan wars in England were guided by the spirit of the Jewish books of Moses. The curse of civilization is meateating. 'The Jewish tribal god found Abel's fatted lamb more savoury than Cain's offering of the produce of the field.' Among one of the silent vegetarian communities founded by Pythagoras, the Saviour was born. The Last Supper was an exhortation to vegetarianism: 'Taste such alone, in memory of me.' 'It is more than doubtful if Jesus himself was of Jewish extraction.' On the swampy margins of Canadian lakes live varieties of vegetarian panthers and tigers. Their African cousins have become blood-thirsty beasts of prey because they live in close proximity to the Sahara. The enormous life-span of Russian peasants is due to their almost exclusively vegetable diet. The Japanese know no other food than vegetables, and are further renowned for their warlike valour and keen intellect. 'In certain American prisons the greatest criminals have been transformed by a wisely-planned botanical diet into the most upright of men.' Less than half of mankind – the degenerate but ruling portion – is flesh eating. 'Should the assumption prove correct that animal food is indispensable to northern climates, what is to prevent our carrying out a sensibly conducted transmigration to those quarters of the globe whose rich fertility is sufficient to sustain the present population of every country in the world, as has been asserted of the South American peninsula itself?' The northern regions could then be abandoned to hunters of boar and big game. The only valid hope for civilization is the regeneration of the human race, not through a new religion, but through art which can reveal the mystery of man's fall and the path to his redemption.

In May Wagner visited Amalfi with Joukowsky and discovered the Moorish Palazzo Rufolo (or Ruffali) which suggested to them the set for Klingsor's castle and magic garden. As the sea air and cold bathing had wrought no improvement on Wagner's health, the family moved to the Villa Torre Fiorentina near Siena, in mid August. This residence was described as 'princely' by Liszt; it had been occupied by Pope Pius VI, and Wagner enjoyed the luxury of an enormous Papal bed. During his visit Liszt played through *Parsifal*, with Wagner singing. In the third act Wagner pointed out a theme which he confessed he had stolen from Liszt's *The Bells of Strassburg*. At Siena Cathedral, Cosima's diary informs us, Wagner was 'moved to tears, the greatest impression a building has ever made on him'. Joukowsky made sketches which were the basis for the Grail temple in *Parsifal*.

On 4 October they settled in Venice at the Palazzo Contarini on the Grand Canal. Here Wagner came to know Count Gobineau really well, and spent hours reading his *Essay on the Inequality of the Human Races*. He determined to use the pages of the *Bayreuther Blätter* to promote Gobineau's theories, seeing in them ethnological evidence to support his own racial prejudice. In 1881 Wagner dedicated a new edition of his prose works to Gobineau and published a number of articles by and about Gobineau in the *Bayreuther Blätter*. After Wagner's death, the paper continued to devote much space to Gobineau and brought him to the attention of the pan-German anti-Semite Ludwig Schemann who took up the cause, reprinted the *Essay*, published huge volumes devoted to

Gobineau's ideology and created a Gobineau cult. With Gobineau and Wagner, the blind led the blind: one muddled thinker misunderstood and misrepresented another. Wagner extended Gobineau's racism into his own theories about redemption, regeneration and racial purification. From the writings of Gobineau and Wagner to those of the proto-Nazis Schemann and Wagner's son-in-law Houston Stewart Chamberlain it is only a short step further to *Mein Kampf*. The tragic sequence began with Wagner's own self-deception: his ignorance and prejudice, his embroidery of half-truths and bigotry, his power to influence his credulous followers, spawned a malevolent gospel. The first supplement to *Religion and Art, What boots this Knowledge?*, was written in Venice and appeared in the *Bayreuther Blätter* in December 1880. Wagner dismisses the Jewish Ten Commandments as lacking any trace of a Christian thought. Love, Faith and Hope are the essence of all Christian virtue. Knowledge of the historic fall of man must lead us to believe in and strive for his regeneration.

Leaving Venice, the family arrived in Munich on 30 October. Wagner attended a number of performances: Beethoven's *Missa Solemnis* under Levi; *The Flying Dutchman*, which Wagner declared he would recast in one single act; *Tristan*; *Lohengrin*, a private performance during which Wagner sat with Ludwig in the royal box; and *The Magic Flute*. On 12 November Wagner met the King for the last time. The occasion was a performance of the *Parsifal* prelude. Wagner wrote an explanatory note which named three main themes, titled 'Love', 'Faith' and 'Hope?' His royal benefactor had already given an assurance that *Parsifal* would be reserved for performance at Bayreuth: only private performances for Ludwig would be permitted in Munich.

Wagner returned to Bayreuth on 17 November and within a few days was back at work on the full score. Joukowsky had brought to Bavaria a young Neapolitan fisherman, Peppino, who helped gladden his life during preparations for the mighty *Bühnenweihfestspiel*. Brandt and the brothers Brückner were to build the *Parsifal* sets from Joukowsky's designs. Much of the coming year was spent in planning the second festival: auditioning singers and supervising the innumerable preparations for the production which was now announced for the summer of 1882. It was an anxious period for Cosima who watched her husband's frequent and agonizing attacks of chest and heart pains: her secret fear was that the combined strain of completing the drama and organizing the festival would prove too great. His temper grew worse as his health declined, and outbursts of vehement anger became more and more frequent as the production approached. 'How should I ever presume to forgive him?' she wrote. 'It is my duty to be good and amicable to Richard just as the hours come round and strike.'

Two more supplements to *Religion and Art* appeared in the *Bayreuther Blätter* during 1881: *Know Thyself* (February/March) and *Hero-dom and*

Richard Wagner

Christendom (September). In May he provided an *Introduction to a work of Count Gobineau*. In *Know Thyself* Wagner spells out the cause of mankind's degeneration – the Jews – and he hints at the only hope for its regeneration – elimination of the Jews. The recent 'conferment of full right upon the Jews to regard themselves in all conceivable respects as Germans', i.e. the bestowal by the Reichstag in 1871 of full German citizenship to Jews, he compares with the situation in Mexico where 'blacks were given *carte blanche* to consider themselves whites'. The Jew is the 'daemon of man's downfall'. The German instinct must wake up to this, for the Jew intermingles everywhere: 'Without a fatherland, a mother-tongue, in the midst of every people's land and language he finds himself again . . . even commixture of blood does not hurt him; if a Jew or Jewess intermarry with the most distant of races, a Jew will always come to birth.' *Hero-dom and Christendom* takes this a step further.

Besides having absorbed the wrong food, the blood of nobler races has been tainted by inferior breeds as set forth by Gobineau in his magnum opus. The world is doomed to destruction and the human species along with it. But must we go to our doom as beasts or gods? Aryan blood is the only truly virtuous strain. Now that this blood has been mixed with that of 'one-time cannibals now trained to be the business leaders of society' (i.e. Jews) the race has deteriorated. This great Aryan race descended from the gods, from the hero-gods Hercules and Siegfried. As rightful rulers of the world the chosen Aryan race descended through the Frankish–German and Hohenstaufen Emperors, and even in periods of degeneracy their spirit was reborn. On the other hand, coloured men, both black and yellow, descended in the Darwinian way from apes. Through the centuries these inferior peoples have drained the Aryans of the purity of their blood. Without Aryan blood in their veins, however, the ignoble races would have achieved nothing. To set right man's fall, his racial degeneration, Christ was born to suffer and die for mankind, redeeming the human race through His blood. Christ's blood was not that of any individual race but a higher fluid, 'a divine sublimate of the species itself', a godlike manifestation of the highest qualities of the Aryan spirit. His blood was a fountainhead of pity which streams through the human species, wiping away the sin of racial decline and redeeming inferior breeds. Only through the true Christian sacrament, the partaking of the blood of Christ, can the very lowest races be raised to the purity of the gods. But the idea of the human species attaining a uniform equality is nonetheless horrifyingly repellent.

It is to be noticed that Wagner does not see any hope of redemption through the sacrament of the Roman Catholic Church, for that body is the property of what he (or Gobineau) calls the Latino-Semite race. Jews too are offered little hope of redemption in Wagner's religious scheme. On the subject of Jews, however, his intellect had never been able to function rationally, and now that his mind had almost totally atrophied outside the creative musical sphere, he blamed them for everything and anything he thought wrong with the world. It is astonishing how obsessed he was with the Jews. He made no secret of his anti-Semitism, which became legendary. But not until the publication of Cosima's diaries was it evident that, in private conversation, the Master hardly ever opened his mouth without insulting the Jews. Every subject he touched upon led to a string of brutal and aggressive remarks about Jewish politicians, Jewish bankers, Jewish journalists, the Jewish stranglehold on Germany. In his last years the attacks became more frequent and more repellent. In 1878 he was told that the international congress in Berlin planned measures to safeguard Jews in Rumania which was threatened by war. 'Let them slaughter one another!' cried Wagner. On another occasion he remarked in what Cosima calls a 'vehement jest': 'All Jews should be burned!'

In the summer of 1880 Wagner declined to sign an anti-Semitic petition to the Reichstag organized by Dr Bernhard Förster, giving as his reason the recent failure of an anti-vivisection petition and declaring he had no faith in such approaches to the government. The real cause of his reluctance to sign was in all probability due to the prominence of Jews among his foremost supporters and assistants – Rubinstein, Levi and Neumann. In private his remarks would indicate that he hated his Jewish friends even more than his imagined Jewish enemies – it became a family joke that Fidi would have to be provided with a hooked nose and Wahnfried turned into a synagogue, there were now so many Jewish adherents – and he never ceased to remind Rubinstein that he was 'cursed with his Jewishness'. The young man who had run to Wagner from the persecution of the outside world was never allowed to forget that he was of vile and inferior origin. In the last years of his life there was much speculation in the press that Wagner himself was a Jew. Cartoons appeared showing him with an exaggeratedly Jewish nose, and depicting audiences of Jews applauding *Parsifal*. He was nicknamed the Rabbi of Bayreuth, running festivals for the benefit of his Jewish kinsmen and admirers. His birth in the Brühl, the Jewish-dominated quarter of Leipzig, was cited as evidence of his Semitic origin. No one then knew what is known today: that detailed investigation has failed to find a single demonstrably Jewish ancestor in the Geyer or the Wagner family trees. Above all, Wagner did not know this. His irrational hatred of the Jews may have increased in the later 1870s as a gesture of self-defence, a vigorous attempt to prove his Aryan purity. The slightest doubt in his mind that Geyer could have been Jewish would explain why he gave no public hint of his belief, so often confided to intimate friends in earlier years, that Ludwig Geyer was his father.

Not only Rubinstein bore the brunt of Wagner's malicious taunts, but Levi too was subjected to degrading insults on account of his faith. Wagner repeatedly urged this conductor, son of a Rabbi, to be baptized. Levi was Kapellmeister at Munich, and by the terms of the 1878 contract between Bayreuth and the King, it was agreed that the *Parsifal* production was to be given with the artistic personnel, orchestra and singers of the Munich court opera. Wagner had the highest praise for Levi's gifts as a conductor and, strangely, he felt respect for his open and honest stance as an orthodox Jew and his refusal to alter his name to 'Löwe' or something more German. Cosima also formed a high opinion of him, and indeed became affectionately attached to the Rabbi's son, maintaining a warm and friendly correspondence with him. Despite this, Wagner's anti-Semitic fixation led to some very tactless behaviour. One day in June 1881, when in Bayreuth supervising the *Parsifal* preparations, Levi arrived at Wahnfried ten minutes late for lunch. Wagner reprimanded him angrily in front of the whole family and told him to go to his room where he would find a letter waiting for him. This document was an anonymous letter sent to Wagner from Munich. It called upon him not to allow the purity of *Parsifal* to be sullied by a Jewish conductor, and accused Levi of amorous relations with Cosima. Levi left Wahnfried at once, and wrote to Wagner asking to be relieved of his duties. The incident was diplomatically resolved, largely thanks to Levi's generous nature and his ability to overlook Wagner's ill-breeding and concentrate on the greatness of his art. At sixty-eight, Wagner indulged in sudden tantrums more characteristic of a six-year-old child. To face Levi with that letter was not only malevolent but foolish: had Levi left Bayreuth for good then it would have confirmed the gossip about Cosima, at any rate in the eyes of the Munich scandal-mongers.

As if to show that he was the most tolerant, broad-minded and open-hearted of humanitarians, Wagner told Ludwig on 19 September, that it meant nothing to him whether *Parsifal* was conducted by a Christian or a Jew, despite the many curious remarks that Levi's post had prompted. To this the King replied with delight, for 'there is nothing so nauseous, so unedifying, as disputes of this sort: basically, all men are brothers whatever their differences of faith.' These were liberal sentiments that Wagner could not bear. He wrote to Ludwig on 22 November pointing out that the King is tolerant of Jews only because he has no personal experience of them. Although Wagner has displayed friendship and compassion towards these people, he knows that 'the Jewish race is the born enemy of pure humanity and all that is noble in it: it is certain that we Germans will go under before them, and perhaps I am the last German who knew how to stand up as an art-loving man against the Judaism that is already getting control of everything'. Jews such as Levi and Rubinstein have caused him much trouble; for these 'unfortunates' are not like 'the rest of us'. One has to exercise great patience with them for they suffer understandable agonies of soul and often contemplate suicide: '. . . if it is a question of humanity towards Jews, I can confidently claim credit on that score.' As late as the final dress rehearsal of *Parsifal*, in July 1882, he was unable to forget Levi's crime of birth. Cosima wrote in her diary that if

Richard 'were playing in the orchestra he wouldn't like to be directed by a Jew'. Yet in that year, Levi could describe Wagner to his father in these words:

> He is the finest and noblest person. It is natural that the world misunderstands and calumniates him; men always blacken anything that shines; Goethe didn't have a better time of it. But posterity will some day acknowledge that Wagner was as great a man as he was an artist, as those now close to him are well aware.

After completing the full orchestral score of *Parsifal* Act One on 25 April 1881, Wagner left with Cosima for Berlin where Neumann was at last able to present the *Ring*, not at the court opera, but at the Viktoria Theatre. The composer assisted at the rehearsals with energy and enthusiasm. Emil Scaria sang Wotan so magnificently that Wagner forgave him his mercenary behaviour in walking out of Bayreuth five years before. Seidl's conducting won his warm approval. Only Ferdinand Jäger as Siegfried disappointed him, and this was due to hoarseness not vocal inability. Wagner remained for the first cycle (5–9 May) which was a triumphant success. The Kaiser, the entire court and all Berlin society attended. Even Hülsen was converted to the tetralogy, admitting that he now believed it to be a practical theatrical proposition. Promising to return for the fourth and final cycle, Wagner left for Bayreuth where he found Gobineau waiting for him, at Wahnfried. Their discussion of the odious beliefs they held in common resulted in Wagner's *Blätter* articles referred to above. The Count was guest of honour at Wagner's birthday celebrations that month and saw the children present their father with the arms from each town where there was a Wagner–Verein, Cosima having commissioned these in secret. Gobineau travelled with the family to Berlin for the last *Ring* cycle on 25–29 May. Jäger had been replaced by Vogl who now sang Siegmund and the Siegfrieds of the last two dramas. After the final *Götterdämmerung* an unfortunate incident occurred. The eighty-four-year-old Kaiser and the Crown Prince being present, Neumann insisted that Wagner appear on stage for speeches and the presentation of a laurel wreath. When he did so, he looked very pale and ill. No sooner had Neumann commenced his speech, with a tribute to the Imperial family, when Wagner turned and walked off the stage. Neumann finished his address in some embarrassment and confusion. There was an outburst of cheering and applause, Vogl stood awkwardly clutching Wagner's huge laurel wreath, the cast in all their finery seemed disappointed and bewildered. At length Wagner appeared in his box to acknowledge the ovation. Neumann attributed Wagner's behaviour to a sudden tantrum, thinking he was offended by the offer of thanks to the Kaiser, and he wrote to the composer expressing indignation at this 'insult' and suggesting that all personal intercourse between them should cease. In fact, Wagner had suffered a slight heart attack which forced him to leave the stage. He explained this to Neumann, but to no avail. The impresario was deaf to any such explanation. The old spirit of friendship was never fully restored: their future relations were confined to matters of business. They met in July, Wagner then expressing anger that Neumann still doubted his word. In his memoirs he recalled leaving Wahnfried:

> We went on in silence down the leafy path to the gate, stood there for a while, and then, without another word, Wagner kissed me and put his arms around me. So we parted. It was fully two years later, when the sad news came up from Venice of the Master's sudden death from heart failure, that I was finally convinced of the tragic sincerity of his words.

The scoring of *Parsifal* Act Two occupied Wagner from 6 June until 19 October. During the summer Karl Brandt worked in Bayreuth devising the machinery and movement for the transformation scenes. The majority of singers had been auditioned and selected by September. Two problems with Bülow were added to Wagner's worries. Hans had sent 40,000 marks to Bayreuth; a considerable sum, realized in part by concert takings but including 12,000 marks from his own savings. He had suggested the money be used to erect a statue of Wagner, but Wagner returned the gift: a statue was in his view a useless gesture, and he suggested Bülow invest the money for his children. This rejection was hardly calculated to win Bülow's sympathy in connection with the other more serious problem. Wagner had long desired to adopt Bülow's daughters Daniela and Blandine: it was sensible, and in their best interests, that they should take his surname, but Hans persistently refused to agree and openly resented the suggestion. In fact he continued to refer to his 'three daughters', never conceding that Isolde was Wagner's child. So anxious was Cosima to resolve the future well-being of her children that she arranged to meet her former husband in Nuremberg in July. Their first encounter in eleven years was painful and melancholy on both sides, and they parted without reaching any understanding.

Driven by the damp weather of Bayreuth to seek health and relief from his pain in a warmer climate, Wagner left for the south, with his family, on 1 November. They travelled through Munich and Rome to Naples where they boarded a ship for Sicily. During the voyage he studied various guide books and had the wild idea of a voyage up the Nile, suggested to him by Gobineau's travel stories. Palermo was their destination, however, and they sailed into the harbour as the breathtaking landscape of terraced gardens and orange groves was lit by the radiant light of dawn. Rubinstein was already there to greet them and conduct them to their hotel, where, in a luxurious suite, Wagner finished *Parsifal*, scoring Act Three between 5 November 1881 and 13 January 1882. As the task drew near completion he was informed of the sudden death of Karl Brandt; the supervision of the technical aspect of the production was now entrusted to his capable son, Fritz Brandt.

Waiting patiently for Wagner to finish *Parsifal* was Auguste Renoir, who had come from Naples in order to paint the Master. At first he was informed that Wagner would not receive him, but then Joukowsky brought the good news that, having finished his work, Wagner would grant him an interview. Renoir recorded his frank good humour, and the craziest of conversations in French and German, during which every conceivable subject was touched upon (including impressionism in music), the artist only managing to interject 'Yes, dear Master', and 'Of course, dear Master'. Wagner punctuated his speech with a succession of gutteral noises, and climaxed in a tirade against the Jews. Renoir's sketch he considered made him look like a Protestant clergyman. The artist was pleased to gain 'some sort of souvenir of that marvellous head', which he later used as the basis for an oil painting.

In February, Wagner left his hotel and settled in the Piazza dei Porazzi. Here, early in March, he wrote a fragment of six bars, which he added to a passage of seven bars rejected from the sketches for *Tristan*. The result was the 'Porazzi melody' which he presented to Cosima on 18 April. The Porazzi villa was cold and damp; Wagner caught a chill and suffered severe cramp in his chest. They left Palermo for Acireali in the third week of March. From his hotel balcony there, Wagner witnessed the dying Garibaldi passing in procession to Palermo, and was greatly moved by the emotional crowd that greeted its hero on his last journey. On 13 April they returned to Naples and arrived in Venice two days later for a fortnight's stay. Here they selected the Palazzo Vendramin-Calergi as a suitable resting place for the coming autumn, after the labours of *Parsifal*. Wagner called at Karl Ritter's home in Venice, but was turned away at the door.

Preparations began in earnest for the second festival on Wagner's return to Wahnfried on the first day of May. Meanwhile, in London, Neumann was presenting the *Ring* at Her Majesty's Theatre. Wagner had thought of visiting England, but his health was too precarious. He had to decline a doctorate offered by Oxford.

The *Open letter to Hans von Wolzogen* (Blätter, April) announced the end of the Patronatverein. Tickets would be available for *Parsifal* in the ordinary way, although two private performances would be given for members of the Verein alone. In July, the *Open letter to Friedrich Schön* answered that gentleman's question as to how he could best aid the Bayreuth scheme. Since he first envisaged a festival at Zurich, three decades before, Wagner had entertained the idea of free admission to the friends of his art. He now proposed a Stipendiary Fund which would provide tickets and travelling expenses to those of limited means, especially the poorer class of students. In one form or another such a system to help young people attend Bayreuth has continued to the present day.

Wagner's sixty-ninth birthday was marked by the familiar tableaux, speeches and serenades. The guests included Humperdinck, Gobineau and Count Biagio Gravina, second son of the Sicilian Prince of Ramacca, who was, with Wagner's warm approval, now engaged to Blandine. Ludwig's gift consisted of two black swans which Wagner named Parsifal and Kundry. Special arrangements were in hand for the King's visit to the Festspielhaus, including a private approach to the theatre, a concealed entrance and a carefully partitioned royal box. It was with grief that Wagner learned early in July, of Ludwig's firm decision not to attend the production. On the King's birthday (celebrated in Bayreuth by the marriage of Blandine and Gravina) he sent him a hurtful quatrain which began 'You scorn the Grail's solace'. (Ludwig did not see *Parsifal* until after Wagner's death, when it was given privately at the Munich court theatre in May 1884.) The King could not bring himself to believe that this would be Wagner's last work – he longed for *Die Sieger* – but Wagner had told Cosima in April that he would write no more operas. He had ideas for instrumental works including symphonies, but he committed nothing to paper.

The weeks of rehearsal were full of alarm for Cosima. She watched Wagner nod off to sleep from sheer exhaustion in his armchair after the day's activity at the theatre. The weather was dismal and 'he cursed Germany, he cursed Franconia, he cursed Bayreuth'. At night he slept badly and dreamt of death.

The singers had arrived in the town by the first day of July. Owing to the large number of performances, and in case of indisposition, it was necessary to allot two or even three alternative singers to the main parts. The principal members of the cast were –

Amfortas	– Theodor Reichmann
Titurel	– August Kindermann
Gurnemanz	– Emil Scaria, Gustav Siehr
Parsifal	– Hermann Winkelmann, Heinrich Gudehus, Ferdinand Jäger
Klingsor	– Karl Hill, Anton Fuchs
Kundry	– Amalie Materna, Marianne Brandt, Therese Malten

Franz Fischer deputized as second conductor to Hermann Levi. In addition there were 29 Flower Maidens, 31 Knights of the Grail, 19 voices from the middle height of the temple, and 50 children's voices in the dome. The orchestra numbered 107. The musical problems were nothing like as complex as those in the *Ring*, but there were difficulties with the stage machinery, particularly during the transformation scenes. To depict Parsifal's progress to Monsalvat, Brandt (or Wagner?) had devised moving scenery. The painted canvas was mounted on vertical rollers standing at each side of the stage, and reeled across to give the effect of changing time and space. When it was tried out in rehearsal, the music ran out long before the scenery had trundled across the stage. Wagner was greatly agitated, and when it was suggested that more music be written, he cried, 'What? Do I now have to write music by the yard?' Observing that little could be done – it was too late to replace the very expensive machinery –

he stormed back to Wahnfried declaring he would have nothing more to do with the rehearsals.

It was Humperdinck who came to the rescue. This young composer had greatly impressed Wagner at their first meeting in Italy in 1879. He had been invited to participate in the production of *Parsifal*, and had been in Bayreuth for a year or so, making a copy of the score from Wagner's manuscript, and afterwards assisting at the rehearsals. He observed the calamitous scene change, ran home and composed a few extra bars of music. Full of apprehension he took his work to Wahnfried and laid it before the Master. Wagner looked at it carefully, gave him a friendly nod and said, 'Well, why not? So be it!' Thus it was that, at the first *Parsifal* and unknown to the audience, a few bars of Humperdinck were heard – and those few bars saved the entire enterprise.

The press resorted to a number of tricks reminiscent of 1876: the defection of Heinrich and Therese Vogl from Bayreuth, as Wagner refused to give them the 'star treatment' they desired, was cited as an example of Wagnerian wickedness. A minor outbreak of smallpox was described as an epidemic which would ensure the cancellation of the festival. On this occasion, however, such reports had no ill effects on the attendance. The private performances for the Patronatverein took place on 26 and 28 July, and the first performance on the 30th. Thirteen performances followed in August. Among the crowds who called at Wahnfried were Bruckner, Dannreuther, Liszt, Malwida, Mathilde Maier, Elizabeth Nietzsche, Countess Schleinitz, Praeger and Stein. Neumann paid a visit and Wagner gave him a free hand to produce the *Ring* anywhere. This most ardent champion toured the work throughout Germany, Belgium, Switzerland, Italy, Hungary, Austria and Russia, within the next three years. The festival made a profit: the gross takings were 240,000 marks. At the first public performance the precedent was established of maintaining silence after the first act, reserving applause until after Act Two, and allowing curtain calls only at the very end. One evening Wagner ignored this sacred convention, burst into applause for the Flower Maidens and cheered loudly. The rest of the audience hissed the unseen and unknown offender. However, Wagner continued to express noisy approval during this scene at every subsequent performance. He was enchanted with the superb quality of singing, and considered the level of performance to be far higher than in 1876. Other features of Bayreuth had also improved. Visitors appreciated the laying of a better road to the theatre hill, more efficient street lighting and the provision of a large restaurant beside the Festspielhaus. Only the weather failed to adapt itself to the festive spirit, although the sun appeared during the last few days. For Wagner the darkest moments were his spasms of intense pain and occasional fits of asthma. On one visit to Wahnfried Scaria was alone with the composer when he suffered an alarming heart attack. Purple in the face, Wagner sank on to a sofa and 'made convulsive movements with his hands as if fighting off an invisible enemy'. Eventually he became still and murmured, 'I have escaped death'.

During the final performance Wagner, unknown to the audience, wriggled his way up through the orchestra pit, took the baton out of Levi's hand and conducted the last act from the transformation scene to the end. Sensing perhaps that this was his farewell not only to Bayreuth, but to his career of music, he directed lovingly, dwelling over every nuance of his score, and adopting a much slower tempo than that to which the singers and orchestra were accustomed. Levi wrote to his father:

> At the end of the work the audience broke into applause that defies description. But the Master did not show himself, but remained with us musicians, making bad jokes, and when the noise of the audience showed no sign of abating after ten minutes, I shouted 'Quiet! Quiet!' at the top of my voice. This was heard up above, and people did quieten down, and then the Master, still at the conductor's desk, began to speak, first to me and the orchestra; then the curtain was raised, the whole company of singers and technical personnel was assembled on the stage, and the Master spoke with such affection that everyone started to weep – it was an unforgettable moment!

Wagner left Bayreuth for the last time on 6 September. The family's progress south to Italy was slow owing to abnormal floods: the railway bridges at Ale and Agide both collapsed half an hour after their train had crossed. No omen could have been more striking.

His last home, the Palazzo Vendramin-Calergi on the Grand Canal, was a sumptuous Renaissance house in which he occupied a suite of about eighteen handsome rooms. The noble villa had been the home of the Loredan family, then passed to the Dukes of Brunswick and Mantua, the families Calergi, Grimani and Vendramin, the Duchess de Berri, and was now the property of the Duke della Grazia. Wagner turned his bedroom into a 'blue grotto' with soft fabrics and delicate scents. In the warmth and luxury of these surroundings he was visited by his most faithful friends and disciples: Liszt, Levi, Stein, Joukowsky, Rubinstein, Humperdinck, the Count and Countess Schleinitz and Heinz Thode, who was to marry Daniela five years later. Gobineau did not come. He died at Turin in October.

Cosima described her father's appearance as like King Lear in those last Venice days. Despite all their differences, he and Wagner were totally reconciled. Liszt could forgive him his outbursts of temper; Wagner dearly loved his friend, despite his irrepressible irritation with Liszt's constant socializing and his lack of sympathy with the experimental late music of Liszt. He wanted him to remain in Venice until the end. This Liszt could not do, but in two strange piano pieces, entitled *Lugubre Gondola* of December 1882, he penned a musical premonition of Wagner's funeral cortège gliding on the lapping waters of the canals of Venice.

Cold winds, rain and more rain followed Wagner to Italy. His cramps around the heart became daily more frequent, and he was prescribed valerian and small amounts of opium for relief. What mattered most to him was not medical treatment, but the presence of Cosima, who lived solely to keep him alive a little longer for his work. From Venice he sent two contributions to the *Bayreuther Blätter*: *Das Bühnenweihfestspiel in Bayreuth* which contains, in addition to words of praise for his singers, a valuable summary of the ideals he aimed for in voice production and acting. The *Open letter to Herr von Stein* was a preface to a volume of dramatic sketches by his young disciple. Wagner's mind returned to thoughts of regeneration and the urgent necessity for the noble German people to colonize some virgin country and breed a pure unsullied race.

He began to plan for another Bayreuth festival in the summer of 1883; Levi visited Venice to discuss the arrangements. A new production of *Tannhäuser* was contemplated, and Wagner expressed the hope that, over the next ten years, all his works from *The Flying Dutchman* onward would be presented at the Festspielhaus. If he could achieve that he would hand over the festival to his son Siegfried who was now showing talent for music and drama.

The score of Wagner's only symphony had disappeared in the direction of Mendelssohn half a century before, but in 1877 the parts used for a Prague performance turned up by chance in a trunk abandoned by Wagner in Dresden. Anton Seidl reconstructed the score from these parts and Wagner planned a performance in Venice to celebrate Cosima's forty-fifth birthday on Christmas Day. Students and professors of the Venice Conservatoire formed the orchestra, and Wagner conducted five rehearsals. On 22 December, at a rehearsal attended by Cosima, Liszt, Joukowsky and the children, he had a heart attack after the first movement. The actual performance, in the Fenice Theatre, took place on Christmas Eve, Wagner conducting the first two movements, Humperdinck the remainder. He sent an account of the event, *On the Performance of a Youthful Work*, to a German musical paper.

On 13 January 1883, Liszt left Venice for Budapest. Wagner spent most of the next month quietly indoors, reading with Cosima their favourite Shakespeare, Goethe and Calderón. Sometimes he would go to the piano and play his beloved Bach fugues or Beethoven's Ninth. On 22 January he played the Shepherd's song and the Pilgrim's Chorus, and remarked to Cosima that he owed the world another *Tannhäuser*. To please the children, he attended the last evening of the winter carnival in Venice on 6 February, but as a result he developed a chill and spent the next day in bed. When he was granted sleep Wagner was a prolific dreamer. Cosima's diary faithfully records all his dreams as well as her own. He frequently dreamt about her, and about many other women, notably Minna. On the night of 9 February 'he dreamt of his mother, whom he meets at the Brockhaus's, but who appears quite youthful, charming, as he could only have remembered her from her portrait, and very elegant too'. On the next night he dreamt about Schröder-Devrient, and said to Cosima at breakfast, 'All my wenches now pass before my eyes'. He then took a walk, but returned after ten minutes with his hands clasped to his heart. Throughout the afternoon he was restless and disturbed, but had recovered sufficiently by the evening to read from Fouqué's *Undine*, of which he dreamed that night, and to begin his last essay, *Über das Weibliche im Menschlichen* (On the Feminine in the Human Race).

This essay, intended for the *Bayreuther Blätter* as the final supplement to *Religion and Art*, occupied him on the next day, 12 February. It survives only as a fragment. Wagner's last thoughts were of the nature of the female, her part in redeeming man; the wrongs of polygamy and loveless marriage; the emancipation of the female sex, and the Buddha's compassion for women. At lunch he discussed his mother with Cosima and later in the day, after a walk with Eva, read more from *Undine*, while Joukowsky sketched him. He played a few bars at the piano – the 'Porazzi melody', some ideas for a scherzo, and the closing chorus of the Rhinemaidens from *Rheingold*: 'Only in the depths is there tenderness and truth: false and cowardly are those who revel above!' And he said to Cosima, 'To think that I knew it so well even then!' Lying in bed he remarked, 'I am very fond of them, those inferior beings of the depths, of those who are full of longing.' With these words, Cosima's diary closes.

'I shall have to take care of myself today,' Wagner said to his valet on the morning of 13 February. He remained in his blue grotto working at his essay, sending word at two o'clock that he did not feel well enough to join the family for lunch. A maid listened in the next room, hearing Wagner sigh and moan as he struggled against the agony in his heart. Suddenly he rang his bell vigorously and asked for Cosima and a doctor. Cosima was seated at the piano playing Schubert's *Lob der Tränen* when the maid entered with the news. Siegfried recalled, 'I shall never forget the way my mother rushed to the door. It expressed the force of a passionate anguish; she ran into the half-open door so hard that it almost split.' She helped Wagner onto a sofa, and as she did so his watch fell out of his pocket. 'My watch!' he cried and, looking in silent love and gratitude at Cosima who embraced him, he died in her arms. At first she thought him only asleep. The doctor arrived at 3 p.m., attempted to massage his heart to no effect, and pronounced the Master dead. For fully twenty-four hours Cosima clung to his body, praying that she too might die. For several days and nights she wept unceasingly and refused to eat anything. Joukowsky wrote to Liszt, 'I am not in a fit state to describe to you the days in Venice during which we were torn this way and that between our sorrow and the profound fear that we might lose your daughter as well.'

To attend to the funeral arrangements and protect Cosima from the inevitable publicity, Hans Richter and Adolf von Gross (Feustel's son-in-law and a devoted friend of Wagner's widow) came to Venice. Unknown to her mother, Daniela gave her consent for a death mask to be made. On Cosima's instructions, she and Isolde cut off Wagner's silver-gold hair and then their mother placed it on his embalmed body as he lay in the coffin.

The cortège of gondolas made its stately way to the station, the gondoliers raising their oars in salute as they passed the villa where *Tristan* was created. On the slow train journey to Bayreuth, Cosima sat in a carriage alone with the coffin, while Gross, Joukowsky and Richter sat with the children. At Innsbruck Levi and Porges joined the funeral train. At Munich, the station was crowded with mourners bearing torches and wreaths. Bayreuth too was filled with thousands who wished to pay their respects when the train reached the town, almost thirty-four hours after it left Venice.

Cosima did not attend the tributes on the following day, 18 February, nor the solemn funeral procession through the town to the grave in the Wahnfried garden. There, as snow fell, the twelve pall bearers, Feustel, Gross, Joukowsky, Levi, Muncker, Niemann, Porges, Richter, Seidl, Standhartner, Wilhelmj and Wolzogen, left the coffin, and withdrew. Cosima then came from the house to join her children at the graveside and watch the coffin being lowered into the vault. Almost half a century was to pass before she was brought to lie there at his side.

Cosima and Siegfried Wagner both died in 1930, the year of the twenty-fifth Bayreuth festival. With Wagner's death the Bayreuth story really only began, and that story is the subject for other books. The creation of a Bayreuth style was Wagner's unfulfilled ambition. It was left to his heirs to carry it out. But the theatre on the green hill by no means monopolized the progress of Wagner's art into the twentieth century. Indeed, Bayreuth's jealous guardianship of the traditions laid down by the Master led to the accusation that the theatre was no more than a mausoleum where creative ideas had become shackled to convention, stylized and fixed. Exciting landmarks in the evolution of the Wagner legacy were the 'pirated' *Parsifal* at the Metropolitan Opera, New York in 1903 (a decade before the work became available to theatres generally), and the pioneering work of the Swiss designer, Adolphe Appia (1862–1928). Appia's remarkable conception of stage design in terms of light and space was all too rarely realized in practice during his lifetime (*Tristan* at Milan, 1923, and *Rheingold* and *Walküre* at Basel, 1924). Cosima rejected his ideas as those of a madman. Wieland Wagner, Richard's grandson, hailed him as the ancestor of stage reform at Bayreuth.

Since 1951 the Bayreuth festivals have occurred annually under the direction of Wieland (1917–66) and his brother Wolfgang Wagner (b. 1919). With vision and courage they opened the doors of the Festspielhaus, for the first time since 1944, to reveal one of the greatest stage experiences of the post-war period, a style of Wagner production that has had an immense effect on theatre design generally. Wieland Wagner once said:

> We have seen and experienced things that our fathers and grandfathers were powerless to prevent: acts of destruction which go far beyond human imagining. If we want to build a new house, we must first dig up the ground in which the foundations are to be laid. My generation has been, and still is, concerned not to luxuriate in aesthetic conceptions as if these were defined immutably for all time, but to seek out the inner laws inherent in a work of genius and to interpret it uncompromisingly, as we find it mirrored in our own souls.

Fifty years separated Wagner's death and the establishment of the Third Reich. And yet in the minds of many people Wagner's art is synonymous with fascism. *Die Meistersinger* is for them a manifestation of power, *Walküre* a hymn to war and violence, *Siegfried* a celebration of fascist youth and strength, *Tristan* pathogenic and morally harmful, *Parsifal* a racist allegory. Not only was Wagner Hitler's favourite composer and the *Ring* his favourite work, but he wrote, 'In order to understand National Socialist Germany, one must know Wagner'. Hitler's association with Bayreuth has undoubtedly raised a moral question. Is Wagner's music 'fascist'? Did he contribute to the events of fifty years after his death?

To answer such questions would fill another volume. However, such is Wagner's posthumous reputation that his biographer cannot shrug off such moral problems. If the reader has reached this point unwearied, then let him take patience for a few more pages before judging the music in terms of the man. It has been the unhappy task of some of these chapters to explore the darker side of Wagner's mind, but not to deny the universal greatness of his art. It is to be hoped that this journey through Wagner's career in all its aspects will lead to a clearer understanding of the historical framework in which he thought and worked. That he was self-centred, avaricious, ruthlessly ambitious and a monster of conceit cannot be denied. That he displayed heartless ingratitude, dishonesty, duplicity and limitless prejudice of the blindest sort is all too evident. An actor and an extremist in all things, he displayed his weaknesses without restraint.

To blame a figure of one historical age for the follies of a later one is, however, another matter. Thomas Mann, writing in the 1930s, considered that 'it is quite unjust to place a contemporary interpretation, the interpretation they would be given today, on Wagner's nationalistic gestures and pronouncements'. One does not blame the founder of the Christian church for the burning of Jews in the middle ages. One does not blame Karl Marx (himself a Jewish anti-Semite) for the persecution of Jews in twentieth-century Russia.

Hitler was musically and culturally illiterate. The hallmarks of fascist Germany were ignorance, prejudice, arrogance and creative sterility. The work of Wieland Wagner emancipated Bayreuth from narrow Teutonic chauvinism and illustrated the universal quality of his grandfather's art. That quality was always there. Those who are blind to it are making exactly the same error as Hitler, and perverting Wagner's art by labelling it Nazi or fascist. Wagner's recent detractors can, unfortunately, see him only through Hitler's eyes. The most vehement of anti-Wagnerites are motivated by a kind of love-hate. Nietzsche was the earliest, and remains the classic example of this. He attacked Wagner's art as 'an outrage on morality' and yet praised the music as profoundly expressive and of the highest importance. How can there be such a contradiction?

If one could approach Wagner's music with as little knowledge of his thoughts and personal prejudices as we have, say, of Bach – would the music strike us as immoral? If one approaches *Parsifal* without any preconceptions would one find there a racist creed? If the *Ring* is a monument to German fascist ideology, which of its characters represent the Aryans, and which the Jews?

However devoutly it may be wished that Wagner had never written *Judaism in Music* or any of his other racist tracts, the fact remains that he did so, and that he felt it urgently necessary to do so. It may be that an artist has to believe in something, even in nonsense, sometimes in dangerous nonsense, in order to stimulate the mysterious processes of creation. The listener does not have to share his beliefs. One does not have to be a Christian to understand and enjoy Bach, an Italian nationalist to appreciate Verdi, a Theosophist to like Scriabin, a Soviet-style communist to admire Shostakovitch. In 1856 Wagner told the King of Saxony that his writings were a sort of poison he had to get out of his system.

In his book, *Richard Wagner, the Man, His Mind and His Music*, Robert Gutman views *Parsifal* in terms of an allegory of racism, purely on the evidence of its verbal text and in the light of Wagner's racial theories as expounded in the later essays. For Gutman, the darkest interpretation of *Parsifal* is as 'the gospel of National Socialism', a drama depicting the redemption of the Aryan race from its sin of mixing with the blood of inferior races, through the annihilation of the Jews and the regeneration of Aryan blood through that of Christ. It is an anti-Christian work: cruel, depraved and demonic. None of this criticism touches upon the music which he concedes to be among Wagner's greatest.

Similarly, Debussy attacked the 'bogus' Christianity of *Parsifal*, the falsity of its religious and moral ideas. For Debussy, Wagner was 'old Klingsor'. Would Shakespeare be 'old Iago'? Yet Debussy makes it very clear that his criticisms apply 'only to the poet we are accustomed to admire in Wagner and have nothing to do with the musical beauty of the opera, which is supreme. It is incomparable and bewildering, splendid and strong. *Parsifal* is one of the loveliest monuments of sound ever raised to the serene glory of music.'

Nietzsche's most famous diatribe against *Parsifal* – 'a work of rancour, of revenge, of the most secret concoction of poisons with which to make an end of the prerequisites of life, a *bad* work . . . an outrage upon morality' – did not prevent him acknowledging the incredible beauty of the music.

If these indictments of the text have any substance, did Wagner merely fling a cover of marvellous and bewitching music over an evil creed? Or is the immorality, the falseness and maliciousness of the text, an illusion? Do we perhaps find in Wagner whatever we want to discover? If so, was Hitler able to find his foul ideas confirmed in Wagner's art?

Before the forest of question marks overwhelms us, let it be admitted that there *is* evil in Wagner's art. That evil is part of his achievement. In his dramas Wagner explored human nature to its utmost depths; he set out, as he himself admitted in *Opera and Drama*, to bring the unconscious part of human nature into consiousness. The *Ring* was to depict reality in all its aspects. He considered that it was the function of art to reveal mythic symbols. As in a dream-world, archetypes of the human psyche appear on the Wagnerian stage. His characters are cosmic entities interwrought with each other in strange ways. His art conquered and controlled unconscious forces, organized them into mythic drama, and revealed them as naked forms of good and evil, darkness and light, love and hate, creation and destruction. Wagner intended that those who looked upon such an art would find there a divine experience. He believed that this experience of his music, akin to that of dreams, could bring about self-awareness and, more than that, an understanding of the divine. It might be added that no two people will find the same experience in his art; if, as Wagner intended, 'the artist succeeds in revealing deep and hidden truths' of symbolic myth, then one may, according to one's point of view, either be given a glimpse of the divine, or a frightening vision of the diabolic. Such a challenge is inherent in any exploration of the human psyche.

The danger, as Wagner once observed to Röckel, is when people foist their own fixed ideas and interpretations on the symbols of his dramas. Hence he avoided naming or explaining the musical leitmotifs of his operas. These motifs become images that reveal far more than words. Wagner was a *musical* dramatist and the greater part of his work can only be fully understood through the music. Most of the prejudice against his art ignores the music completely. Commenting on the adverse reaction caused by *Judaism in Music*, Wagner said in *Mein Leben*: ' . . . it cannot be adequately explained on the mere ground of a theoretical or practical dislike of my opinions or artistic works'. He came to imagine that the Jews were conspiring everywhere to destroy his art. Today, we can examine his life and see that this fear was irrational and fanciful.

If we can look Wagner in the face as a man, and look into his music to see there one of the profoundest explorations of humanity in all art, then the twin aspect of man and artist no longer seems an irreconcilable dichotomy. The passion of the man, the universal passion of his works, together teach us much about the weaknesses and strength of human nature, the sufferings and greatness of the individual and the universal.

Glossary

Abt, Franz (1819–85) German composer of songs, part-songs and piano music. Conductor in Zurich (1841–52); thereafter at Brunswick Court Theatre until 1882.

d'Agoult, Marie Catherine Sophie, Countess (1805–76) *née* Flavigny. Born in France, descended from wealthy Jewish banking family, Bethmann of Frankfort. Married Comte Charles d'Agoult, 1827. Mistress of Liszt (1835–44) and mother of his three children, Cosima, Blandine and Daniel. As 'Daniel Stern' she wrote a biographical novel, *Nélida* (1846), designed to expose Liszt's weaknesses and damage his reputation. She also wrote political and historical essays.

Ander, Aloys (1817–64) Tenor at Vienna Court Opera. Much admired by Wagner until he selected him for the projected Vienna *Tristan*. Then Ander developed chronic hoarseness which was widely attributed to the impossible nature of Wagner's music. In fact Ander was exhibiting signs of mental illness. He subsequently forgot his music during a performance of *William Tell* and never recovered his sanity.

Anders, Gottfried Engelbert (1795–1866) German who worked (from 1833) at the Bibliothèque Nationale, Paris. His real surname, supposedly a noble one, is unknown. Close friend of Wagner during the first Paris stay. Contributor to the *Gazette Musicale*.

Apel, Theodor (1811–67) German poet and landowner at Ermlitz near Leipzig. Son of August Apel, dramatist and poet, whose *Freischütz* was the basis of Weber's opera. Fellow member with Wagner of student Saxonia Club, Leipzig, and class-mate at St Nicholas School. Gave Wagner considerable financial support before suffering a riding accident (1836) which left him blind. Wagner's *Columbus* overture was written for one of his plays, and Wagner set some of his lyrics.

Auber, Daniel François Esprit (1782–1871) French composer of *c.* 50 operas, mainly to libretti by Scribe. Director of Paris Conservatoire from 1842. His *Masaniello* and *Fra Diavolo* influenced the young Wagner. In later years they became friends and Wagner wrote a tribute upon Auber's death.

Bakunin, Mikhail (1814–76) Russian anarchist. After resigning a commission in the Imperial Guard as a protest against Czarist rule, he travelled widely in Europe. Refusing a summons to return to Russia, his estates were forfeited. Meanwhile he studied Hegel and came to know Marx and Proudhon. In 1848 he took part in the Paris revolution and attempted to organize a revolution in Prague. In 1849 he participated in the Dresden revolt, was arrested and imprisoned in Russia. He was transferred to Siberia in 1857 but escaped in 1861 and returned to Europe by way of Japan and the USA. In 1862 he joined an expatriate revolutionary group in London, founded the Social Democratic Alliance (1869) and

321

the Russian secret society 'Land and Liberty' which became the spearhead of the populist movement.

Berlioz, Hector (1803–69) French composer, conductor and critic. Works include operas, *Benvenuto Cellini, Beatrice and Benedict, The Trojans*; choral works, *The Damnation of Faust, The Childhood of Christ, Requiem*; symphonies, *Romeo and Juliet, Symphonie Fantastique, Lélio, Harold in Italy*; songs, overtures, etc. His memoirs contain an account of Wagner's early days at Dresden.

Betz, Franz (1835–1900) German baritone. At Berlin Court Opera, 1859–97. The first Hans Sachs and the first Bayreuth Wotan.

Brandt, Karl (1828–81) German theatre machinist. Worked in his native Darmstadt. Supervised technical aspects of the first Bayreuth *Ring*. Died while at work on the first *Parsifal* production and was succeeded as machinist by his son Fritz (1854–95). Karl's brother, Friedrich Carl (1846–1927; also known as 'Fritz'), was technical director at the Munich Opera (1865–76) and was responsible for the stage machinery for the first *Meistersinger, Rheingold* and *Walküre* productions there.

Brockhaus, Friedrich (1800–65) Publisher and bookseller in Leipzig; retired to Dresden, 1850. Married Wagner's sister Luise in 1828.

Brockhaus, Heinrich (1804–74) Publisher and bookseller in Leipzig; brother of above. Also parliamentarian. Confiscated Wagner's library after Dresden uprising, in lieu of an unpaid debt.

Brockhaus, Hermann (1806–77) Philologist and professor of Sanskrit; brother of above. Married Wagner's sister Ottilie in 1836.

Bülow, Hans Guido von (1830–94) German pianist, composer, teacher and conductor. Son of Eduard, Baron von Bülow, poet and radical political writer. Pupil of Friedrich Wieck and Moritz Hauptmann. Married Cosima Liszt in 1857; they were divorced in 1870. Father of Daniela (1860–1940) and Blandine (1862–1941). [Isolde (1865–1921), Eva (1867–1942) and Siegfried (1869–1930) were all born illegitimately to Wagner and Cosima.] Conducted first *Tristan* and *Meistersinger*. Arranged piano score of *Tristan*. After leaving his post at the Munich Opera he lived for a time in Florence and made many concert tours notably in Britain and the USA. Appointed conductor at Hanover (1878), Meiningen (1880), and later in Berlin and Hamburg. An enthusiastic advocate of Brahms in his later years. Married the actress Marie Schanzer, 1882. Died while convalescing in Cairo. Compositions include works for orchestra and piano solo.

Cornelius, Peter (1824–74) German composer and writer. Pupil of Liszt; colleague of Wagner in Munich. Works include operas, *The Barber of Baghdad, Der Cid*, and *Gunlöd*; songs and part-songs.

Dannreuther, Edward George (1844-1905) English pianist, teacher, conductor and writer on music, of German descent. Resident in London where his pupils included Parry. Prominent English champion of Wagner, translator of his prose works and founder of the London Wagner Society in 1872.

Devrient, Eduard (1801–77) Member of famous German acting family; singer, actor, theatre manager and writer. Historian of the German stage. Librettist of *Hans Heiling* (Marschner; originally intended for Mendelssohn). Director of drama at Dresden Court Theatre (1844–6) and director of Karlsruhe Court Theatre (1852–69).

Glossary

Dietsch, Pierre Louis Philippe (1808–65) French organist, composer and conductor. Wrote church music and operas, including *Le Vaisseau Fantôme*, the French version of Wagner's *Flying Dutchman* libretto, adapted by Paul Foucher and Bénédict Henri Révoil. Appointed conductor of Paris Opéra 1860; conducted ill-fated *Tannhäuser* there; dismissed from his post 1863.

Dingelstedt, Franz (1814–81) German producer, writer and dramatist. Director of Munich Court Theatre (1850–7) and Weimar Court Theatre (1857–67).

Dorn, Heinrich (1804–92) German composer, teacher and conductor. Held appointments at Leipzig (1829–32) where he conducted Wagner's early Overture in B flat, Hamburg, Riga (1833–43) where he and Wagner quarrelled, Cologne (1843–9) and Berlin (1849–69). Teacher of Schumann. Works include opera *The Nibelungs* (1854). His memoirs, *Aus meinem Leben* cast light on his relationship with Wagner.

Düfflipp, Lorenz, Hofrath von Bavarian politician. Succeeded Pfistermeister as Cabinet Secretary to Ludwig II. Later Court Secretary; retired 1878. Succeeded by Ludwig von Bürkel.

Eckert, Karl Anton Florian (1820–79) German violinist, pianist, composer and conductor. From 1853 at Vienna; Stuttgart (1860–7); succeeded Dorn at Berlin (1869). Works include three operas, orchestral music and church music.

Esser, Heinrich (1818–72) German conductor and composer of operas and vocal music. Kapellmeister at Vienna Opera (1847–69). Afterwards retired to Salzburg. Made piano score of *Meistersinger*; introduced Hans Richter to Wagner.

Feuerbach, Ludwig Andreas (1804–72) German philosopher. Important influence on Wagner. Follower of Hegel; influenced 'Young Germany' movement prior to 1848. Author of *Philosophy and Christianity* (1839), *The Essence of Christianity* (1841) and *The Essence of Religion* (1845). His tendency towards materialism and the subjectivization of Christianity influenced Marx.

Fischer, Franz (1849–1918) German cellist and conductor. Member of the 'Nibelungen Chancellory' 1875–6. Shared conducting of *Parsifal* with Levi, 1882. Conductor at Mannheim (1877–9) and Munich (1879–1912).

Fischer, Wilhelm (1789–1859) German bass singer, later chorus master at Leipzig and then at the Dresden Opera (from 1831). Also stage manager. Collector of early polyphonic music. Invaluable in helping to mount the first *Rienzi*. After his death, Wagner wrote a tribute to him.

Frantz (Gustav Adolph) Constantin (1817–91) Prussian political writer of nationalist and anti-Semite persuasion. Influenced Wagner (they met at Tribschen, summer 1866) who corresponded with him and dedicated to him the 1868 edition of *Opera and Drama*.

Fricke, Richard (1818–1903) German choreographer, attached to Dessau Court Theatre. Assisted in production of the first Bayreuth *Ring*. His valuable recollections of the rehearsals were published posthumously. His duties included giving lessons in dancing and deportment to the Wagner children.

Fröbel, Julius (1805–93) Professor of Mineralogy at Zurich (1833–44). Involved in 1848 revolutionary movement. After period of exile in America (1849–57) he lived in Vienna. Appointed editor of *Süddeutsche Presse*, Munich, 1867. From 1873–90 in consular service of the German Empire.

Frommann, Alwine (1800–75) German painter; reader to Princess Augusta of Prussia (later Empress of Germany) in which capacity she did much to advance the cause of Wagner.

Gast, Peter (1854–1918) Pseudonym of Johann Heinrich Köselitz, German composer of four operas, including *Der Löwe von Venedig*. None of his works achieved success. Close friend of Nietzsche.

Gautier (Louise) Judith (1850–1917) French writer; daughter of Théophile Gautier. A passionate admirer of Wagner's music, she visited Tribschen and Wahnfried many times, indulging in a love affair by correspondence with Wagner, 1877–8. She translated some of his writings into French, notably the libretto of *Parsifal*. Married Catulle Mendès.

Gobineau, Joseph Arthur, Count de (1816–82) French diplomat, writer and racial theorist. He held posts in the French cabinet and at Berne, Hanover, Frankfort, Tehran, Athens, Rio de Janeiro (where he was a friend of the Brazilian Emperor Dom Pedro II) and Stockholm. He retired to Italy in 1876. A royalist who despised democracy, he was the first to propound the theory of Aryan superiority on a 'scientific' basis, in his *Essay on the Inequality of the Human Races* (1853–5). His other literary work is considerable; a novel, *The Pleiads* (1874) being his finest work of fiction. Wagner and the Bayreuth circle popularized his racist theories, and Wagner's son-in-law Houston Stewart Chamberlain (1855–1927; married Eva Wagner) elaborated them in various books.

Gutzkow, Karl Ferdinand (1811–78) German poet, novelist and dramatist. Associated with Laube in leading the 'Young Germany' movement of 1830s. 'Antiromantic' in style, he pioneered the social novel. Works include *Wally, die Zweiflerin*, *Die Ritter vom Geiste* and *Uriel Acosta*. As dramatic director at Dresden Court Theatre (1847–50) he quarrelled with Wagner.

Habeneck, François Antoine (1781–1849) French violinist, conductor and composer, of German descent. Founder of the Société des Concerts du Conservatoire. Director of Paris Opéra (1821–2) and conductor there (1824–46). Wagner was greatly impressed with his interpretations of the Beethoven symphonies.

Halévy, Jacques François Fromental Élie (1799–1862) French composer of Jewish descent. Wrote over thirty operas including *La Juive* (1835) and *La Reine de Chypre* (1841). Wagner greatly admired the former, and was warmly attached to Halévy as a man. Bizet married Halévy's daughter.

Hanslick, Eduard (1821–1904) Viennese critic, born in Prague. Studied piano with Tomašék. Left Austrian Civil Service in 1856 to become a lecturer in aesthetics and musical history at the University of Vienna, becoming a professor in 1870. Wrote for the *Wiener Zeitung* and the *Neue Freie Presse*. His major book, *Vom Musikalisch-Schönen* was a landmark in the evolution of musical aesthetics. His championship of Brahms and his enmity towards Liszt, Wagner and Bruckner are legendary. Wagner caricatured him as Beckmesser in *Die Meistersinger*.

Heckel, Emil (1831–1908) Music publisher in Mannheim. Founder-President of the Richard Wagner-Vereine and a member of the Bayreuth Festival Committee.

Heine, Ferdinand Actor in Dresden; colleague and friend of Ludwig Geyer. Later costume designer at Court Theatre during Wagner's period as Kapellmeister, when they were close friends.

Heine, Heinrich (1797–1856) German-Jewish poet and journalist. Settled in Paris in the early 1830s. Friend of Chopin and Liszt. His version of the 'Flying Dutchman' story was Wagner's main source for his opera. They were acquainted during Wagner's first Paris stay: Heine's witty prose style influenced Wagner's writings of that time, and Wagner set Heine's poem *Die beide Grenadieren*. His lyric verses were set by countless composers from Schubert to Richard Strauss.

Herwegh, Georg (1817–75) German poet. Author of *Gedichte eines Lebendigen*. Involved in the 1848 uprising in Baden, he fled to Zurich where he became Wagner's friend. Heine called him 'the iron lark of the revolution'.

Heubner, Otto Leonhardt (1812–93) Saxon politician. District officer in Freiberg from 1843. Led the Dresden uprising in 1849, for which he served ten years in prison. After 1871 a magistrate in Dresden.

Hey, Julius (1831–1909) German teacher of singing; pupil of Friedrich Schmitt. Employed at Munich Music School and assisted at rehearsals for first Bayreuth festival. Author of *Deutscher Gesangsunterricht* and a valuable memoir of Wagner.

Hill, Karl (1840–93) German bass baritone, resident at Schwerin. The first Bayreuth Alberich, and the first Klingsor. He died insane.

Hiller, Ferdinand (1811–85) German pianist, conductor, teacher, composer and writer on music. Pupil of Hummel. In Paris (1828–34) he was a friend of Liszt and Berlioz. In Dresden (1844–7) he became an enemy of Wagner. Kapellmeister at Düsseldorf (1847–50) and at Cologne (1850–84) where he helped found the conservatoire.

Hoffmann, Ernst Theodor Amadeus (1776–1822) German romantic novelist, essayist, composer and critic. His literary works inspired or suggested countless musical works and Wagner was one of many nineteenth-century composers to be greatly influenced by his lively style which ranged in its mastery from the whimsical to the macabre. He was the composer of several operas (the last being *Undine*, 1816), chamber music, piano sonatas and vocal works. In addition he wrote poetry, conducted, managed a theatre and was a capable civil servant. He was acquainted with Ludwig Geyer and Adolf Wagner.

Hohenlohe-Schillingsfürst, Prince Chlodwig von (*Prince of Ratibor and Korvei*) (1819–1901) Minister-President of Bavaria (1866–70). German Ambassador to Paris, 1874. Governor of Alsace-Lorraine, 1885. Imperial Chancellor and Prime Minister of Prussia (1894–1901). (He is not to be confused with Prince Konstantin von Hohenlohe-Schillingsfürst who married Princess Marie Sayn-Wittgenstein.)

Holtei, Karl Eduard von (1798–1880) German actor, poet, dramatist and theatre manager. Appointed Wagner conductor at Riga where they soon became enemies.

Hornstein, Robert, Baron von (1833–90) Minor German composer and *littérateur*. Lived latterly in Munich. His memoirs are revealing on the subject of his stormy acquaintance with Wagner.

Hülsen, Botho von (1815–86) Sometime lieutenant of grenadiers in the Prussian army; helped crush 1849 Dresden uprising. Succeeded Küstner as Intendant of the Royal Court Opera, Berlin, in 1851, and remained in that post until 1886. His early intense antipathy towards Wagner's works gradually mellowed until he latterly displayed a genuine, and often financially generous, regard for them.

Humperdinck, Englebert (1854–1921) German composer, teacher and writer on music. Pupil of Hiller, Lachner and Rheinberger. Assisted Wagner with *Parsifal* production. Of his seven operas, *Hänsel und Gretel*, the best known, clearly shows Wagner's influence.

Jachmann-Wagner, Johanna (1826–94) Wagner's niece. A distinguished and highly successful singer. The first Elisabeth in *Tannhäuser*. The parts of Elsa (in *Lohengrin*) and Brünnhilde (in *Walküre*) were composed with her in mind. She annoyed Wagner by devoting her talents to works like Dorn's *Nibelungen* and the operas of Meyerbeer. At Bayreuth they were reconciled: she sang the alto solo in his performance of Beethoven's Ninth, and Schwertleite and the 2nd Norn at the first Bayreuth festival. She also taught, and among her pupils was Mrs Mary Burrell.

Joachim, Joseph (1831–1907) Jewish, Austro-Hungarian violinist, conductor and composer. Liszt's orchestra leader at Weimar (1849–53). Friend of Mendelssohn, Schumann and, especially, Brahms. Founded the Joachim Quartet, 1869.

Joukowsky, Paul Russian painter; son of Vasili Joukowsky, poet, translator, tutor to the Czar and friend of Goethe. Joined Wagner's circle in 1880. Designed sets for first *Parsifal*.

Kietz, Ernst Benedikt (1815–92) German painter, resident in Paris. A close friend of Wagner's first Paris sojourn, they remained friends, largely by correspondence, for over thirty years.

Kietz, Gustav Adolf (1824–1908) German sculptor. Friend of Wagner's Dresden Opera years. His memoirs describe that period and the preparations for the first Bayreuth festival, which he attended. Brother of above.

Kittl, Johann Friedrich (Jan Bedřich) (1809–68) Bohemian composer and teacher. Pupil of Tomašék. Succeeded Dionýs Weber as director of Prague Conservatory (1843–65) and conductor of orchestra there. Friend of Wagner, Liszt and Berlioz. Composer of *Bianca und Giuseppe*, to a libretto by Wagner, which had great success and was frequently revived.

Klindworth, Karl (1830–1916) German pianist, composer, conductor and teacher. Pupil of Liszt. Resident in London from 1854. Joined Moscow Conservatory (1868), subsequently returning to Germany as conductor of Berlin Philharmonic Orchestra. Retired to Potsdam, 1893. Skilled arranger (e.g. his version of Alkan's Concerto in G sharp minor), he made the standard piano versions of Wagner's operas from the *Ring* onwards. His critical edition of Chopin's works (1882) is notable. Late in life he and his wife adopted an English girl, Winifred Williams (born 1897) who married Wagner's son, Siegfried, in 1916.

Küstner, Karl Theodor von (1784–1864) Intendant of Munich Court Theatre (1835–42) and of Berlin Court Theatre (1842–51).

Lachner, Franz (1803–90) Bavarian composer and conductor. Friend of Schubert and pupil of Sechter. Conductor at Kärntnertor Theatre, Vienna (1827–34) and at Munich Court Opera (1836–65). Works include eight symphonies, several operas, oratorios, church music.

Laube, Heinrich (1806–84) German novelist, dramatist and theatre director. A leader of the 1830s 'Young Germany' movement. An early champion of Wagner, later a bitter foe.

Lehmann, Lilli (1848–1929) German soprano; daughter of Marie Löwe-Lehmann and sister of Marie Lehmann (1851–1931). Her career spanned over half a century and her repertoire ranged from the principal Wagnerian rôles to Italian bel canto. She and her sister took part in the first Bayreuth festival as Rhinemaidens and Valkyries. Her autobiography recalls her association with Wagner.

Lehrs, Samuel (1806–43) German-Jewish philologist. Born in Königsberg; settled in Paris, where he became the closest friend of Wagner's first French visit. A scholar with a leaning towards German medieval literature, he directed Wagner to the sources of many of his later libretti.

Levi, Hermann (1831–1900) German-Jewish conductor, composer and editor. Kapellmeister at Karlsruhe from 1864, and at Munich (1872–96). Conducted the first *Parsifal*.

Lipinski, Karl (1790–1861) Polish violin virtuoso; also conductor and composer. Friend and, later, rival of Paganini. Friend of Berlioz and Schumann. He abandoned a touring career as soloist to become Konzertmeister at Dresden (1839–60).

Liszt, Franz (1811–86) Hungarian pianist, composer and teacher, also writer on music; noted champion of new composers. From early childhood pursued a virtuoso touring career, which he abandoned in 1847. From 1835–44 lived mainly with the Countess d'Agoult; one of their children, Cosima, becoming Wagner's mistress and later (1870) wife. In 1847 he formed a liaison with Princess Carolyne Sayn-Wittgenstein. About that time his real friendship for Wagner began – and his subsequent devotion to Wagner, his encouragement, his financial aid, his unsparing effort to assist in promoting performances, his advice, sacrifices and example in artistic matters, resulted in a collaboration of two great musicians that is rare if not unequalled in history. Liszt's works of the Weimar period (when he was court conductor and gave the first *Lohengrin* performance) considerably influenced Wagner. Throughout his career Liszt was a harmonic innovator in all branches of his art: whether piano solo, orchestral, choral or in transcribed music. In 1866 he took minor orders in the Roman Catholic Church. Wagner had little sympathy with his later music or with his religious beliefs but they remained friends to the end, despite an estrangement during the 1860s caused largely by Wagner's relationship with Cosima. Liszt died at Bayreuth in July 1886, having developed pneumonia after attending a festival performance of *Tristan und Isolde*. 'Tristan' was the last word he spoke.

Lüttichau, Wolf Adolf August, Baron von (1786–1863) Member of the Royal Court of Saxony. During the imprisonment of the royal family (1813–15) he was hunting page to Prince (later King) Friedrich August (II), and subsequently became Master of Forests. In 1824 he resigned that post owing to illness and was appointed Intendant of the Royal Court Theatre, Dresden.

Marschner, Heinrich August (1795–1861) German composer and conductor. Assistant to Weber at Dresden Opera for a time. Works include operas, *Der Vampyr*, *The Templar and the Jewess*, *Hans Heiling*, etc.; songs, orchestral works, choruses, etc.

Materna, Amalie (1844–1918) Austrian soprano. The first Bayreuth Brünnhilde and Kundry.

Mendelssohn (-Bartholdy) (Jakob Ludwig) Felix (1809–47) German composer, pianist, conductor and amateur painter. Grandson of Moses Mendelssohn the

German-Jewish philosopher, and son of Abraham Mendelssohn the banker. Child prodigy. Composer of symphonies, overtures, oratorios, concertos, incidental music to *A Midsummer Night's Dream*, chamber music, piano works, songs, etc. Conductor of Leipzig Gewandhaus Orchestra (from 1835) and head of Leipzig Conservatory (from 1843). Visited Britain many times, where he established an enormous popular following.

Mendès, Catulle (1841–1909) Portugese Jew, naturalized Frenchman. Writer and librettist. Friend of Wagner from the time of the Paris *Tannhäuser*; contributor to *Revue Wagnérienne* (from 1885). Member of the Parnassian group of poets; author of many plays and novels. Supplied Chabrier with the libretto for his *Gwendoline* (1886) and *Briséïs* (unfinished); and Debussy with the libretto for his first opera *Rodrigue et Chimène*. Other composers who set his poetry included Bizet, Fauré, Goldschmidt, Hahn, Massanet, Paderewski, Roussel and Saint-Saëns. He was married for a time to Judith Gautier.

Metternich, Pauline, Princess von (1836–1921) Grand-daughter of Prince Clemens Metternich, Austrian Chancellor. In 1856 she married his son (her uncle), Prince Richard von Metternich-Winneburg, who became Austrian Ambassador to Paris, 1860. Persuaded Napoleon III to commision the *Tannhäuser* production. Her memoirs (published 1920) contain a very inaccurate account of Wagner in Paris.

Meyerbeer, Giacomo (1791–1864) German-Jewish composer of operas, church music, marches, songs, etc. Settled in Paris 1826; also acted as musical director to the King of Prussia from 1842. Collaborating mainly with the librettist Scribe, he wrote spectacular grand operas in an eclectic style, exploiting popular elements of the Italian and French schools. These include *Robert le diable* (1831), *Les Huguenots* (1836), *Le Prophète* (1849), *Dinorah* (1859), and *L'Africaine* (first performed 1865).

Meyer-Dustmann, Luise (1831–99) Soprano at the Vienna Court Theatre. Sister of Friedericke Meyer. Studied the part of Isolde for the proposed Vienna *Tristan* (rehearsals abandoned, 1863).

Meysenbug, Malwida von (1816–1903) German feminist, writer and translator. Daughter of Hessian politician Baron Phillip Rivalier. Involved with emancipation of women and the revolutionary movements of the 1840s. Joined Fröbel's College for Women in Hamburg until it was closed by reactionary authorities. Fled Germany 1848; settled in London where she met Alexander Herzen, the Russian writer and champion of socialist ideas. She was governess to his children (his wife having run off with Georg Herwegh, Wagner's Zurich neighbour), translator of his memoirs (into German), and she adopted Herzen's daughter, Olga. Lived later in Paris, Florence and Rome (from 1870). Lived briefly in Bayreuth (1873) but the climate did not suit her. Close friend of Nietzsche from May 1872. Author of *The Memoirs of an Idealist* (1876).

Montez, Lola (1818–61) Born in Ireland; real name Marie Dolores Eliza Rosanna Gilbert. Educated in India, Scotland, London, Bath and Paris. After a stormy marriage to an officer in the British-Indian army, she began her career as a dancer in London in 1843, from that time onwards using her pseudonym and adopting the identity of an Andalusian dancer. She toured Europe from Paris to St Petersburg creating a sensation with her good looks and legendary fiery temper. Riots and duels followed in her wake and many men fell under her spell from the Czar of Russia and the King of Prussia to Alexandre Dumas and the poets of the Paris boulevards. Liszt had a notorious affair with her, and together they attended a Dresden performance of *Rienzi*. Wagner felt repelled by her, considering her 'a painted and jewelled woman with bold, bad eyes' and describing her after her death as 'demonic and heartless'. In 1846 she became the mistress of Ludwig I of Bavaria, who created her Baroness von Rosenthal and Countess von Landsfeld. She lived in astonishing luxury in Munich and gained complete political power, fomenting an anti-Catholic movement. When she forced Ludwig to close the University in 1848 there was a revolt, leading to her exile and the King's abdication. After a bigamous marriage in England she made further tours of Europe, and settled in the USA in 1851, becoming involved in the gold-rush in California, social reform, spiritualism, feminism and religious revivalism. After a final world tour she died, a penitent, in New York.

Mottl, Felix (1856–1911) Austrian conductor and composer. Member of the 'Nibelungen Chancellory' 1876. Conducted the first Bayreuth *Tristan* (1886); Kapellmeister at Karlsruhe (1881–1903), afterwards director of opera at Munich. Instrumental in mounting the first *Parsifal* outside Bayreuth, New York, 1903. Composer of three operas, chamber music and songs.

Muchanoff, Marie (1823–74) *née* Countess Nesselrode; niece of Russian Chancellor Count Nesselrode. Pupil of Chopin, and an excellent pianist. Married (1st) a Greek diplomat, Johann von Kalergis (1839), and (2nd) Herr von Muchanoff (1864). Friend of Delacroix, Berlioz, Heine and Théophile Gautier, the last two having left written testaments to her beauty. Liszt had an affair with her. She was a staunch and influential supporter of Wagner's music, but disdained his writings.

Müller, Christian Gottlieb (1800–63) Wagner's first composition teacher (1828–31). Member of Leipzig orchestra. Organist at Altenburg after 1838.

Neumann, Angelo (1838–1910) German-Jewish tenor, later impresario and theatre manager in Prague, Leipzig and Vienna. He was the first to mount extensive tours of Wagner's operas, notably the *Ring*. Published a memoir of Wagner in 1907.

Niemann, Albert (1831–1917) German tenor, at Hanover and then Berlin (1866–88). Sang Tannhäuser in Paris (1861) and the first Bayreuth Siegmund.

Nietzsche, Friedrich Wilhelm (1844–1900) German philosopher; son of a Lutheran pastor. Entered University of Leipzig, 1865. Professor of Classical Philology at Basel (1869–79). Lived mainly in France, Italy and Switzerland until 1889 when he became insane. His principal works are *The Birth of Tragedy* (1872; dedicated to Wagner), *Thoughts Out of Season* (1873–6), *Human, all too Human* (1878–80), *The Dawn* (1881), *Thus Spake Zarathustra* (1882–4), *Beyond Good and Evil* (1885), *The Genealogy of Morals* (1887), and in 1888: *The Anti-Christ, The Wagner Case, The Twilight of the Idols, Ecce Homo, Nietzsche-contra-Wagner* and *The Dithyrambs of Dionysos*. His notes and sketches for *The Will to Power* were published posthumously.

Ollivier, Emile (1825–1912) French lawyer and politician. Member of parliament from 1857. Married Blandine Liszt, 1857. Became Prime Minister of France, January 1870.

Paul, Jean (1763–1825) Pseudonym of Johann Paul Friedrich Richter; German writer and poet. Lived at Bayreuth from August 1804. Books include *Die Unsichtbare Loge* (1793), *Hesperus* (1795), *Titan* (1800–3), *Flegeljahre* (1804–5), and *Levana* (1807).

Pecht, Friedrich (1814–1903) German painter. Friend of Wagner in Paris, Dresden and Munich. Recalled Wagner in his memoirs (published 1894).

Perfall, Karl, Baron von (1824–1907) German composer of four operas etc. Also dramatist. Intendant of court music in Munich, 1864; Intendant of Court Theatre there, 1867–93.

Pfistermeister, Franz Seraph von (1820–1912) Cabinet secretary to Ludwig II of Bavaria; resigned 1866 as he was blamed for the handling of the Seven Weeks' War.

Pfordten, Ludwig Karl, Baron von der (1811–88) Bavarian politician. From 1843 Professor of Jurisprudence at Leipzig. Appointed Saxon Minister of Education, 1848. In ministerial service of Bavaria, 1849–59. Appointed Minister-President of Bavaria, 1864. Resigned after Seven Week's War, 1866.

Pohl, Richard (1826–96) German critic and composer. Resident in Weimar and (from 1864) in Baden-Baden. Co-editor of *Neue Zeitschrift für Musik* and author of books on Wagner, Liszt and Berlioz.

Porges, Heinrich (1837–1900) German-Jewish writer on music and choral conductor; co-editor of *Neue Zeitschrift für Musik* from 1863. Assisted Wagner in Vienna, followed him to Munich, and helped in the preparations for the Bayreuth festivals of 1876 and 1882. He wrote much in support of Wagner, including *On Performing the Ninth Symphony under Wagner* (1872), *The Stage Rehearsals for the 1876 Festival* (1877) and *Tristan und Isolde* (published 1906). In the last-named book (written 1866–7) he referred, with Wagner's approval, to the themes of the opera as 'Hauptmotiven' (synonymous with 'Leitmotiven').

Praeger, Ferdinand (1815–91) German pianist, composer and writer on music. Settled in London, 1834. Schumann selected him to be a correspondent of the *Neue Zeitschrift für Musik*. His *Wagner as I knew him* (1892) is a tissue of untruths and exaggerations. (The facts are set right in Vol. 5 of Ellis's *Life of Wagner*.)

Pruckner, Dionys (1834–96) German pianist, pupil of Liszt. Professor at Stuttgart Conservatory from 1859.

Pusinelli, Anton (1815–78) Doctor of medicine in Dresden. Devoted friend of Wagner; assisted him financially and supervised publication of his scores.

Raff, Joachim (1822–82) Swiss composer, pianist and critic. Friend of Mendelssohn and Bülow; disciple of Liszt. Wrote eleven symphonies, operas, concertos, church music, chamber works, etc. Author of *Die Wagner-Frage* (1854).

Redern, Wilhelm, Count von (1802–83) German composer, resident in Berlin. Prussian Court Chamberlain (1825), Intendant of Court Theatre (1828), General Intendant of Court Music (1830–42).

Reissiger, Gottlieb (1798–1859) German composer of operas, church music and chamber works. After pursuing a career as singer, pianist and teacher in Germany, Italy and Holland, he succeeded Marschner as musical director of German opera at Dresden in 1828, later rising to the rank of Kapellmeister.

Rellstab, Ludwig (1799–1860) German critic, novelist, essayist, poet, translator and composer.

Glossary

Remenyi, Eduard (1830–98) Hungarian violinist; friend of Liszt. Solo violinist to Queen Victoria, 1854.

Richter, Hans (1843–1916) Austro-Hungarian conductor. Joined Wagner's circle as copyist for *Meistersinger*, 1866. Conductor in Pest (from 1871) and Vienna (from 1875). Conducted first *Ring* cycle, Bayreuth 1876. Later championed the symphonies of both Bruckner and Brahms. A frequent visitor to England, he was conductor of the Hallé Orchestra, Manchester (1897–1911) and the dedicatee of Elgar's first symphony. He retired to Bayreuth in 1912.

Ringelhardt, Friedrich Sebald (1785–1855) Director of Stadt-Theater, Leipzig (1832–44).

Ritter, Julie (1794–1869) Widow of a merchant of Narva, Russia; owned estates in the Crimea. Settled in Dresden in 1840s. Supplied Wagner with a pension throughout his Zurich years. Her second son, Alexander, married Wagner's niece Francisca (Albert's daughter).

Ritter, Karl (1830–91) German poet and musician. Pupil of Hiller and Schumann. Elder son of above.

Röckel, August (1814–76) Music director at Dresden Court Theatre (1843–8). A leader of the 1849 Dresden uprising, he was subsequently imprisoned at Waldheim, Saxony. Upon his release in 1862 he returned to radical political journalism in Coburg, Frankfort, Munich (where he mingled in Wagnerian politics) and Vienna. After a paralytic stroke in 1871 he retired to Pest.

Rubinstein, Joseph (1847–84) Russian-Jewish pianist and composer. Wagner's musical assistant from 1872. He made a notorious attack on Schumann and Brahms in the *Bayreuther Blätter*. He committed suicide.

Sainton, Prosper Philippe Catherine (1813–90) French violinist and orchestral leader. Composer of works for violin. Resident in London from 1845; professor at the Royal Academy of Music.

Sayn-Wittgenstein, Carolyne, Princess von (1819–87) *née* Ivanovski; daughter of a Polish landowner. At age seventeen married Prince Nicholas Sayn-Wittgenstein, adjutant to the Czar. Met Liszt in Kiev (1847) and became his mistress. After a lengthy attempt to annul her marriage, involving negotiations with the Czar, the Russian Orthodox Church, and the Vatican, they planned to wed in October 1861. On the eve of the wedding the Pope refused to annul her Russian marriage. From 1860 until her death she lived in Rome, Liszt going his separate way but often visiting her. A strong-willed intellectual, she exercised enormous influence on Liszt, as also on Berlioz whose opera *The Trojans* was written at her suggestion. Her championship of Berlioz (and many of Liszt's grander projects) may well have been part of her plan to oppose Wagner. In her lonely eccentric old age she occupied a darkened room, smoked strong black cigars and wrote her monumental theological opus, *Interior Causes of the Exterior Weakness of the Roman Catholic Church*, which ran to twenty-four volumes.

Sayn-Wittgenstein, Marie, Princess von (1837–1920) Daughter of above. Wagner called her 'the Child' and she inspired the figure of Freia in Rheingold. First met Wagner in 1853. After her marriage to Prince Konstantin von Hohenlohe-Schillingsfürst (1859) they never met again, and Wagner later had a sour opinion of her. One of the great intellectual beauties of the nineteenth-century, her praises were sung by many of the distinguished men of her era.

Scaria, Emil (1838–86) German bass. Engaged at Vienna Court Opera. Sang

Gurnemanz in the first *Parsifal*, 1882. At the first London *Ring* earlier that year (when he sang Wotan) he was already displaying signs of alarming forgetfulness. He died insane.

Schindelmeisser, Louis (1811–64) German clarinettist, conductor and composer of operas. Kapellmeister at Königstadt Theatre Berlin, Wiesbaden (from 1851) and Darmstadt (from 1853). Friend and admirer of Wagner from Leipzig student days. Step-brother of Heinrich Dorn.

Schleinitz, Marie, Countess von (1842–1912) *née* von Buch. (Later became Countess Wolkenstein.) Friend and confidante of Cosima from the early years of her marriage to Bülow. Her husband was Minister of the Royal House of Prussia. A powerful Berlin ally of Wagner during the preparations for Bayreuth.

Schlesinger, Moritz Adolf (1798–1871) German publisher in Paris. Son of Berlin publisher Adolf Martin Schlesinger (d. 1839). Settled in Paris 1819 and *c.* two years later founded his own firm there, publishing the music of Berlioz, Chopin, Liszt; later Franck etc., and important editions of Weber, Hummel and Beethoven. He founded the weekly *Gazette Musicale* (1834–80) to which Wagner contributed. Wagner also worked as transcriber of scores for Schlesinger. He promoted concerts of new music, at one of which Wagner's *Columbus* overture was heard. He retired in 1846.

Schmitt, Friedrich (1812–84) German tenor. Colleague of Wagner at Magdeburg. Later summoned to Munich by Wagner as teacher of singing. Author of *Grosse Gesangschule für Deutschland*.

Schnorr von Carolsfeld, Ludwig (1836–65) German tenor, also pianist, composer, arranger of songs, poet and painter. Son of the painter Julius Schnorr (1794–1872). Sang at Karlsruhe (1854–60) and Dresden (1860 onwards). At Karlsruhe he became associated with the soprano Malvina Garrigues (1825–1904) whom he married in 1860. They were the first Tristan and Isolde (1865). After Ludwig's death Malvina sang at Hamburg and at Karlsruhe, where she settled as a singing teacher. She published a volume of poetry by herself and her late husband.

Schopenhauer, Arthur (1788–1860) German philosopher. Author of *The World as Will and Idea* (1818) and *Parerga und Paralipomena* (published 1862). His line of thought developed from Kant and Indian philosophy, and his pessimism and emphasis on the primacy of the will influenced Wagner and the young Nietzsche in addition to many artists and writers.

Schott, Franz (1811–74) German publisher; director of the firm founded 1773. Published Wagner's *Meistersinger*, *Ring* and *Parsifal*. He and his wife Betty (1820–75) were noted patrons of music in Mainz.

Schröder-Devrient, Wilhelmine (1804–60) German soprano. Daughter of Friedrich Schröder (baritone) and Antoinette Sophie Burger (actress). Sang Leonore in the revised version of *Fidelio* (1822) and received the highest praise from Beethoven, who intended to create another rôle specially for her. Associated with Dresden from 1823. Married the actor Karl Devrient (1823; divorced 1828). She had two subsequent marriages and many love affairs. Wagner first heard her in 1829 and regarded the experience as the most powerful influence upon his entire career. She sang to Goethe in 1830. Nicknamed 'the Queen of Tears' she had her critics as well as her devotees, and her powers began to decline after 1837. Sang the first Adriano, Senta and Venus, all at Dresden.

Schumann, Robert Alexander (1810–56) German composer and writer on music.

Married Clara Wieck (1840). Founder and editor (1833–44) of *Neue Zeitschrift für Musik*. Resident in Dresden during 1840s. After throwing himself into the Rhine (1854) he was confined to a mental asylum where he died. He had little sympathy with Wagner and was grieved when his successor as editor of the *Neue Zeitschrift*, Franz Brendel, began to champion Liszt and Wagner. Works include many piano pieces, songs, chamber music, concertos, four symphonies, opera *Genoveva*, and various choral works.

Schuré, Edouard (1841–1929) Alsatian writer and critic. Prominent advocate of Wagner's cause in Paris. Author of essays on music and theosophy, novels, poems and plays. Contributor to *Revue Wagnérienne* (after 1885).

Scribe, Auguste Eugène (1791–1861) French dramatist and prolific librettist. Among the composers to whom he supplied libretti are Auber (over thirty), Donizetti, Meyerbeer, Rossini and Verdi.

Seidl, Anton (1850–98) Austro-Hungarian conductor. At Bayreuth with Wagner from 1872. Conductor for Angelo Neumann's tours of Wagner. From 1885 at New York Metropolitan Opera.

Semper, Gottfried (1803–79) German architect; associated with Wagner in Dresden, Zurich and Munich. Designed or collaborated on the work of many famous buildings in Dresden, London (the South Kensington Museum), Vienna (the Burgtheater) and Zurich.

Sgambati, Giovanni (1841–1914) Italian composer and pianist. Pupil of Liszt. Composer of two symphonies, piano and chamber music, choral works, etc.

Spohr, Louis (1784–1859) German composer, violinist, conductor and writer on music. Composer of seventeen violin concertos, eleven operas, oratorios, ten symphonies, chamber music including thirty-four string quartets, etc. Wagner wrote a 'recollection' of him upon his death.

Spontini, Gasparo Luigi Pacifico (1774–1851) Italian composer and conductor. Resident in Paris (1803–30); court music director in Berlin (1820–42). Wrote many operas on heroic and historical subjects including *La Vestale* (1807) and *Ferdinand Cortez* (1809). Wagner wrote a 'recollection' of him upon his death.

Stein, Karl Heinrich, Baron von, zu Nord- und Ostheim (1857–87) German philosopher and poet. Member of Wagner's circle from 1879 (acting as Siegfried's tutor). Works include *Helden und Welt* (1883) and *Die Entstehung der neuen Aesthetik* (1886).

Tausig, Karl (1841–71) Polish Jewish pianist. Favourite pupil of Liszt. Also wrote piano studies and transcriptions. Noted interpreter of Chopin. Stayed with Wagner at the 'Asyl'. Before his death from typhoid fever at twenty-nine he helped organize the appeals for the Bayreuth festival scheme.

Tichatscheck, Joseph Aloys (1807–86) German tenor; mainly at Dresden Opera. The first Rienzi and the first Tannhäuser. He retired in 1872.

Tomašék, Václav Jan (Wenzel Johann; 1774–1850) Bohemian composer, pianist and teacher. Friend of Goethe. Wrote operas, church music, piano works, songs, etc.

Uhlig, Theodor (1822–53) German violinist, composer and author of theoretical works. Close friend of Wagner at Dresden and important correspondent thereafter.

Unger, Georg (1837–87) German tenor. The first Siegfried.

Viardot-Garcia (Michelle Ferdinande) Pauline (1821–1910) Franco-Spanish mezzo-soprano; also pianist. Daughter of Manuel Garcia (tenor); sister of Manuel Garcia (inventor of laryngoscope and teacher at Royal Academy of Music; died 1906, aged 101) and Marcia Malibran (soprano). A distinguished artist and intellectual, she had fluent command of at least five languages. Mistress of Turgenev.

Villiers de l'Isle Adam, Count Philippe Auguste (1838–89) French writer of poetry, plays, essays on freemasonry, occultism and theosophy. Admirer of Wagner.

Vogl, Heinrich (1845–1900) German tenor, engaged at Munich. The first Loge at Munich and Bayreuth. Married Therese Thoma. Together they were the first Siegmund and Sieglinde (Munich, 1870).

Weber, Bedřich Dionýs (1766–1842) Bohemian composer, conductor, teacher and writer of theoretical works. Founded Prague Conservatory and conducted Wagner's early symphony there (1832).

Weber, Carl Maria Friedrich Ernst von (1786–1826) German composer and writer. Director of German Opera at Dresden Court Theatre from 1817. Friend of Ludwig Geyer. Died in London after supervising first production of his opera *Oberon*. Wagner was instrumental in having his remains returned to Dresden. Works include operas, *Der Freischütz, Abu Hassan, Euryanthe*, concertos, piano music, songs, incidental music, etc.

Weinlig, Christian Theodor (1780–1842) German musician, theorist and teacher. Cantor at Holy Cross, Dresden (1814–17) and at St Thomas, Leipzig (from 1823 until his death). Teacher of Wagner.

Weissheimer, Wendelin (1838–1910) German composer, theatre conductor and writer on music. Author of *Experiences of Richard Wagner, Franz Liszt, etc.* (1898).

Winkler, Hofrath (1775–1856) Saxon writer (using pseudonym Theodor Hell), court official and theatre manager. Intendant and later secretary of Dresden Court Theatre. Friend of Ludwig and Johanna Geyer. Proprietor of *Dresden Abendzeitung*.

Wolf, Hugo (1860–1907) Austrian composer and critic. Wrote mainly songs; also one opera, *Der Corregidor*, an *Italian Serenade*, etc. Became insane 1897.

Wolzogen, Hans Paul Baron von (1848–1938) German writer on music. Editor of *Bayreuther Blätter* and author of many studies of Wagner. He named the 'Leitmotiven' in Wagner's dramas.

Zumpe, Hermann (1850–1903) German composer and conductor. Member of 'Nibelungen Chancellory'. From 1877 Kapellmeister at Schwerin, and from 1900 general music director in Munich.

Select Bibliography

ABRAHAM, Gerald. *A Hundred Years of Music*, London, 1938.

'A lost Wagner Aria', *Musical Times*, vol. 110, 1969.

BAILEY, Robert. 'Wagner's musical sketches for 'Siegfrieds Tod' ' in: *Studies in Music History: Essays for Oliver Strunk*, ed. H. Powers, Princeton, 1968.

BARTH, Herbert. *Internationale Wagner-Bibliographie: 1945–55*, Bayreuth, 1956; adds. by Henrik Barth (1955–60), Bayreuth, 1961.

(ed. with Dietrich Mack and Egon Voss) *Wagner, a Documentary study* (transl. R. J. Ford and M. Whittall. Preface by P. Boulez.), London, 1975.

BARZUN, Jacques Martin. *Darwin, Marx, Wagner: critique of a heritage* (2nd edition), New York, 1958.

BECKETT, Lucy. 'Parsifal as Drama', *Music & Letters*, vol. 52, 1971.

BEKKER, Paul. *Richard Wagner, his life in his work* (transl. M. M. Bozman), London, 1931.

BERLIOZ, Hector. *Memoirs* (transl. D. Cairns), London, 1969.

BIDDISS, Michael D. *Father of Racist Ideology: the social and political thought of Count Gobineau*, London, 1970.

BLISSETT, William. 'Ernest Newman and English Wagnerism', *Music & Letters*, vol. 40, 1959.

BLUNT, Wilfred. *The Dream King: Ludwig II of Bavaria*, London, 1970.

BUESST, Aylmer. *Richard Wagner: the Nibelung's Ring* (2nd edition), London, 1952.

BURRELL, The Hon. Mary. *Richard Wagner's Life and Works 1813–34*, London, 1898.

CHAMBERLAIN, Houston Stewart. *Die Grundlagen des 19. Jahrhunderts*, 2 vols, Munich, 1932.

Richard Wagner, Munich, 1896; transl. G. A. Hight, London, 1897.

COOKE, Deryck. ' "Parsifal": the Moral Question', *The Listener*, 6 May 1971.

CORNELIUS, Peter. *Ausgewählte Briefe*, 2 vols, Leipzig, 1904–5.

DAHLHAUS, Carl. (ed.) *Das Drama Richard Wagners als musikalisches Kunstwerk*, Regensburg, 1971.

(ed.) *Richard Wagner: Werk und Wirkung*, Regensburg, 1971.

(with Westernhagen, C. von) 'Wagner, Richard' in *Grove's Dictionary of Music and Musicians*, 6th Edition.

DEATHRIDGE, John. *Wagner's Rienzi: a reappraisal based on a study of the sketches and drafts*, Oxford, 1977.

DONNINGTON, Robert. *Wagner's 'Ring' and its Symbols* (2nd edition), London, 1969.

DORN, Heinrich. *Aus meinem Leben*, 3 vols, Berlin, 1870–2.

DU MOULIN ECKART, Richard. *Cosima Wagner*, 2 vols, Munich, 1929–31; transl. C. A. Phillips, London, 1930.

ELLIS, William Ashton. *Life of Richard Wagner*, 6 vols, London, 1900–8.

FISCHER-DIESKAU, Dietrich. *Wagner and Nietzsche*, New York, 1976.

Richard Wagner

FÖRSTER-NIETZSCHE, Elizabeth. *The Nietzsche-Wagner Correspondence* (transl. C. V. Kerr), New York, 1921.

FRICKE, Richard. *Bayreuth vor dreissig Jahren: Erinnerungen an Wahnfried und aus dem Festspielhause*, Dresden, 1906.

GAL, Hans. *Richard Wagner: Versuch einer Würdigung*, Frankfurt-am-Main, 1963; transl. H. H. Schönzeler, London, 1976.

GAUTIER, Judith. *Wagner at Home* (transl. E. D. Massie), London, 1910.

GECK, Martin. *Die Bildnisse Richard Wagners*, Munich, 1970.

GIDDINGS, Robert. 'Wagner and the Revolutionaries', *Music & Letters*, vol. 45, 1964.

GLASENAPP, Carl Friedrich. *Das Leben Richard Wagners*, 6 vols, Leipzig, 1894–1911.

GOBINEAU, Joseph Arthur, Comte de. *Essai sur l'Inégalité des Races humaines*, 4 vols, Paris, 1853–5.

GOLLANCZ, Victor. *The Ring at Bayreuth* (with an afterword by Wieland Wagner), London, 1960.

GUTMAN, Robert W. *Richard Wagner, the man, his mind and his music*, London, 1968.

HANSLICK, Eduard. *Vienna's Golden Years of Music* (ed. and transl. by Henry Pleasants III), New York, 1950.

HEY, Julius. *Richard Wagner als Vortragsmeister, 1864–76*, Leipzig, 1911.

HILL, Ralph. 'On Hanslick and Wagner', *The Chestarian*, vol. 12, 1931.

HOLLINRAKE, Roger. 'Nietzsche, Wagner and Ernest Newman', *Music & Letters*, vol. 41, 1960.

HOPKINSON, Cecil. *Tannhäuser: an examination of 36 editions*, Tutzing, 1973.

HORNSTEIN, Robert von. *Memoiren*, Munich, 1908.

JACOBS, Robert L. *Wagner* (Master Musicians Series), London, 1947.
'Wagner and Judith Gautier', *Music & Letters*, vol. 18, 1937.
'A Freudian View of the Ring', *Music Review*, vol. 26, 1965.

KAPP, Julius. *Richard Wagner*, Berlin, 1922.
The Women in Wagner's Life (transl. H. Waller), London, 1932.

KIETZ, Gustav Adolph. *Richard Wagner in den Jahren 1842–9 und 1873–5*, Dresden, 1905.

KLEIN, John W. 'Bizet and Wagner', *Music & Letters*, vol. 28, 1947.

KNUST, Herbert. *Wagner, the King and 'The Waste Land'*, Pennsylvania, 1967.

LEHMANN, Lilli. *Mein Weg*, Leipzig, 1913.

LIPPERT, Woldemar. *Wagner in Exile*, London, 1930.

LIPPMAN, Edward Arthur. 'The Esthetic Theories of Richard Wagner', *Musical Quarterly*, vol. 44, 1958.

LISZT, Franz. *Gesammelte Schriften*, vol. III, Leipzig, 1881.

LOCKSPEISER, Edward. 'The Renoir Portraits of Wagner', *Music & Letters*, vol. 18, 1937.

LORENZ, Alfred Ottokar. *Das Geheimnis der Form bei Richard Wagner*, 4 vols, Berlin, 1924–33.

MAGEE, Bryan. *Aspects of Wagner*, London, 1968.

MANDER, R. and MITCHESON J. *The Wagner Companion*, London, 1977.

MANN, Thomas. *Essays of Three Decades* (transl. H. T. Lowe-Porter), New York, 1947.

MENDÈS, Catulle. *Richard Wagner*, Paris, 1886.

MEYSENBUG, Malwida von. *Memoiren einer Idealisten und ihr Nachtrag. Der Lebensabend einer Idealisten*, 2 vols, Berlin, n.d.

Select Bibliography

MICHOTTE, Edmond. *Richard Wagner's visit to Rossini* (transl. H. Weinstock), London, 1968.

NEUMANN, Angelo. *Personal Recollections of Wagner* (transl. E. Livermore), London, 1909.

NEWMAN, Ernest. *The Life of Wagner*, 4 vols, London, 1933–47.

Wagner as Man and Artist (2nd edition), London, 1923.

Wagner Nights, London, 1949.

NIETZSCHE, Friedrich Wilhelm. *Werke in drei Bänden* (ed. K. Schlechta), Munich, 1960.

Complete Works (ed. O. Levy), 18 vols, Edinburgh, 1909–13.

OREL, Alfred. 'Richard Wagner in Vienna', *Musical Quarterly*, vol. 19, 1933.

PANOFSKY, Walter. *Wagner: a pictorial biography* (transl. R. Rickett), London, 1963.

PECHT, Friedrich. *Aus meiner Zeit: Lebenserinnerungen*, 2 vols, Munich, 1894.

POHL, Richard. *Richard Wagner, ein Lebensbild*, Leipzig, 1883.

PORTNOY, Julius. *The Philosopher and Music*, New York, 1954.

PRAEGER, Ferdinand. *Wagner as I knew him*, London, 1892.

RÖCKL, Sebastian. *Ludwig II and Richard Wagner*, 2 vols, Munich, 1913–20.

SCHAFER, R. Murray. *E. T. A. Hoffmann and Music*, Toronto, 1975.

SCHURÉ, Edouard. *La Drame Musical*, 2 vols, Paris, 1875.

Richard Wagner, son oeuvre et son idée, Paris, 1930.

SHAW, George Bernard. *The Perfect Wagnerite*, London, 1898.

SIEGEL, Linda. 'Wagner and the Romanticism of E. T. A. Hoffmann', *Musical Quarterly*, vol. 51, 1965.

SKELTON, Geoffrey. *Wagner at Bayreuth* (with forword by Wieland Wagner), London, 1965.

SPENCER, Stewart. (ed.) *Wagner 1976, a celebration of the Bayreuth Festival*, Wagner Society, London.

STEIN, Jack M. *Richard Wagner and the Synthesis of the Arts*, Detroit, 1960.

STROBEL, Otto. *Richard Wagner: Leben und Schaffen: Eine Zeittafel*, Bayreuth, 1952.

THATCHER, David S. 'Nietzsche and Brahms: a forgotten relationship', *Music & Letters*, vol. 54, 1973.

VOSS, Egon. *Studien zur Instrumentation Richard Wagners*, Regensburg, 1970.

WAGNER, Cosima. *Briefe an ihre Tochter Daniela von Bülow, 1866–85* (ed. M. F. von Waldberg), Berlin, 1933.

Briefe an Friedrich Nietzsche (ed. E. Thierbach), 2 vols, Weimar, 1938–40.

Die Tagebücher (ed. M. Gregor-Dellin and D. Mack), 2 vols, Munich, 1976–7.

WAGNER, Friedelind. *The Royal Family of Bayreuth*, London, 1948.

WAGNER, Richard. *Gesammelte Schriften und Dichtungen*, 12 vols, Leipzig, 1907.

Richard Wagner's Prose Works (transl. W. A. Ellis), 8 vols, London, 1892–9.

Sämtliche Werke (ed. C. Dahlhaus), 30 vols (projected), Mainz, 1970–

Das braune Buch (ed. J. Bergfeld), Zurich, 1975.

Mein Leben: Erste authentische Veröffentlichung (ed. M. Gregor-Dellin), Munich, 1963.

My Life, 2 vols, London, 1911.

Richard Wagners Gesammelte Briefe (ed. Kapp and Kastner), Leipzig, 1914 (incomplete).

Richard Wagner

Sämtliche Briefe (ed. G. Strobel and W. Wolf; 15 vols projected), vols 1–3, Leipzig, 1967–71.

Briefe, Die Sammlung Burrell (ed. J. N. Burk), Frankfort-on-Main, 1953.

Letters of Richard Wagner: The Burrell Collection (ed. J. N. Burk), New York, 1950.

Richard Wagners Briefe (ed. W. Altmann), 2 vols, Leipzig, 1933.

Letters of Richard Wagner (ed. W. Altmann; transl. M. M. Bozman), 2 vols, London, 1927.

Family Letters of Richard Wagner (transl. W. A. Ellis), London, 1911.

Richard Wagner an Freunde und Zeitgenossen (ed. E. Kloss), Berlin, 1909.

Richard Wagner an seine Künstler (ed. E. Kloss), Berlin, 1908.

Richard Wagner an Theodor Apel (ed. T. Apel, jr), Leipzig, 1910.

Briefe an Hans von Bülow, Jena, 1916.

Briefe an Judith Gautier (ed. W. Schuh), Zurich, 1936.

Letters of Richard Wagner to Emil Heckel (ed. K. Heckel; transl. W. A. Ellis), London, 1899.

Zwei unveröffentliche Briefe Richard Wagners an Robert von Hornstein (ed. F. von Hornstein), Munich, 1911.

Correspondence of Wagner and Liszt (transl. F. Hueffer), 2 vols, London, 1888.

König Ludwig II und Richard Wagner: Briefwechsel (ed. O. Strobel), 5 vols, Karlsruhe, 1936–9.

Richard Wagner an Mathilde Maier (ed. H. Scholz), Leipzig, 1930.

Richard Wagner an Ferdinand Praeger (ed. H. S. Chamberlain), Berlin, 1908.

The Letters of Richard Wagner to Anton Pusinelli (ed. and transl. E. Lenrow), New York, 1932.

Briefe Richard Wagners an eine Putzmacherin (ed. D. Spitzer), Vienna, 1906.

Briefe an Hans Richter (ed. L. Karpath), Berlin, 1924.

Richard Wagners Briefe an Frau Julie Ritter (ed. S. von Hausseger), Munich, 1920.

Richard Wagner's Letters to August Roeckel (transl. E. C. Sellar), Bristol, 1897.

Richard Wagner's Letters to his Dresden Friends, Theodor Uhlig, Wilhelm Fischer and Ferdinand Heine (transl. J. S. Shedlock), London, 1890.

Richard Wagner to Minna Wagner (transl. W. A. Ellis), 2 vols, London, 1919.

Richard Wagner to Mathilde Wesendonck (transl. W. A. Ellis), London, 1905.

Briefe Richard Wagners an Otto Wesendonck, Berlin, 1905.

The Nibelung's Ring (transl. W. Mann), London, 1964.

The Ring (transl. A. Porter), Folkestone, 1976.

Wagner writes from Paris (ed. and transl. R. L. Jacobs and G. Skelton), London, 1973.

WAGNER, Siegfried. *Erinnerungen*, Stuttgart, 1923.

WALKER, Frank. *Hugo Wolf* (2nd edition), London, 1968.

WALLACE, William. *Liszt, Wagner and the Princess*, London, 1927.

WATSON, Derek. *Bruckner* (Master Musicians Series), London, 1975.

WEISSHEIMER, Wendelin. *Erlebnisse mit Richard Wagner, Franz Liszt, usw.*, Stuttgart, 1898.

WESTERNHAGEN, Curt von. *Richard Wagner: Sein Werk, sein Wesen, seine Welt*, Zurich, 1956.

The Forging of the 'Ring' (transl. A. and M. Whittall), London, 1976.

WILLE, Eliza. *Fünfzehn Briefe von Richard Wagner nebst Erinnerungen und Erläuterungen von Eliza Wille, geb. Sloman*, Berlin, 1894.

Select Bibliography

WOLZOGEN, Hans Paul von. *Thematische Leitfaden durch die Musik zu Rich. Wagners Festspiel Der Ring des Nibelungen*, Leipzig, 1876; trans. E. von Wolzogen, London, 1882.

Erinnerungen an Richard Wagner, Vienna, 1894; transl. A. and C. Simpson, Bayreuth, 1894.

ZUCKERMAN, Elliot. *The First Hundred Years of Wagner's Tristan*, London, 1964.

Index

340

Index

Biebrich, 184–90
Bilz, Herr, 239
Bilz-Planer, see Planer, Ernestine Natalie
Birth of Tragedy (Nietzsche), 250, 255–6, 260,
  282, 286
Bischoff, Prof., 165
Bismarck, Otto von, 22, 198, 210, 218, 227,
  240, 248ff., 253, 260, 262
Bissing, Henriette von, 193–4
Bizet, Georges, 235, 247, 286, 288, 324
Bluebeard (Grétry), 74
Blum, Carl, 53
Blunt, Wilfred, 275
Bohème, La (Puccini), 67
Böhme, Rudolph, 27
Boieldieu, François Adrien, 53
Boïto, Arrigo, 255
Bologna, 255, 281
Bonfantini, G. A., 14, 245
Bordeaux, 112–14
Borromean Is., 127, 238
Bösendorfer, Ludwig, 278
Boulogne, 60
Bourgault-Ducoudray, Louis, 177
Brackel, Harald von, 54
Brahms, Johannes, 182, 191, 194, 200, 247,
  262, 266, 270, 274, 282, 286, 299f.
Brandt, Friedrich Carl, 240, 322
Brandt, Fritz, 308, 322
Brandt, Karl, 258, 260, 265, 269, 271, 276,
  279f., 303, 308, 310, 322
Brandt, Marianne, 310
Breitkopf und Härtel, 33, 85–7, 94, 98, 123f.,
  134, 148f., 158f., 168
Brendel, Franz, 119, 180, 333
Breslau, 23–4, 100, 127
Brestenberg, 155
Brix, Herr, 66
Brockhaus, Friedrich, 29ff., 45, 61, 131, 190,
  322
Brockhaus, Heinrich, 111, 261, 322
Brockhaus, Hermann, 52, 72, 77, 93, 238, 322
Brockhaus, Luise, 22, 24, 27, 29, 61, 72, 186,
  263
Brockhaus, Ottilie, 22, 24, 27, 52, 72, 238
Browning, Robert, 294
Bruckner, Anton, 213, 274, 278, 311
Brückner, Max & Gotthold, 265, 269, 280,
  303
Brückwald, Otto, 258
Bruneau, Alfred, 177
Brünn, 34
Brunswick, 270, 298
Brussels, 30, 168
Buch, Marie von, see Schleinitz
Bucher, Lothar, 261
Budapest, see Pest
Buest, Count von, 102
Bülow, Blandine von, 204, 227, 239, 254,
  308, 310, 322
Bülow, Cosima von, see Wagner, Cosima
Bülow, Daniela von, 204, 219, 223, 227, 239,
  254, 308, 315, 322

Bülow, Hans Guido von, 92–3, 101, 122,
  133, 140, 145, 150–2, 155, 161, 173–6, 180,
  184, 187–9, 193, 202–3, 205, 207, 210–17,
  219, 222–33 *passim*, 236–9, 241–2, 244,
  247–8, 256, 278, 282, 287, 308, 322
Bülow, Isolde von, see Wagner, Isolde
Bulwer-Lytton, Edward George, 17, 51,
  59–60
Bungert, August, 286
Bürkel, Ludwig von, 297
Burne-Jones, Sir Edward Coley, 294
Burrell, Mary, 14–16, 21, 24, 30, 51, 58, 224,
  239, 245, 326
Büsching, J. G., 35
Byron, George Gordon, Lord, 111, 145

Cairns, David, 144
Calderón de la Barca, Pedro, 152, 157, 207,
  313
Calzado, M., 164
Camilla (Paer), 37
Capriccio (R. Strauss), 121
Carlsbad, 45
Carmen (Bizet), 274, 286
Carvahlo, Léon, 163
Cassel, 85, 93
Cenerentola, La (Rossini), 26
Cerf, Karl Friedrich, 46, 48–9
Cézanne, Paul, 177
Chabrier, Emmanuel, 177
Chamberlain, Eva, see Wagner, Eva
Chamberlain, Houston Stewart, 13–14, 303,
  324
Champfleury (Jules Fleury-Husson), 167
Chausson, Ernest, 177
Chemnitz, 106–7
Cherubini, Maria Luigi Carlo Zenobio
  Salvatore, 37, 43, 57, 142
Chicago, 254
Chopin, Frédéric François, 142
Chorley, H. F., 243
Christ, Jesus, 50, 298, 302, 304, 316
Christus (Liszt), 205, 259, 262
Cid, Der (Cornelius), 181, 203–4
Coburg, 108, 269
Cocteau, Jean, 291
Cologne, 260, 298
Communist Manifesto (Marx & Engels), 97
Como, 238
Constitutioneller Zeitung (Dresden), 164
Coriolan Overture (Beethoven), 33
Cornelius, Peter, 133, 180–5, 188, 191–4,
  203–4, 208, 218, 221–2, 232, 236, 258,
  262–3, 322
Cornet, Julius, 88
Costa, Sir Michael, 140, 142
Covent Garden, 143–4
Czerny, Carl, 31

Dame blanche, La (Boieldieu), 53, 122
Damrosch, Leopold, 180, 213, 278
Danckelmann, Count & Countess, 278
Dangl, Frau, 211

341

Index

344

Index